TASLIMA NASRIN is an eminent writer and secular humanist who has been subjected to forced banishment and multiple fatwas. Her writings have been deemed controversial time and again because of their unflinching preoccupation with gender and communal politics. She has been living in exile since 1994.

MAHARGHYA CHAKRABORTY is a teacher, literary translator and social media and communications consultant. His interests in cinema and archiving included a tenure of working as a digital archivist in the Media Lab of Jadavpur University, as well as working as a writer of film subtitles.

PRAISE FOR THE BOOK

'What shines through the book [is] the immense anger Nasrin feels. Not just at her plight, but her anger over the treatment of women and minorities, at misportrayals by the media, at political compromises of leaders'—*The Hindu*

'*Split* impresses not just because of the turn of events that she records so faithfully, but more because her voice and reality are still relevant. . . . It remains an important record of the fate of those who dare to walk the road of truth'—*Financial Express*

'Nasrin is the quintessential rebel . . . She uses her pen to rise up against the status quo'—*Open*

'*Split* is an important read . . . Nasrin's raw emotions of love, lust, happiness, fear, anger, betrayal, all come through with a rare authenticity that deserves a salute . . . Her prose [tackles] upfront matters that are easily swept under the carpets, namely communal tensions and gender politics, and how integrated they are to our mundane life whether or not we choose to acknowledge them'—*Free Press Journal*

'*Split* asserts the power of the printed word and the reaction it triggers in those who fear the word'—*Deccan Chronicle*

'*Split* is a powerful book [and] an intense read . . . There is a wry sense of humour and satire that flows throughout the book. . . . There is a lyrical quality to the prose . . . The book also reveals Taslima Nasrin's grasp of human psychology'—Bookedforlife.in

'*Split* is a searing account of the challenges Taslima Nasrin has faced . . . It is a heartfelt account of Nasrin's life, experiences, and revelations from her life in Mymensingh and Dhaka . . . Nasrin bares open her soul . . . The extremely personal, and sometimes, heart-wrenching revelations and confessions [make] the reader feel they are closer to her'—Womensweb.in

BY THE SAME AUTHOR

Lajja
French Lover
Exile

SPLIT

A Life

TASLIMA NASRIN

TRANSLATED FROM THE BENGALI BY
MAHARGHYA CHAKRABORTY

PENGUIN BOOKS

An imprint of Penguin Random House

PENGUIN BOOKS

USA | Canada | UK | Ireland | Australia
New Zealand | India | South Africa | China

Penguin Books is part of the Penguin Random House group of companies
whose addresses can be found at global.penguinrandomhouse.com

Published by Penguin Random House India Pvt. Ltd
4th Floor, Capital Tower 1, MG Road,
Gurugram 122 002, Haryana, India

Penguin
Random House
India

First published in Hamish Hamilton by Penguin Random House India 2018
Published in paperback in Penguin Books 2021

Copyright © Taslima Nasrin 2018
Translation copyright © Maharghya Chakraborty 2018

10 9 8 7 6 5 4 3 2 1

ISBN 9780143426530

Typeset in Adobe Caslon Pro by Manipal Digital Systems, Manipal
Printed at Replika Press Pvt. Ltd, India

www.penguin.co.in

MIX
Paper from
responsible sources
FSC® C016779

Contents

Contents

By the Brahmaputra

It was not long before the cholera outbreak, after ravaging the villages, spread to the cities. We began boiling our drinking water, and water purification pills started being distributed freely by hospitals and municipal offices. There were loudspeaker announcements explaining in detail how to dissolve the pills in water, door-to-door campaigns by municipal agents to distribute them—but nothing managed to stymie the onset of an epidemic. Homes piled up with cholera patients, the dead spilling out on to the streets. There were not enough beds in the hospitals; some patients had to be laid out on the floor with needles attached to bottles of cholera saline stuck in their hands. Doctors, nurses—none had a moment to lose. At Suryakanta Hospital I was terribly busy, running from one patient to the next with bottles of saline. The infected were streaming in like flotsam after the tide; what with the wards already overflowing most ended up on the crowded floor of the corridor. Despite the saline running day and night few patients actually recovered. Cots, for the dead to be carried away on, were heaped in front of the hospital. All the cemeteries and crematoria were crowded. Vultures were circling above.

I had my hands so full that the days were a blur. I usually got back home well past evening; occasionally in the afternoon if I was too tired. Father had spread bleaching powder in the gutters of our home, Abakash, while pills were crushed into the drinking water, the bathwater and even the water kept aside for washing clothes and doing dishes. As soon as I stepped into the house Mother took my apron away to be washed.

That afternoon, however, I could not take the apron off. Father informed me that I was to go out on a call. He would have gone but he had to instead attend to another seriously ailing patient. I had never attended a call before. I asked him for the address and he told me to look out for a white house on my left, three houses past the Metharpatty rail line on the Naumahal route. Yasmin's friend Rehana's house. I set off on my first call as a doctor with Yasmin in tow, a stethoscope in the pocket of my apron, besides a blood pressure monitor and a few life-saving injections.

At Rehana's house they were expecting Father. But since I had gone in his stead, and since I too was a doctor, I was allowed to attend to the patient—Rehana's younger brother. His eyes had sunk into hollows, his lips were dry as peeling paper, and I quickly examined him for signs of dehydration and advised the patient be admitted to a hospital at once. One of the uninfected brothers reminded me that the hospitals were so full that patients were being turned away. Seeing that no one in the family was keen on taking the boy to a hospital, I wrote a prescription for five bags of cholera saline, a saline set, butterfly needles and some medicines. Rehana immediately sent the healthy brother off with some money to make the arrangements.

The room we were in, one of the two small ones on the second floor, was in complete disarray. Rehana's father was sitting on a chair, a look of utter bafflement on his face; her mother was standing by the door, her face pale, Barrister—the youngest of Rehana's three brothers—in her lap. Barrister had already been through two bouts of diarrhoea and his sister was worried that he too had the disease. After the saline arrived I set everything up and showed them how to change the bags. Having advised them yet again to take both the uninfected brother and Barrister to a hospital I made my way down the stairs, Rehana close at my heels. Yasmin had gone ahead and hailed a rickshaw. The two had been close friends since school. Some girls are married off while they are still in school; Rehana had been one such girl. She had a daughter too, about a year and a half old, and she had had to drop everything in her own home to rush to her brothers' aid. In fact, for two days she had been unable to visit her own daughter. Neither was it advisable to bring the child there. Almost at the foot of the stairs, Rehana extended the consultation fee towards me. Sixty taka, my first earnings from a call, I confessed gleefully to Yasmin as I got on to the rickshaw. Yasmin, her brows drawn together, stared at my overjoyed face for a long while with a stunned expression and then exclaimed, 'You took money from Rehana?'

Still smiling, I replied, 'Yes! I did. Should I not have? But she gave it to me! I attended to the patient, why shouldn't I take the money?'

'Rehana is my friend. Two of her brothers are suffering from cholera. How could you take money from her at such a time?'

When Rehana had extended the money towards me, perhaps out of a sheer lack of habit, I had stiffened a bit. Rehana was Yasmin's friend, but I didn't know her at all! If we were to go around the city we would have found a friend of mine or Yasmin, some friend of our brothers or some distant acquaintance of both my parents, in perhaps every other house. It would have been impossible to make a living as a doctor for much longer in that case! I was on a call, I had paid for my rickshaw, I had treated the patient, put in my labour, wasn't I entitled to the fee then? All doctors were! I had toughened myself up with such arguments and taken the money from her in the end despite a dogged sense of discomfort, an instinctive lowering of the eyes and a coldness spreading in the heart. Yasmin remained silent the entire way back, her brows still drawn together. I asked her if she wanted sweets from Shri Krishna, or if she wanted to go watch a film, but she refused both. I had thought that at least everyone at home would be happy at my first earnings from a call, however, I could not spy any sign of happiness on any of their faces, least of all Father's. 'I don't take money,' he told me. 'I consult them for free.' Father used to consult many patients for free across the city; it did not mean I had to do the same.

The next day Father informed us that both Barrister and the healthy brother were down with cholera. All three patients had been shipped off to a hospital, leaving Rehana and her father to run around handling the entire situation. We could hardly believe the news he had for us the day after: 'The three brothers have recovered and have been discharged. Rehana and her father are dead. They were rushed to the hospital urgently in the dead of night but nothing could be done. He died on the way; she died half an hour after reaching. While she had been taking care of her brothers she had begun to vomit. Since there would be no one to take care of the sick or take them to a hospital if she too was laid up, she hadn't said a word to anyone. She hadn't wanted anyone to get upset over her. That's what the father had done too; he hadn't wanted anyone to know. He had wished for his sons to get well first before taking care of himself.'

Rehana's father had been the sole earning member of their household. He had been a man of principle, which explained why despite being a lawyer he had been unable to alleviate the poverty of his own home his entire life. Rehana had always tried to chip in, somehow saving something or the other for them from her husband's income. What was going to happen to them now? As everyone at Abakash gathered to discuss their future I sat stunned, Rehana's fair round face transfixed in my thoughts, her anxious but lively face, pale and yet so charming. I kept asking myself the one question—why had I taken her money? What need did I have of the money?

Perhaps she had assumed I would refuse the money, seeing how I was her friend's sister, how Father used to treat her family for free. Selfishly and inconsiderately I had taken the money with scant regard for the cholera-afflicted family and what they must have been going through. She must have been surprised and quite hurt. Why did I have to go and hurt a girl who was to die in only a couple of days? Why did I have to do that! She must have saved that 60 taka with a lot of effort. There is so much that I spend without reason, without ever keeping track of my finances. Would it have even mattered if I had refused to take money from a family in such dire straits? Would I have died? Gone hungry? No, I wouldn't have. I didn't really need the money. I had taken it because I had wanted to, because it had made me happy. I had taken it because I was a proud doctor. On a house call how could I justify being a doctor without taking a fee! That's why I had taken it. Unable to forgive myself, I couldn't bear to look at my own reflection in the mirror, so ugly it appeared, so replete with hate. Hate at my macabre, cruel hands that had taken that money. My disgrace made me fling accusations at myself—'How could you take the money? Shame! Are you so greedy? Shame!'

Mother had never met Rehana but she went to their house with Yasmin nevertheless. I couldn't go, I didn't have the courage. Mother returned from their house, her eyes puffy and red from crying. Post the incident Yasmin became so terrified of water that she would shriek and run at the mere sight of it; she wouldn't drink water even when thirsty, would refuse to take a shower even when the heat and the summer made it necessary. Irrespective of how hard I tried I couldn't go back to the way things were before the incident either. My guilt had me ensconced in an intimate embrace, present with me wherever I went, sitting with me in pensive silence and showing no signs of freeing me from its clutches.

Soon enough, the cholera epidemic bid farewell to the city. The young Rehana, barely in her twenties, was no longer among us and nothing was ever going to bring her back. Neither would I ever get a chance of fixing my mistake. Days passed as they usually do but I found myself in a sort of a stupor. I had sent 200 taka with Mother to give to Rehana's mother, but that had not managed to rid me of my self-loathing one bit. Rehana did not know what I had done, she would never know. I kept trying to tell myself that taking the money from her had been nothing but a nightmare. A scene kept replaying in my thoughts, taking place on the stairs of their house. Rehana offering me the money, and I, my hand on her shoulder, chiding her, 'Have you gone crazy! Why will I take money? Keep it, it will come to some use.' Rehana smiling, her eyes awash with tears. 'Thank you, Nasrin aapa! You have been a saviour! You treated my brother. I will never be able to repay the debt I owe you.' Yet more scenes soon joined the reel. Rehana playing ludo with her brothers, both of them healthy again; her daughter sitting beside them, watching them at play; the clouds of despair parting and Rehana's fair, restless face awash with laughter, as well as her ebony eyes.

~

There was not much work at Suryakanta Hospital after the epidemic passed. I went to the Zilla Health Centre of Mymensingh to request a transfer to a new place. Nurul Haque, the director of the centre, opined, 'Join family planning. There's a post open for a doctor.' I joined the family planning department simply to ensure a measure of preoccupation in my life. But this new office refused to let me into its closed little world. I wished to enter this world but an invisible sentinel kept me at bay. The thing was that I understood a 500 cc syringe as a 500 cc syringe, not as a 25 cc one; since I could not comprehend the subtle fix between a 5 and a 25, they never picked me for their team. Left on the sidelines I sat by myself or tried to find work on my own. And then finally it dawned on me that there was nothing for me to do there. There was no office for me, no separate table or chair, nor were there patients for me to cure. The clerks sat at their desks, behind piles of paper, pens and documents of various colours; the more I tried to fathom what those documents were and how the office ran, the more I began to feel like a colossal fool. I felt foolish because I realize I had no rights to know anything about the organization. I was asked to sit still, and keep doing simply that.

Gradually, I began to feel unnecessary. And I *was* unnecessary; the true masthead of the organization was the family planning officer, the tall, fair and stately Mujibar Rehman. Of course, he was not a doctor. Far from it, in fact, and yet the office was his fiefdom while my role was purely ornamental. There was one other doctor there besides me, the portly Saidul Islam. He was quite thick with Rehman and I would notice their sniggering and whispering. I also noticed that Saidul Islam's function there wasn't remotely as decorative as mine. A doctor from the office of the deputy director of family planning, he would only drop by at the centre on occasions. Otherwise he was always on the move on his motorcycle for shipments of medicines or for signatures.

The family planning office was on Kalibari Road—it comprised a large tin hut by the road, on the other side of which a flight of stairs led down to a low courtyard past the edge of the road. The square courtyard had three relatively smaller tin sheds in three corners. One of the sheds used to be empty and the other was used to stock medicines; the third shed was reserved for Ayesha Khatun. Among Khatun's many duties was the charge of handing out condoms and contraceptive pills, and helping women put in or take out contraceptive coils, albeit discreetly behind a curtain. Ayesha Khatun and Mother had been in the same class when they were in school and when I came to be aware of this startling fact I could not help but compare the two—one was slogging away in the kitchen trying to keep the home fires burning while the other was dressing pretty and heading to work. Perhaps the latter had been the backbencher, the one who hung her head when asked the English word for gobar. While Idulwarah, always the good student, had quickly supplied the right answer, only to now be reduced to making fuel cakes out of cow dung for her clay oven. The large tin hut had been partitioned with a thick paper wall into two rooms, the smaller for Mujibar Rehman and the larger for four clerks, one of whom was Ambiya Begum, the accountant—starkly painted lips, a hint of pink rouge on her cheeks, wearing a spotless, crisp sari. Nearly every day, at least twice or thrice, Rehman would take the accountant to the storeroom to check the stock of medicines. Hours would pass but their stocktaking would not end. Unable to restrain myself I had inquired of the only other person there of my species—the other doctor, Saidul Islam—as to what was happening. 'What is happening? Let's see if you can guess what is happening,' he had said, laughing. That has always been my biggest drawback, my lack of imagination. Expectedly, I failed to comprehend what exactly was happening. Other than checking stock so thoroughly the rest of Rehman's hours at the office would be spent on lording over his subordinates and having furtive conversations with Ambiya in his private office. Both Rehman and Islam would come and go whenever they pleased while the clerks would dutifully sit at their desks from ten to five, regardless of whether they had anything to do or not. Since she had the boss's attention Ambiya had more perks among the staff—she could go home much before five if she wanted.

After a few days I finally figured out what my job there was after all. If Ayesha Khatun faced any issues while putting in a coil, or if someone had had an adverse reaction to contraceptives for which she was unable to find a solution, I was to offer my services. Khatun was an experienced professional; in effect, she knew much more about these things than I did. And yet I was her boss, although I never did have too much faith in that word. Instead I gradually began to develop a rapport with the family planning officers employed by the centre—hundreds of agents spread over the neighbouring villages and district towns whose job, besides distributing condoms free of cost and encouraging people to consider permanent contraception, was to spread awareness regarding family planning through a door-to-door campaign in their designated localities. Many of these agents would often visit the office, to attend meetings or to procure more supplies, money, condoms, pills, etc. Some of them had basic school degrees and there were also a few college graduates. In fact, there was a hierarchy in place among the officers—some ranked lower than others. Most were women, though there were a handful of men in the job too. It didn't escape my notice that the men, despite being of a lower rank, were perfectly adept at throwing their weight around. Like Rehman, for instance. Almost inevitably we ended up clashing over a homeless couple with children who I had given shelter to in the unused shed. Rehman wanted them out and I tried reasoning with him.

'There is no harm if they stay here! This room isn't being used, so what if they stay here?'

'No, they can't stay. They have to leave,' he responded, an edge of steel in his voice.

'Where will they go? They don't have any place they can go to. What harm is there if they stay?'

'Yes, there is. There is a lot of harm if they stay.'

Rehman could not explain to me what exactly would happen if they were to be allowed to stay. Suffice it to say I lost the argument because Rehman had more authority than I did—he was a man. While Mujibar Rehman and Saidul Islam, on account of being men and officers, continued to terrorize their colleagues and employees, I was pushed to the sidelines with the clerks and subordinates despite being of equal rank. Gradually, I began to feel less like an officer and more as one of the underpaid clerical staff at the centre, growing ever closer to them like their neighbour or maybe even a close first cousin. The agents would instinctively tell me about the minutest things in their lives and I would patiently listen. Because I was the youngest person in the office, whenever I entered a room colleagues twice or even thrice my age used to promptly stand up and greet me with a 'Salaam-waleikum, madam'. I was so uncomfortable with it that I pleaded with them repeatedly to not do it. Even Ayesha Khatun, who was Mother's age, was the same, and I remember telling her bluntly that I would stop entering the room if she stood up. An easy camaraderie, conversations, jokes—such things made me happy, and the more popular I grew with these people the more I fell out of favour with the powers that be. I was an officer and yet I was not one. The peon wanted to get his daughter admitted to a school. He didn't have the money so I gave him some. Similarly I gave money to others in need, often wilfully forgetting the loan. I made arrangements for people who were not getting adequate treatment so they would get more care. Since there was no work for me to do, I went around trying to find work and doing things of my own accord. One such job was part of Saidul Islam's itinerary—organizing sterilization camps with the agents of the family planning office in the remote villages and district towns. They would set up camp in a schoolroom of a village and the agents would muster people for ligations and vasectomies. I too began visiting these camps—by boat, rickshaw or bullock cart, and sometimes even on foot.

Most of the patients brought in for vasectomies were eighty–ninety-year-old poor men; the agents probably found them lying by the roadside clutching their palpitating hearts and brought them in en masse to be sterilized. Men of all ages are usually similar in their fondness for their family jewels. Women, regardless of age, made up the majority of the patients in the camp. I learnt about women who were willing to be sterilized after enduring the physical strain of bearing nearly six or seven children but were unable to do so because their husbands were not allowing them. The husbands usually had one reason—children were a gift of Allah and to do anything to refuse that gift was an insult to Allah Himself. I learnt about families who made so little that they were unable to feed their children twice a day, let alone educate them—yet they would have children every year but refuse to get sterilized for fear of upsetting Allah. Their answers to the agents were the same: 'Allah is granting us children; He will feed them.'

I learnt about women who were being forced into pregnancy for the seventh or eighth time because their husbands were waiting for a male child. I also noticed how many women came for a ligation simply because they wanted the sari and the cash incentive of 120 taka given as gifts by the government. I learnt that despite laws forbidding women who did not have at least two children, of whom the youngest was not yet five, from undergoing ligation, many came nonetheless to the camp and lied about sterilization because they were too poor and wanted the handouts promised to them in exchange for the procedure. I became aware of touts at the family planning centre demanding a cut from even this paltry amount of 120 taka. I realized that some of the women who were claiming to be thirty or thirty-five and the mother of two children were in fact childless and barely sixteen or seventeen. They came to the camps to get sterilized for life in exchange for a cheap cotton sari and 120 taka.

I discovered my country's poverty in these camps. I trembled and I wept.

Particulars

CS and I became friends during the last few months of college. CS had two distinct qualities—her sense of humour, which was intensely attractive, and her constant anxiety about things, which was equally repellant. Suppose someone in class was found studying liver diseases; CS's anxieties would increase swiftly. Why was the girl reading up on liver ailments? Perhaps there would be questions based on that in the paper! Immediately CS would begin staying up nights reading up on the same. Or perhaps someone was to mention that staying in a hostel was far more conducive to studying than staying at home. CS would immediately pack her bags and set off for a hostel despite facing no issues whatsoever at home. Her study partner had been a boy with the reputation of being a good student. When some other boys became more known for their academic performance CS began sulking because she did not have them as her study partners! Nothing seemed to satisfy her.

A native of the city, she lived with her mother, who worked at Agricultural University, in the old Bombay Colony, near the jail that was right past Khagdaha. Her father had abandoned them long back. Hailing from Chapai Nababgunje, her mother had travelled all over with a transferable job before finally settling down in Mymensingh. I used to feel a surge of respect whenever I met the woman—I have hardly ever known a more self-reliant and confident mother. CS graduated from Vidyamoyee[1] and Ananda Mohan[2] and got admitted as a medical student. Despite being from the city she used to talk in the Rajshahi dialect, far cleaner and sweeter than the one we used in Mymensingh. The staccato beats of our verbs—'aibam', 'jaibam', 'khaibam'—were too difficult for her to get used to; she was still stuck on the plain utterances—'ashbo', 'jabo', 'khabo'. Be that as it may, it suited her best when she was being herself. Although only a couple of inches taller than me, in mass and bulk she was way ahead and could easily overshadow my reputation as the tallest girl in the class. It was something that hardly ever affected me.

Other than the occasional visits to the camps, my job at family planning usually involved a lot of waiting. So CS and I began to meet often and the conversations gradually grew longer. None of our other batchmates were working out of the city; CS was at the clinic for the disabled on Boundary Road and she didn't have any work either. Usually if there was a big hospital in the city most people would never go to the smaller clinics. We were of the last batch of doctors from the medical college to have gotten government jobs right after graduating; the rules were changed from the following year and doctors no longer remained eligible for an immediate posting after finishing their degree. Many new doctors did the rounds of private clinics while others had to sit for the BCS exam in order to get government employment. This peculiar exam, meant for anyone seeking a government job, had previously exempted the medical profession, but the new rules overturned all that and supplied a further caveat—even those already in government jobs would have to pass the exam!

We could not help but wonder why despite already having government jobs we still had to appear for the test. It was explained to us that we needed to take the test to make our posts permanent. I had never heard of an impermanent government job; thus far we had always known that government jobs were the only things that were permanent. CS, as usual, got anxious. Soon enough a big fat BCS guidebook was procured and she had sat down to study. I procured a book too but scarcely managed to turn the pages. I had no desire to practise close reading and write essays on cows like girls in the fifth grade, and the BCS exam was a giant quagmire of everything from Bengali, English, Mathematics, History and Geography to Home Science and General Knowledge. I wanted to be a doctor and it was enough that I knew how to do that well. Why did I have to take a plunge into this mess! The government was in a bind; it was no longer able to employ new doctors and this was simply a ploy to get out of that problem. If the BCS exam turned out to be unsuccessful, perhaps there would have been a 400 metre race with the promise of government employment for the final winner! It was as if the country had been overrun by doctors, and there was no longer any space left to accommodate new ones. Expectedly, an excuse was extended that there were no funds left in government coffers. There was barely one doctor for every few thousand citizens to share and yet the government could not pay for doctors!

CS and I travelled to Dhaka to appear for the BCS examination. If not about cows we at least had to write about goats. Charting new mathematical frontiers, inventing a fictional date of birth for Kazi Nazrul Islam, answering a unitary method problem—if the milkman mixes 2 litres of water to every 5 litres of milk how much water would there be in 28 litres of milk—with the confident answer of 'three buckets', and boldly proposing that Lake Baikal was in Bagura, we managed to pass both the written and oral exams to ensure a final seal of approval on the permanence of our jobs. Our work remained the same as it had been before the exam. In fact, the ones who failed the exam didn't face any issues with their jobs either.

Two things happened in CS's life around that time. She and her mother left their place in Bombay Colony to move to the teachers' quarters in Agricultural University; and CS fell in love. The second was a rather remarkable incident, especially because it was her first tryst with the emotion—she fell for a doctor named M. He was married and so was CS. Her husband used to live in Moscow. Right after finishing our degrees, seeing the other girls in the batch getting married to doctors and settling down, CS had characteristically gotten anxious. This had led to the realization that if others were doing it, marriage must not be too bad a thing and that she should get married too. The catch had been that one needed a groom to get married to. CS, try as she might, could not bring herself to like any of the doctors left around her—this thing or that, there was always something wrong with each of them. If at all there was someone she liked, she would go around asking other people about them; if someone ended up saying something unpleasant, it would promptly deflate her enthusiasm. Finally, one day she had asked me, the concern apparent in her voice, 'What do you think I should do? There is no one that I can marry!'

'Why do you have to get married right now? There are so many who still haven't yet,' I had replied. This succeeded in mollifying CS for a few days, but only till she received the news that the homeliest girl in the batch too had gotten hitched. I had still tried persisting with a few more examples of attractive girls who were yet to find grooms, especially mentioning Halida in the list. Scoffing at the mention, CS had replied, 'Don't talk about her. She has already said she does not wish to ever get married.'

Eventually, after much indecision, CS had managed to locate a first cousin—an aunt's son—who was of marriageable age. As was the need of the hour she had immediately begun to think of ways she could find out more about him. As it turned out, the man in question lived in Moscow where he had gone to get his orthodontist's degree. CS had been quick to act: 'Do you think I should write to Humayun? Should I tell him that I want to marry him?'

'You saw him last when the two of you were children. Would you be compatible now? Think about it carefully,' I had advised again.

CS had indeed taken my advice to heart. She had thought about it long and hard. Humayun was only a dentist, but he was a dentist in Moscow. That was not such a bad thing at all! Usually doctors for human beings don't really pay too much attention to dentists and veterinarians. But CS had grown so desperate that she had written a letter to Humayun in Moscow. Without any prevarication, based essentially on whatever faded fascination Humayun may have had for her a long time ago, the letter had been quite forthright in voicing her intentions: 'I want to marry you.' When Humayun had agreed CS had seen no reason to waste further time. She had taken a flight to Moscow, gotten married there, spent two months with her husband in his hostel and then come back home pregnant with his child. Her child was delivered under the care of Zobayed Hussain who had taken one look at the newborn and declared, 'An elephant's given birth to a rat!' CS had named her newborn Ananda.

While Ananda was happily growing up in his grandmother's care, CS's life went on as usual, with her job and her growing closeness to M. He had a son too, Hriday. I must confess that I had been rather surprised by the choice of name given the sort of person M was. He might have been handsome, his body might have been tough and lean, but his speech betrayed the provincial character innate to Mymensingh, which stood in stark contrast to CS's clean utterances and pronunciation.

Besides, neither did he share any of CS's literary or cultural interests. In fact, when M used to zoom around the city on his motorcycle—two inches shorter than CS with the dark, stocky build so unique to Mymensingh—it would have been difficult to convince anyone that he really was a doctor and not a goon. His eyes especially were particularly bovine, the sort of eyes that do not really go very well with a masculine face. Perhaps that's why, precisely because of the softness of the eyes, the hardness of his body was never immediately apparent.

CS seemed to have forgotten everything—that she had a husband who could have come back any day, that he could have nurtured dreams of settling down as a happy family with his wife and son. She was not worried about Humayun, she was concerned only about M and whether he truly loved her. She would ask me what I thought about whether he loved her, although I had no clue about it whatsoever. I had only met the man once when CS had introduced us and he had abruptly cut off her introduction with 'Oh yes, I know her'. With an all-knowing sideways glance at me and a passing remark—'Dr Rajab Ali is your father, isn't he'—he had looked away to glance at CS's face and then again at a piece of paper in his hand; a mere scrap but it had been so very interesting to him at that moment. CS had been smiling sweetly while beads of sweat clung to his forehead; he should have wiped them away but he hadn't. While I could never be certain if M truly had any feelings for CS, their affair gradually spread beyond the confines of the office. CS's footsteps frequently began to find their way to Abakash and M's red motorcycle routinely began to trample the grass on the field.

In the beginning their conversations would take place in our living room—all their arguments, bellyaches, anger, laughter, tears, jokes, fights and meeting plans for the next day. Soon, M's motorcycle found its destructive way right up to the field of the housing cooperative of Agricultural University where CS lived, putting the grass there through the same torture and crushing the life out of it for good. By then their relationship had become unabashedly sexual. M would return home from her quarter late in the night. Her mother would usually be in the next room, a silent witness to everything, the roar of the motorcycle as well as their cries of pleasure. She had never interfered in her daughter's life and her daughter too had categorically told her that she was no longer interested in any physical intimacy with Humayun; that her husband had never been able to sexually satisfy her. CS had given me a blow-by-blow account of her husband's performance in bed—he would climb atop her and be done even before she had time to grasp what was happening. CS was no longer willing to waste her body on Humayun.

Even after Humayun's return to the country for good, her affair with M continued. M kept visiting their house and CS could not help getting close to him, joking and laughing with him and whispering in his ear with her husband right in front of them. Try as she might she could not keep her fiery passion for M a secret and her desire would reveal itself brazenly irrespective of who was with them. At night she would go back to her husband's bed and they would sleep beside each other like siblings; let alone Humayun touching her, even a passing shadow of his hand on her body would trigger her anger and exasperation.

Soon after, Humayun left to set up a dental clinic in Rajshahi. Such was her obsession with M that CS was not willing to expend even a passing thought on him. M had promised her that he would leave his wife and marry her; CS had believed him. What she had not known about was his rather decent relationship with his simple, god-fearing wife Shireen, also a doctor, and that he had another doctor, Anu, on the side as his mistress. He exploited three women every day telling each of them that he loved them, while CS failed to recognize the one single kernel of truth in all this—that he loved only himself. I had come to find out about M from Yasmin who had heard all this from her classmate Milan, M's younger brother. Was there any better proof than that? Once, Milan had even met CS and on hearing this M had flown into a screaming rage. 'Why did you go to meet her? She's a bad woman. She would make a pass at you too.' This was who M was, someone who made promises of love to CS while calling her names behind her back.

I warned CS, asked her to control herself. I told her M didn't love her, that he only wanted to exploit her.

'But he told me he loves me,' she protested.

'He lied to you,' I countered.

CS never lied and so it was unfathomable to her that other people did.

'He sleeps with you, then goes to Anu's house to have sex with her, and then goes back to sleep with his wife Shireen.'

'M has told me that he is not sexually involved with anyone else other than me.'

Eventually, CS set out to find the truth. M had sworn on the Quran that he had nothing to do with Anu. Let alone speak to her, he had claimed they did not even run into each other. Although CS did not believe in the Quran, M did and she was convinced that a believer would never lie in the name of the holy book. One fine day CS decided to do something outlandish. Donning a black burqa she took a bus to the Muktagacha Health Centre where M and Anu used to work. Standing in the queue with the other patients she kept an eye on the pair from behind the veil, observing their laughter and banter. The objective was not simply to observe them; it was as much about a surprise reveal. Reaching M and Anu, CS abruptly ripped off her veil in front of a flabbergasted M. Their relationship should have perhaps ended right then, but it didn't. M managed to grovel and snivel his way back into CS's confidence.

What I could not come to terms with was how much CS had changed—the same girl who used to watch every step and fret about the smallest things! While doctors our age were busy preparing for the FCPS exam, staying up nights to study, CS remained completely unperturbed by it. She had stopped eating and one could see it progressively taking a toll on her body, her beautiful face marked by dark lines. She used to have a hearty laugh and loved making other people smile with her sharp sense of humour. Instead she would sit around like a tree felled by the storm, her vacant eyes staring fixedly at the paint peeling off the walls and occasionally weeping desperately for M. The resolute and self-confident girl I had known was allowing herself to be abused by a dishonest gold-digger. Meanwhile, M had opened a new chamber by the river. He had also employed rickshaw-pullers and local touts at the Gudaraghat jetty to prey on patients who travelled from the villages to the city in search of doctors. These hapless patients were brought to his chamber and there he prescribed them a series of unnecessary blood, stool and urine tests, simply to siphon a lot of money off them. CS knew about everything but still chose to remain silent. Neither was she concerned about all that people were saying about her and everything she was doing. All she wanted, at the expense of everything if need be, was M. M, for his part, had kept deferring his promised divorce from his wife Shireen for well over a year. Did CS not know anything? She must have known that he had been lying to her, that he would never leave his wife for her! I felt nothing but annoyance at her senseless love for the man.

She came to our house one day and just sat there for a long time. She cried for a while, then sighed and said, 'At least once I want to know what an orgasm feels like.' Utterly surprised I asked, 'What are you saying! You have never had an orgasm?' She confessed she hadn't. Humayun was out of the question. Since M was great in bed and could go on for even two hours if he wished to, he was the only who could probably give her one. As annoyed as I was I could not feel anything but compassion for her.

I had later learnt via a survey conducted on female orgasms that most women do not know what they are. CS had known that there was such a thing as an orgasm and so she had wished to experience it. Those who don't know what it is don't desire it either.

~

My life went on as it had to with or without CS's woes. I was determined to make something of my medical expertise and to that end I got a signboard painted with my name, degrees and chamber timings and hung it from the main gate of Abakash. I even got letterheads specially printed from Jaman Printers. Patients did start coming in but they were usually from the locality and mostly known faces. Whenever they would stretch their hand towards me with the consultation fee my ears would start burning. No matter how hard I tried I could not stop it from happening every time. Unable to take money from these people I would hurriedly write the prescription and proceed to keep my hands folded under the table. Besides, I was soon overcome by yet another whimsical fancy—a dream to open a clinic of my own. I wanted to use the room in front of Abakash to make a small clinic that would provide pregnant women a chance to have a painless childbirth.

There was a large piece of tin lying in the courtyard which I took to Shilpasree, Jayanta Talukdar's shop in Golpukur, to have it cleaned and painted, and got 'Dr Taslima Nasrin, MBBS, BHS (Upper). Especially trained in gynaecology and childbirth. We use painkillers here for delivery', etc. written on it. The day I hung the new signboard in front of Abakash, that very day Father brought it down, stowed it away in the balcony and informed me that one needed a proper licence to start a medical clinic. Instead, much to my delight, seeing my immense enthusiasm for the medical profession he ended up offering me a job. He got a small room constructed for a pathological laboratory just outside his clinic, complete with a microscope and myriad red and blue bottles of chemicals. I was to sit there in the afternoon to test the laboratory samples he sent my way for 20 taka per test. We grew quite close during this time—after returning home at night we would often play chess, though Father would best me every time without much effort. In fact these chess matches were a thing of wonder in the house, with everyone else usually on my side and Father holding his own fort. Mother especially desired to see me defeat him and whenever he would capture one of my pieces she would get agitated: 'See, you should have moved your knight! Your father gave it thought before capturing it. Why do you move pieces without a thought?' If I lost she would usually be more depressed than me.

The work at the pathology lab saw a slight slump when I began getting calls from Popular Clinic, off C.K. Ghosh Road. Jahangir, my brother's childhood friend, owned the clinic, where women used to come for what we call menstrual regulation, or MR in medical terms—in laymen's terms it can be called an abortion. I was paid 300 taka for every MR; the remaining 1000 or 1200 went to the clinic. It was not as if I was experienced in the MR procedure, especially because it had never been a major component of the medical degree. A large syringe had to be inserted into the vagina to draw out the foetus; the nurses usually kept the patients ready on the operating table and I only had to go in to complete the procedure. For the first few patients the procedure was not completed fully. Suffering from vaginal infections some had to come back to finish the procedure and I could not help but feel terribly guilty. Gradually, I became more experienced at it and began getting calls from Seba Nursing Home near Chhayabani Cinema too. I was earning more and Father too was keen on fanning my interest in the medical profession. He was not happy with me being stuck in an everyday job or earning a few extra bucks by doing abortions, though—he wished for me to study further. A doctor with only an MBBS degree was not hard to find and the degree itself hardly mattered much in the long run—with it one had to be satisfied with only being a doctor in a remote village somewhere.

To become a doctor of importance I set myself diligently to the task of preparing for my FCPS degree, without which a simple MBBS degree amounted to nothing. Ironically, though I did pore over books, it was poetry that I was studying and not medicine. Every day Father would return with fresh news regarding another old batchmate moving to PG Hospital in Calcutta for a postgraduate degree. This would be in tandem with his laments about my uncertain future. He had always encouraged my fantasies of becoming a doctor; rather, he had never been actively opposed to it. However, his lack of opposition was what I had taken to be encouragement and this was something he had begun to dislike. So began the pointed jibes regarding the 300 taka I was making from Popular Clinic and Seba Nursing Home: 'If you pass the FCPS you can easily earn nearly three lakh from a single operation.' He would tell me about his life, how as a poor farmer's son he had chosen to not follow his father's profession and had worked hard to become a doctor instead. He was a doctor with an MBBS degree, why should his children remain stuck with the same? They should become FCPS doctors, even go abroad to get their FRCS and FRCP degrees. He could not come to terms with how I was bent on wasting such a glorious opportunity for higher education and so he would go on and on about the wrong choices I was making and how time and prospects once lost could never be retrieved.

Nevertheless, no matter what he said I could not continue studying for my FCPS exam. Although I was still a doctor, I was also acutely aware that I was tired of the life it entailed; that I wanted to do something different. And one fine day I did manage to do something different. I founded a cultural organization called the Shokal Kabita Parisad (Morning Poetry Council), with its offices in the room in front of Abakash where I had initially planned to set up my clinic.

Lives

My life was split between two cities—Mymensingh, with my home, my family and my job, and Dhaka, with its literature, its culture and my friends. Dhaka was always special; I would get on a train or a bus bound for the city whenever I had some money. There was another reason for visiting Dhaka so frequently—Suhrid. It had not been easy sending Suhrid to Dhaka. Chotda, my elder brother, had tried forcing him away once, amid screams and tears, to get him admitted to a school there. Mother too had given up and confessed that she could not look after him by herself any more, although later it was she who had gone and begged Chotda and Geeta to send Suhrid back. Not that she had had to implore much—Geeta had been more than happy to send the boy away again. In fact, Geeta had been rather taken aback by the boy's behaviour. Suhrid was her son. She had carried him for nine months and given birth to him. If the boy was supposed to feel a connection to someone it ought to have been his own mother. However, let alone answering her when called or jumping on to her lap, Suhrid would run to his grandfather or to his aunts.

Geeta could not fathom how her own son could dare ignore her so. Livid, she had sat and fumed and screamed. 'My son's gotten spoilt because of this infernal family. If they want a son so bad why don't they get one of their daughters married?' And my Chotda had knelt in front of her and implored, 'Geeta, come what may I will bring your son to you.' Geeta had remained unimpressed and my brother continued; he had had to admit that everything was his fault, that he was the cause of Geeta's suffering, and that he should not have sent the boy to Abakash after his birth in the first place. He had had to accept that because of him their son did not want Geeta as a mother. He had blamed his mother and his sisters for how the boy had turned out and finally admitted that only Geeta was the right person to take care of Suhrid. Mollified, Geeta had finally stopped screaming and gotten up to pour herself a glass of water. She had then pushed Chotda out, locked the bedroom door and, walking up to the cupboard stuffed with saris, jewellery and money, fished out a photo album from under a stack of ironed plain cotton saris, proceeding to destroy all photos of Suhrid taken with us at Abakash and sparing only the photos with her in them.

Joy usually knew no bounds in Abakash as far as Suhrid was concerned. We used to frequently have him pose for photographs. Yasmin had located a friend's brother who owned a photo studio and she had gotten his camera and taken numerous photographs of Suhrid. The day she brought the photographs home, we had fought over who would get to see them first. Geeta had arrived with Chotda from Dhaka around the same time. She had had scant real interest in the photos, although she had managed to express some enthusiasm nonetheless. In fact, she had requested that the photographs be given to her, presumably because we had Suhrid for real while she had to make do with his memories via photographs. Not that she had said it in as many words; it had not been difficult to deduce the insinuation. On the basis of that deduction we had handed over all of Suhrid's photos to her, an act behind which Mother's sympathies for her had played a significant part.

That very afternoon, when Yasmin's friend Krishti had come over and Yasmin had wanted to show her the photographs, Geeta had categorically refused to hand them over. She had taken them with her to Dhaka and later torn them up. In fact she even tore up the negatives and dumped them in the bin in the kitchen. It may have calmed her down for the moment but it had not succeeded in getting rid of the animosity she felt for us: Mother, Yasmin and I. The feeling had made her hands itch and wish to tear us bloody with her talons. What had we done? According to her, we had formed a hold over someone else's child—that had been our fault. Even without the love and attention showered on him Suhrid had always been an energetic child. Mother would keep calling for him and he would not even look back, running like the wind, stealthy and swift, racing up to the roof or off to the field. Mother would constantly worry about him falling and getting hurt somewhere. Geeta had been adamant that her son had to listen to her. So when he refused to do as asked, refused to sit down when told to or stand up when ordered, she would get displeased and angry. For her it did not matter if Suhrid did not listen to anyone else in the world; he had to automatically listen to her. Did he not know who she was?

Geeta would stomp about ferociously and yank Suhrid towards her, her eyes red with rage and her teeth bare, and demand, 'Do you know I am your mother? Do you know there's no one closer to you than me? Why don't you come to me as soon as I call you? Why? From now whenever I call you have to be in front of me immediately!' Suhrid, dumbfounded, would tilt his head in agreement and then run to Mother to hide behind her and weep helplessly. His tears used to break us. Mother would try teaching him every day to love his parents. One day she had even tried speaking to Geeta. 'Why don't you try it nicely . . .' she began in a placatory tone. 'I will decide how I speak to my son,' Geeta thundered. Mother had gone quiet and so had we. After a long while she had spoken again. 'He stays here and so he considers us family. He comes to us, is attached to us. When you take him with you he will form a similar bond with you. Then he won't even want to leave you and come visit us.'

During her brief visits to Abakash, while Geeta's only concern would be to make Suhrid listen to her, the little boy would constantly struggle to escape her clutches. Whenever they suggested taking him away to Dhaka he would clutch at one of us in fear and whisper in our ear to hide him somewhere and not let him go. If we did not comply he would go ahead and find a hiding place himself; once he had gone and hidden in one of the paper boxes under the bed in the tin room. Geeta would notice how close he was to us and how much he loved the people at Abakash; she would notice how he did not love her as he loved us. To the boy she was terror personified, a nightmarish ordeal and nothing else. Every time she visited us she would drag him to a separate room and tell him, 'You have no one else in this world other than me.' He would stare at her and then try to run away, failing to do so because of her vice-like grip on his neck. He would end up crying and driving his mother to thoughts of murder.

In all this Suhrid was the one who got dragged around. Once, while he had been playing badminton, Chotda had arrived from Dhaka without any advance notice and taken him away from the field. The little boy had kept crying for help as he was being taken away. A few days later he was brought back to us again and it seemed the little boy had been given a fresh lease on life. We got him admitted to a school called Notun Kuri (Tender Buds). I used to take him to school and fetch him back while Mother took on the task of teaching him English and vernacular alphabets at home, and how to draw and spell and recite nursery rhymes, shaping him into the brightest boy in his class. He was growing up enveloped in our love and care. The day Chotda arrived again to take him to Dhaka for good, this time by any means necessary, Yasmin had fled with the boy. By the time she had returned in the evening Chotda had left after waiting for them the whole day, but not before soundly admonishing us regarding our role in spoiling Suhrid and warning us that they would cut off all ties with Abakash unless we agreed to send Suhrid to Dhaka the next day. A meeting was called that night and Father decided that it was best to comply. There were good schools in Dhaka and he would get a lot of opportunities. It broke our hearts into pieces to have to do such a thing but we had to consider the bright future ahead of him and gather our emotions.

It would have been impossible for Chotda and Geeta to take him to Dhaka, though; even if they were to tie him up in the car he would have attempted to jump off the moving vehicle. So it was decided that Yasmin and I would take him. Since he would have refused to go with us if he had known we were going to hand him over to his parents, we had to lie to him about visiting a fair in Dhaka and about returning the very same day. We took the morning train, got off at Kamalapur station in Dhaka and hailed a rickshaw for Nayapaltan. Suhrid had been expecting the fair we had promised him and it was only when we reached Nayapaltan that he had finally figured out our ruse, beginning to scream and cry immediately and demanding why we had brought him there instead of taking him to the fair. The more we had tried convincing him that we would simply drop by for a while and leave, the more he had cried that he did not wish to go at all. We had gotten off, bought him ice cream and walked with him for a long time, telling a him a bunch of lies—that we had run out of money and had to go see Chotda to borrow some in order to be able to visit the fair and return to Mymensingh at night, and so on. The beloved boy had believed everything we told him that day and entered the house with us. Chotda had been away but Geeta was there. One look at her and Suhrid would not let go of us. Geeta could not stand it, his insolent attachment to us that made him refuse to obey his mother's orders. She had wrenched him away by his wrist and thrown him to the floor. Shocked, we had tried to intervene; she had lunged at him again and slapped him across the face. Terrified, he had tried running towards us but she had grabbed hold of his collar, yanked him back and roared, 'Where are you going? Come here. One step without my orders from now and I will murder you.'

We could see him trembling in terror. No one had ever laid even a finger on him in Abakash, let alone strike him or push him. Neither had he ever heard anyone speak to him like that. He had started crying in fear and was rewarded with another slap and a blow on his back. 'Not a single sound,' Geeta had screeched. Silent sobs were racking his frame while we stood in a corner weeping, unable to do or say anything. Even the mildest protest from us would have resulted in revenge in the form of another blow—he was within her grasp to do as she pleased with him. If she wanted she could tear him to pieces. The boy who used to be treated like a prince in Abakash, whose well-being had been our primary concern, who was smothered in attention and fed with love every hour—chicken soup, fruit juice, pure milk, cream, fish koftas, carrot halva, puddings with eggs and so much more—was not allowed to eat anything the entire day. We could not stand it. We had returned to Mymensingh that day, both of us crying the entire way back. We had asked ourselves repeatedly whether Geeta had truly ever wanted Suhrid with them in Dhaka, since it had not seemed so to me. She had been happier when he had been away; he had been the perfect weapon for her to manipulate Chotda's guilty conscience with and keep him compliant.

~

We kept going back to Nayapaltan despite Geeta's misbehaviour in order to see Suhrid; he seemed to come back to life whenever he saw us. Geeta would quickly usher him to another room when he tried to come near and not allow him to talk to us. He would be locked up in another room from where he would stare at us through the crack between the door. If Geeta allowed him to get a drink of water or go to the toilet, and our eyes would meet for an instant, all our love used to be exchanged in that one fleeting glance. He would keep trying to be let out just for that. We did not dare protest. We had no choice but to stay silent, like deer hiding from a stalking predator.

Or Geeta would have to be enticed with gifts to thaw her, for her to allow us a brief meeting with Suhrid. He would approach us cautiously, his eyes glistening with joy. The boy who used to laugh out loud and do as he pleased, who used to run like the wind and speak nineteen to the dozen, was no longer allowed to smile or cry. Forced to speak in whispers, his voice grew hollow, his entire mien terrified and lifeless. He would keep saying the same thing to us: 'Stay. Don't go.' If he were to see the return tickets in our hands, his eyes would well up and he would try and snatch them away. Even if we were not allowed to talk to him, our presence in the house gave him comfort, the fact that we were there near him in one of the rooms.

His face would be a mask of fear, dread clouding his eyes all the time. Geeta's terror loomed over him like a shadow. At Abakash whenever he refused to eat we used to tell him stories to entice him. With Geeta he was not allowed to touch any food even if he were to die of hunger. There would be food in the refrigerator and on the table but he had strict instructions not to lay a finger on anything. He was only allowed to eat when Geeta would feed him—bad, often rotten, stale and inedible food. We saw him grow skeletal gradually, his plump, cherubic frame withering under her onslaught. At least when Chotda used to be home he would gather everyone at the dinner table for meals and Geeta would have to feed him meat and other things despite her reluctance. Before outsiders she maintained the perfect maternal facade, her love for her son shining forth bright, but few remained unaware of her conniving nature for too long. Geeta was a cunning woman; she could hide her true vicious nature all too well beneath layers of affect to be able to manipulate and control anyone for her own gains. However, none of the relationships stood the test

of time; she would be gone like the wind as soon as her purpose was
served.

Unable to stay away we would go back to Nayapaltan time and
again just for a fleeting glance of Suhrid. Mother would take chicken
for him and lots of fruits, but Geeta would take everything from her
and hide it all away, not breathing a word about it to Suhrid. Earlier,
as soon I got my salary I used to take him out and buy him the toys
he wanted. I continued doing so, buying clothes and toys and taking
them to Dhaka, but the same thing happened and Geeta would lock
everything away in the cupboard, neither telling him nor giving him
anything. She instead gave everything to Parama, who had her sole
attention. The love and care Suhrid used to get at Abakash was now
reserved for her daughter. The little girl even had the right to abuse
her older brother, hit him or kick him and he had to endure it all
silently. The two siblings were being brought up in different ways in
the same house. Suhrid had never taken showers on his own; instead,
Mother used to bathe him with soap and lukewarm water, massage
him with olive oil and comb his hair neatly. Living in Dhaka he had
to learn to bathe on his own; most days he would just pour some
water over his head and come out. Geeta would bathe Parama, give
her new clothes, shoes and toys, reserving the old hand-me-downs for
Suhrid. He had a hard mattress to sleep on while Parama got a soft
bed. She got the kisses while the blows were for him. Geeta would
rub baby lotion on the girl, comb her hair, and coo, 'Do you want
some grapes, princess?'

'No.'

'Please, just a little.'

'No.'

'My little darling, please, only a little.'

The girl would nod in acceptance. Immediately Geeta would
yell for Suhrid to fetch Parama grapes. Suhrid would run to obey his
mother.

He would ask, 'Can I have some too, Mother?'

'No!' she would bark. Or perhaps Parama wanted to put on her
shoes. Geeta would call, 'Suhrid, get her shoes.' He would get the
shoes and be rewarded with a blow on his back. 'Go clean them first!'
Geeta would bark again. Then she would say, 'Go put them on her

feet.' If he were to complain, 'Am I her slave?' Geeta would instantly lunge at him, brandishing her slippers and beating him, and scream, 'Yes, you are her slave. You help her wear them every other day so how dare you complain today? What is making you so brave? Who? Do you think anyone will be able to save you from me?' All this would happen in front of me and unable to bear it I would leave the room to go to the balcony and cry, struggling believe the scene I had witnessed with my own eyes. Could a mother ever behave in such a manner with her own child? I have often heard stories of evil stepmothers but all such tales paled in comparison to how Geeta used to behave. Mother used to say, 'She didn't clean his shit or his piss, nor did she teach him to walk or talk. She got a tailor-made son after six years, so of course there is no attachment.' I have always wondered why, though. Do mothers who have been reunited with their children after many years of separation love them less intensely? Father would visit Suhrid too and Geeta would not let him meet the boy either. He would struggle, wanting to come near Father but would be restrained with punches, slaps and dire warnings. Each time Father would return to Abakash broken-hearted—'Has Geeta completely forgotten that Suhrid is her own child?'

~

After each visit we returned from Dhaka, with our hearts heavy and distressed about what was happening right in front of us. It often happened that we would turn up at Nayapaltan but Geeta would not open the door to let us in. Once, braving a terrible heat wave, Mother went to Nayapaltan, enduring the dust and the soot of the unruly and crowded bus from Mymensingh to Dhaka, only to end up waiting in front of their door for nearly four hours before returning home. Geeta had been at home that day but she had refused to open the door. Another time Suhrid had seen Mother through the window and called out to Geeta to open the door, but she had not responded. Suhrid had dragged a chair to the door all by himself and unlatched the door. Obviously, for this act of defiance there had been severe consequences for him over the next few days. On many an occasion I too had to return from Dhaka empty-handed. Even if Geeta were to open the door she would not tell us to sit or offer us any food. We usually got food from outside and spent the night on the couch, only for Suhrid. Often we thought to simply stop going, only to change our minds later—we kept going because of Suhrid, because our visits never failed to make him happy.

To ensure our visits continued unimpeded we showered Geeta with gifts so it would appear we loved her dearly, took the entire family out to the restaurant, or the theatre, and to fairs and markets, wherever she wanted to go, as if she was the kindest person in the entire world. We tried hard to make sure she did not sense that we were doing everything only for Suhrid's sake, so that he would be allowed to meet us and to ensure he had some respite from his otherwise suffocating existence. Geeta understood everything, of course, and I knew that she did. She never said anything, neither did she let Suhrid sense anything. It often happened that I would leave my purse stuffed with money in the living room to go to the toilet, only to find it empty when I returned. The same happened to the earrings I once took off before going for a shower. I was sure about one thing—if such things made Geeta happy then I was fine with letting this continue just so she would refrain from thinking of new ways of tormenting Suhrid. I regretted my losses in silence and did not utter a word aloud. We had to flatter Parama too, pick her up and coo about her prettiness when she was anything but, besides giving her gifts because it made Geeta happy. If Geeta was happy she would ask us to sit or even let us meet Suhrid, at the very least let us have a glimpse of him or a moment of respite when he could quickly come and touch us. Even a fleeting touch was very important to him. Geeta's mother and siblings would often stay over with them and I saw them fawn over Parama and abuse Suhrid as well. Making Geeta happy was obviously her family's primary economic necessity.

This one time Suhrid fell and broke his hand and Geeta refused to take him to a doctor; in the end I had to. The doctor took an X-ray and detected a broken bone. Suhrid's hand was put in a plaster and placed in a sling, with the doctor warning us that it would take nearly a month to heal completely. No sooner had we returned to their place than Geeta tore open the plaster and sling and declared, 'Nothing's happened to him. It's all an act.' We tolerated everything Geeta did, all the time praying that she would direct her ire at us and not him. Suhrid too understood everything and the six-year-old endured all her cruelty so she would not misbehave with us. Quashing all his emotions and natural exuberance ruthlessly he picked up lessons in deviousness. He tried his best to make his mother happy, say things that pleased her; he learnt to put on an act simply to gain some sympathy from his own mother.

Chotda would return from his job in the airlines every two weeks or so. As soon as he entered Geeta's complaints would begin—Suhrid was bad, he never listened to anything she said, there were complaints against him from school, he had hit Parama, and more such figments of her imagination. She was happy when Chotda scolded Suhrid; she encouraged him to fawn over Parama instead, placing her in his lap and praising her to the skies—Parama was good in studies and in recitation, skilful at games as well as taking over people's lives, and so on and so forth. There was no end to things she wanted, especially since everything was about her. Chotda did notice that Suhrid was being mistreated but he did not possess the courage to stand up to Geeta. He gave all his money to her and it was his duty to follow everything she decreed—not just Suhrid, Chotda too was terrified of her. Geeta had long since resigned from her job as a receptionist in the airlines office and transitioned to being a full-time housewife. It was not as if she led the life of a housewife, though—she had a swanky lifestyle, she drove her own car and went where she pleased, to play tennis or swim. Despite being a housewife Geeta led the sort of independent lifestyle that most independent and affluent working women could only dream of. Her fearlessness and self-assurance used to amaze me while her lack of generosity, her cruelty and her misbehaviour troubled me as much.

Mother was worried that all this would affect Suhrid's brain, since he was not getting a chance to have a normal childhood. She also believed Geeta would eventually begin to love the boy. In fact, we believed that too, but we were foolish in thinking so. At the very centre of it all there was one reason why she hated Suhrid—she hated him because he did not love her, he loved us. That love had not diminished an ounce even after they had separated him from us; this realization further stoked her rage. Her envy, her obstinacy and her pettiness had stamped out every last bit of common sense.

It happened that we went months without visiting Suhrid, only to give their relationship a chance to become normal and to ensure Suhrid got a chance at growing up like any other child of his age. Whenever Chotda came to Abakash with them during Eid Suhrid would come back to life. He brightened up at once, playing, running, laughing and crying like before simply because we were near him again. All this would change in an instant if Geeta was around. It was the same every Eid; he refused to go back to Dhaka with them at the end of the day. He would go and hide, trembling in fear. They always found him in the end and beat him into submission, dragging him to the car. His screams of pain while being dragged away left scars on Abakash and the entire neighbourhood.

Geeta could never love Suhrid and neither could Suhrid ever love his mother.

~

Without Suhrid, for long stretches of time Abakash remained lifeless, a ghostly fortress that once used to be full of laughter and joy. For days on end there would be nothing to keep us company but the silent sighs emanating from the spectral house.

I Could Never Touch You

The ashes of an incredible dream—a life with R, a life for the two of us together—clung to me like skin. I knew it was no longer possible to live with him; I was well aware that we had both definitively turned towards different lives away from each other. That the time had come to clean the ash and grit off and start afresh. Yet time rolled by, the days burnt out silently, the nights kept howling by like monitors shrieking in the dark, and I remained stuck all by myself like wreckage cast aside. I could not fathom which new direction I should choose, which way I should go where his crushing absence would not immediately set off after me like a maniac in pursuit. Life felt like a feather at one moment and heavy as a stone the very next. I had never really felt this weight before, the full weight of life, and before I could make sense of things it had crept down my back and slowly bent my spine. I could not recognize this life; it was mine and yet it was not. Without pausing to consider I had given away everything life had offered to me to another. Later, racked with thirst, I had reached out and found that there was nothing left for me.

My life was spread out in front of me like an arid wasteland. Every day I would run to the door on hearing the postman—like I used to previously, but not exactly like that either—despite knowing for certain there would be no letters for me. I searched among the pile for the one letter whose words magically arise from the page and dance like dreams in front of my eyes, their silvery shimmer falling on me like rain. I knew I would receive no letters like I used to once but the desire buried deep inside me would frequently resurface without warning, like a boisterous gaggle of adolescent girls. It was not me; rather it was some other entity inside me, searching for a familiar handwriting on the envelopes. It was not me; it was someone else who sighed when there was no letter to be found. Every day I would stare after the departing back of the postman, the letters he had left behind in my hand, the sighs surrounding me. Not mine, someone else's. I tried casting this unknown person aside, struggled to keep the entity hidden in some dark dungeon deep within. Every day, over and over, I tried to forget that I would never get another letter from R. On my knees in the ash I helplessly sat searching, hoping to unearth even a few shards of the incredible dream that might have been left behind by mistake.

Come February, every afternoon I ran into many poets and writers while strolling down the book fair on the grounds of the Bangla Academy in Dhaka. Many conversations, many hours spent in the tea stalls over adda, although through it all my eyes searched tirelessly for one particular face and a familiar pair of eyes. Every night I returned home unfulfilled. Then suddenly there he was one day and I found myself walking up to him, my feet driven by some unrecognizable part of me. I wanted to ask him, 'Are you well? If you are, will you tell me how? I have not been well. You seem happy. How do you seem happy? I have not been happy for a long, long time.' I said nothing as he stood there surrounded by friends. Instead, I quietly watched him for a long time, wanting to break through the barrier to go stand in front of him and stroll through the book fair with him like we used to. I turned my desires over in my mind, played hide-and-seek with them a little, blindfolding them and running away. And then, safely at a distance, I would stop to turn around and laugh, the laughter ringing out like a hollow wail even to my ears.

His new book of poems was out but I could be a part of the joyous celebrations only from a distance. When I did manage to buy his book *Diyechile Shokol Akash* (You Had Given Me All the Sky) and approach him for an autograph he stared at me coldly for a while before scribbling on the front page—'To Anyone'. Somewhere down the line I had become just like anyone to him. I stood there numb with the book in my hand, and I could feel my thoughts pounding in my head like a tribe of monkeys trying to tear me apart. Had R known how much I had hoped he would ask about me? How was I, when did I reach Dhaka, how long was I going to stay, and more. All my acquaintances had asked me these questions. Were R and I not even acquaintances any more? How could he be so thoughtless? Could someone forget a person they once loved so soon? Riding pillion on my desires the unanswered questions returned home with me.

Towards the end of the book fair we finally managed to talk, sit down and have tea together. I asked him about his leg and he told me he was finally able to walk short distances.

'Did you stop smoking?'

'That will be quite impossible,' he laughed and replied. I did not ask if he had managed to quit other things too, afraid he was going to say those would be quite impossible to quit too. Gazing intently into my eyes for a while he asked me in a deep voice, 'Come with me to Jhinaidaha tomorrow, early in the morning.' He did not know if I wanted to go nor did he wish to; he asked me as if he still had the right to ask me, as if he knew I would agree. As if the moment he touched me I would cry out like a stubborn girl. I was supposed to return to Mymensingh the day after and there I was being offered a trip to Jhinaidaha instead. There was a poetry event being organized there and other poets were going to attend as well. The last time, when our separation had not yet been finalized, we had gone to Cox's Bazar where we had bathed in the sea and read out poetry to each other on the beach in the twilight. The poets Mahadev Saha and Nasir Ahmed had been there too—Saha in a lungi and a kurta with a *gamchha* over his shoulder, R and Nasir Ahmed in long trousers and me in a kangaroo-yellow tee and jeans. We had waded into the sea, our clothes had gotten wet and heavy and the waves had tried to draw us further in over and over again. It had been wonderful! I decided to go to Jhinaidaha, not to be a part of the celebration but only because I wanted to be with R. We were divorced, we were no longer in a domestic partnership, but there was no one closer to me in the world than R and there was no greater friend. We had grown close over many years and he had become my entire world. He had hurt me but I could not deny that I still loved him.

There was a bus for Jhinaidaha from the Bangla Academy. On the way we spoke about the smallest incidents and accidents that had happened in our lives in the meantime. The only thing I hid was my pain, never telling him how in the cold mornings I usually awoke to a frozen lifelessness. Suddenly he asked, 'You want to listen to a poem?'

Was it even possible that I would turn down one of my favourite poets? Sitting beside me in the bus R read the poem out aloud—it was called 'Dure achho dure' (The farthest you are from me).

> I could never touch you, the part which makes you, you—
> I have sifted through warm bodies in search of happiness,
> We have dug into each other in search of solitude,
> But I have never been able to touch you.
>
> The way they break oysters to find pearls,
> You have only found disease in me,
> And an eternal river of flames.
>
> In ecstasy,
> I have read the startling secrets in your eyes—
> But I have never been able to touch you.
>
> Trusting hands have slackened, like creepers, and let go—
> On my way to these unmindful revelries
> I have brushed past my heart; or tissue as I call it now.
>
> I could never touch you, the part of you that was mine—
> Driven to madness, I have upset the calm,
> Laid the quiet sky to waste,
> And my soul has walked in the relentless rain.
>
> To this day I have not been able to reach the part that makes you, you.

I kept staring for a long time at the flamboyant tree outside, laden with red blossoms, the sultry breeze brushing my skin softly. R was reading his poems, telling me how he had been writing with both hands, a lot of political poetry and a verse drama. At my behest he even handed me his notebook of new poems; I noticed that besides the radical, anti-establishment verses there was a new and different kind of poetry too, one of personal insight. Although it had taken him time and effort to arrive at this new form, nevertheless I was happy to note that he had broken out of time-worn shackles. This new poetry gradually transported me to a fantastic and exquisite world where R appeared more committed and more sincere.

On stage at the conference at Jhinaidaha, we read our own revolutionary poems against untruth, inequity, autocracy, injustice and oppression. The louder the voice of outrage grew, the louder was the applause—the most politically subversive poems drew the widest praise. This is a fairly well-known trend in poetry—those who only write poems of personal grief and happiness are not usually considered socially conscious enough. I had seen this in R too. He used to be much prouder of his political poems than he was of his other work, perhaps more so because in a time of social and national crisis such poetry becomes a clarion call for casting one's personal grievances aside and coming out into the open, to reconnect and reconcile with humanity, and to compose lyrics reflecting collective desires.

Poets do not exist outside society. Just like others it is their duty too to attempt to find a cure for an ailing social order. Poets were very popular in Bangladesh; hundreds of people gathered at poetry conferences to listen to them and the poets would use this platform to call for social revolution. R too had taken on such a challenge and he was more than equal to the task, his fiery poems attacking the dictatorial government mercilessly. I was left wondering as to how someone with such a commanding voice and such a formidable ability to conjure blistering verses could be so icy otherwise. Off stage, on our way to somewhere else, I could sense R falling behind because of his slow, measured steps. He was walking a short stretch and then stopping to recover from the strain; every time I extended my shoulder in support. I felt so helpless seeing him it made me want to brush away his illnesses in the wink of an eye, grab him by the hand and start running—two mad, earnest and excited hearts leaving everyone else behind to bite the dust.

While my desires were being trampled under the feet of the people walking ahead, in the house of the director of the Jhinaidaha Cultural Association, the poet Asad Choudhury, was beginning an informal debate with his numerous admirers. Like most debates of the time the theme was rather topical—Hussain Muhammad Ershad[3] and how he could be deposed. Critical arguments were bandied about on whether the political parties were succeeding in their anti-Ershad campaigns, whether Khaleda Zia and Sheikh Hasina were making any mistakes in their political strategies. R's excitement about contributing to the discussion was palpable; I was intrigued too but I knew that any input would be impossible for me. I have never been very well versed in heavy political jargon and neither was I very good at exposition. It had taken me days to comprehend the meaning of the term 'socio-economic'. What I knew for certain was that in order to create a healthy and safe environment all steps had to be taken to ensure the necessary sustenance, shelter, education and health care for all. There had to be equality between men and women, fair distribution of wealth, the eradication of superstition, bigotry, violence and ruthlessness from society. And all this required an efficient and honest leadership. Who was going to lead the nation?

Some were in favour of Sheikh Hasina while others wanted Khaleda Zia and various reasons were being discussed for and against both candidates among their supporters. The brightest spot in all this was the fact that both women had joined hands to fight Ershad. We were used to seeing the two at odds with each other, exchanging insults at random, but here they were united under one common goal, having set aside their differences at least for the time being. Of course, as much as this was a credit to both of them, the biggest effort had been put in by the intellectuals who had advised and inspired the two leaders to come together for the sake of democracy. Despite having gotten used to experiencing inequality, in effect all around me a new dream of a just and unbiased society was gradually beginning to take hold. Life is usually the most uncertain of all things; not just for a select few, it is so for everyone. That night in Jhinaidaha had managed to unearth a secret trove of hope, despair, new dreams and fresh nightmares.

One of the guests had informed our host that R and I were no longer married; while making arrangements for the night two separate rooms were allotted to us. We politely refused the gesture and slept on the same bed. After what seemed like ages R touched me again that night, kissed me again, our two bodies joining and converging at a point, an incredibly intimate moment after being apart for aeons. The morning after brought with it curious and speculative stares from the others. I did not feel the guilt everyone was expecting me to feel and nor was I perturbed by the disapproval. I might have separated from R in legal terms but if there was a man whom I considered my own it was R. There was not an iota of artifice or untruth in the fact that R was the only man I loved, regardless of the many hurts I nursed against him. I kept that love well hidden; it was the same useless sensation that made me place my hands on his warm, dark hands, made me sit by myself in solitude, did not allow me to make plans for my life and stopped me from thinking about my future altogether. On our way back to Dhaka, while engrossed in talking about poetry and reading stray lines to each other, R began reciting a very old poem of his. It seemed as if his time was slowly and irrevocably decomposing—

> Take off my clothes.
> These artifices, the skin on my flesh,
> This crumbling casing of beauty—
> Take off this shroud that the sun places on the day.
> Time and every instant, like molten tar, is melting
> Just like a woman or a child's untainted feelings,
> And Man's faith, and love.
> I cannot undo the relentless loss of civilization,
> The wetness of self-stimulation, or flowers swept away by the currents,
> Or dying children; I cannot turn back the epidemic,
> The murder of embryos, predatory hands in the dark . . .
> Unforgivable failures have piled high and become a mountain,
> With a valley of golden indolence at its feet,
> And a few stray, pale defeated demons.
> Rip my consciousness to pieces,
> Whip my static trustful body blood,
> Throw my soul to a hungry lion.
> I can't rip off their original masks—
> I can only burn,
> And I can save some fire from the night,
> To burn the morning.

I could sense a new grief stealthily approaching me. Brushing my pain aside impatiently R was telling me about a girl called Shimul he

had met the year before at the book fair, about whom he had written
a number of poems. 'What kind of poems?' I could not help but ask.

> During dark summer storms,
> I feel like holding another girl's hand,
> And losing myself in the remoteness.
> My dreams take flight in the rain and the wind.
> I wish I could bloom like a spray of shimul.

'And then?'

> In the scorching afternoon heat,
> I wish I could touch the solitary mole on her chin,
> With love; blue eyes, and a body made of moonlight—
> I wish I could feel the fine tendrils of memory,
> Through my fingers, and move aside the locks falling lightly
> Over a forehead of dreams.

'What else do you wish for?'

> I wish I could walk down the middle
> Of the orderly city road,
> And sweep aside all the prohibition.
> I too wish I could cry.

'Isn't that a happy thing? What's with the tears then? Why do you
want to cry?'
        'Listen to me first,' he laughed and replied.
        'Fine, tell me first.' I laughed too.

> I wish I could take the cuffs off,
> I wish I could maul all the intrigue,
> I too wish I could break your body into fragments.

'Why do you sound like a butcher? Whose body do you want to cut
into pieces?'
        Before my faux ire could betray itself, with a smile R continued,
'Have you read the verse dramas? They are about Shimul.'

I don't know your name,
But I know you.
Where do I look for you now?
Where do I go and search?

In ceramic woods, or among the brick she-oak,
Where do I go and search for you?

Where are your placid mornings and serene days?
Where are your fulsome afternoons and lonely nights?
Where do I look for you? In the fallen leaves,
The evenings spread out in the grass? Where do I look for you?

'You have looked enough. In the second verse drama you mention having lost sleep while looking for her and only realizing it in the morning. It's the same in the third. You have crossed rivers, oceans and vast fields, mountains and forests and what not! You have even searched the sky but have you managed to find her after all?' R smiled brightly and told me he had found her—he had found his Shimul. Apparently Shimul had been hesitant at first, had been cautious about opening herself up to him. R had done his best to coax her hesitations aside.

Be a little indiscreet in this cavalcade.
Why a little? Why only a little indiscreet?
You could open your heart to me,
Let your ebony tresses loose,
And you could reveal your deepest shame to me,
The still-fresh memory of the wound on your brow,
And your dreams of tomorrow.
You could simply brush aside the memory-fossils,
Let the silk-cotton float in the air,
And brush past the noisy afternoons, riding on the clouds.
You could toss the green paper,
On which you wrote your dreams to me,
Into the water under the bridge.
You could spread out your hand and ask for a summer storm,
Walk on the fragrant wet earth, and ask life to change for you.

Sensing the tears about to spill I turned towards the window to hide my face. As if specks of dust carried by the wind through the open window had gotten into my eye and I was trying to wipe them off. I did not want R to see how hurt I was. What reason did I have to be sad? Our lives were different. He was allowed to fall in love with someone else, even marry someone else if he wished to. Smiling as if his new-found love was quite amusing to me, as if it was making me deliriously happy, I asked, 'And the girl is ready to change her life?'

'Yes, Shimul has agreed to get married. But she wants to wait for a while.'

'The two of you must be together all the time.'

'Yes, we are.'

'What does she look like?'

'She's young. Pretty.'

'Great.'

'What is great?'

R's eyes lit up with a stunning light, his dreams reflected deep in them.

'Have you kissed her?'

'Yes.'

'Have you had sex?'

'She wanted to. I said no.'

'You said no! What are you saying! Why?'

'I told her I wanted to wait till after we are married.'

'She really wanted to sleep with you?'

'Yes, she did.'

I was surprised to hear this. Bengali girls do not usually go out of their way to ask their boyfriends for sex, especially before marriage.

'Then?'

'What then?'

'Do you honestly love Shimul?'

R was staring, numerous red shimul flowers blossoming in his eyes. Averting his gaze to rest upon the flamboyant tree in full bloom outside, perhaps hoping to chance upon a shimul among their mix, he answered in a happy voice, 'Yes, I do.'

'Truly?'

'Truly.'

'Why did you ask?' he inquired.

My eyes fixed on the barren slice of land in the distance, I replied, 'Just like that.' R was beginning to appear distant; a friend still but not the same as before. We were close but not that close any more.

We reached Dhaka in the middle of the night and R took me to his newly rented house on Indira Road to spend the rest of the night. Following him up to his room on the second floor I was faced with a completely unknown space done up in a totally unfamiliar style. The only objects from before were the bed, the old sheets and the old blue mosquito net—all familiar things and yet so very unfamiliar to me. While he slept soundly I spent the rest of the night sleepless beside him on that bed. R had slept with countless women but he had always maintained that he was not in love with any of them; he had had no emotional ties to them. The same man was freely confessing his love for another person to me, unhesitatingly telling me their love story. Looking around among the shifting shadows in the room I was struck by a thought—surely Shimul must have been there, surely this was where their love-struck gazes had met and held.

In the morning I got up and placed two kisses on R's forehead, ruffled his thick hair fondly and said to him, 'Be happy.' He nodded and replied, 'I hope you will be happy too.' Leaving him in bed I waved him goodbye and left. I was meant to leave anyway.

I walked out of the house and kept walking looking for a rickshaw. The balmy morning air was caressing my skin but it seemed as if a violent summer storm was bent on upsetting everything inside me, destroying everything and leaving me destitute. I felt alone all of a sudden, so very alone. It seemed there was not another soul on the road except me. Unaware as to where I was going I marched on aimlessly with a horde of my own memories in close pursuit—memories of Mymensingh, the college campus, the canteen, the Press Club and the Botanical Garden, those days of intense passion and dreams strung together with love. I suddenly found it impossible to disentangle myself from the hold my memories had on me. The tentacles, like those of an octopus, were gradually coiling around me, they had me in their chokehold and I could not breathe.

The Holy Carrot

To combat the growing menace of the Ershad Hatao movement, he dangled a holy carrot in front of the people. A new clause was unilaterally added to the constitution—a state religion—and consequently, Islam was declared the state religion of Bangladesh. Were there demands in public to instate Islam as the state religion? No, there had been no such demands. Were Muslims finding it difficult to practise their religion without the proviso? Nothing of that sort had happened and everything had been going on as usual. The Muslims were fine, they were constructing masjids and madrasas in every conceivable corner of the nation, seers and soothsayers were cropping up a dime a dozen and everything had been going to hell anyway. The only things missing had been the President's personal interventions, which were finally at hand. By playing the religion card Ershad was effectively contributing to the din already audible everywhere.

Do nations need a religion? It is the people who need it. The nation is not one individual; it is a guarantor of safety for people of all religious and ethnic identities. If the nation is not impartial, if a nation shows communal tendencies, then is it surprising that its people will protest and create disruption? This is something that is bound to happen. In an Islamic state a non-Muslim citizen is bound to feel insecure. The one true path to civilization lies in the separation of the state and religion—almost all developed nations have followed that path. The time when religion had been all-powerful has historically been regarded as the Dark Ages—a time when millions of people were burnt alive, when there had been no such thing as freedom of speech. I was worried that my country too was slipping back into such a time of darkness. I was anxious that the citizens of my country were about to be infected by a fatal virus that had been dispersed in the air. Ershad was coming up with fresh ruses to sustain his position. He had dissolved the assembly and conducted a sham election with some small and independent political parties as his opponents, since all the other major political parties had withdrawn from the contest. The bogus vote was meant to foreground the legitimacy of his claim to power but it had hardly managed to convince anyone. Such was his greed for power that on realizing the precarious nature of his seat he resorted to state religion to bail him out. Hence the divine carrot dangled in front of everyone's noses to bring the faithful under his control.

The opposition parties had joined forces to form a coalition and many cultural organizations from the villages as well as the cities were joining their ranks to unite and combat Ershad. But it was not as if these coalitions were speaking out strongly enough against the idea of a state religion. The simple thing was that Islam had such a firm hold on people that most did not possess the courage to speak out against it. Nonetheless a few political and non-political organizations committed to social justice had taken to protesting the contentious eighth amendment to the constitution. A handful of writers and journalists too were writing against the idea of a state religion. That was—more or less—it.

In 1971 Bengali Muslims had revolted and waged war against their non-Bengali Muslim overlords to prove irrevocably that being a Muslim was not the only criterion for cohabitation. In 1971 Bengalis had proved that the partition of India on the basis of the two-nation theory had been a momentous mistake. The Bengalis who had participated in the Mukti Juddho (Liberation War) of 1971 had dreamt of driving back the non-Bengali Muslims and forming a nation called Bangladesh premised on their love for the Bengali language and culture. After a bloody nine-month-long war the country was liberated and Sheikh Mujibur Rahman assumed the leadership of the emergent nation. He may have had a hundred faults, despite being enormously popular he may have made many mistakes as an administrator, but he had also charted a robust constitution where Bengali nationalism and socialism had found pride of place alongside the ideals of secularism. It was Major Zia who had usurped power and effectively forced secular thought out of the ambit of governance. Following in his footsteps another military dictator had committed an even greater crime and added a poisonous clause to the constitution under the ruse of an amendment. Had that been our lot? The Hindus, Buddhists, Christians and Muslims—we had all been Bengali. Yet it was impossible to sing about communal harmony any longer. On 7 June 1988, a black day in the history of Bengal, they snuffed out the glorious prospect of a non-communal and just society in cold blood. After having made significant progress and achieving significant things, it was a day of regression, of relapsing to untruth, injustice and obscurity. That day we rewound the clock not by a couple of years but almost a millennium.

~

Sheikh Hasina was our only recourse. She had returned to Bangladesh in 1981 as the president of the Awami League. The people had been thoroughly displeased with Ziaur Rahman[4] for letting traitors and mass murderers like Golam Azam,[5] convicted of war crimes during the Liberation War, back into the country and paving the way towards the legitimization of communal politics. Besides, there were other infractions like adding 'Bismillah' to the constitution and undermining secular ideals, all of which ensured that the people were glad to see her back and many felt they could pin their hopes on her. However, Sheikh Hasina had been taken in by Ershad's con and formed an alliance with the Bangladesh Jamaat-e-Islami[6] for the 1986 general elections. Khaleda Zia on the other hand had steadfastly resisted being duped by Ershad's tricks. Although Sheikh Hasina too had figured out the workings of the sham vote soon enough and broken from the assembly, it had not been easy living down the mistakes resulting from a single imprudent decision.

Regardless, progressive citizens were hopeful that if she were to come to power she would reinstate the ideas her father had instilled in the constitution. The immediate strategy, however, was simple: to support the anti-Ershad coalition front so that the ensuing social revolt could successfully depose the corrupt and autocratic government. Ershad had captured power seven years earlier and was only growing more adamant with each passing day about consolidating his failing influence. The people did not want him but that hardly bothered the despot—he had the guns and he had religion, and he was using them to suppress dissent and stay in power.

I had never been a part of any political organization but at such a moment of crisis I too was willing to start nurturing the faint possibility of change. I too had begun to place my faith in these women who were promising us a better future against all odds.

~

A combined cultural coalition was created by merging the Mymensingh Sahitya Parisad, the Shokal Kabita Parisad and a number of other independent literary and cultural outfits. It comprised poets, writers, singers, dancers and theatre artists among many other performers, each and every person inspired by the spirit of the Liberation War, with shared concerns over social justice, political stability, democracy, a healthy social structure and the betterment of the people. Amir Hossain Ratan was elected leader of the coalition, a truly influential person and dedicated worker who had, with his own efforts and his own money, started a school called Mukul Niketan on Maharaja Road. It had not taken time for the school to graduate from a makeshift bamboo structure to a proper building. The number of attendees too was increasing with each passing year and Ratan had dedicated himself to the task of whipping the recruited asses into shape. His favourite word was 'discipline'—besides formal education he was dedicated to instilling this discipline among his students.

During the National Day parades on the Circuit House grounds one could not help but stare in wonder at the students from Mukul marching past. During the deadly floods in Mymensingh—when houses were swept away by the angry river, with cattle dying and the people's last resources being washed away—Ratan and his students had been there helping in the rescue and rehabilitation efforts. On any given day Ratan usually had so much work he barely had time for other equally important things—for instance, taking a shower, eating, or even sleeping. However, bowing to our collective plea he agreed to assume the leadership of the coalition in addition to his numerous other responsibilities. Work was what made Ratan—Ratanda to everyone—the happiest. At a rather advanced age his relatives had coerced him into getting married, but even his beautiful young wife had been unable to tie him down at home. Perhaps I was not as audacious as him but a significant portion of my life too was spent outside domestic confines.

There were many poets in the Shokal Kabita Parisad; but since most of them were not very good at recitation we took on new members, not poets exactly but those who could recite poetry beautifully. Our primary mission was to compile our fiery subversive poems into a compendium and teach everyone the rules and tropes of choral poetry. Poring over hundreds of books of poetry, we spent nights compiling the manuscripts; in the afternoons rehearsals were held in the room in front of Abakash with all the new recruits. As for me, my recitation skills were threatening to overshadow the poet in me. From Kazi Sabyasachi to the more recent Jayanta Chattopadhyay, there were numerous poets being discussed in the room. Not just writing poems, being able to recite poems properly is a form of art too. Consequently, the work we did was quite satisfying. Be it the solo recitals or the group performances, the poems of the Shokal Kabita Parisad managed to move our listeners and the group rapidly gained popularity in the city. Besides the Town Hall and the Public Hall, we were invited by a number of big and small cultural organizations for their events.

In fact Shokal was a significant component even within the cultural coalition and at times people argued that without Shokal the alliance would not have had the same impact. At a time of political crisis we felt the need for poems which would inspire and incite, exactly what the poets of the Shokal Kabita Parisad were doing. Most of the poems were by R, Nirmalendu Goon, Shamsur Rahman and Mahadev Saha. Usually, poets from West Bengal were not known for their politically subversive poems and consequently there were not too many that were finally selected for the compilation. As the group became more famous, more people started trickling in and we had to tighten the selection procedure. We even organized a debate in the conference room of the Press Club on 'Poetry for Social Change', entirely executed by me but from behind the scenes. We asked HSS to be the chief guest and he promptly agreed to come down from Dhaka for the occasion. HSS was a great speaker and he had the audience in his thrall as expected. Events like 'Poetry for Resistance', 'Poetry for Peace', among others, were being organized and we were recalling old alliances formed on special days like 25 March[7] or 16 December[8] and holding silent protest marches. It had been a while since I had been in Mymensingh during the 21 February celebrations, and that particular morning would usually witness me waking up to the iconic 'Amar bhaier rokte rangano ekushe February, ami ki bhulite pari'[9] without fail. There was nothing more evocative and pure on earth than the sight of a mass of people dressed in white, barefoot and holding flowers in their palms, singing and marching to the Sahid Minar. This scene did not just wake me up, it infused my life with a new sense of vitality. I was proud of Rafiq–Salam–Barkat[10] for their sacrifice and I was proud to call myself a Bengali. The morning would carry the strains of the mournful song on its wings, having such an effect on me that I would be reduced to tears. To this day the song never fails to make me cry.

While marching down the streets of Mymensingh on 16 December, our palms cupping flowers to be offered at the Martyrs' Memorial, we were singing songs of victory and independence. At the end of one song Jatin Sarkar[11] suggested we sing 'Joy Bangla' (Long Live Bengal). No sooner had the song begun than a murmur of protest arose from one section of the crowd. As we turned to the dissenters we realized that the cause of the disagreement was that 'Joy Bangla' and 'Ekti Mujiber theke lokkhyo Mujiber dhoni protidhoni' (One Mujib echoes another thousand waiting in the wings) were Awami League songs. We were celebrating Victory Day together regardless of our individual political affiliations and so it was unseemly to some that we sang songs of one particular political party.

Jatin Sarkar countered immediately, 'Why should these be Awami League songs? These are songs from the Liberation War!' I could not help but hang my head in shame. The songs which used to play over the radio from Swadhin Bangla Betar Kendra[12] during the 1971 war, songs which inspired the *muktijoddhas* to continue their fight for independence, songs which stirred them to sacrifice their lives without hesitation in order to save the country from Pakistani forces, could there be anything more shameful than denying their legacy? These songs belonged to all of us, the people of Bangladesh. It was not difficult to figure out that there were certain conservative nationalist elements among us. Pigeonholing songs was not a new strategy. During Ziaur Rahman's stint in power Shahnaz Rehmatullah's 'Prothom Bangladesh amar shesh Bangladesh' (First Bangladesh, my last Bangladesh) used to be played before every radio and television newscast, to the extent that it gradually took on the mantle of a nationalist song. Ershad had followed this example and adopted another song for similar purposes. Such a travesty! Songs were no longer autonomous; they had to toe the line of some political party or the other! At the Martyrs' Memorial, Jatin Sarkar and I were asked to offer flowers. It was an immense privilege to have been asked to perform such a prestigious task alongside such a remarkable individual; I was acutely aware that I barely had any credentials to be associated with such an erudite man.

Of the few people whose long speeches I ever wished to listen to Jatin Sarkar was one of the most significant. He had the innate ability to talk on any topic effortlessly for hours, and not simply for the sake of speaking. From the definition to an in-depth critique, he could explain a topic better than anyone else I knew. Previously a professor of Bangla at Nasirabad College, Sarkar was the author of many remarkable books on socialism. He was always clad in white, whether at home or elsewhere. It was easy to stereotype him as merely a dhoti-clad Hindu but there was not a more secular person than him in Bangladesh in my knowledge. An atheist through and through, a staunch Marxist besides that, he used to wear the dhoti because of his love for the garment.

I had heard his long speeches in front of the public library on countless occasions during the birthday celebrations of Rabindranath Tagore, Kazi Nazrul Islam and Sukanta Bhattacharya. His favourite used to be Nazrul, though, and he could fluently converse in the local dialect of Netrakona. He was the product of a very simple life, almost to the point of having trouble making ends meet; I was well aware that despite being inspired by his ideals it would never be possible for me to renounce everything like he had. It is easier to pontificate about renouncing wealth and material possessions than actually practising it in life. Nevertheless, people still respected such ideals. People on the road used to move aside and let Sarkar pass and even seek his blessings. The only person I knew who had not spared Sarkar even a glance was Shakti Chattopadhyay. He had been visiting Dhaka and HSS had suggested a visit to Mymensingh; Shakti had readily agreed. Having called and informed Yasmin in advance they arrived at Mymensingh within a day. I had been in Dhaka and they picked me up along the way. Yasmin had gone on a cleaning and decorating spree; my older brother had always had a fixation for eminent poets and authors and had splurged on fish for the occasion—koi, tiger prawns, hilsa, rui—from the new local market.

Mother had cooked up a feast and at lunch a grand spread was laid out on the huge table in the dining room. In the afternoon I had invited Jatin Sarkar and poet Pranab Roy to come and meet Shakti Chattopadhyay. After the initial round of introductions HSS at least uttered a 'Hello, how are you?' Shakti on the other hand did not spare even two words, carrying on a private conversation with HSS the entire time instead. Sarkar and Roy sat there for a while, had tea and biscuits, skimmed through some of the magazines on the table and then left, leaving my plans for an animated literary discussion in tatters. Shakti spent the entire time burping, perhaps a sign of a few extra drinks from the night before. To be fair, being unused to alcohol myself I could not be quite sure if a hangover could make someone burp so strangely! We fed him well and took him around Maharaja Shashikanta's house and Satyajit Ray's grandfather's school before finally saying our goodbyes in the evening.

It would have been impossible to host them if Dada, my eldest brother, had not come to my rescue; my brother had always been extremely stingy except when the situation involved poets or writers. Once when Humayun Ahmed was visiting Dhaka he had suddenly turned up at our house, despite not having my address. For some reason Ahmed had formed the impression from my writing that I had a red house by the Brahmaputra. Accordingly, he had arrived and knocked on the doors of some of the other houses in the vicinity asking about me. After several failed attempts he had asked his way to Abakash much to Dada's stunned disbelief. After a long, incredulous silence at the door Dada had gathered his wits and launched into a flurry of questions—'Please come inside and sit. What do you want to have for lunch? Do you like fish? My wife will cook. She cooks so well. If only I had known from before, I would have called over a few friends too.' He had run to the market immediately to buy fresh fish. At lunch Humayun Ahmed had regaled us with stories—not stories about others but his own and we were left clutching our sides in laughter. Dada was firmly of the opinion that those who could tell good stories could write good stories too. I was never good at telling stories although I had already written a few by then, some of which I had sent off to the daily newspaper and they had been published on the 'Women's Page'. I was not really comfortable with the idea of a Women's Page—it's not as if newspapers had a separate Men's Page too. Women were discriminated against just as children, the elderly or the differently abled were, with the simplest assumption being they were weak. Since I was not an established writer every story I sent to the literary section of the newspaper was tossed aside into an irrelevant heap.

The meetings of the political coalition were on as usual and the city was racked time and again by the din of protest marches. Student unions in the universities too were playing a crucial role in the movement. Ershad's police forces had allegedly murdered a number of innocent protestors by letting loose a truck on one such march organized by the students of University of Dhaka; the bloodstains there were still fresh.[13] The cultural front too was tirelessly conducting protest meets. We were striving for the glimmer of hope we could spy across the stark darkness of the world around us, still unsure whether it was the light at the end of the tunnel or a mirage like everything else. Jatin Sarkar was hopeful about the future; he was convinced that should a democratic party come to power they would again consign Ershad's divine carrot to the hereafter where it belonged. However, we could not be sure when such a party would come to power.

Gradually the united front had shrunk to a size smaller than even the Jamaat. After Comrade Farhad passed away a huge funeral process as per Islamic rites was organized. If communists were unable to extricate themselves from religious rituals—even if it was for show—then how were the rest of the parties supposed to resist the lure! Religion is a devastating force. It does not matter if you are not a believer because if you try and eradicate it the consequences can be dangerous. Lack of education and awareness is at the root of the superstitions that sustain religion—these beliefs have no logical correspondence and neither do they concern themselves with free thought. If Islam was going to remain as the state religion nothing could stop the democratic country of Bangladesh from becoming an Islamic republic. Religion is like cancer.

Once it takes root it systematically corrodes the entire state apparatus and there is no way to arrest its growth; nor can it be cured. With the investiture of a single state religion all other religious identities—Hindus, Christians and Buddhists—and even non-believers could be instantly reduced to second-class citizens.

Consequently, if someone wished to become a true Muslim they only had to cite the Quran for legitimacy of their actions—that one must not be a friend to those of other lesser religions for fear of facing the wrath of Allah. In addition to this it would also legitimize violence on other religious beliefs—kill those who believe in other gods or in a single stroke maim non-believers entirely. Invariably, all Muslims would not be very happy with such developments and there would be other ways of making them toe the line. Religious coercion would be used to systematically subjugate Muslim women and new rules would be instituted to dehumanize women into nothing but a mass of flesh and blood.

Like a golden virus born in blood,
That marks the skin, the flesh with putrid wounds,
I see a hopeless disease growing in the veins of my people.
It grows and manifests
As demonic bigots and merchants of providence,
Who scatter and infect like corrosive cancer.
A bigot has no religion, only greed, and foul cunning,
They break the world into a thousand fragments,
And they break people, in the name of God—
In His name they claim the right to kill.
Blindness! Stupidity! Where is God!
In a thousand years they have raised storms,
And flowed rivers of blood and offered it to their God.
Where is Paradise? The promised angels? The flowing rivers of wine?
In their endless hunger for sex over eternal time
They have become ravenous feral beasts!
Is there another *dozakh*[14] more terrifying?
Does hunger burn less than *hawiya*[15]?
Does hunger burn any less than passion?

Those who raise hell for their eternity,
Let them find their way to Paradise—
Let us live here on Earth,
In this blue world—so we may dream of tomorrow,
And sow equality
Along the draught of our belligerent times.
Religion had brought us light once.
Today some selfish foul people,
Hawk its bones and rotting flesh—

R must have been livid. He had used the swearword 'foul' without a
pause in the poem. He used to speak with a lot of cusswords anyway.
Despite the word 'foul' giving me a moment's pause I kept repeating
the last couplet to myself—

They plug the gaps left in time with fables,
Not opium, religion is hemlock.
We would have invariably fought over this had he been nearby.

*Note: The book was originally banned in West Bengal because
of accusations that certain sections might incite communal tensions.
Despite the injunction being later revoked by the Calcutta High Court
persistent concerns over renewed communal tensions have forced
the author to excise the section from further Bengali publications
and leave a blank page in its stead.*

The state of Bangladesh too was in the doldrums. Having read the writing on the wall Ershad was trying to use religion to save his own skin.

> He has hung a holy carrot in front of us,
> A smokescreen for his greed and fear.
> So wear the blindfold,
> The more unseeing, the more faithful—
> More benevolent will be the Light.
> Pluck out your eyes and toss them aside,
> Padlock all rational thought in your brain.
> Bravo! And so you become loyal.

Other Worlds

Much happened in 1989, a few good things, quite a few bad ones and some which were neither. In the latter category I can immediately consign the publication of my own book of poetry, *Nirbashito Bahire Ontore* (Exiled Without and Within), published by Shokal Prakashani and financed entirely by me. This publishing house had been an earlier venture, much before the Shokal Kabita Parisad, and its first publication had been a verse drama by the poet HA. One would have to retrace one's steps further by two years to talk about HA. I had just begun working at Mymensingh around that time, having been transferred there almost magically after working at the Nakla Health Centre for only a fortnight. Friends from college had all moved to various parts of the country. R had been busy with his prawn farm in Mongla port and rarely, if ever, came to Dhaka.

When one is alone one is ready to socialize with anyone. I had socialized with HA, a poet hailing from Sirajgunje, whom I had met hardly twice before in Dhaka. Since I used to publish poetry in my literary journal, *Senjuti*, R had sent me across a host of poetry by many young poets; Awlad had been one among them. After finishing college many of R's friends—Ikhtiar Choudhury, Kamal Choudhury, HA, Mohammed Sadiq, Farooq Moinuddin—had given up on their dreams of writing poems and short stories, rid themselves of the stench of alcohol and weed and got crewcuts and shaves, acquired nicely fitted suits and, mustering their most serious expressions, joined magisterial posts. One morning I had gone to the Circuit House grounds for an interstate sports meet—not as a spectator but as a doctor for the injured athletes—when I heard my name being called. Turning to see who it was I was greeted by the sight of a man in a suit, his hair neatly combed and parted, smiling sweetly at me. I had had no trouble in recognizing HA.

'Oh, fancy seeing you here!'

'Yes, I work here. It's only been a few days since I have come here, to join as the information officer. How are you? Where is R? Is he well?'

'I work here too. I don't know where he is, or how he is.'

He had smiled widely and left with an invitation for me to drop by the information office at Gulkibari.

One day soon, while on one of my usual afternoon rickshaw rounds through the city with Yasmin, I had decided to take HA up on his invitation. At the information centre—a yellow single-storey house with a small meadow—HA had wrapped up his work and patiently listened to me narrate the tale of the demise of my relationship with R. As for himself, he had mostly stuck to his poetry and the verse drama which he had been quite hopeful about and had resolved to get published. R used to sing praises of his poems; I was convinced he was a good poet. Besides my duties as a doctor this was what occupied me—a desire to form a society of poets or bring out poetry magazines, or even seriously getting into publishing. I was earning, getting my salary every month, living with my parents and feeding off them, while spending my money caring for artists and writers. As if everyone and everything, in art as well as literature, had been ailing without my assistance! Doctor care for thy patient, let literature be! But it was easier said than done. Old habits were hard to beat and they goaded me to take HA's precious verse drama to the German Printers one fine day. HA had given me his word that he would arrange for the sale of the books. Without even trying to fathom the merits of the verse drama I had gone ahead and gotten it published. The new publication house was named Shokal[16] (Morning), the nickname no one called me by any more. This particular morning had no sunshine though; as it turned out it was beset with darkness and foreboding from the outset.

Bandi Debota (Captive God), HA's verse drama, was published by Shokal Prakashani after I had proofread it and spent money out of my own pocket for it. HA had promised to buy the first two hundred copies himself; the remaining three hundred had ended up under my bed, of which a few I had later given to R to sell. I had also taken him to HA's house but their meeting had not made R happy. In fact, he had been so enraged that on returning to Dhaka he had written a filthy short story about it called 'Itor' (The Foul) accusing me of sleeping around with random men, including HA. Unfortunately I was the only one who knew the truth—that I had never considered HA anything other than a friend and nor had I entertained the possibility of anything more. It was becoming difficult to keep calling HA a friend anyway, especially since I had begun to notice certain oddities in his behaviour. He used to come across as indifferent but he had not been entirely so. He would be perennially in a haze, keep talking ceaselessly, sometimes laughing out loud without reason or playing a plaintive tune on the harmonium. Just as suddenly he would go absolutely quiet and nothing would be able to stir him. Even amidst a din he would be lost in his own thoughts.

He would go on long drives in the office car, working the driver to death all night, while on other days he would give the man some money and casually give him a day off with a smile. The same HA had many faces and it was too difficult to discern which one was real. I also found out about his frequent visits to a pir in Shambhugunje; they would sit and smoke weed, and rumour had it HA was giving the man money too. I noticed he was becoming unpopular in his office with every passing day, unable to remain on cordial terms with his colleagues. It had not been possible for me to solve his work problems but there was one problem I did try to solve—when he fixed his sixteen-year-old maid Miriam's marriage to a seventy-year-old man. The latter used to be a peon in his office and HA had claimed since the two were madly in love he had decided to get them hitched. I did try talking to Miriam separately to ask her why she was going along with the plan but Miriam had only smiled; the bashful smile a girl smiles when her paramour is mentioned.

Regardless, I had not been convinced that Miriam and the toothless Abdul Hamid were madly in love. It was possible that the man had some money and a piece of land and so the poor girl's father had agreed to the match thinking his daughter would be well cared for. Despite my best efforts, however, I had been unable to stop the wedding. Instead I had attended the marriage of a doddering old man with a girl the age of his granddaughter and even had dinner there. Ever since this incident I had been convinced that HA was hiding something, but he never revealed his secrets, remaining an impenetrable puzzle behind a smokescreen. I would later get to know that HA had beaten his wife and thrown her out of the house and the poor woman had taken the children to Sirajgunje. She used to sing beautifully and he had married her when they had been very young. They had had children early too, much before most of his friends. Whenever I used to ask about his wife, his son or his daughter, he would confess to have no news of them. Neither did he ever send them any money. I could not fail to notice that he did not have an iota of kindness in him for them; to him his wife had been disobedient and so he had punished her. He was the husband so he had the right to do as he pleased. He had been a poet and a thinker, he was this and he was that. He was a lord and a zamindar and I lost all interest in keeping tabs on him. I had been more concerned with the unknown wife, having seriously begun to empathize with her situation.

Nearly a year passed, the Shokal Kabita Parisad happened and many poets and orators began joining us. At someone's suggestion that we should invite HA to join our group I had tried looking him up, only to discover to my utter shock that he had morphed into a completely different person. Gone was the suited clean-shaven man, only to be replaced by a homeless destitute, having given away all his belongings to the seer from Shambhugunje with whom he used to smoke pot. He had lost his job as well as his sanity. Barefoot, his clothes filthy, face almost hidden behind a bushy beard, he would turn up at Arogya Bitan and beg Dada for a few spare bucks. He even came to me one day asking for money and stricken with pity I had ended up giving him some. He used to roam about with a big bound notebook under his arm, telling everyone he had written a new verse drama which he was convinced, if printed, was going to cause a sensation the world over. From a first-class gazetted officer and son of the zamindar of Sirajgunje, HA had been reduced to a beggar within the span of a year. What could I have done for someone who had brought this upon himself? I had decided I was not going to entertain his problems and neither was I going to give him any more money. My money was better spent in other endeavours.

Tariq Sujat took on the responsibility of completing one such endeavour, the one that was neither good nor bad: my book of poems. A young man with a boyish face, Tariq Sujat was one of the poets who had spent sleepless nights when the Shokal Kabita Parisad was being formed. Starting the Parisad, organizing a National Poetry Festival on the crossroads in front of the university—at such an exciting and invigorating juncture R and I had gotten to know many such young poets like Tariq Sujat, Mozammel Babu and Shimul Mohammed. My relationship with R was rapidly deteriorating at that point of time. Even when the relationship was almost over, in its last painful stages I had been in touch with some of them. Mozammel Babu was an engineer; he used to publish a fortnightly literary journal called *Saili* (Craft) out of an office on the first floor of the stadium. His dedication to the world of literature had made him forsake the material world; despite being a rich father's son his appearance was exceptionally plain. Even Tariq Sujat was the same. I would travel to Dhaka to give him the money for the print job in instalments. To my delight the cover was being made by Khalid Ehsan. Hailing from Chattagram, Khalid, a poet in his own right, used to travel to Dhaka before the book fair to illustrate covers of the books about to be published.

Unfortunately, not only did I not get the printed books on the promised date, but nearly a month passed with no sign of them. Tariq too was nowhere to be found. After turning the world upside down searching when I finally did find him it was to learn that work on the book was not over yet. Of course I realized immediately that it had been a mistake dumping the entire responsibility on someone who was dividing his time among a hundred things at the same time. When the books finally emerged from the press it was almost the end of February—Mother Language Day was over and the book fair was nearly in its home stretch. I stashed most of the packets of books under the bed in Chotda's house. Although I did send some to a few shops in the book fair, I usually avoided passing by them, embarrassed and anxious that I would find my books lying on the shelf unwanted! Neither did I keep track of any sales or inquire about my share of the proceeds. Instead I passed my entire time there chatting at the tea stall, before returning to Mymensingh with the sack of books after the end of the fair.

I also sent some books to the Kabir Library and Parul Library by the Ganginar, to be put up for sale, and I frequently visited the libraries to glance at my unsold books and sigh. It was NM who

brought me out of my depression. I had met NM through SHA.
SHA, who used to write beautiful rhymes, had come to Mymensingh
for a poetry recital. He used to be on good terms with poet Ataul
Kareem Shafeeq of Mymensingh. Ataul Kareem had brought him
along to a Poetry of Resistance event organized by the Shokal Kabita
Parisad in the courtyard of the Town Hall. SHA was to recite a poem
there. There were not too many people in the audience that day.
Nevertheless, SHA had been so impressed by the group recital by
members of the Shokal that he had gone back to Dhaka and informed
Swarasruti, a leading poetry association. Swarasruti had been in the
middle of preparations for a big event in the auditorium of the British
Council, with leading and talented poets from both sides of the
border scheduled to attend. Invitations were being sent out to various
artists and groups of both Bengals for solo and group recitation events
and Shokal Kabita Parisad had received one too.

Medical college student Pasha, Rosalyn who used to study at
Agricultural University, small and bespectacled budding intellectual
Dolan, Yasmin and I—with unbound energy we had set ourselves
to preparing for the programme. The rehearsals were conducted at
Abakash where our voices rang out with lyrics on equality, equity and
a society free of discrimination. The girls clad in *jamdani* saris and the
boys in white kurtas, we had arrived at Dhaka for the recital. We had
gone up to the stage and recited our poems, some solos, some with
two of us or three, and even the entire group. There had been not one
mistake, not one nervous tic and our little recitation team from the
suburbs had received thunderous applause from the audience. Usually
a team from the suburbs got a raw deal at Dhaka; the city's poets
and artists have always been bullies to a degree. However, paying no
attention to any sort of bullying, we had long and stirring get-togethers
with our poet friends from Dhaka on the British Council grounds. It
was at one such gathering that SHA had introduced me to NM.

Rather unattractive, with raised teeth, a raised forehead and
unkempt hair which had begun to grey rather early, NM could best
be described as a bag of bones. He gesticulated wildly while speaking
and his tiny ass in his tiny fifty kilo frame would sway whenever
he moved. NM was the editor of a weekly literary magazine called
Khabarer Kagaj (Newspaper) which published articles on a mix of

topics—politics, literature, society, culture—and which had slowly built up quite a reputation. He published it cheap too, on newsprint. Of the few dozen weeklies published across the country *Khabarer Kagaj* was the most different. Many renowned poets and writers had contributed to various issues of the journal; we had always felt the need for something just as ingenious in our country. As the journal gained popularity, NM too was becoming more well known in literary circles. A journalism student could not have suddenly gotten into the good graces of poets and literary figures just like that unless he had talent of his own, irrespective of how he looked.

Just like Tariq, NM too was always trying to do multiple things at the same time. He was the president at Swarasruti, or something of that nature, even though he was not a poet; nor was he someone known for his recitation skills. He had one exceptional quality though: he had no qualms about admitting his shortcomings. That is not to say he was any less proud of his achievements either—his pride would become apparent from time to time, sometimes unobtrusive and sometimes too stark to miss. At first glance there had been no reason for me to like this man who spoke in a strong Komilla dialect. But it did not take long for our meeting to advance into acquaintance and from there to friendship. To be fair it was NM who had decided that he was going to be friends with me at any cost and he usually had a way of getting what he wanted. Another quality of his that I admired was his enthusiasm about doing new things. He was always planning new things and then jumping head-first into implementing them. A passionate, earnest, tireless and hard-working man, NM, like SHA, was the same age as me. Our tête-à-têtes too used to be especially engaging.

Despite having left the medical profession, SHA had done well for himself—he had started an advertising agency called Gati. He used to say Gati was for sustaining his life and literature was for sustaining his soul—to his credit he was managing both just fine. SHA's friend Sayed Al Farooq had a garments business; he was a poet too and used to publish his poetry with his own money. The two of them used to also run a poetry journal together. After they had a falling out SHA would often say the most vicious and unkind things about Al Farooq. Despite their numerous differences this was one aspect where both NM and SHA were remarkably similar—if they were to like someone they considered that person to be the best in the world, their respect for them almost reverential as it were. However, if they were to dislike someone then they would not hesitate to verbally eviscerate the person. Not that I figured all this out immediately; it took me a long time to understand these things.

Eventually it so happened that despite having met him through SHA I was meeting NM more often than the former; the latter's enthusiasm too was partly to blame for that. As for SHA, our meetings became less frequent solely because of his own actions. One day he invited me to his house. On reaching there I realized his wife was away from Dhaka and we were alone in the house. At first the conversation was fairly staid, until I suddenly found him right next to me praising my beauty and trying to kiss me. I tried pushing him away discreetly, repeatedly, even tried moving and sitting elsewhere and each time he kept trying to come nearer and touch me. I tried explaining to him that I was not interested in letting him kiss me, that he should not destroy the beautiful friendship we had. When he still refused to back down, refused to keep his hands to himself, I was left with no choice but to leave. After kissing me perhaps he would have gone back to his wife, Muniya, and, chanting the Hajar al-Aswad, performed a penitent lover's Hajj by kissing her on her black lips.

I never faced something like this with NM. Despite spending hours together alone he never made any advances and soon we became very close friends. A true friend is one you can trust, who will be there by your side through the good times and the bad. While telling NM about the old days I told him about Chandana one day. As soon as he got to know that Chandana lived in Komilla he suggested we take his car and immediately drive there. MHI was there; he too joined in and the three of us set off for Komilla. A while ago NM had surprised me by turning up at Abakash with MHI. In fact, this was something he liked to do—surprise people. Since I was a bit like that too I loved his impromptu decision to drive to Komilla. If something struck my fancy I wished to do it immediately and not leave it aside for later; waiting and considering were not things I was good at. When we finally located Chandana's house in Komilla I was faced with the realization that she was the docile daughter-in-law of the house, her head covered with her sari; she was also a mother to an infant. This was Chandana, my Chandana; she had been so close and yet she had seemed so far away that day, so much so that when I touched her I could not be sure if she felt it.

'I had gone to Rangamati. I kept thinking about you. You remember we had planned to go? You had promised you would show me around. We were going to have so much fun. Do you remember?' I could not be sure if Chandana remembered anything. When I suggested we go somewhere, anywhere, Mymensingh or Dhaka, she only laughed at what was clearly my madness. She did not laugh loudly though, neither did she talk loudly. There was an immense sense of *control* about her—she walked stealthily, spoke in whispers and talked mainly about her little rose garden in the attic. She had read MHI's stories before; in fact she used to call herself Sajani after reading his story 'O sajani'. But even he failed to inspire any excitement in Chandana; she only kept staring at him impassively, like someone standing before a complete stranger. I met MHI fairly often after that day. Soon a friendship developed and the passage from the formal pronouns of address to the informal ones was traversed with startling ease.

My friends were increasing as much in literary circles as in the non-literary ones. In family planning, Dr Saidul Islam, who had nothing at all to do with literature, had already become a good friend. I was never too choosy about my friends. That did not mean I welcomed anyone I found standing at my door. There were many writers I rejected, even if not on our very first meeting then definitely by the second: Haroon Rasheed, for instance. He was a talented boy who I had known since the time when *Senjuti* was still being published. In fact I used to be quite an admirer of his poetry. We would keep in touch through letters and he had even come down to meet me once. You take quinine for malaria but what medicine can you take for quinine? He could have come to meet me a thousand times, but as a shy girl from the suburbs I did not have the courage to reciprocate. When Haroon returned again a few years later, R and I had parted ways and I was battling loneliness on a daily basis.

His intentions were clear right off the bat—since I was alone there was no way I could turn away a handsome man such as him—and he seemed completely convinced by the reasonableness of his expectations. The more he looked at me with love in his gaze, the more I had to look away, towards the coconut tree laden with coconuts, the grille on the window, or the betel nut tree that had been struck by lightning the past monsoon. There was nothing I could say to Haroon. On the other hand I had much more to talk about when speaking to Farid Kabir, a poet who resembled an emaciated tree-dwelling ghost; I had met him through Haroon when the latter had brought him to Abakash. I faced the same uncomfortable situation with Haroon again while visiting his house in Dhaka. Despite my best efforts we could not sustain even the most cordial of relationships.

Not that the people I eventually accepted as friends were the only ones suitable while the ones I turned away were not worthy. For instance, I could scarcely have imagined that my relationship with HH was going to end on such a sour note. The truth is, when you abruptly try to twist an existing relationship into something foreign, something alien, everything sort of gets upended in the process. I had known HH for a long time, having first met him to ask for a few of his poems for *Senjuti*. Whenever I had some free time to spare and I was bored sitting at home, I would go meet him at the Press Club. It would inevitably lead us to a restaurant and him ordering lunch for two instead of one. The two of us would sit in the crowded restaurant and eat and he would steadfastly refuse to allow me to chip in with the bill. However, if I took a gift for him in return he would coldly tell me he never accepted any gifts and that I should take it away and use it myself or give it to someone else. We mostly talked about my family. He would ask about Father, Mother, he would ask how my brothers were doing and my sister too, and so on. A bachelor, he lived alone and had worked for a newspaper. When that shut down he did not seek another job, instead choosing to mostly spend his days gambling. The latter he could do very well and he would win most of the time. I too had taken to gambling at one point of time but that had not lasted long.

Every evening there used to be a gambling party at Parveen's house—Parveen was the sister of Hasina, Dada's wife, although people knew they were cousins. Many professional gamblers used to be there with wads of currency notes stuffed inside their pockets. Parveen and her gambler friends had taught me how to play flush. However, every time we played, after a small peek into a hopeful fortune, I would lose badly, all my money seemingly evaporating into thin air. Each time I would think that I was going to win and of course each time I lost, often so badly that I would not even have the money for a rickshaw to return home. Back home, to my utter consternation, I would have to ask family members for money. I would never have figured out that I was being successfully conned at these games because I was an amateur. Thankfully, Father had stepped in and at his behest my brother took me aside for a long lecture that succeeded in weaning me off the habit. Despite losing at gambling so many times I must admit that it had been very exciting. Money is transient, it comes and goes, but can it ever give such a rush? It cannot. For HH gambling was like a regular nine-to-five occupation. As someone who had forsaken domesticity it suited him perfectly. He could conveniently bypass social expectations or not let those expectations touch him in any way. That was perhaps why these qualities used to attract me so much. What if I could have been indifferent like him? I knew, however, that it was not something everyone could do.

So even when I began receiving phone calls from Dhaka almost every day I did not have the faintest idea that he wished to be anything else to me other than the revered older brother I had always thought of him as. My suspicions were first aroused by a poem he wrote for me and a new nickname he gave me. Then, out of the blue, the man who was known to have never gone anywhere other than his own house and the Press Club—no social invitations, not even friends' houses—came down to Mymensingh to celebrate my birthday on 25 August. Another time while I was in Dhaka he even overcame his hesitations and turned up at Chotda's house to meet me. Whenever I sensed his emotional and love-struck gaze on me I would look away deliberately. The day he held my hands for the first time I tried discreetly snatching them away. He did not understand my reluctance, though, and kept trying to grab hold of my hands. I did not like it because I did not wish to see him in such a light. He seemed so peculiar when he suddenly began—

Suddenly one day,
If love comes to you and asks,

Let us go then, you and I—
Would you?

The man speaking to me was not the HH I knew; the poet whose one
poem in 1969 had inspired thousands of people to take to the streets
in solidarity—

To the ones who are young now, this is the finest time to rally,
To the ones who are young now, this is the finest time to go to war.

He was not the same HH whose indifference towards society, whose
reflective and contemplative nature, had moved me so. Neither was
he exactly that poet, the melancholy in whose poems used to permeate
my being.

I had never imagined HH as a possible lover. He was someone I
revered, someone I was in awe of. If someone you worship wishes to climb
down from their pedestal and roll in the same dirt as you that is bound to
lead to heartache for both parties involved. My hesitant eyes would cloud
over with darkness whenever they met his pleading gaze. The person
inside me who had never imagined facing such a scenario would get
angry, her voice would harden, cruelty toughening her natural kindness
and making her inhuman and brutal. Then one day, the transformation
finally achieved, I threw the innocent man out of my house.

'HH bhai, you must leave. You must leave right now.'

There had been pain in my voice that day, perhaps a bit of despair
and a hint of hate too. He had walked out wiping his eyes. I had
steadfastly refused to look at him leave, the unsentimental person
within me struggling to remain impassive and unaffected by the
unrequited love that had taught the man to acknowledge his self—

Sometimes I desperately want everyone to know—I still am.
Love rings in my head, and in my heart,
Like a bee in a bonnet.
I have to write to her:
One of these days do come and tell me,
How happy are you that I cry.

I could never go and tell him. I could only read his poetry from a distance and sigh. I had never wished to hurt him, nor had I ever wished to fall in love with him.

> I have loved you and called you Tana.
> If you cannot love me,
> Raise your fangs and strike me with your venom.

It had been a clever rhyme but I was never a venomous snake that wished to poison an innocent solitary person like HH. Irrespective of the person, if I have ever become friends with someone I have always been the one who would rather preserve a relationship than destroy it. However, my association with HH was beyond repair. He may have asked me to strike him with my venom if I could not love him but he had lashed out in anger as well—

> If you wish to go, go—
> I will be the path under your feet,
> Not to turn you back,
> But lead you to the icy flames.

> Or,
> I had handed you endless possibilities,
> But are you so extraordinary any more?
> Or is your pain cheap?
> Perhaps it is for the best, my devious darling,
> That you have cut these silken ties that bind us.

His kind soul could not rest after abusing me so. So he had also mentioned how generous he could be—

> You turn me down and walk away
> With such savage grace—
> Have you hurt yourself?
> Chipped the pretty nail on your left foot?
> How terrible! Come sit a while,

As I wipe your wounds with mercy,
And salve them with my antiseptic kisses.

After the remarkable success of his book *Ekhon Jouban Jaar* (The Young Ones) the wounded poet was about to publish his second book of poems, *Je Joley Agun Jwole* (Burning Water). The name of a proposed third book—although none of the poems for that collection had been written yet—he had told me in confidence: *Kar Ki Noshto Korechilam* (Had I Harmed Anyone)! Meanwhile, *Achal Premer Podyo* (Lyrics for a Hopeless Love) was published, illustrated by Dhruva Esh. I read the poems and was deeply saddened by the realization that he had been so hurt. Why did he have to fall in love like that? What need had there been to get hurt and to hurt in return? I knew that despite the impression of indifference he had cultivated around others, HH was a deeply committed man. None of the women he had loved had ever loved him back. He could never have the family he had always dreamt of. No one had been aware of the dreams he must have nurtured over the years. It was not always apparent but he was a neat and organized man. He would only wear well-ironed clothes, clean sandals, with a thick cloth *jhola* by his side containing pens, some paper and packets of cigarettes, all neatly arranged. My bag was never so organized. There is a tendency to assume a bearded man with a jhola is a poet, somewhat detached and a little scattered, but it is not always so. Some people like being hurt while some others like to make sacrifices. HH himself had once written, after parting ways with a woman he had loved, 'After paying this price in pain, life has finally learnt that love is radiant in separation and pales when reciprocated.' He hawked pain. Long before we ever met, like a true hawker, he had sung out:

Do you want some pain?
I have some of various shades, red, or blue—
Pain of refusal and indifference,
Pain of loving the wrong woman,
Pain of public rallies of the wrong politicians,
Or the pain of two jokers high on hydrogen.
Do you want some pain?

Who else is there to sell you the purest kind?
There is none other like me, having lost it all,
There is none other like me to get you the best!

He loved in secrecy and those he loved never grasped his true intentions. In secrecy he sat alone with his loneliness, asking about his beloved. If she were to remain unresponsive he would declare with wounded pride:

. . . if nothing else, forget me with care.
Why should you care about my loss?
Perhaps I have erred in falling in love,
Perhaps I have erred in lying on withering flowers,
And in broad daylight,
Murdering my own solitude. Who cares?

He loved his sister in Netrakona too but never visited her. She was in his blood, in every fibre of his being, like death and life cohabit side by side, camouflaged.

~

While sacrifice, pain and separation were the sort of treasures the ascetic poet HH desired, I knew another poet for whom consumption was primary and life nothing but a great game. Life was a stage and he a mere player on it, performing every waking moment. Sometimes it was difficult to differentiate between when he was being his true self and when he was lying or acting. So I assumed everything was the truth, which is perhaps why he used to like me so much. His most famous work was *Khelaram Khele Ja* (Khelaram at Play) where he had deftly drawn the astonishing character of a conman called Babar Ali. Had I not spent a long time in his company I would never have understood that the character of Ali, universally reviled as a shameless scoundrel, was a reflection of its creator HSS himself.

After my break-up with R, HSS had taken it upon himself, of his own volition, to mend my broken heart. One day he took me to Rangamati; I had never been there before. Sitting on the grass by the lake at the foot of the tall mountains HSS confessed to me how he too often felt terribly lonely. While speaking he would use such startlingly beautiful words that I could not help but be amazed. In comparison to him my vocabulary was light as a feather; even an insect could have done a decent translation of what I had to say, my sentences so fragile that often he would have to lean in closer just to discern what I was saying. Taking me to a colourful hotel somewhere in the middle of Rangamati he dipped his head closer and whispered to me, 'We should just take one room, shouldn't we?'

If I had said 'No, we shouldn't', perhaps it would have seemed I was suspicious of his motives, that I was making assumptions about his moral character. Since there was no question of asking questions, almost to convince him that I was not apprehensive of him, I answered in an impassive, indifferent voice, as if responding to a passing how-are-you, 'Yes, of course we can.'

'Tell me if you are having second thoughts. We can take two separate rooms.'

I replied simply, 'Why should I be having second thoughts? No, I'm not having second thoughts.'

'Are you sure?'

I suppressed all my doubts brutally, my face a mask of serenity. Simply because I was convinced that there was nothing that could tarnish the innocent and unsullied relationship we had, I answered, 'Of course.'

Placing his hands gently on my back HSS said, 'This is one thing I like about you. You never say no to anything.'

That was true, I never said no. A man who was my father's age, who could easily have been my father, my older brother, an older male relative or simply a friend—I did not think I had to say no to him especially. Why should I have said no? I was not a provincial and conservative person like others, nor was I bigoted, narrow-minded or completely implicated within the familial matrix! Another time HSS had taken me and Yasmin on a sojourn to the sal forests of Komilla and we had put up at the guest house of the forest department—Yasmin and I in one room and he in another. We had gotten up in the morning, had breakfast in the dining room of the guest house and gone out to roam the sal forests, before returning to Dhaka later. Throughout the trip it was HSS who had mostly spoken—about his childhood and youth, the poverty he had faced growing up, suffering from tuberculosis, Dr Anwara who had saved him in the TB hospital, their courtship and eventual marriage, their two children, his writings, besides the shameless and unscrupulous nature of people around him about which he had spoken without any hesitation.

Whenever the talk veered towards literature he would enthusiastically ask me about my work. I had been extremely embarrassed by the attention, had almost curled up in mortification. I wrote poems purely out of my own fancy; I did not dare share my amateur efforts with someone as illustrious as HSS. Instead, I admired this man's kindness, his generosity, the sense of stability he exuded. He had stayed abroad for long and had an upmarket life, with a house and a car in the upscale locality of Gulshan in Dhaka. He was a writer renowned all over the country, he travelled all over, was a huge scholar. He knew so much but was still so inquisitive that he was constantly looking to unearth new things; such was his lust for life. He had also been so warm and welcoming with me and Yasmin, two simple girls from the suburbs, that we were delighted and awkward at the same time. However, there was one thing that I could not fail to notice eventually. As large-hearted and hospitable as he was, despite the number of times we had welcomed him into our house in Mymensingh, not once did he invite us to his house in Dhaka. He preferred staying over at a place for the night only if it was far away from Dhaka. Not that I did not wish to visit faraway places. There were so many places in the country I was yet to visit, so many things I was yet to see, still so many new regions I had to explore. And it was not as if I was getting any younger.

Rangamati's beauty reminded me of only one person again and again: Chandana. Chandana must have walked on that field, she must have sat beside that lake, she must have played under that tree as a child—that was all I could think. I wondered what games Chandana used to play when she was little. Did she ever play *gollachhut*?[17] Even if she did not, life had played it with her. She was the one who had been tagged and flung out from the Chakma way of life in Rangamati into a Bengali household in an alien place. Was she happy? I badly wished to know the answer to that question. It seemed I had not seen her for a thousand years. The last we met it had been in R's dilapidated house in Muhammadpur. She had come with her son, but at that time there had been nothing for me to welcome her with; I could not even take her out to lunch. Once I had visited her at her sister-in-law's house in Dhaka and seen for myself how awkward and withdrawn Chandana was at home. She had a small room to herself and her infant son and seeing her I had refused to believe that she slept there with a man. This was Chandana, the same girl who could not stand the sight of a bare-chested man or see a man chewing food! And here I was supposed to believe she had become a loyal and devoted housewife? I could not shake off the thought that no matter in whose arms she was, she was not happy. I had kept wondering if she still wrote poems like she used to.

HSS made plans of travelling to Kaptai from Rangamati. He was going to meet some of his admirers there and they wished to host us. I was not prepared for the trick he pulled after reaching Kaptai; he introduced me to his admirers as his daughter. They had never met his daughter so it was not hard convincing them. We were on a boat in the middle of the lake and he was sitting with his fans and answering their questions about his new book and what he was writing then. One of his devotees happened to be sitting beside me. Perhaps thinking that not talking to HSS's daughter could be considered rude, the man smiled shyly at me and asked, 'Is this your first time at Kaptai?'

'Yes, the first time.'

'Your house is in Gulshan, isn't it?'

I heard my own heart beating erratically and I turned towards the water pretending to have not heard his question. He asked again.

'You must have read everything your father has ever written.'

I looked at him. 'Excuse me, what?'

'I was saying, you must have read all of HSS's works?'

'Oh. Not all, I've read some.'

I turned to stare at the water again, hoping against hope that the man would be dissuaded from asking any more questions by my intense interest in watching the lake. Unfortunately, another admirer joined the first to keep me company.

'Are you returning to London soon?'

Trembling helplessly on the inside, I steadfastly stared at the water, unable to think of any suitable answer to the question. It was as if I had not heard anything, that I was hard of hearing. HSS may have been a renowned author, he may have had all his faculties intact, but it still did not guarantee that his daughter had to have the same. For a moment I wished I could simply jump into the lake if that would have saved me from the questions.

'What is your daughter's name, HSS?' someone asked.

Smiling sweetly he replied, 'Her name is Adwitiya.'

'Such a beautiful name,' the same voice said again.

'I gave her the name.'

HSS was looking at his Adwitiya fondly. He was looking at her sad eyes, at the tears threatening to gather in the corners. He saw all that but the smile on his face did not slip. He said over that smile, 'Her mother calls her by another name. Why aren't you talking, Adwitiya? Don't you like it here?'

Nodding to indicate that I did like it there—saying otherwise was not an option at the risk of ruining such a wonderful boat ride—I turned my gaze back to the water. At least no one noticed the tears.

Frequently, HSS would unbutton his shirt to reveal a long scar from his throat to his belly, the result of a cardiac operation, and claim he was not of this world for much longer. This reminder of his mortality used to make me feel even more partial towards him. It was these feelings perhaps that had stopped me that day from calling my *father's* bluff. It made me cautious while talking lest I addressed him wrong and spoiled the game. Had I been a better actress I would perhaps have been able to ask him that day, with a boat full of people as my captive audience, 'Father, did you take your medicines after lunch?'

HSS wrote plays; in fact, he had written quite a few for the People's Theatre. Around that time he was translating Shakespeare's plays, to be staged by an English theatre director. But HSS did not just write plays, he performed them in real life too. What else had that trip been but a staged play? He could have introduced me as someone who was *like his daughter*. Instead he had said I *was* his daughter. Not once had he been anxious that I might deny being his daughter! Nor had he been apprehensive about what could happen to his reputation should the truth come out. Despite being tempted repeatedly I did not tell a soul anything that day, I did not because I did not want to tarnish his reputation. I did not respect him any less than the others, then why did he have to put me under the spotlight and toy with me so? He had his own name, his own identity, while mine had to be hidden away! I could not address him formally, nor could I call him 'HSS bhai'. The words would almost slip past my lips before I gulped them back down again, the words dissolving on my tongue and leaving it dry as parchment.

After the boat ride and a visit to the Kaptai dam, HSS went on a long tour of the navy base, with the deaf and mute Adwitiya struggling in his wake. We had a dinner invitation at a naval officer's house in the evening where, in front of the whole house, my new identity was reinforced—HSS's daughter Adwitiya. When the naval officer addressed me formally HSS intervened swiftly, 'Don't be so formal with her! She isn't even twenty-one yet. Are you twenty-one yet?' Twenty-five years old when this was happening, I had lowered my head to count the toes on my feet, then the fingers on my hand, and then back again to my feet. By then HSS had begun drinking.

'Your daughter doesn't talk a lot, does she?'

'You're right. She talks very little. I don't know where she gets it. Where do you get it from? From Mymensingh?' HSS winked at me as he finished. None of the others knew anything about Mymensingh.

The wife of the naval officer had put in a lot of care into her appearance for the evening. Smiling gratefully at HSS, she approached us for a photograph. The other people in the house wanted photos too, even the neighbours did, and HSS made me sit beside him for each one.

'Does your daughter write too?' inquired the naval officer's wife.

'Yes, she does. Very beautiful poems she writes. Why don't you read out one of your poems for them, Adwitiya!'

I shook my head in refusal immediately.

'So naughty! She's very naughty!' HSS laughed, slapping me on the back.

Everyone present confessed that they had previously seen HSS on television. Even while sitting down for the lavish dinner that is what they continued to talk about—who had seen him when and in which show. Only one person proudly declared that he had read a book too, *Adidiganta Nagna Padadwani* (Barefoot Across Eternity). The name astounded me, especially because it was not HSS's work at all, it was a book by Shamsur Rahman! Not once did HSS protest and rectify the error that it was not his work! Instead he looked at me once, winked, and it seemed as if the entire thing was all too amusing for him. Perhaps that too was a side effect of 'not being of this world for too long'; it made one susceptible to finding joy at making others dance to their tunes. His joy was short-lived though, what with the urgent bathroom runs he had to make throughout the evening. When I finally went to the bathroom after dinner I immediately figured out the reason for his frequent visits. The entire place was covered in vomit, the sink was overflowing and the drainage system too was entirely clogged. Not that HSS was sick and unconscious somewhere. He was still holding court, that same old smile fixed on his lips, a smile whose secrets I could never interpret.

At the Kaptai guest house, HSS had ultimately booked one room—primarily to save money and also because it would not have been odd for a daughter to share a room with her father. Despite it being a big room, with two beds on either side, I was petrified about sleeping there that night. HSS was drunk out of his senses by then and I had no wish to spend the night in the same room as him. At least if I could have slept in the corridor outside, or even on a mat spread out under the tree, I would have been more at peace. Instead, pretending as if he had not touched alcohol that evening and as if I was his daughter for real and everything was not a lie, I used my own imaginary excuses as a shield to bolster my courage. Entering the room I headed straight for the bed and the blanket on it, which I proceeded to cover myself with from head to toe. As odd as that was in the heat, there was nothing else I could have done that night. To me the blanket was the only thing that could have protected me like a force shield from any untoward incidents. So I held on to its edges for dear life, afraid that any moment a bandit would barge in and attack. My own heartbeat was making a din in my ear, anxious that soon Khelaram would be in the room looking for Sharifa's bed.

'Are you asleep?'

I did not answer. Instead I pretended to be asleep; a sleeping person would be spared from answering questions. Lying still on the bed like a dead log, I pretended to have not heard his query. Stealthily parting the covers in the darkness—as if it had moved while turning—I peered out from underneath to see him walking about in the room. Why was he walking about? Why was he not going to bed? What did he want? Did he have ulterior motives in bringing me so far away from Dhaka? Despite there being empty rooms in the guest house and even after the naval officer had offered to book separate rooms for us, he had booked one single room and introduced me as his daughter for no apparent reason. The entire night all I did was listen to my own heartbeat and hear the sounds of HSS, awake, walking about and mumbling to himself. A girl from the suburbs such as I could not fathom what was real and what was not in how this renowned author from Dhaka behaved that night.

The next morning we drove to the airport and took our flight back to Dhaka. He did not take the baby taxi to his house, afraid that his wife or someone else would see us together and there would be talk that he had been away cavorting with a younger woman. He got off near Gulshan and I took the taxi to Nayapaltan. Nearing my house I heaved a sigh of relief, the kind an amateur actress would have after finally being allowed to get off the stage. All he wished to do was avoid gossip and so the only recourse left for him was to keep doing what he was doing in secrecy. It was possible that he had been angry with me that day because he had not gotten from me what he had probably hoped for. Perhaps he had been angry with himself too for having spent so much money on the trip in vain. Like how in his novel Babar Ali had only managed to seduce his girlfriend after much subterfuge and after taking her from one corner of the country to the other. Did his own creation Babar Ali live somewhere within him? For the first time I felt it was definitely possible that it was so. On our way back he barely spoke a word. He was beginning to resemble someone I barely knew, as if he had only heard my name or heard about me but we had not yet met formally. Was it because he had not succeeded in having his way with me? Or had he been thinking about his writing? Or was it because he had been reluctant to let his co-passengers in the flight know that he had been away on vacation with a younger woman he was not related to? At least in my behaviour there had been no sign that I was struggling to trust him, or that I was suspicious about his motives. Pretending to not understand a gesture was something I could do well, especially in the middle of uncomfortable situations. When men pretend to know more than they actually do it can get very sticky if women do not counter this by pretending they do not know things. Since intuition has always been a stronger trait in women, they find it easier to sense looming danger. I mention women in plural here because later I got to know very similar things from Yasmin. She too had managed to ignore many an illicit offer simply by pretending to not understand the pass made at her in the first place.

It was possible that HSS had had no ulterior motives for taking me with him. It was possible he had taken me with him just as a kind gesture. However, introducing me as his daughter was something I could not accept. He did not have to hide my true identity. I might not have been a famous poet like him but I had my own name, my own self. I might not have been a poet but I still wrote poetry. So what had been the reason for the charade? It was not as if he had been having a scandalous extramarital love affair with me!

Once, while visiting us in Mymensingh, HSS had called Shamsur Rahman from our house somewhat unnecessarily. After a few initial polite questions asking after his health, HSS had informed Rahman that he was travelling away from Dhaka. He had asked Rahman to guess where he was and when Rahman failed to guess correctly, HSS had smugly informed the former that he was only 120 miles from Dhaka and surrounded by beautiful women. Done passing on this news he had looked at me and smiled. 'I hope you heard, I did not tell him where I am or under whose roof.' I had failed to grasp why that had to be a secret.

'You could have said you are in my house.'

'What are you saying! Everyone in Dhaka will get to know!'

'So? Why is that a problem?'

He had only laughed mysteriously at that. I still don't know why he had lied on the phone that day. He had regaled me with stories of the many women Shamsur Rahman had had affairs with and while telling me these stories I had seen his jaws tighten; it had convinced me that he was secretly envious of Rahman. Envy had him in its grasp; all he wished for was to be as big a poet as Shamsur Rahman and acquire the adulation of as many female admirers. He loved the word too—envy! Once, while on a trip to the flooded Brahmaputra plains, he had pointed to a tree on a tiny stump of land and said, 'Do you know what that tree is called? It's called Envy.' Strangled by his own jealousies he had told me about his doomed love affair with his sister-in-law who had grown up in his house. They had been in love, or so he told me, and their relationship had progressed as far as a relationship could go. Later, the sister-in-law had met a young wastrel and eloped. HSS had been unable to process the fact that she had left him. He had confessed that he often visited the sister-in-law and bought her everything she might require to take care of a family. He had gone on about how deeply she had hurt him by going ahead with this marriage, how she had left him completely alone.

I could never fathom why he had chosen to reveal such details of his personal life to me. Sometimes it seemed he was very lonely, that he had no one whom he could talk to about his joys and sorrows. It made me feel sorry for him. I could also not shake off the thought that perhaps authors were inherently like that: they told as many engrossing stories as they wrote and fact had very little to do with those. HSS had once told me a story from his childhood. Once as a boy he had entered his house through the back door and told everyone that there was a huge dog at the front gate. Of course there had been no such thing, but he had said it nonetheless. There had been no reason, neither had he wanted to scare anyone—he had said it because he wanted to.

'Just like that?'

'Yes, just like that.'

Perhaps that had been the first hint as to his future vocation as a writer. HSS lied quite frequently, often without any particular reason, perhaps because to him life had always been like a short story. Regardless of what he believed, or what tales he told, I must confess that he used to speak beautifully and his stories were always amazing. I have always been in awe of this quality in him.

~

HSS was greeted with a grand reception at Abakash only once, when he had come to Mymensingh for a programme organized by Shokal Kabita Parisad. I had made arrangements for his stay at Abakash without previously considering how Father was going to react to the news—he was going to scream the house down, or perhaps he was going to throw HSS out summarily. Admittedly it had been a risk. I had set Mother the task of convincing him that HSS was one of the foremost authors and intellectuals in the country and so he had to refrain from behaving like an animal with the man. Dada was asked to praise HSS in front of Father as much as possible. The objective was to convince Father to allow us to host HSS at Abakash for two days. In the end Father had consented and we immediately set ourselves to preparing the house for the visit. Every conceivable sort of exotic item of food was bought from the market and the kitchen almost became a warzone. My room was cleaned and set up nicely for the esteemed guest. Let alone misbehaving, Father had put on his suit to sit and have dinner with HSS and for two days, instead of coming home and shouting as was his usual routine, he had done his best to behave like a civilized human being.

The second time, however, we were not so lucky and it was all because of Chotda. The feeling of gratitude everyone had been nurturing ever since HSS's first visit was brutally dispelled by him when he snidely remarked to Father, 'The whole of Dhaka knows this HSS's shenanigans. He has quite the colourful reputation with women. That rat bastard.' Almost immediately HSS was declared persona non grata at Abakash. Nevertheless, it was not as if he stopped coming to Mymensingh after that. He visited again and stayed at the guest quarters of the Circuit House. He used to tell me about his travels all over the country—that travel broadened the horizons of experience and that one needed to study people because there was nothing more fascinating than them. How people talked, how they laughed or cried, how they got embarrassed or felt fear—everything was an object of study. I remember sitting near his feet and listening to him philosophize with awe.

Once, he had turned up at Chotda's house to meet me but Chotda had not shown him even the most basic of courtesies. I had been livid with my brother that day. When Chotda alleged that the entire city

knew about HSS's affairs I understood the words were not his own—
he was repeating stories heard from a colleague on a flight or from
some washed-up tabloid journalist. Neither was there any logic to
the claim that the entire city knew. Most people in the city, the ones
completely unconcerned about literary circles, did not know who HSS
was. Of the rest the ones who were from the literary world respected
HSS a great deal. Regardless, I was unable to clear HSS's name that
day and he remained unwelcome at Abakash. Consequently, because
of this unjust ban I was even more partial to him. I used to go visit
him wherever he would ask me to, be it the Circuit House, or some
restaurant, or even on a short trip to Muktagacha. When he was busy
making a documentary on Kuddus Boyati by the river, I visited him
there too.

My relationship with HSS was built on admiration and
affection. He had the sort of benevolence for me that a renowned
writer often has for literature enthusiasts who are also amateur poets.
This slowly became more personal, especially after he expressed his
interest in knowing why I was divorcing R and even came down
to Mymensingh because of it. Be it literary or not, irrespective of
whatever conversations the two of us were having, he was always the
primary speaker. Somehow the role suited him. He could coax even
the shy and blushing Yasmin with a 'hey, how are you, what are you
doing, come and sit here', and tell her numerous stories and give her
much advice. The advice even I got—advice on how to write poems,
how to make the ear alert to sounds rather than counting the words
for the rhyme, and so on. He used to read all my poems and say
something or the other about every one of them—the good ones,
the ones that could be improved, and words that could sound better
instead of the ones I had used. There was no artifice in all this.

When he heard about Yasmin's disappearance he was as
devastated by it as I was and I remember him crying helplessly, much
to my surprise. Later, he even visited Yasmin's new house quite a
few times to see her. Once, while I was in Dhaka, he took a young
paramour of his to see Yasmin. He spent the whole day canoodling
with the young girl, hugging her and kissing her, much to Yasmin's
discomfort. In her new house she had to face uncomfortable questions
regarding what her senior male guest was up to inside the room with

a nearly underage girl. Both Yasmin and I saw the girl later when HSS's translation of *The Tempest* was being performed at the British Council. The three of us, me, Yasmin and the girl, were seated together while HSS was behind us. Every single time I turned back I noticed that his eyes were fixed on the girl instead of the stage. This girl had once tried to commit suicide by leaping to her death off a fifth-floor balcony, such had been her mental anguish. He had brought her out of that state, helped her see life in a new light and inspired her to love again. He had told me all about it.

~

Sometimes he was inundating me with well-meaning advice like a concerned father, sometimes he was protecting me like an older brother, sometimes he was making risqué jokes like a friend and sometimes his eyes were flashing with a sinister lupine smile. Besides one could never be sure if he truly had less-than-noble intentions or not. When he had forced me to sleep in the same room with him in Rangamati and Kaptai it had seemed the Babar Ali inside him had taken over; later I had not been so sure about that. Before we became close there were many instances when I had been in two minds about him. I remember how in a restaurant in Mymensingh, after knowing why I was leaving R he had placed his hand on my back in sympathy. His hand had fallen just over the clasp of my bra and my back had arched almost immediately, involuntarily, attempting to shake off the soft gesture of comfort. It had seemed that Khelaram had come so far only to toy with me. As deeply as I respected him, my apprehensions regarding him were equally acute.

He had written a wonderful article in the newspaper about Shokal and my literary endeavours. The same man had invited me to his house and showed me around the empty place, before taking me to his painting studio and shutting the door behind us as if he had finally managed to get me where he had wanted all along. Cold with fright, I had sidestepped him, unlocked the door and walked out. This was the same man who had called me from London before his heart surgery to let me know that I was the first person back home he was calling. This was the same man who had been so impressed by my poetry that he had written to his publisher in Dhaka to publish my book and had advised NM to get me to write a column in *Khabarer Kagaj*. Even after all this I was unable to worship this godlike man—it had had more to do with my inability to treat him as a god rather than any uncouth behaviour on his part. Sometimes I felt that all these emotions were nothing more than baseless anxieties and fears and that HSS was as generous and magnanimous as everyone made him out to be. Nevertheless when the time came for his columns to be compiled into a book, he carefully expunged all mention of Taslima Nasrin's literary talents and all his earlier praise of the Shokal Kabita Parisad from therein. That is another story, though. Let me come back to 1989.

Of all the bad things that happened in 1989, Yasmin's disappearance was perhaps the most devastating. I went into severe depression and began craving a change of scene—just to get away to a completely unknown place. I loved Mymensingh but at that moment it seemed to me the city was my mortal foe. No other city could have seemed so empty—I could not bear the sight of an abandoned *Gitabitan* slowly gathering dust on the harmonium, or her clothes, her favorite knick-knacks and the books of poetry lying around. So I left the city for some time. Soon after, I found myself sitting dejected by the Sitalkha, MHI right by my side. I had known MHI for long; we had been in touch through letters since the time of *Senjuti*. He used to write beautiful romantic letters, soaked in touching words of love and devotion. Not just me, he used to write such letters to many other women.

Once while in Tangail for a programme he had met Mukti and fallen in love with her, especially after hearing her sing Tagore's 'Amar mukti aloi aloi' (My freedom is written in the light). Mukti used to be an amateur poet. Their relationship had lasted for quite some time, that is, until the day it ended. I had even written a soppy story of star-crossed love called 'Nikosito Prem' (A Tried and Tested Love) for the magazine *Sandhani* (The Seeker), with MHI, Mukti and a third fictional character called Lima. Many who read the story assumed that Lima was a manifestation of me. Had I not based the character on me? Yes, I had. At such a young age I must admit I used to have romantic fantasies regarding MHI, like any other curious girl interested in a romantic boy. R used to be friends with MHI; he became even better friends with Mukti eventually. When we were still together I remember meeting MHI at the book fair and we would end up having a cursory conversation. MHI had later gotten married to a simple homely girl while I had relinquished all my domestic dreams and broken out of the family cage to live as a free bird—hurt, tired, alone, with nowhere to go, but free nonetheless.

MHI used to tell me about this magical kingdom across the seven seas. My only desire was to go away, somewhere far away, although I had no idea how far would actually be far enough. Thinking of the only place in the world that could be called heaven on earth and not wishing to look at this scorched, tired world around me for a moment longer, I turned to MHI and suggested, 'Let's go to Kashmir.' He agreed immediately. 'Yes. Let's go!' Throwing a cool glance at the unruffled waters of the Sitalkha, MHI told me, 'We'd need almost thirty to thirty-five thousand for this by the way.' I did not have so much money. My monthly salary was 2000 taka and all my savings had been spent in publishing my book. So I borrowed the money that would allow me to lose myself and find that faraway place, to try and forget my pain and be free. Chotda was there at the airport to see me off.

Everyone at home knew that I was going to India alone to meet my friend Atashi in Calcutta, and that the two of us were planning a trip. I told the actual truth to no one; that would have been a disaster. If they knew I was going with a friend called MHI, that I was going to lose myself in an unknown land, they would have immediately put me in chains and locked me away. It was fine if I was going around with another man as long as movement was limited to within the country. Crossing the border with a strange man would have been an entirely different matter. One could argue that if we were allowed to sit beside each other by the Sitalkha then what was so wrong with doing the same by the Ganga? There was a difference because the Sitalkha and the Ganga were not the same things. With the Sitalkha there had been the reassurance that irrespective of whether I was swimming in the river or up to something else, I was going to be home at night. With the Ganga there was no guarantee where the night would lead me. Everyone was afraid of the night and so was I, which is why I insisted on two separate rooms for the two of us in the hotel at Calcutta. The same in Delhi, and then again in Agra. The two of us got busy sightseeing or generally strolling about like tourists, visiting the Victoria Memorial Hall, the Red Fort, the India Gate or the Taj Mahal. During one such sojourn, while out on a walk holding hands in the balmy afternoon air, I was struck with the abrupt realization that I was in love with MHI. Perhaps it was because I loved him that I had taken off my own gold chain and hung it around his neck in the Rajdhani Express. I was in love and if someone was going to ask me to leap off the Himalayas, I would probably have done so. I wanted to tell MHI all my stories of pain and joy, I wanted to look into his eyes, kiss him lightly on his eyelids and tell him that I loved him. Obviously, I could not do that and even before I could say anything, something happened that changed our equation irrevocably.

Tucked away in Jammu, away from the prying eyes of the rest of the world, MHI made love to me, his touch shaking me to my very core. On a princely houseboat floating on the Dal Lake in Srinagar, basking in the welcome warmth of the roaring fireplace, I found myself drowning in my love for him. My relationship with R had ended long back. I had not realized how much I had missed a man's touch. Wrapped in MHI's embrace, covered in the pristine white sheets he pulled over us, I felt myself come alive again. Reservations long ingrained in me—that sex was forbidden with anyone other than my husband—were tossed aside in the stormy winds blowing in from the Shalimar Gardens. There was no one dearer to me than MHI at that moment, so much so that I almost forgot the life he already had back in Bangladesh. I was reminded of it with a rude jolt after returning to Calcutta when MHI had to go to Treasure Island to buy clothes, jewellery and gifts for his wife and child. That he had a world of his own where I was not welcome became clearer when he told me that he had made an appointment to go visit Sunil Gangopadhyay by himself, leaving me to relive the feelings of soul-crushing emptiness I had experienced after Yasmin's disappearance.

The flight from Calcutta to Dhaka took half an hour. The half hour was almost up and MHI was still not telling me when we were going to meet again and where, or when we were going to be together again. He was not telling me that he loved me either. In fact, he was saying nothing. He looked happy, content at the prospect of returning home to his family. Desperate and unwilling to let him hear me sigh, a helpless woman trapped by love yet again, I placed my hand on his, hoping against hope that my touch would convey the pain wrenching my gut. Surprised, MHI turned towards me. 'What is it? Why are you behaving like that?'

I was looking at him, all my vulnerability reflected in my gaze.

Drawing his brows together as if he had comprehended what I was trying to convey, MHI reassured me, 'Oh, are you afraid? Is this your first time on an airplane? Don't worry, it happens.'

Slowly I moved my hand away from his.

Back in the city MHI took a baby taxi to his house in Old Dhaka while I made my way to Nayapaltan. When he was about to leave it would have been impossible for anyone to tell that he had spent the past several days with me. It seemed as if he had simply run into me while walking on the road, an old acquaintance and nothing more.

The book fair had started in the meantime. One day, from a distance, I spied MHI wandering in the fair grounds with his wife in tow; she was wearing the sari he had bought for her from Treasure Island. I was far away from them, completely out of place in such a happy image, best relegated to the shadows.

~

Not that this managed to completely cure my obsession with him all at once. There was still a bit of it left somewhere deep inside me. A few days later MHI met me at the Mouchak crossroads and took me to his friend's house. He did not have much time that day for anything except sex—he did not have time to spend the day talking about love, nor did he have time to cast a fleeting glance at my feelings for him. That day I finally tore all my rosy fantasies of love to shreds and let them be washed away by my tears.

Thus We Are Swept Away

Mahakali School was not too far from Abakash and every Friday Yasmin would walk to the school for her classes. On holidays music classes were conducted there by Anandadhwani; all the students would join in and sing Rabindrasangeet at the top of their voices. Young or old, five or seventy-five, no one was refused entry. I was absolutely delighted to see Yasmin singing such beautiful Rabindrasangeet. And how beautifully she had learnt to recite poems! I had taught her but she had long surpassed me. She was the best at the Shokal Kabita Parisad when it came to recitation and I was proud of her. I had a dream for her future—she was going to become a great singer and I was going to send her to Santiniketan for better training. I nurtured this dream carefully—a beautiful blue lake and my hopes gliding on it like a swan.

Yasmin knew everything, of course. I was ready to do anything to ensure a bright future for her, be it at the cost of my own life. Since there was not much work at the family planning office, I used to spend most of my time at home with Yasmin as my constant companion and best friend. Not just at home, I needed her with me even when I had to go somewhere—to roam the city, to visit Suhrid in Dhaka if Mymensingh was becoming too intolerable or even to socialize within the literary and cultural circles on certain occasions. Obviously, there were boundaries too in this relationship, lines neither of us ever crossed. Like I never told her why I had left R and neither did she ever tell me why she often got late returning home. In order to live a healthy life both of us had resolved that there was no space for anything illicit between us. However, perhaps Yasmin's definition of illicit had been different. Why else would she lie about being at her friend Rinku's on getting late because she had stopped to chat with two boys from her class? There was nothing wrong with talking to boys, of course; she used to lie to me out of fear that I would be displeased with her or judge her or misinterpret what was happening. Not that I ever told her not to talk to any of her male friends. They used to come to Abakash to chat and spend time with her and sometimes I too would join in.

Despite being so close, Yasmin was never able to overcome this awkwardness between the two of us. She used to love me and fear me in equal measure. So I never realized that she had gradually grown very tired of meeting my friends, reciting the poems I asked her to recite, singing the songs I liked to hear and trying to get used to my idea of what life was. I never realized that she had begun to suffer from a crisis of identity and neither did I grasp the fact that no matter how inconsequential my social status and fame was to me, I was still making my own decisions while she had to depend on me for everything. Her independence had begun to erode, resulting in a feeling of loneliness that I never noticed. I did not understand that I was inadvertently parading my beauty, my maturity and my aesthetically organized life constantly in front of her, a life where I was the queen and she had been dragged into it and made to play the part of a pawn. I loved the pawn, make no mistake, and I gave her what I felt she needed quite generously. But I failed to sense her isolation. She understood that I did not wish for her to just finish her studies, get married and become a good housewife like other women around her. I wished for her to be her own person, to have a life defined entirely by her own choices and tastes—she knew all that and yet she suffered from low self-esteem and this too I was blind to. We were so close, we shared the same bed, but I never saw her wounds. I was trying to build a beautiful life for her, notwithstanding Father's cruelty, my brother's and his wife's selfishness and Mother's indifference, but I did not realize in time that the project was doomed.

One night she did not come back home. We waited for her till late but she did not return. Unable to hold out for much longer I went to see all her friends in the city in search of her. I even went to her acquaintances and to our relatives, but there was simply no sign of her anywhere. Mother and I spent a sleepless night, watching Father pace up and down the room, the same question plaguing all of us: where could she have gone? She had gone to college like the other days. Even if she ever got late, she usually came back home by afternoon. A full day had passed, dawn was about to break, but there was no sign of Yasmin. I was terrified. Mother had spread out the prayer mat on the floor and was reading one namaz after another, begging Allah to ensure her daughter's safety no matter where she was. Early in the morning I went out and sat near the black main gate of Abakash waiting for her. The second day also passed without any sign of her. Father kept calling from his chamber to ask about her while Mother had gone to the mazar of the old pir to pray for a miracle. I was having trouble breathing from the anxiety and I could not go on trying to think of new places to go look for her. Late in the night of the second day we finally received news of her whereabouts via Jahangir, her friend who used to live on Ishan Chakraborty Road. She was in Sankipara, in her friend Milan's house. Dada and I set off immediately to bring her back. We found her at Milan's house curled up on the bed, her face buried between her curled up knees. Unable to understand what was happening to her I ran to her and took hold of her hand. Wrenching it from my grasp, she cried, 'No, don't touch me!'

I could not fathom what was wrong. What had happened? Had someone said something to her? Why was she angry?

'Let's go home.'

'No.'

What was that supposed to mean?

It was M, Milan's older brother, who explained to us what it meant. Yasmin wished to marry Milan, that too immediately. I have never been as flabbergasted by anything in my entire life as I was that day on receiving this news! Stunned into silence, there was only one thing I was certain of—Yasmin and Milan did not have a romantic relationship. As a result, no matter how hard I tried, I could not comprehend why she was suddenly talking about things like marriage and why she was so shamelessly demanding it for herself out of the blue. Yasmin had meanwhile declared that she was not going back to Abakash with us. She was set on her decision and no amount of coaxing and cajoling—short of dragging her out forcibly, kicking and screaming—was going to change her mind. Her body was taut as steel and somehow she had managed to beat her spirit into steely determination too; neither of us mattered to her in that moment. While this dramatic exchange was under way Milan had not put a foot inside the room and was standing at the door, his head hanging low. Yasmin had left home the day before in a salwar and kurta; she was wearing a blue sari when we found her. There was no apparent reason for her odd behaviour, at least not one I could think of that could explain the entire situation.

Since M did not have any answer either, Dada tried reasoning with her. 'This is not how you get married. Let's go home for now, we can fix a wedding for later.'

'If you are fixed on the idea of marrying Milan, finish your studies first and then you can marry him,' I joined in. In response Yasmin gave us three days to make all the necessary arrangements for her wedding. I remember crying helplessly like a baby in front of the entire household. Yasmin saw me crying but it did not change her mind. By the time the situation was somewhat resolved it was well past midnight. I did not hear Yasmin's verdict myself; she conveyed her decision to us via Milan's sibling. They were closer to her suddenly, passing on any information she wanted to get across to us since she did not want to speak to me directly, although I could not understand the reason behind her sudden anger. What had I done to deserve such ire?

That night I could not return to Abakash. Dada left while I spent yet another sleepless night in an unknown house beside a silent Yasmin. I tried talking to her, tried coaxing her to tell me what was wrong. Every time I placed my hand lightly on her shoulder to coax her to talk, she firmly moved it away. She did not fall asleep, though, and I was sure that there was something mysterious behind the entire charade. The next morning I somehow managed to convince Yasmin to return home with me, with the promise that we would get her married to Milan, if not immediately, if not the day after, then soon. Frankly, there was no way she would have agreed otherwise. She remained stone-faced throughout the journey, not looking at me even once. This behaviour continued after we reached Abakash. She spent the day in bed, staring at the wall. When Dada returned home in the evening, she shamelessly started screaming to remind us about her wedding. I asked her a thousand questions only to be met with unnerving silence. She told us nothing about what had happened the night she had not returned, not even where she had been. Neither did she reveal the reason behind her insistence on marrying Milan at such short notice! Not a soul in the house managed to unearth the secret.

Later, years later—she was a full-blown housewife with a husband and children and had managed to overcome her adolescent awkwardness with me—she told me what had happened that day. Her classmate and friend Milan had taken his older brother's motorcycle to college. After class he had invited Yasmin for a ride to Madhupur and Yasmin had not refused. Besides, the obvious lure of a long ride on a motorcycle had been altogether too tempting. They had reached Madhupur, and both being students of botany, gone on a stroll through the botanical gardens. After naming numerous trees, enumerating the diseases plaguing the various plants and collecting plant and root samples for later study, while on their way back to Madhupur Cottage where the motorcycle had been parked, they were stopped by a fat policeman. He had smirked at them and asked, 'What are you two doing here?' On learning they were college students on a visit to the botanical gardens, he had laughed loudly, looked around to see if they were being watched and barked, 'Give me 5000 taka.' Before they could question him about the sudden and exorbitant demand, he had continued, 'Doing dirty things in the jungle, eh? If you don't pay I won't let you leave.'

They had vehemently denied the dirty accusations, but to no avail. Instead, the man had leered at Yasmin and winked. 'This one's a whore. I knew the moment I saw her.' He had said it despite having known absolutely nothing of the sort. Milan had told the man that they had no money and would have to return to the city to get some. The man had grabbed hold of Yasmin's wrist and told Milan, 'You go to the city. Leave this one here.' Yasmin had tried wresting her hands from his chubby, rough paws, pitifully begging Milan to not leave her alone with the man. One can beg all one wants but not everyone is easily moved by someone's plight. They think of themselves first and foremost, a fact Milan had been well aware of. At that moment, Yasmin's fate was entirely dependent on him. She had known that if he were to leave it would be irrelevant whether he returned with the money or not. The man would probably have raped her and disappeared inside the jungle and her shame would have driven her to suicide. Her eyes tightly shut, a litany of these thoughts had been running through Yasmin's mind. She had been afraid that any moment Milan was going to start his motorcycle and drive off. Terrified and trembling on the inside, she had tried shutting her ears to the devastating sound of the rolling engine. That day Milan could have refused to answer her call for help. He could have easily ridden off without a glance backwards; the policeman had let him go anyway. Yasmin had not been his lover whose honour he should have felt compelled to protect. But Milan had not left. Not only that, he had told the fat policeman, 'Keep the motorcycle, sir. Let us go, we will go to the city and get the money.'

The man had no interest in the motorcycle. He had been after Yasmin, waiting for night to fall so he could do what he wanted with her. Beside a petrified Yasmin, Milan had steadfastly refused to leave her at the policeman's mercy. As if she had been granted a new lease of life Yasmin had cried helplessly. In the evening when darkness had swooped down upon the forest in the blink of an eye, the man had locked them up in the house of a forest department officer, ensuring they understood that they had to arrange for the money by morning if they wished to be set free. He had taken the motorcycle with him as insurance.

When they asked Yasmin for her name and address she had given them a bunch of fake names—father, Abdur Rafiq, businessman from Kachijhuli. She had been terrified of revealing that her father was the renowned Dr Rajab Ali and sullying his reputation in the process. Not only had she failed to return home at night, she had also been apprehended by the police with a boy—in her head there could be no greater shame than that. Yasmin had been kept in the room for the children and had not slept a wink that night. In a room on the balcony, Milan too had stayed awake. He had called a friend from the house and asked them to arrange for 5000 taka and come to the forest officer's quarters as early as possible the next morning. As agreed, once the money had been paid, Milan had got his motorcycle back and they had finally managed to return to Dhaka. Once in the city, the enormity of the situation had hit Yasmin! How was she going to live down the shame! The shame of having spent the night outside with a man! Milan had advised her that other than an immediate wedding there was nothing else they could do to avoid scandal. Yasmin had not agreed to the proposal, though she had first sought shelter at her friend Jahangir's house near Abakash. There she had spent the entire day trying to decide whether she was going to return home or not.

She had known that the moment she returned everyone was going to ask her questions about the previous night, to which she had no answer. She had not been to her grandmother's house or her aunt's, nor had she been with a female friend; everyone at Abakash had already found all that out the night before. She had walked from Jahangir's house to Abakash's black gate, stood there for a long time, torn between walking in and walking away. She had stood there and waited for something, perhaps a sign, though she herself had not been sure what that would be—perhaps a ray of light to wash away the darkness looming over her. Or perhaps she had wished for magic, for everyone to go back in time and start the day again! How could she have known that she had nothing to be ashamed of? Pure self-loathing had inspired the scene we had witnessed at Milan's house. She had been so ashamed that she had kept her face buried between her knees when we went to get her back.

She was forced to show us her face eventually but she refused to meet anyone's eyes even after that, mostly staring at the wall or the ceiling. She was convinced that she was no longer the old Yasmin, no longer family to us, no longer the youngest daughter of the house. I remember feeling terribly sorry for her despite being quite angry at her behaviour. One day, after she had kept refusing to speak even after being asked repeatedly why she wanted to get married in such a hurry, I simply sat down at her door. Looking away towards the darkening courtyard and keeping my voice loud enough so she could hear from the bed even if she refused to turn towards me, I kept talking. 'You have one life. If an accident happened that night then it's not a problem. So many accidents happen in life! You don't have to get married because of that! What relationship do you have with Milan? If you have been going around in secret, so much so that you imagine you can't live without him, then go ahead. Get married if that makes you happy! But remember one thing. It's not right deciding these things in haste. Finish your degree, get a job, and only then think about getting married. Be self-sufficient; don't become dependent on someone else so soon. Get your master's in botany, do a PhD, get a job as a teacher! You will be eligible to teach at Agricultural University. And if you are really dying to get married then why does it have to be Milan? What does he know? What can he do? Can he even speak a proper sentence? Besides, he's M's brother, how good can such a demon's brother be? So many good boys come to this house. Choose one of them. Rather, there are so many doctor friends of mine who would consider themselves lucky to be able to marry you.'

I was afraid that if we did not go through with our promise of arranging her wedding with Milan she was going to do something horribly drastic. However, nothing of that sort happened and much to my relief I soon began to see flashes of the old Yasmin again. Her friends were visiting her at the house once more and she started visiting them too. Let alone thinking about marriage, she stopped taking Milan's phone calls altogether. She did speak to him on one occasion only, just to firmly tell him that her marriage had been fixed elsewhere by her family and he should not call her again. Soon, a handsome boy called Rana, from the locality surrounding Agricultural University, began visiting—he was an older brother of Raka, a friend of Yasmin's close friend Krishti. Finding them sitting in the living room and chatting at length managed to restore some of my sanity; at least she had gotten over the madness of wanting to marry Milan. Besides, Rana was far more suitable for her than Milan in looks, prospects as well as talent. She would speak to him in hushed, muted tones over the phone and he would often drive his own car to Abakash to show off and also take Yasmin out for drives. Of course, in the end, he would take the money for petrol from Yasmin. In fact, sometimes he would even take money from her to pay the rickshaw.

This went on for a while until one fine day Yasmin abruptly broke off her affair with the greedy Rana. She started going to college and coming back home straight after class. Otherwise, recitation at Shokal or musical programmes by Anandadhwani kept her occupied. Everything she wanted, even things she needed which Father did not want to spend money on, I would buy for her. Her shame over the incident with Milan eventually faded but something else took its place: the growing feeling that no one liked her. Whenever any of my acquaintances or friends used to visit the house, be it the doctors or the writers, they usually showered me with attention without even sparing a glance at her.

However, one day her complaints about these things vanished in their entirety when Ataul Karim Shafeeq began to notice her. Shafeeq was my age, a handsome, refined and polite man from tip to toe and dedicated to literature. Not that he had chosen a life of poverty for that reason. He had finished his studies, earned his BCS degree and was working as a deputy magistrate. His interest in Yasmin was reassuring to me, not that I ever actively set her on him deliberately. However, when he would come to meet her I used to eagerly call her outside. When she dressed up or put on lipstick or neatly did her hair before meeting him I never discouraged her or said, 'Why are you dressing up so much? What's the matter? Go as you are!' When they would sit and talk for hours I never interrupted them. In fact, I used to become even more indifferent, often making an excuse and leaving them alone to talk. I would also ask someone else to get them some tea and snacks or take it to them myself. After he left I would ask her, 'What did Shafeeq say?' Yasmin used to smile sweetly and reply, 'He said I looked beautiful.'

'And?'

'He asked me if I wanted to go somewhere for a few days.'

When Shafeeq offered to take Yasmin out she came to me with a shy smile on her face to ask for my permission. 'Of course! You can go.' I let them go because the incident with Milan and her sudden demand for marriage was still terrifyingly fresh in my mind, stalking me like a predator waiting for a chance to pounce. I had always been different from the others. Besides, I had always envisioned that Yasmin and I would be together always, with our music and our poetry to accompany us. If not for that incident, Yasmin getting married was not a scenario that would ever have caused me concern. A marriage, if it had to be, should be for love; it should not be based on a mistake or an accident.

After Yasmin returned I asked her, 'Where did you go? What did Shafeeq say?' She replied, 'He took me to Agricultural University,' to the first question but evaded the second with a shake of her head and a 'nothing much'. I wanted to know if he had said something like 'I love you and I want to marry you'. My parents were asking about him already and I had told them, 'He is a very good boy, one in a million, and he really likes Yasmin.' For my parents it did not matter in the least that he was dedicated to literature. What mattered was that he had a good job.

I noticed after a few days that Yasmin was starting to avoid Shafeeq. She would not go to meet him even if I asked her to. If I tried pushing her to go and see him she would free her hand forcefully from my grasp and say, 'Don't push me! I don't want to go!' She did not tell me what had brought about her sudden change of mood. Only once, later, she had confessed, 'The scoundrel keeps trying to touch me.'

'What!' My ears were ringing. 'What do you mean he keeps trying to touch you?'

'What else does that mean?'

'He wants to hold your hand?'

'Yes.'

The ringing reduced a fraction. 'So? Holding hands is not such a bad thing.'

Yasmin had not said anything more that day. Not that she could have; there had always been an invisible chasm between us preventing us from talking about our bodies. Perhaps that day she had been unable to tell me anything more.

Years later, when she was already raising a family with her husband and children, she had laughed out loud at the mention of the educated, handsome and cultured Shafeeq's name and told me that she had managed to catch a glimpse of the devil under the handsome deity's guise. The pain such a realization had caused her, plus the inability to reveal anything to anyone, had shown up so many years later as dark lines creasing the fair skin on her forehead while reminiscing. Shafeeq's interest in her had initially reassured her that their marriage would finally make everyone in the family happy, besides forever eliminating any lingering fear of public shame from the incident with Milan. But when Shafeeq should have said 'I love you', when they should have been walking hand in hand in some garden somewhere, when they should have been sitting by the river gazing at the greenery around them and dreaming about their future, he had instead taken her to an empty room and tried to grab her breasts. Not just that, one afternoon when no one else had been home at Abakash he had pounced upon her and tried to rip off her clothes. After her screams had woken up Sufi sleeping in the veranda, she had abused and thrown him out of the house, locked herself in her bedroom and wept with her face buried in a pillow. That incident had strengthened her conviction that no one loved her; most just wanted her body.

Our bodies are very cheap. When there is nothing else in us to love men think our bodies too will be easy to violate. Like the young poet Kajal Shahnawaz, whose hostel room Shafeeq had taken Yasmin to. He had spent a long time chatting with me about literature at Abakash over tea, and on his way out winked at Yasmin and asked her to visit his hostel room alone sometime. I also remember the elephantine Abdul Karim, Hasina's brother, who had grown quite close to us. He would often visit Abakash with his wife and children and Mother used to cook and feed them. He had cornered Yasmin once and offered to pay her 1000 taka—totalling a nice, tidy sum of 4000 a month—if she would agree to sleep with him once a week. Yasmin had been stunned by his audacity but she had not uttered a word of the incident to me.

Had she not said anything because she had been afraid that I would judge her or accuse her, or demand to know why such things happened only to her? Had she been anxious or ashamed that saying anything would only make people point out that she was not as beautiful or talented as me? Had she just been too humiliated by the man's uncouth behaviour to ever mention the event to anyone? Or perhaps she had not said anything because she knew I had put her on a pedestal and she had hesitated to jeopardize my foolish fancies. She had been aware of the dreams I was nurturing for her, she had not wanted to shatter them and cause me hurt. She had chosen to play the part of the sister I was familiar with and loved, continued singing my favourite songs and reading the same old poems. She had chosen to spare my shitty fragile pride and avoided revealing her own pain lest it hurt me too. She had nurtured my dreams with music and poetry, given my desires wings and herself receded into the shadows to lick her wounds.

Months went by and life at Abakash plodded on by a series of fine negotiations with happiness, discontent and age. The people of the house were used to spreading their joys around and nurturing their hurts in isolation. The pomegranate tree grew heavy with fruit and Mother, absolutely delighted, gave us some of the fruit and also took some to my grandmother's. Everyone there was all praises for the beautiful fruit her tree had borne and she was so inspired that she brought home two more saplings to join the one in the courtyard. Everyone saw her joy; no one noticed her agony. Yasmin's honours examination results had been declared and she had done very well, so much so that the professors were sure that if she worked hard she would get first class marks in her master's. Yasmin came home and relayed the happy news to us for all of us to share in her joy, and we sat together and rejoiced in her success. No one noticed her despair; that burden was for her to bear alone.

And then that day arrived, that terrifying day. I had gone to Dhaka two days before to inquire about my book and I came back home to find Yasmin missing. She had left the night before without telling anyone. There was a piece of paper lying on my table.

Bubu, I'm leaving. I will not stay in this house any more. Don't try to look for me.

Mother was sitting quietly.

'Where has she gone? Why? What happened?' I screamed.

She did not respond. An icy wave passed over my skin. Sufi—Father's sister's daughter, our cousin and basically the resident domestic help—informed us that Yasmin had left at dawn wearing a black sari. Suddenly, Mother spoke. 'Your father beat her so much! Of course she left! She has finally escaped this house.' Weeping softly, she told me about the unimaginably cruel act that the house had witnessed the night before—Father had whipped Yasmin, his own daughter, like an animal. Not an inch on her body had been spared from the assault of the whip. Clumps of hair had come off, so hard had he pulled at them. He had dragged her so roughly that her clothes had ripped off, revealing angry red welts on her body. What had she done to deserve such violence? She had returned home at midnight. Father had been waiting for her impatiently, pacing up and down the veranda. Seeing the car he had run up to the front gate to see two boys sitting inside the car that had dropped Yasmin off. If he had waited he would have found out that those two boys were Prabir and Shakeel. To them Yasmin was like an older sister; she used to attend all their religious occasions and was a friend to them. Years younger than her, they had hired a car from somewhere and implored her to join them on a day trip to Dhaka. Prabir had never seen Dhaka before and they had meant to come back by the afternoon anyway. They would have too, had the car not broken down midway. Hence, the late return, the whipping and her subsequent disappearance.

I sat and listened, my blood having long frozen in my veins. When we—Mother and I—set out to look for her, it was afternoon already. At our first stop, Nani's house, we found out that Yasmin had indeed stayed there the night before. She had been glum but she had not said a word to anyone about what had transpired at Abakash. No one at Nani's house had suspected anything either; they had simply assumed she wanted to spend the night at her grandmother's. That afternoon she had taken the black sari off, borrowed clothes from Hasem mama's daughter and left. We went to many other relatives, to her friends, but did not find any clue regarding her whereabouts. We went back home hoping she would eventually return. The next day we went out in search again and made telephone calls to a bunch of places asking about her. Amidst mounting anxiety, we searched for her by asking our relatives and friends in Dhaka over the next few days. Sleepless, not having had a morsel of food or a drop of water, I was beginning to feel like a fish being tossed about in a stormy sea.

Another day passed without any sign of her. Her good friend Sobur from Agricultural University came to ask about her and accompanied us in our search. Father had never liked Sobur before but we saw him softening towards the boy and going up to him to ask about Yasmin. Unable to locate a single clue anywhere Sobur even went to the hospitals to check. Three days later we finally received word from Milan's house that Yasmin was in Phoolpur with him, in her classmate Jaman's house. Milan had called to inform us that Yasmin and he were married. The news arrived late and I spent the rest of the night pacing the room impatiently, trying to calm myself down, trying to convince myself that this was all another act, another dramatic scene that she wanted to stage like before. I prayed again and again to let the news be wrong. Since Hasina was from Phoolpur and taking her would make it easier to find the house, she accompanied me early the next morning as we set out to bring Yasmin back home.

Crossing the Brahmaputra, we took a rickety tin bus to the Phoolpur bus station, jostling for space and trying to save our heads from being bashed against the tin roof as the bus bounced over rough terrain, all the while battling a toxic cocktail of human sweat and the combined smells of spit–piss–shit from children. At Phoolpur bazaar we asked after Jaman and followed the directions we were given, over a long walking trail that was partly built and partly a rough track, to a tin house. Hasina went inside and came back to confirm that Yasmin was in the house and that she had indeed married Milan the day before. I could not—rather, I did not—want to believe it. Convinced it was all a lie, I helplessly glanced around to find someone who could reassure me so.

We entered the house to find ourselves facing two unmade beds, two pillows lying side by side and Yasmin's hairclip beside one. I was shocked to realize that this was the bed on which she had slept with Milan the night before. So was it really true? Had she truly gotten married? Still not wanting to believe what was staring back at me all I could do was pray for the sky to fall on our heads or a massive flood from the Brahmaputra to wash Phoolpur away. I began to babble. 'Yasmin, come with me. Let's go. Quickly! It's me! You were angry with him, that's fine. Now let's go home.' No one paid any heed to my rant. I saw her from across the courtyard, wearing a different sari, her face and head covered. For a moment something swept across my soul, as if I had been trying to protect something soft and fragile for a long time from a pack of ravenous hyenas and the feral beasts had finally won.

Hasina and Jaman tried to intervene. 'If they are already married . . .' What did that even mean! Married?! In my head all I knew was that I had come to take her away and she had to come back with me. Hasina went to tell her I was asking her to come out so we could leave; she came back with an unequivocal reply: No. My lost sister was right in front of me but I had to leave without her and this harsh realization broke my heart. I could not bear it—she did not want to come out in front of me, let alone talk to me or go anywhere with me.

That day, till the last ounce of energy was left in my body, I begged her, even ordered her to come with me. It was fine that they had married, let Milan go back to his house and let Yasmin come home, I suggested. Let them finish their studies and then we could arrange a grand public ceremony and confirm the union. However, Yasmin was unwilling to listen to any of my arguments. If she did not wish to finish her degree that was fine, but they were young so we could take some time at least to figure out how to set them up in a home of their own. When that failed to elicit a response, I suggested we arrange a wedding the day after but she had to come home first. No matter what I said Yasmin refused to listen to anything, steadfast as she was in her decision to stay with Milan, her new husband. I realized that her relatives, her parents, her siblings, no one meant anything to Yasmin more than her husband any more.

And so, in the end I walked away from her and left Phoolpur in tears. She had turned me back, and in the process unleashed a storm in my world that was bent on sweeping away all the dreams I had carefully nurtured for so long: a life with Yasmin filled with music and poetry. It felt as if the earth had been snatched away from under my feet and the aftershocks were tearing down the few remaining edifices that were my life's work. Feeling utterly impoverished, I boarded the bus headed for Mymensingh and returned home enveloped in the gloom of the bus horn and the grease, the loud yells and the quiet sighs. The house was empty. It had never seemed so empty before. Father, Mother, Dada, everyone was there, but still it seemed there was not a single soul left in the house. I was alone and I could hear myself crying. I had always actively distanced myself from the various ailments in the house: Father was afflicted with masculinity, Mother suffered from religion and Dada was obsessed with his wife Mumu. The only person I had been close to was Yasmin. The girl who had been gradually blossoming into a poet, an artist, much more beautiful and gifted than many of her peers, such a talented girl, had chosen a boy to whom neither poems nor songs meant anything more than a mere jumble of letters. I was racked with despair and anxiety about how she was going to cope. She was just beginning to sense what it meant to be independent, just learning its ropes, but she was bent on turning her back to that and deliberately choosing a life of servitude.

The courtyard was white with the light of the moon. I sat alone in one corner. There was no one to sing a song to the full moon, no one to call me 'Bubu'. Mother was weeping softly. Father was sitting with his fingers pressed against the veins on his temple. Pain, immense and mute, was perched heavily on the spine of Abakash.

Many, many years later, Yasmin told me how hurt she had been when she had left Abakash that dawn in a black sari she had taken from my cupboard. Father's mercilessness had manifested in terrible self-loathing that had forced her to leave the house. She had gone to college instead, attended her classes and spent a long time in Prabir's house after class before making her way back to Abakash eventually. She had stood there in front of the black gate for a long time wondering whether she ought to go in. Her hurt and outrage had returned in full force and she had turned back, hailed a rickshaw and spent the night at Nani's, hoping someone from Abakash would turn up in search of her to take her back home. No one had come.

She had considered going to Dhaka but she had no money and had been too ashamed to borrow. She had gone back to college the next day and then back to Abakash in the evening to stand immobile in front of the black gate before turning away yet again. Unable to think of a place where she could seek refuge she had finally gone to her classmate Jaman, who had a small rented place on College Street. She had gone there and sat for a long time without telling him anything about what was wrong. She had finally come to the realization that if she did not wish to return home, if she wished to avenge the violence that Father had unfairly brought down upon her, then the only course open for her was to get married. She had considered suicide but had been too afraid; besides, it would have been too much work to procure poison. So the only course had been the one available to most women if they wished to escape their father's house—exchange it for their husband's.

However, this resolution had an immediate snag. Whom was she to marry? Whom could she so shamelessly propose marriage to?

She had been afraid that whoever she had thought of initially would reject her if she were to ask. It was then that she had thought of the long-forgotten Milan. She had instantly set out to look for him. She had not wasted a moment after finding him, telling him in no uncertain terms that she wished to get married immediately and he had to make up his mind quickly if he wished to marry her too, or lose the chance forever. An astonished Milan had asked her about the prospective groom of her parents' choice she had told him about. Unwilling to dig up past hurts she had evaded the question and that very night they had left with Jaman for the latter's house in Phoolpur. The next day, afraid of getting married at Phoolpur lest someone recognize Yasmin as Dr Rajab Ali's daughter, they had accompanied Jaman to Haluaghat to the marriage registrar's office there to sign the relevant documents. That had not been easy either. The officer had been suspicious that Yasmin had been abducted under false pretences by Milan and Jaman; they had had to bribe the man to get their work done.

After returning home I cried and asked Mother why none of them had gone to look for Yasmin at Nani's the night before. Tortured by guilt Mother keened like a madwoman and replied, 'If only I knew! I did not know she had gone there.'

'If you had gone and brought her back none of this would have happened.'

She kept crying and saying the same thing over and over, 'If only I knew. I thought she would come back after her anger subsided. I've lost her for good—'

Yasmin's life had changed; she was not the same old girl any more. She was not going to roam around Abakash singing her favourite song 'Amra emni eshe bheshe jai' (Thus we are swept away), she was not going to recite poems like before, she was not going to go to college and then come back home in the afternoon, she was no longer going to accompany me on our afternoon rickshaw rides through the city. She had willingly given up on the endless possibilities in her future and her chance to live independently. She had left Abakash and married a classmate who could not string together a single sentence properly; this to me was as good as receiving news of her death. The girl who used to be my shadow was no longer by my side and the pain of losing her was akin to feeling as if she were dead. Everything around me was crumbling and I had never felt so alone in my life. Abakash, the entire city, everything seemed desolate and lifeless.

I took a few days off and escaped to Dhaka. Quashing all her pain and sorrow deep within, Mother went to see Yasmin at Milan's house after they returned to the city. HSS came down to Mymensingh on hearing about Yasmin's disappearance. He stayed for a day at the Circuit House and spoke to Yasmin over the phone from there. He requested her to reconsider, to go back home and not destroy her own life, but his pleas fell on deaf ears. I had nursed the hope that she would return eventually. It often happens, people realize they have made a mistake and come back after things have cooled down. So many people return, Yasmin never did.

~

After returning from Calcutta I found myself completely alone in Abakash. There was no one there to listen to my stories of the places I had visited and the things I had done. There was no one with whom I could sit and listen to the music and poetry cassettes bought from Calcutta. My suitcase lay abandoned; there was no one to grab it from me with a 'Show me what you have got from there', or, 'I want this . . . no . . . give me that!' One afternoon as I lay on my bed listening to Shantideb Ghosh's rendition of 'Ami kaan pete roi' (I wait to hear from you), the only thing I could think of was how much Yasmin would have been moved by the song. On a sudden impulse I made a telephone call to Milan's house. On recognizing her voice at the other end I lowered the receiver and turned it towards the song playing in my room. After the song was over when I put the receiver back up to my ear again, hoping to hear someone breathe if only to reassure myself that someone indeed had been listening, I heard her choked sobs from the other end. Was it any wonder that a natural-born singer like her would be moved by such a plaintive tune?

Since she was married, since she was not going to come back home, everyone at Abakash eventually re-established communication with Yasmin—everyone except me. Yasmin too began visiting Abakash, often accompanied by Milan dressed in a kurta pyjama. She would usually stay for half an hour to an hour at the most, chatting over tea and biscuits like any other visiting acquaintance. While she was at home I usually stayed in my room behind closed doors. The day Father finally relented to Mother's tireless requests with a series of heavy sighs and decided to accept their alliance, so much so that they bought Yasmin a red Benarasi sari and jewellery and arranged for a private dinner with some of Milan's relatives, even that day my door remained firmly shut. She was a different Yasmin and I could not pretend that everything was fine in front of her; neither could she. She was married and she was someone else's wife and daughter-in-law.

I occasionally got news about the strict regime she had to maintain at her in-laws', how she was managing to forge bonds with her mother-in-law, with her older brother-in-law and his wife, with her husband and even with the other relatives. She had become party to their joys and sorrows and they were of the utmost concern to her. People she had barely known for twenty-two days were suddenly more important to her than someone she had lived with for twenty-two years. She was learning how to be a dutiful housewife, how to pull the drape of her sari over her head in front of elders, how to carry out their every order and wait on them hand and foot. She was training in the kitchen with her mother-in-law, learning how to cook and feed her husband meat and fish. She was learning how to wait for him quietly in her room, how to pull the drape lower over her head at the sight of her brother-in-law and how to speak softly and demurely to everyone in her new family. She was being trained to keep the house pretty and dream of home and hearth and furniture. She was being taught how to forget her ambitions, aspirations, music and poetry so she could easily let go of the last strains of melody left in her life once and for all.

Without, Within

NM came and took away the packets of *Nirbashito Bahire Ontore* that had been lying with me to send to the distributors of *Khabarer Kagaj*; they were going to take charge of the sales, much to my relief. It was all good paying for the printing and binding of one's own book, it could ensure a first-class publication but all of that amounted to nothing without a suitable distributor. This was something I had learnt the hard way, effectively curing me of ever wanting to handle this on my own. Besides, I found out later that the book had sold well at the book fair and if it had reached the stands on time it would probably have sold even more. I received a confidential piece of news from the poet Mohammed Sadiq, who was a bureaucrat too, about a ploy in motion in the upper echelons to ban the book. The accusation: the poem 'Niyati' (Fate) had been deemed obscene. All the poems of the collection were from the time when my relationship with R had been in its last stages. The poem in question was about his behaviour on one such occasion.

> Every night an impotent man comes to my bed.
> He kisses,
> My eyes
> Lips
> My chin,
> And he grabs my breasts,
> He suckles.
> My thirsty skin, on edge,
> Begs and whimpers for the sea.
>
> His fingers pass through my curls

Leaving fire in their wake
And I am a ball of fire he plays with,
While my body cries,
For this man's body to break and get bent
And rivers emerge therein.

The winter full moon hangs on the sky.
Lying peacefully in her lap,
He sets me on flames
And as I burn,
The impotent man turns over and sleeps.
Parched,
I prod the still sleeping man
And I cry for a drop of water.

When the poem had been published in *Robbar* (Sunday) the magazine had not been banned. So I could not fathom why they wished to ban the book! Who had the last word in what was obscene and what was not? To me the poem was not offensive at all! SHA advised, 'You should expunge that "he suckles" bit.' Why? Because that bit about suckling a woman's breasts was too offensive? Ha! The same SHA who had tried every trick in the book to do the same to me was trying to explain lewdness to me! I could not find a single reason why I should remove that line—to me it seemed essential in underlining the notion of a person's skin craving another's touch. Of course my male friends were not happy with my logic even though most of them were always fantasizing about *every woman* they knew, imagining grabbing and sucking on their breasts, lying in wait to turn the fantasy into reality with someone they could succeed in hoodwinking. Take Mozammel for instance. Such a handsome and talented man! He was younger than me and used to call me 'aapa'. He had been seeing a very pretty girl for a few years and they were about to get married. One night, having managed to find me alone, Mozammel tried to get fresh with me! Thankfully I managed to settle the matter rather quickly!

Another poem from the collection, 'Dudhraj Kabi' (The Ophidian Poet), also caused some stir. People whispered that the poet was in fact R. Irrespective of whom it refers to, the first and primary concern about a poem should be how it works as a poem, nothing else! People always pale in comparison to words. It did not matter if I had written the poem with R in mind. What mattered to me was the poem.

> I should have just gotten a dog instead.
> Even foxes can be tamed,
> And I have raised a poet with milk and bananas—
> It bit me
> Before turning tail and slithering away.

In reply R wrote a poem of his own—

> Yes, you better get a dog.
> To spend your profound time playing fetch,
> Or perhaps a cat,
> Yes, a cat would be best.
> You never saw what was good and pure,
> But now you have found the best thing for you,
> Yes my darling, get a dog or a cat.

> Pigs could work just as well,
> Given the mutual love for filth,
> I see how nothing makes you happier.
> Yes, that's the perfect watering hole for you,
> With your water and your kind of dirt,
> With no fear of getting your hair wet,
> It's the perfect place for your kind of games.

> There, in the murky depths,
> You will be properly invisible!
> You could even go fishing,
> And find your kind of catch in the mud!
> Let your habits grow roots instead,
> Waste no more time on trifle dreams,
> Silly little sickness such as they are—
> Yes, you better get a dog, and a cat.

Dogs are faithful, cats are pampered,
Where else will you find such perfect harmony?

Despite being deeply hurt by his poem I could not help but wish I
knew how R was, what he was doing, if he was well! Whenever I
travelled from Mymensingh to Dhaka this wish would often lead me
to Asim Saha's Ityadi to speak at length with Saha and Nirmalendu
Goon and learn if R was still in Mongla or if he was busy with Shimul.
Was his leg okay? Was he walking properly again? I was told he was,
but with effort. I listened to them, careful not to show too much
concern, even if on the inside my heart would be about to burst with
more questions. Did he think about me or ask about me? Not that I
could ask such questions or even sigh in response any more! When
a marriage ends, couples often turn bitter enemies. Not once had I
imagined that R and I would ever be enemies. I had forgiven even the
friends who had tried to take advantage of my broken marriage and
seduce me, only because I had no desire to destroy friendships.

NM had published a few advertisements for *Nirbashito Bahire
Ontore* in the newspapers. A few days later he informed me that his
distributors had sent him word that the book was doing well. I was so
happy to hear the news, so moved by NM's generosity, that I could
not ask him about the proceeds of the sales. Around the same time
I witnessed yet another instance of his broad-mindedness. I had not
told anyone about my trip to Calcutta with MHI. However, despite
finding out about it from somewhere, NM did not make a single sly
comment about it to me.

After returning from Calcutta, SHA had inquired with faux
innocence, 'How was India?' and I had answered in the same way, 'It
was great.'

'Where did you go?'

'Oh, so many places! I met Atashi too. Such a lovely girl!'

Immediately there had been another innocent question, 'I hope
the nights with MHI in Astor were good!'

I confess the directness had caught me off guard. SHA had
somehow found out, presumably from Atashi. As soon as he had
heard about Calcutta he had given me Atashi's address and asked
me to meet and tell her I was his friend. I had met the poet Subhash

Mukhopadhyay's daughter Atashi and ended up having a lovely time with her. In fact I had developed lovely equations with everyone in their household, including the renowned poet himself. I had not gone to their house alone—MHI had been with me. SHA could have said it differently but he had chosen to use the information as a sting. That was how SHA was; he could hurt someone without batting an eyelid. NM was not like that at all. Rather, one day he casually informed me he had found out about MHI's visit to Calcutta from the latter's wife after we had left. He had simply made the connections and deduced we had gone together.

Could I have gone alone? Yes, I could have. Wherever I visited in India I could have easily done so alone. It's just that I would not have loved it as much. There were so many things I did not like doing alone and going somewhere by myself was right there at the top of the list. Yasmin used to get angry and say, 'It's your friend, you go! Why drag me along?' I used to drag her with me to visit R when he would come down to Mymensingh. If Yasmin was not there I would take Suhrid. R used to get angry and ask me why I could not come alone. Of course I could have! I was going to college and returning home on my own all the time. It was just that I preferred going with someone, someone close to me.

Not even a month had passed after my visit to Calcutta when NM suddenly suggested we go there again. 'Let's go to Calcutta for seven days.' He refused to tell me why. When I insisted he informed me there was some business work regarding the magazine that he had to attend to. He was going to be busy with his own work and I would be free to do as I pleased and go where I wished to. I did not need to be asked twice! Besides, Mymensingh was becoming intolerable without Suhrid and Yasmin. In the house I felt like a corpse, like a crushing loneliness was waiting to rip me apart. My work could have given me some respite. However, since that too was a life of indolence the feelings of despair were only intensifying. So we set off for Calcutta. Before leaving I had to make sure to pack some beef for Subhash Mukhopadhyay. Last time he had expressed a wish to eat beef and I had promised to get some for him during my next visit.

The first thing we did as soon as we reached Calcutta was to go to the information centre to meet Soumitra Mitra so he could arrange two rooms for us in a government guest house on Hungerford Street. Stashing our luggage in the rooms we set off to follow our itinerary, with a young boy named Siddhartha Sinha in tow. Siddhartha was a member of Soumitra's poetry group, Abrittilok, a true disciple of the latter and a talented reciter himself. Besides, he had another connection with NM—he was the Calcutta correspondent for *Khabarer Kagaj* and it was his duty to collect new work from writers and send it to Dhaka. He was to be our guide. Our first stop—to take the beef to Subhash Mukhopadhyay. Suffice it to say Mukhopadhyay was in shock that I had actually gotten him the Eid special sacrificial beef from Bangladesh that he had wanted. Elated, he called his wife Geeta to come and see the gift. He was determined to eat beef and had Geeta cook the meat for him the same day.

The previous time when I had visited him he had enthusiastically welcomed me, cooked *baticharchari*[18] for me, shown me around Calcutta and taken me to the Grand Hotel for the Ananda Puraskar where Sunil Gangopadhyay and Sailesh Kumar Bandopadhyay were felicitated. Hearing our plans of visiting Delhi, Agra and Kashmir he had been less than pleased and advised us, 'What do you want to see there? Come with me. We will go to Tangra, Budge Budge.' Surprised by these names I had asked him, 'What is there to see in Tangra and Budge Budge!' He had smiled and replied, 'People.' At that moment I had found myself hard-pressed to recognize the cheerful public persona he used to maintain, the man who was always up to no good with his family and who could easily be the life of a party fuelled only by baticharchari and a glass of rum. His everyday sins may have been too many to count but no matter how much they piled up nothing could obscure the innate greatness of such a man. When the true Subhash Mukhopadhyay emerged from beneath the trappings it was impossible to do anything but revere the man.

NM had a surprise in store for me after we left Subhash Mukhopadhyay's house. He took me to the offices of *Anandabazar Patrika* and *Desh* on 6 Prafulla Sarkar Street. He was scheduled to meet Sunil Gangopadhyay, Sanjib Chattopadhyay, Sirshendu Mukhopadhyay and Sankarlal Bhattacharya to request them to contribute to his weekly. The opportunity to encounter so many renowned litterateurs was to me akin to visiting a place of worship

and being given a chance to meet my deities in person. I had formed
an image of them in my head from their writings. When one meets
a person one has always imagined it happens quite often that the
real and the imagined do not always compare favourably. The small
defects can be easily forgiven, like I could forgive Sirshendu's bright
pink socks matched with a pair of staid black sandals. Instead, I
found myself engrossed in his reminiscences of Mymensingh. Back
in Dhaka I was an avid reader of *Desh* and I firmly believed it was
the best literary journal in Bengali. So I was shocked to realize that
I was sitting in the room from where *Desh* was published, talking to
the same people who were the editors of the magazine, who regularly
wrote for it and whose writings I had voraciously consumed since I
was little.

Sitting behind a pile of papers, Sunil Gangopadhyay graciously
spoke to us at length despite his busy schedule. Sanjib Chattopadhyay
was famous for his humorous stories but in person he would hardly
ever be seen smiling, although NM did not hesitate for a moment
before asking him to write a column for *Khabarer Kagaj*. We also
went to meet the poet Nirendranath Chakraborty who I had last run
into in Dhaka. He shared his office with Gourkishor Ghosh who was
so gracious, as if we were old acquaintances, that I was deeply moved.
I also noticed that those who were originally from East Bengal, who
had had to migrate to West Bengal after the partition, were decidedly
warm and friendly when meeting someone from Bangladesh. Perhaps
we reminded them of a life they had been forced to leave behind
and they could not help but talk about their old house, the gardens
around it, their village or their town, or ask how the Brahmaputra or
the Meghna looked. We met Sankarlal Bhattacharya at the *Sananda*
office and he took us to the roof and spoke to us about what he was
reading and writing and the ideas he was grappling with. Everywhere
I was the mute listener, it was impossible for me to be anything more.

Soumitra Mitra took us around to many places. We had lunch at
the famous poetry reciter Debdulal Bandyopadhyay's house, a grand
affair with numerous preparations of fish. NM had asked Debdulal
for a column too. If possible he would have even asked Jyoti Basu
to write for his journal! Soumitra also took us to the poet Shakti
Chattopadhyay's house. We reached and were greeted by a shirtless

Shakti waiting for us in his drawing room. We ended up having a lengthy conversation while being plied with food. I knew Shakti from before; he had visited Abakash with his wife and son. He showed us a small room on the first floor and told me to come and stay there when I visited next. He had gotten the room made especially for spending time with friends. Shakti had a reputation of being apathetic, so much so that he would often misplace his own poems, but NM barely flinched before asking him to write for *Khabarer Kagaj*! Shakti too agreed instantly and even gave his word to get it done by the week after.

NM had another surprise in store for me—a dinner invitation at Sunil Gangopadhyay's house. I had met him twice before that in Dhaka. The first time had been at a poetry recital by Swarasruti where he had attended as the chief guest. Mozammel Babu, SHA, MHI and I were chatting on the British Council grounds when we had spied him nearby, surrounded by his admirers and in the middle of giving autographs to the numerous fans approaching him. Mozammel had quipped, 'He is giving everyone his autograph, what if we go and give him our autographs instead!' It was a funny suggestion and we had all laughed, though none of us had the guts to go and do it. Mozammel had looked at me. 'Let's go, aapa! We will give our autographs to Sunilda!' Not one to lose out on a chance at tomfoolery I had gone along with the harebrained plan. We had approached Sunil and when he had looked at us expecting to see an extended notebook or a piece of paper, Babu had blurted out, 'Sunilda, we are here to give you our autographs.' While I tried hiding my flaming face, Sunil had not missed a beat. Instead of getting uncomfortable he had smiled congenially and replied, 'But I don't have paper.' We had gotten paper and the two of us signed it and one of Bengal's biggest poets and novelists had neatly folded the tattered sheet and carefully put it in his pocket. After getting together with our friends, everyone had pounced on us to tell them what had happened. The second meeting had only been a passing encounter and we had not really spoken much.

On this particular occasion it did not seem to me that Sunil remembered the incident about the autograph and I did not dare remind him of it. A grand party had been organized at his residence in Mandevilla Gardens. His wife Swati was a soft-spoken beautiful woman. Soumitra too had brought along his beautiful wife Moonmoon. Both Swati and Moonmoon were nonchalantly drinking alcohol. I had never seen women drink before and since my own capacity was restricted to softer drinks I was happily nursing my glass of Limca. At some point in the evening a collective conspiracy resulted in the addition of a few drops of fiery bitterness in my soft drink. I could feel a slight dizziness coming on after a few sips which soon turned to a pleasant buzz as everyone started to sing. They were all singing their own songs, set to their own tunes, while Sunil seemed determined to finish all the songs in *Gitabitan* over the course of the night.

As the party rolled on till midnight I could not help but reflect on the last time I had been in Calcutta. MHI had felt ashamed to bring me to Sunil's house along with him while NM had not thought twice about it. Thanks to him I had met Sunil personally and even got to know him as a friend. This feeling of happiness enveloped me over the next few days. A few days later I received an invitation to recite poetry alongside famous poets like Sunil, Shakti Chattopadhyay and Sankha Ghosh in a programme organized by Soumitra's Abrittilok. I styled my hair beautifully with jasmine blossoms and, in the presence of these and many other luminaries of the literary world, went on the stage, swallowed my apprehensions and recited my poem. Was I grateful? Yes, I was. People have dreams that reach for the sky; mine had never even dared to reach for that stage!

Siddhartha informed me that NM had given him a few copies of my book to put up for sale at Papyrus Books on College Street. A small advertisement for the book had also been arranged in *Desh*. I could not ask if any sales had happened at Papyrus, embarrassed that they would say not a single copy had been sold. While there was no end to my awkwardness, HH had once told me that I had a fair bit of pride. When the book was published HH had spoken to his own publisher Najmul Haque of Anindya Prakashani about it. Haque had been hesitant at first and when he had finally relented, albeit not wholeheartedly, I had surprised everyone by refusing to give the book to Anindya and declaring that I was going to publish it myself. After Haque's departure HH had told me that he liked my pride. Why should I have given my book to someone who had not been sure about it in the first place? What is a person without a little bit of pride and self-respect?

~

NM's audacity surprised me from time to time. He could casually ask renowned poets and authors to write for his journal. In fact, he went to visit Purnendu Patri for the same reason, something I would never have dared to attempt. I knew the words from Patri's 'Kothopokothon' (Conversations) and 'Amra Abohoman Dhongsho o Nirmaner' (We Float on the Backs of Love and Death) by heart. When I met him all I could do was recite in my head what Subhankar somewhere must have said to his Nandini:

> People, Nandini, only people,
> In the raging storm
> And the trembling shadows of the kerosene lamp,
> The faces of a wretched people;
> Their skins reek of diesel and harvest,
> Their sweat of salt,
> Their palms glisten with mica, and
> Scars left by spades and engine wheels.
> When I look at these people
> I see the sky, the clouds, and the sunrise behind the peaks,
> I see new trees growing,
> And a bustling metropolis growing around it.

Since I was an admirer of Patri's poems NM spoke to Soumitra and arranged for a meeting. He ought to have been busy with his own work but instead he was busy giving me these unexpected surprises. I noticed how concerned he was with my happiness, how considerate he was about what would please me or bring me joy. If he could have he would perhaps have plucked the moon from the sky for me! I had never experienced such dedication from any of my friends before. Let alone friends, even R, the one person I had loved to distraction, had hardly ever cared about what made me happy.

As I stared at Purnendu Patri in fascination—not speaking lest I say something silly—NM coolly asked the latter, that too in his thick Komilla dialect as if he and Patri were first cousins, to contribute a column to *Khabarer Kagaj*. It was as if he was asking a columnist from any random newspaper! NM would never pause to think before speaking to prominent poets and writers. To him asking them to write for his journal was as simple as demanding, 'Hey, how's the writing going! Finish it as soon as you can, tomorrow if possible.' He never read anything nor did he consider any of them especially important. An ambitious man, his sole objective was to ensure that the columns written by renowned literary figures automatically increased the circulation and readership of his magazine and established him as a publisher of reckoning. So he did not wish to know if someone had time to write a column or if they at all wanted to write for a new journal published in Bangladesh. He would tell them about the remuneration without even stopping to consider if they were at all interested in such a nominal amount to begin with. Nevertheless, many people wrote for his journal, perhaps more out of their love for East Bengal than anything else.

~

One could not be sure how many things Soumitra was busy doing at any given moment. Whenever I saw him he was in the middle of something or the other. Besides reciting poetry he also had a government job as an officer in the information department. He spoke to an acquaintance of his, Kumud Manna, and made arrangements for us to go on a boat ride on the Ganga at night. I had always wanted to see the Ganga. Sitting in the boat with my legs dangling over the edge, the rustling water lapping at my feet, I could find no discernible difference between the Ganga and the Brahmaputra. While I was lost in my thoughts, NM had his back to the river, perhaps thinking about how he could overwhelm and astonish me further.

Suddenly, one morning, NM told me, 'Get ready quickly. We have to go somewhere.' Yet again he did not say where we were going. It was only later when we were aboard a train and I realized Soumitra too was coming with us that he revealed we were headed towards

Santiniketan. At the very mention of the name a feeling of peace descended upon my heart and NM could easily see the joy flashing in my eyes. Every day he was blessing me with one surprise after another and I could not even begin to imagine when and how he had made all the arrangements for the trip. In a way I fulfilled my destiny with this visit to Santiniketan. The soft-spoken reticent poet Sankha Ghosh was there around the same time. As usual, I was struck dumb at the sight of a favourite poet and author and remained mute most of the time we were around him. Almost in a daze I spent my hours roaming around town, visiting Rabindranath Tagore's house and the iconic mango and devil tree groves beneath which he used to hold classes.

Thanks to the efforts of the vice chancellor we were even allowed access to the parts of Santiniketan not open to visitors. NM wanted to take a photo of me sitting on Tagore's chair but I did not possess the courage to pull off something like that; so I chose to sit on the floor instead to pose for the photograph. To me the entire visit was a dream and back in the guest house at night I could not help but cry when reminded of Tagore's magnanimity and selflessness. It was like crying at the feet of a deity, only in this instance the deity was not imaginary and my tears were not meant to beg that he absolve me of my sins. Neither were they tears of joy or sorrow. The tears were a manifestation of my depth of feeling for the great poet; obviously, NM failed to grasp why I was suddenly hysterical. To reassure me he kept his hand on my shoulder and a few moments later I could feel the faint slide of the hand downwards. Suspicious that the hand was trying to find its way to the zipper of my pants, I quickly shrugged it off. Perhaps he had assumed that as a woman who was willing to disappear for days on end with an unknown man and not bat an eyelid about spending the night in a hotel I would be sexually liberated.

As for me, I had taken NM to be unlike other men. However, feeling his hand slide down my back, I could not help but relegate him to the long list of men who find it difficult to control themselves around women. Is there a man anywhere who can spend a night beside a woman without being overcome by desire? Perhaps not. Nevertheless, I liked the other aspects of NM's character so much that I chose to overlook his dirty wayward hand. Neither did I let him realize that I had sensed his intentions. For his part, NM too pretended that he had casually slid his hand down my back without any ulterior motive.

~

After returning from Calcutta, NM asked me to contribute a column to his journal. Till then I had only written poems and short stories and never a column of any sort. I tried brushing him off, saying I did not know how to write a column, but NM simply waved aside my protests and asked me not to get flummoxed, advising me to write whatever I felt like. But that was easier said than done! How was I supposed to write a column when I had never written one before? NM was quite adamant. 'You have to. HSS has told me that I must ask you to write one.' I knew HSS was fond of me. In fact, after reading my poems he had spoken to his publisher Mujibur Rahman Khoka of Vidyaprakash about getting my book published. To that end he had even written a letter on my behalf to Khoka. I had met Khoka, only for the latter to inform me, 'We don't publish new poets. If you pay for it we can get it published.' Angered, I had walked away, resolving that if I had to pay to get my book published then I was going to do it myself.

Khabarer Kagaj was a rather unique magazine. It had completely broken away from the template for the weekly journal as set by *Bichitra* and followed by later publications like *Sandhani* and *Robbar*. It was printed on newsprint, the cover was newsprint too and the costs were not too high, so everyone could afford it. It contained no poetry or stories, or film gossip. The only news it cared about was political news, and the rest consisted of columns written by renowned writers, intellectuals and political scientists on society, politics and literature. Writers who had never written columns before began doing so after associating with *Khabarer Kagaj*. To be able to gather so many popular writers in one publication was indeed unprecedented and *Khabarer Kagaj* had ushered in a revolution in the domain of Bengali journals.

Some invitations are truly beyond one's wildest expectations; I had never thought such a radical journal would invite me to contribute. It was fortuitous that a well-regarded platform wished to

print my opinions but fortune only ever favours the brave. Providence
was at my door asking to be let in but I was unsure about taking
the plunge. However, NM's enthusiasm and repeated reminders
finally succeeded in forcing my hand. As I sat down to write, trying
to rack my brains to come up with a theme and rubbing my palms
on my arms in exasperation, my eyes strayed to the tiny mark on my
right arm—a tiny round scar, an old memory of a burning cigarette
touching my skin. In a flash my mind was back at the incident years
ago, a stranger on the road stubbing a burning cigarette on my skin
and laughing hysterically. As I was reminded of the scene, I felt as if
I could taste the pain again. There was a blank sheet of paper in front
of me and I was reliving an old wound—perhaps it was a combination
of the two that made me write about that fateful day. I had left the
film theatre and just got on to a rickshaw. As the rickshaw gradually
picked up speed I suddenly felt a sharp blinding pain on my right
arm—a boy of twelve or thirteen was pressing a half-smoked burning
cigarette on my arm.

'I wanted to scream, gather the people and demand justice. I did
nothing. I was afraid that people would only gather around me to
watch, to witness the spectacle of my pain, my screams, my rage and
my tears. The scar remains on my skin to this day, a reminder of that
violence that I carry. I also feel fortunate that no one has yet thrown
acid at me, I have not been blinded and I am especially grateful that
a group of men has not ambushed me on a road and raped me. I am
grateful to be alive. What is my great crime for which I fear such
horrific retribution? I am a *woman*. My education, my taste, my
talents, they have failed to make me *human*; I have sadly *remained* a
woman,' I wrote with a flourish.

NM came to Mymensingh to pick up the article while I was still
contemplating whether I should submit it for publication or not. I
was also afraid they were going to read it and say it did not work for
their journal. Eventually, I decided to hand it in with a caveat: 'I don't
know what the rules for writing a column are. I have only written
about a personal experience.' I was convinced that a *strong* piece of
writing composed of difficult words was never going to be my cup
of tea. NM took the article away despite my suspicions that it was
never going to be published. He, of course, was a master of shocks;

the day the issue was to become available he came to Mymensingh with a copy. I could hardly believe my eyes when I saw my name printed alongside so many renowned writers. After that I had to write a column every week. Fortunately, I no longer had to lose my mind over what to write. Letters began pouring into the office of *Khabarer Kagaj* after my column was published, with praise as well as reproach, the former mostly outweighing the latter. Some said it was fantastic, some said it was outrageous and some agreed as to how true it was. Some called me brave while some confessed to have cried after reading the column. Some pinched their noses in distaste—such things were personal, they said—while others labelled me a man-hater. Anyone who read it had something or the other to say.

Sometime later NM informed me that my article had inspired a veritable tide of conversations at newspaper offices, press clubs and literary circles. Readers too were 'consuming' it well. Truth be told, what made readers want to consume something, what made them decide against another, was not something I was aware of. My objective was not to 'feed' my readers either. Every column that I wrote made my eyes well up with tears, every sentence and every word was written from the heart. Pain that had been pent up inside for a long time found a vent in these columns and I wrote about things I had witnessed around me. AZ, a professor in a university and the author of numerous collections of essays, had recently published a volume of axioms, his macabre and obscene comments about women masquerading as a book. For AZ, one of the leading intellectuals of the country, every woman in the university was a prostitute. Obviously, such statements earned him praises galore from his admirers and he used to revel in such praise, his face brightening up with a smarmy smile. He may have been a formidable writer but I did not spare him in my column.

In fact, I even wrote about the unsavoury side of HSS I had witnessed and my views on it. I had a simple objective for doing so— all I wanted to do was show that many distinguished luminaries of the literary world were often no better than the worst patriarchal rascals, both in opinion and behaviour. I believed if I could reveal even a sliver of the world I moved around in through my own experiences, it could serve to foreground the normalized patriarchal oppression of women in society. My personal experiences then would cease to remain merely personal; they would take on a social dimension. I did not particularly notice it but a lot of readers pointed out that my language was particularly sharp and although many people had written many things about women till date, none had done so quite like me.

NM told me that whenever my columns were published his magazine sales shot up, an admission so strange that I could not believe him at first. Was it even possible? I soon learnt that it was indeed so. AZ's column in *Khabarer Kagaj* was quite popular. Readers wrote to the magazine in response to his writings and these responses were published too. As my columns grew popular and people began to respond to my articles, the responses to my writings too started getting published. One day AZ complained to the editors of the magazine asking why more letters about my writings were being published than about his. The editors firmly but politely informed him that, should he wish to, he was welcome to visit their offices to check the piles of letters so he could be convinced that more people were writing in response to my column 'Without, Within' than in response to his. I later learnt that he had gone on shouting at them in rage. He was so famous already but he was still greedy for more fame. He was convinced that except him no other author in Bangladesh was worthy of any consideration, that he was the only worthwhile one, besides being the only poet worth any consideration. Ultimately, things came to such a state that he began writing letters to *Khabarer Kagaj* under an alias praising his own writings. The same person who was the bearer of his articles to the *Khabarer Kagaj* office used to bring the second set of letters too. It was a total travesty, a giant in his field reduced to such petty envy by someone as inconsequential as me!

Many other incredible things happened because of the columns in *Khabarer Kagaj*. Khoka of Vidyaprakash expressed his interest in publishing my work and began to hound me. Other journals were approaching me to write columns for them. Honouring NM's special request I refrained from taking up any of these offers but Khoka did manage to convince me to publish with Vidyaprakash. Not one but two books: *Nirbashito Bahire Ontore* and *Amar Kichu Jai Ashe Na* (It Does Not Bother Me). Since the former had already been published by Shokal I initially decided against giving it to Khoka. But after submitting the second manuscript he insisted that I allow him to publish *Nirbashito* too. The two collections of poetry were sold out almost as soon as they were published, leading to Khoka immediately starting work on the next edition which sold out just as fast. Soon the craze became such that the publishers were left struggling to meet the demand. There was chatter that no one had seen collections of poetry sell so much in the Bengali publishing world in the recent past. In fact, HSS visited the Vidyaprakash stall at the book fair to express his ire that my books were more in demand than his. I could not believe that someone of his stature would be annoyed by my success. Such was his formidable reputation that we could scarcely be compared. Once, he had written to Vidyaprakash on my behalf to recommend the publication of my books, so he should have been happy that my book was doing well. Khoka informed me that HSS was not happy at all.

NM had expressed his desire to start a daily newspaper after the success of *Khabarer Kagaj*. As was his nature, if he planned to do something, he would see it through till the end. One fine day, true to his plans, he launched his daily newspaper, *Ajker Kagaj* (Today's Paper). The small room on the first floor of Kazi Sahid Ahmad's palatial house in Dhanmandi that used to be the office of *Khabarer Kagaj* began to grow in size till it was huge and had amassed an army of tables, chairs and journalists. Like its weekly counterpart, *Ajker Kagaj* soon became very popular among readers.

My two collections of poetry were unprecedented successes. The sales of *Khabarer Kagaj* were at an all-time high because of my column and thousands of letters were pouring in on a daily basis. While all this was happening, things at Mymensingh were drastically different. Since NM used to visit me in Mymensingh quite frequently, Father had run into him on several occasions at Abakash. After a few such encounters Father began asking questions: 'Who's this boy? Why does she go around with him so often? Didn't she shame us once already, didn't she blacken our faces when she got married? What happened to that? She couldn't live with him for two days. Now who's this she has found? Everyone will call her a whore. I don't want any strange men coming into my house.' Mother simply replied, 'This NM is apparently her friend.'

Father ground his teeth and snapped, 'What is a friend? What is it? I don't want to see her with any boys. If she has to go around with someone ask her to get married. If I see a random man in my house I'm going to kick both of them out.' While I squirmed in shame and indignation, Mother took over from him. 'Your father has asked you to get married. You are going around with these men despite being a single woman. What are people going to say? They are going to call you names.' It became quite obvious that she was simply parroting a less harsh version of Father's words. 'Think about your life. If NM is a good boy, if you like him, then think about getting married. That has to happen eventually, isn't it? Do you plan to be alone your entire life?'

When NM called I told him not to come to Mymensingh any more. A few days later I received a phone call from him; he told me to wait outside the black gate at six the next morning. He refused to reveal anything of what he was planning or why I had to wait so early in the morning. The next morning I went out to the main gate of Abakash and found NM waiting outside wishing to talk to me. The same thing happened the next day, and then again the next. Every morning he would take a train from Dhaka to Mymensingh and stand outside Abakash simply to catch a glimpse of me. Consequently, I had to get up at the crack of dawn and stealthily open the door while everyone else was sleeping, often with my toothbrush in hand in order to make it seem like I was out on a morning stroll. Since this was not an uncommon sight in the locality, the ruse worked. I would tiptoe my way out of the black gate and talk to NM for five–ten minutes as we walked—nothing especially significant, just general conversation—before he had to leave for Dhaka by the next train. He was being quite mad and I remember telling him, 'Why are you pursuing this madness? There is no point travelling like this every day. Isn't the journey tiring too?' NM had simply denied it, saying that the journey did not cause him any trouble. Rather, he had claimed that he quite liked the sleepy quietness of dawn. It was not always possible for me to successfully slip out of Abakash. Some days I overslept or woke up to find Father up and about. On such days NM would wait for a long time before leaving disappointed. His behaviour made me pause to consider if he was in love with me, or was it that he had no other close friend except me? Even if it was the former, he never confessed his feelings to me.

Meanwhile, Abakash was becoming intolerable. Unable to stand even the slightest of comments, harsh or otherwise, I was overwhelmed by an urge to move out and live elsewhere on my own terms. After Yasmin's departure there was no one in the house I could talk to and neither was my beloved Suhrid there. The house seemed mostly desolate, as if not a soul was around. Mother's world was restricted to the kitchen and the pir's tomb. As for Father, except perhaps my older brother there was no place for anyone else in his world. After taking over the duties of the Arogya Niketan, Dada did indeed grow closer to Father.

One night there was a burglary at the Arogya Niketan and both of them suspected Saraf mama was behind it. Tutu mama had once taken money from Dada and failed to return it and Dada used to often complain about it to Mother, just as a pretext to further abuse her family in front of her. In a way he was remarkably similar to Father—just as he never liked anyone from Nani's house neither did Dada. Blood, as they say, always tells. My Hasem mama was the chairperson of the Aqua Union Parisad. Despite having been a brave muktijoddha he could never advance further than the council chairmanship simply because he was not a great public speaker. Since he lacked oratorical skill, he could not articulate the promises they required of him, even the blatantly false ones candidates make to ask for votes before elections. He used to run a small hotel where his friends would gather around to discuss politics. The shop was his only source of income with which he took care of his family of six, comprising his wife and five daughters, all crammed into their single-room home. Despite such adversities he sent all his daughters to school. Suman, his only son, was in jail with some other boys of his age awaiting trial on a murder charge. Much of Hasem mama's earnings used to be spent on trying to lodge a case in the high court to prove his son's innocence. He did not wish to arrange for the money through unfair means, which he could have done easily if he had wished to.

Among all my uncles it was only Hasem mama who had any interest in reading my books. Whenever we met he would tell me, 'Do you have books coming out again? Give me one!' One day

Hasem mama borrowed 500 taka from me. He did not want to, but the legal case was becoming impossibly expensive. Mother did not take the news well, that he had borrowed money from his own niece. Perhaps she was apprehensive that if my father and brother were to find out all hell would break loose. She loved Hasem mama dearly, especially because of his principles. He used to be the sort of person who did not spare his own family when it came to his moral code. Why should such a person borrow money from his own niece? Mother would have rather had him starve if it came to that than ask anyone for money. Despite how she tried to defend her family, she was also embarrassed by them. Mother was very alone, she was the only person in her small world. She was summoned only in case of an accident in the house, or if Father wanted to complain about someone, or if he wished to extract information about one of her children. Around this time Father's new preoccupation was grilling her to find out about my movements, my thoughts, what I was doing and whether I was going to take a decision regarding my future. He wanted to know if I was going to keep living my life like I was doing, shuttling between Dhaka and Mymensingh without any cares or restrictions. Unfortunately, Mother knew too little to disclose anything of my eventual plans to him.

He used to come home and, knowing that I was within earshot, pretend as if he was speaking to Mother. 'It's becoming impossible to show my face around the city. Even today, this one man comes up to me and asks, your daughter is a doctor, right? Has she gotten married? Is your son-in-law a doctor too? Most people already know that she was married once. Why did she marry that alcoholic, skirt-chasing rascal without finding out anything about him first? Now who is going to marry her? All these men will simply have fun with her, take her around. None of them will marry her. I can't go out in front of people because of her; they ask me why I am not getting my daughter married even though she is of age. They want to know! What am I supposed to tell them? I have nothing to say so I hang my head in shame. How can I tell them that my daughter married of her own choice, the guy has left her and now she goes around with other men! Do they not know? Of course they do! And they talk too. Wouldn't it have been better if she had married some doctor?

She could have already had a couple of children and be settled by now.' Mother would nod in agreement. Yes, I should have married a doctor. Munni, who was my age, was already married, had children and was busy with her family like a good little girl, she would add. This bit about the good Munni usually served as a teachable moment; of course, there was no dearth of those. Whichever direction she looked, Mother could only see girls my age or even younger than me married and happy with their lot. Everyone except me, that is.

Eventually, things came to a head. Every waking moment they were battering me. Who called? Who wrote that letter to you? Who is that who came to meet you? How do you know him? If you know him well then why are you not married to him yet! I got so annoyed that I informed everyone that I was going to spend the rest of my life alone and never get married. In response Father issued a stern warning—I was welcome to never marry since there were many women who did not get married. However, I would have to stop all interactions with my male friends, although my female friends were allowed. Not willing to stop there he declared a state of emergency, adding that the first male friend to set foot into the house was going to be forced to marry me. He had beaten Yasmin out of the house. He did not physically beat me but all the lashes were on my soul, forcing me to double over in pain. There was no Yasmin nearby for me to go out with to clear my head, to simply hail a rickshaw and roam around the city, go to a dance or a poetry recital, or a musical event somewhere. I did not feel like going anywhere alone and the Shokal Kabita Parisad too had mostly fallen apart since her departure. Every day I was being reminded in new ways that I was the immoral idiot of the house.

No one at home had ever liked R and they had initially been happy after I left him and returned home. When my status as a divorcee became my most prominent signifier, they could no longer tolerate my husbandless life. Obviously, I was not attractive enough without a cage around me; what if some vicious predator somewhere gobbled me up? Or so they feared, I guess. Why was I uninterested in the FCPS exam? Why was I hell-bent on destroying all my future prospects? So irritated was Father with these anxieties that he did not hesitate to say the most uncouth things to me. It was becoming clearer to me every day that the only way to prove a woman was capable of living without a husband or a family was to earn something significant or renounce everything in life. Earn an extra qualification or find an extra area of expertise, or renounce good food, material comforts and live like a widow. Renounce the world and become a nun. Or commit suicide and be returned to dust. Perhaps I could become unbelievably successful in something, reach the top of my field and be promoted to a top post. Or pass the FCPS!

In the end it was behind the veil of the FCPS that I finally resolved to hide the shame of my husbandless life. In order to make my unnatural life more bearable I had to showcase incredible talent. Ageing without a husband and children was a sin and the only way to find absolution was to work like an idiot and earn a huge degree. Being unmarried was an ugly festering wound that I had to cover up with a colourful degree-shaped shroud. Being myself was not going to be enough to wash away my sins or earn me forgiveness. Other women did not need this extra qualification; they were not called names without it. But since I had walked out on my husband I had to put in extra effort just to be judged at par with other women. And in the end did it truly make a difference? Otherwise why did no one ever show the same concern for a girl working her body to death at her middle-school dropout husband's house and why was I subjected to such scrutiny despite being a qualified and practising doctor?

~

The family planning office, always a place of disarray, was in dire straits. Medicines were being pilfered, money was being stolen, the male employees were in charge of everything and the pretty female employees always had to be careful about wayward hands. While trying to speak out against such rampant violations I realized mine was the only voice crying out aloud. I was losing and the male overseers were waiting for an opportunity to get back at me. The only time I was happy was during the ligation or tubectomy camps organized in far-off villages. When I was immersed in work my domestic woes would temporarily vanish. When there were no camps to attend the only thing to do was to go to the office every day and just sit there—to see how everyone was doing, what they were saying—while swatting at a few flies occasionally. On one such day RH, the boss and deputy director, DD for short, turned up at the tin hut on Kalibari Road for an inspection while out on a pleasure stroll in the evening, his lips red with the paan in his mouth and shades covering his eyes. Mujibar Rehman was there in his office, Ambiya in his amorous embrace. Everyone else had left for the day, including Saidul Islam. The DD found a hundred reasons that justified Saidul's absence but found absolutely none that explained mine and he lodged a complaint against me with the health department head office in Dhaka. Not satisfied with doing so once, he lodged the complaint repeatedly. He could not wait to teach me a lesson for turning down his amorous advances on a previous occasion. He used to often ask me to visit his Aqua office and I had gone one day. He had welcomed me in, sat me down, rung for the waiter and asked, 'What do you want? Tea with milk, or without?'

'Without.'

He glanced at the waiter. 'One with, one without.' The waiter turned around and left.

'Why do you have red tea? It destroys skin colour. You women, you have to think about your skin colour, don't you!' Rows of teeth were on display, like thirty-two dried seeds stuck on a big pumpkin.

'It's a habit. I don't think about skin colour that much.'

'Of course, beautiful women don't need to worry so much either.' Another round of laughter.

Wishing to change the topic I deliberately added, 'You asked me to come. Is there something you need me to do, sir?'

'What work would I have? Is there any work at all in family planning?' More laughter.

'Then? Is there something else you need?'

'Come, sit down. Let's chat for a while. My wife and kids have gone to Dhaka for a few days. In a way you are happier. You can enjoy your life. One can't enjoy life with a family in tow.'

I lowered my eyes and concentrated on my tea.

'Are you very shy?'

I raised my eyes again. 'Not really.'

'If you are so shy, imagine what other women will be like.'

My eyes were on the wall, fixed on the pictures hanging on it. Not much was visible in the pictures from so far but I kept my eyes fixed on them as if I had to memorize the details immediately.

'Now tell me something about yourself. You don't want to talk at all, it seems! Your life is very interesting, isn't it?'

'Not really. My life is fairly simple . . .'

'What are you saying! I have heard from people that you have a very interesting life. You have a devil-may-care attitude. It's a good thing though.' The teeth, like dried pumpkin seeds, flashed with amusement.

'Sir, is there going to be a camp soon?' I knew there was a camp scheduled for the following Wednesday but I still asked.

'Camp? Yes, there is one! You can come with me in my car for the next camp. Reach here in the morning. We can go together.'

'It's not really a problem for me, sir . . .'

'You went with Dr Saidul on his motorcycle that one time . . . [laughter] . . . a jeep is much better. Much more comfortable.'

I did not respond.

'So, tell me. What are your plans in life?'

'I don't have any plans as such.'

'No plans! You don't want to get married?'

'No!'

'What are you saying! You are going to let your youth go to waste?'

'Why should it go to waste? I am writing in my free time. It's good this way.'

The pumpkin had begun to roll in mirth. 'Oh, of course, you are a poet! An intellectual.' Raucous laughter.

That day, he had made me sit in front of him for even longer, speaking nonsense and laughing unnecessarily. Every time I had tried making an excuse to leave he made me sit down. Finally, I had lied to him about an urgent engagement in order to escape. On my way out, he had added, 'Come here day after tomorrow in the afternoon. I will get my work done early and be free. My wife will be away for seven more days. There's no problem.' Not just the day after, I had never gone back to his office again. Justifiably he could not tolerate my audacity. Neither could he bear the fact that I was instigating the other female employees to follow suit and not respond to his lewd proposals. So he was obsessed with forcing me to leave Mymensingh and was cooking up all sorts of troubles to that end. The DD's opposition at office, Father at home—a veritable assault of these combined forces drove me to such a state that I seriously began contemplating suicide.

Deciding to put all my hurt and grievances aside, I visited Yasmin one day. Seeing her I was reminded of those restless, lively days of long ago, the ones we could never go back to again. I wanted to grab her and run away, from the house and from our lives, but she was so inextricably connected to her domesticity, had made so many compromises, that it was impossible to go anywhere with her. 'Let's go somewhere, like we used to. Let's talk, and laugh, like we used to.' My words fell on deaf ears. The dutiful housewife had definitively drawn the blinds on her old life; the life she had chosen might not have been the one she had dreamt about but she did not wish to be subject to any more social censure.

It was enough that one sister's irresponsible lifestyle was subject to so much disapproval, perhaps it was only right that the other sister should have to make amends with her own life. So she was fine being confined within the four walls of her husband's house and she did not want me to visit her too often either. Perhaps she wished to avoid the salacious gossip that my visits led to. Everyone my age was married except me. I was the odd one out, the unnatural one, and so on. I had a broken marriage, I was a sinner and an amoral woman. How could a good housewife be associated with someone like me! So she studiously avoided associating with me, busy as she was with her in-laws and deeply concerned about their happiness. She convinced Father to invite all the people from her in-laws' side to Abakash for which Mother spent the entire day in the kitchen cooking. A few days later she came over to Abakash again to have lunch—with her husband, her mother-in-law, her brothers-in-law and their wives. I gave her all the things I had bought in India; it seemed to make her happy. I was not particularly attached to my gold jewellery either, so I gave that to her too—this time I could clearly see in her sparkling eyes that she was happy.

Although bad times can be relentless, usually there are thresholds after which things seem to turn around. For me, never-ending misfortunes were piling up one on top of another. The final devastating blow came one fateful morning. Abdul Karim, whom I had borrowed 30,000 taka from, turned up at Abakash and made an unbelievable scene, all because I had only managed to pay him back 5000 thus far. He screamed about how I had borrowed money from him to pay for a holiday in India, how I was a disgusting woman, how he had never met another person like me, and much more drivel. I *had* borrowed money from him before my trip to India, on the condition that I was going to pay him back on a monthly basis after receiving my salary. Although he had agreed to the terms then, he came to the house with the sudden demand that I pay him back the entire money all at once. This was the same man who never used to miss an opportunity to make a pass at me and I always pretended to not notice his overtures.

Once he had invited me to a businessman's house in Chhota Bazaar to show me some flowers and seedling samples. Not being suspicious I had gone and found Abdul Karim sitting in a dimly lit room with a middle-aged businessman wearing a green kurta—the sort who carries wads of currency notes in his pockets. When Abdul Karim had launched into platitudes—the businessman in green was very rich, he was going to give me money whenever I needed it, I would not even have to worry about paying him back—I had pretended to not understand their hints, smiled, drank tea, spoken to the man in green about farming for a few moments and then excused myself with urgent hospital business in order to leave. Another time Karim had turned up at Abakash and told me, 'Doctor, I have an ailment. What should I do?' When I had asked what was wrong with him, he had lowered his voice and whispered that he was suffering from excessive sexual desire. Neither of his two wives were able to satisfy him because he could *stay* for long but they usually *finished* too soon; the more he wanted the more they were unable to meet his expectations. I had listened to the entire diatribe and pretended it was a common complaint among people, like the flu, indigestion or dysentery. Doing my best to keep my face and my expression impassive I had calmly spoken to the bald, corrupt man, his teeth stained with paan and his belly shaking with laughter, to tell him about possible ways of treatment.

'This is nothing too serious! Go see a venereologist. You will get the best treatment there. I am not a specialist in venereal diseases.'

'What are you saying! You're a doctor and you're saying you can't treat me!'

'You need a specialist for what ails you, Karim bhai.'

'Oh no, you are so dear to me, almost like a relative. How can I say such things to an unfamiliar doctor?'

'Why can't you? A disease is a disease!'

'No, a doctor can't help me.'

'But I'm a doctor. Why did you tell me then?'

Cackling with glee, he replied, 'I know what medicine I need.' When I steadfastly refused to ask any further questions he ventured to share the information regardless: 'I need a young girl.'

'Well, there's Kiran and Kumud, your daughters. Both are young.'

He immediately stuck out his tongue in shame. 'They are my children. I want a young girl for myself.'

'Oh, so that's what you mean!'

Unfortunately there had been nothing else for me to do but pretend that I did not understand what he was trying to tell me. I could not have thrown a shoe at him; he was a family friend after all. But I had been adamant about not giving him the satisfaction of knowing that he had managed to get his indecent point across. If he had figured it out, it would have probably provided him with his much-needed sexual satisfaction immediately. Besides, I had also wished to convince him that I respected him despite his indiscretions and that I could never imagine he would make such an offer to me. My sole hope had been that he would take the hint and never try to broach the topic ever again.

The very same Abdul Karim was at Abakash shouting the house down about how I was a *bad* woman—I had taken a man on vacation and done unsayable things with his money, women of weak character like me were easily available to any man, and so on. Mother barked at him to stop. 'What nonsense! If she's borrowed money from you, she's going to return it. If not today, she'll return it tomorrow. How dare you say such things because of that?' That shut him up finally. Hasina had been standing at the door all this while. She had not uttered a word of protest while the scene had been unfolding, perhaps secretly delighted that such things were being said about me. It would have been silly of her to ignore such an immensely entertaining moment.

By the time Yasmin arrived with Milan, Karim had left. Taking her with me I gathered all my remaining jewellery and took it to the jeweller's. The jeweller offered me half the fair price but even that came to just 20,000 taka. Yasmin borrowed another 5000 from Milan and I handed over the sum to Hasina to return to her brother-in-law Karim immediately. The debt, however, failed to evoke any sign of relief in Hasina. To me it seemed she would have been happier had I suffered under its weight for some more time.

I escaped from Mymensingh, in search of a place where I would be able to, at the very least, breathe freely. In Dhaka Geeta's misbehaviour went on unabated. She would not let me into the house and if she did, she would not ask me to stay. She would also deliberately restrain Suhrid from coming anywhere near me. She was a different person during the good times and another when things were going south and I could not even begin to understand the number of ways in which she was capable of insulting someone. So I went to NM with my broken heart. He had not an ounce of her meanness, selfishness and malice. Besides, he was forever trying to prove to me irrefutably that he was intelligent, that he was not a bigot, that he believed in equity between men and women and that he was a firm proponent of progressive politics, free thought and religious tolerance. He was constantly trying to do or say things that would convince me he was a kind, transparent, lively and easy-going man, so that I too would get attracted to him, although despite his best efforts I could never think of him that way. Even the day my long-abandoned, unloved and numb body woke up to his touch I remained impassive to any feelings of love for NM. That very afternoon he told me: 'Let's get married.' The way he said it, it was as if he could have been saying something regular—let's have tea, let's go to the fair, let's go for a stroll. Although the words failed to surprise me, I did agree to his proposal because I knew he was my friend and the only person in the world who would never wish for any harm to come to me.

NM was not a cage to me; he was rather like a force of freedom in a stuffy world full of cruelty and abuse.

That afternoon, out in a rickshaw near Dhanmandi, NM had us stop in front of a small shack by the road. The board hanging at the entrance revealed it was the office of the notary public. There was a spectral old man sitting in the dark and dank room whom NM asked about the formalities required for us to get married. Two signatures apiece and some money was all that was needed. All the formalities were completed in five minutes and that night we returned to NM's house in Iskaton and slept together for the very first time. Did we *have* to sign a document to be able to sleep together? I was never one to place too much importance on signatures. I used to sign documents in the office whenever they asked me to. I was an insignificant person so I could never understand how my signature was of any special value. We still signed the documents given by the notary public because it mattered to NM. It was a compromise we reached for the sake of his moral compunctions about us sleeping together.

In the end we ended up spending, if not the entire night, at least half the night in NM's house, surrounded by his parents, siblings and their spouses. It was NM's house and he had the right to do as he pleased. He was the one who used to look after his family and pay the rent; in other words he was the master of the house and no one had any say in any decision he took. His friends used to visit his house often, to eat, party and stay over. In fact, even I had once spent the night there and he had given up his bedroom for me to use. This time it was different though; a signature had authorized my presence even if it did not make much of a difference to me personally. NM remained the same friend he already was and our way of addressing each other remained informal.

Meanwhile, the DD of Mymensingh—the one with the shades, the paan-stained teeth and the roving eye—finally succeeded in getting his complaints against me across to the authorities. Consequently, I was transferred to Chauddagram and in one fell swoop the health department sought to deal me a killing blow. Oddly enough I was not terribly unhappy with the course that things had taken. I had been wishing to get away from it all for the longest time—from Abakash and the toxic atmosphere of the family planning department that had no antidote. Mother was upset and started crying the moment she heard about the transfer. Nevertheless, blessed with a transferable job, there was no way I could have avoided the shift. After joining the health centre at Chauddagram I began commuting to work from NM's house in Komilla. NM would go stay the night there too before heading back to Dhaka early in the morning.

NM was not out of surprises though. One fine day he suddenly handed me a piece of paper—it was another transfer letter. Within two weeks of joining Chauddagram he had managed to get another transfer for me. I was to join as a medical officer in the blood bank of Salimullah Medical College and Mitford Hospital in Dhaka. I could not believe my eyes. So this was what influence could do! Left to my own devices I would never have managed to get a posting somewhere that good. There were only two medical college hospitals in Dhaka and the popular opinion was that the only way to get work in such places was to exploit the authority of influential uncles. None of my uncles were from such prominent circles so I would have to be satisfied with Chauddagram and its ilk. Who would have known that the editor of a weekly literary journal could work his influence not just at the newspaper offices but in the Ministry of Health too!

However, despite this one surprise magnificent enough to trump all the other ones NM had sprung on me, our relationship, defined as it was by a couple of signatures, barely lasted two months. NM wanted to host a grand reception to tell everyone about our marriage in the presence of all his friends and acquaintances. Sadly, that was never meant to be. One day, again while on my way to Dhanmandi in a rickshaw, I suddenly got off at the notary's. I slipped him some money and signed another document, this one the opposite of the one I had signed with NM. Whether the signature remained on a document or not it scarcely mattered to me, I remained the way I was. I had neither gained nor lost anything. When I had signed the document the first time I had been unaffected, it was just the same the second time around. To me a signature meant very little when compared to a friendship; if the friendship was no longer the way it used to be then there was nothing a signature could do to change things.

It did not take me long after the first signature to finally see NM's true nature—his narrow-minded, rancorous, mean and jealous self. And the more I saw this new NM the more ashamed I was to realize that I had considered him my closest friend. Having acquired me he became obsessed with trying to control me. For instance, I would wish to go to Mymensingh but that idea would be shot down immediately.

'No, you don't need to go now.'

'What do you mean?'

'I mean you don't need to go now.'

'Then when do I need to go?'

'Later.'

'When?'

'I'll tell you.'

I was expected to wait for him to tell me when I could go to Mymensingh. I was also expected to wait for him to take me wherever I wanted to go.

While earlier he had always been concerned with what made me happy, after signing the papers it became apparent that his happiness lay in confining me within a cage. When I refused to be caged he raved and railed against me, the vein on his forehead angry and throbbing. Previously he would let me drive his car on occasion; after our marriage I was banned from ever sitting in the driver's seat. Hitherto he had been extremely keen on publishing my articles every week; soon that interest waned entirely. Gradually, I was becoming a puppet for him to play with as he pleased. If I wanted a pen he would get me ten but he would not let me go and get one by myself. He wanted to be the one to fulfil all my desires, leaving me with nothing to do on my own. He did not want me to be proud of myself, he reserved all of that pride for himself. He wanted all my duties, wanted to fulfil them for me while I was not allowed to have any say.

As his desire to be the one who was superior in every aspect grew more desperate, he began belittling all my achievements, the same accomplishments he had been instrumental in fostering. The self-deprecating man I had known, always saying things like 'I don't know anything, I have no clue, I'm an idiot', changed so much that he would not hesitate to claim that he was wiser, more erudite and more talented than almost everyone else. Neither would he stop boasting about his generosity. I soon became convinced that the NM I had known was a mask the real man had put on to win me over. Masks can be tricky things; they tend to slip off sooner or later. He had managed to coax and cajole me into his grasp. Once that happens, when a woman comes under a man's control, no man wants to let her get ahead of him. At the end of the day, NM was a man after all.

~

NM was exceedingly proud of his father and he often mentioned how his father used to be a member of Parliament for East Pakistan. I did not believe he had any reason to be proud of the fact. His father had not only been a leader of the Muslim League[19] in Devidar, a sub-unit of Komilla, during the Liberation War, the man had also been a leading figure of both the Razakar[20] and the Shanti Committee.[21] NM never suffered from any remorse due to his father's past and I never heard him accept the unkind truth that his father had been wrong. Such was his obsessive love for his father that he would make me check the man's blood pressure for no reason at all. Even after assuring him repeatedly that there was nothing to worry about, he would make me check again the very next day and then again the next. Surprised, I would ask him, 'Why?' 'No reason,' he would reply simply. There was no reason to check someone's blood pressure every single day when the person had no related complaints. His father was hale and hearty and neither did he have fluctuating blood pressure. Just because he loved his father did not mean I had to share his unreasonable anxieties. So I would refuse and NM would fly into a rage. His fingers used to tremble and when he was angry his entire person would be racked with tremors, his eyes threatening to pop out of their sockets.

Irrespective of how NM was, everyone else in his family was very nice. His mother was a stunningly beautiful woman living with a hideously unattractive husband. Nevertheless, as long as I stayed in that house, this unattractive man was always sweet to me. In fact each and every person in the house was nothing but warm and affectionate. If only that had been enough! Everyone was easily taken in by NM's humility but I knew he had a strong core of arrogance in him too. And this arrogance was not just limited to himself, it extended to his father as well. Gradually I grew to question his political positions. Before taking on the responsibility of *Khabarer Kagaj* he used to work for *Inquilab*, an out-and-out conservative magazine whose editor-publisher Maulana Mannan had been a well-known Razakar. *Inquilab* was vocal against those in favour of freedom and was playing a huge role in the systematic propagation of Islam in the country. Although NM had very little to say about the magazine itself, he could not hide his glowing admiration for their set-up, their style and their printing press. In fact, *Khabarer Kagaj* was printed in the highly modernized printing press of *Inquilab*, which I even visited with him on one occasion. By then the country had already split in two—the fundamentalists and those opposing them.

As the editor of *Khabarer Kagaj*, even though he was closely associated with many who were directly involved in fighting fanaticism, NM never chose a clear side for himself. He had walked away from the darkness of *Inquilab* and discovered a world of light, but despite holding a university degree in journalism NM never wrote a single editorial for either *Khabarer Kagaj* or *Ajker Kagaj*. He usually got it written by one of the minor journalists who were always around him. Neither did he ever conduct an interview or write an article about a political or social leader, or even a poet or a writer. This was not part of his field of expertise; his skill lay in business. Kazi Sahid Ahmed liked him and had appointed him the editor of *Khabarer Kagaj*. In exchange NM had successfully coaxed many renowned writers to write for the magazine which had resulted in increased sales as well as unprecedented popularity for the journal. NM might have infiltrated the literary world from outside but he deserved many accolades for his achievements—it could not have been easy as an outsider to successfully break into this world and create such an impact.

An incident, or an accident, happened soon after NM and I started sleeping together, something that had never happened with R—I became pregnant. I could feel something different in my body and in my heart, the discernible presence of someone other than me. All of a sudden I could barely recognize myself, these startling changes occurring within me making me quake; a maelstrom of fear, shame and happiness, and dreams, threatened to sweep me off my feet. NM was always adept at springing surprises but his reaction to this unexpected news was markedly different from anything he had tried before.

'Let's go to the clinic.'

'Why the clinic?'

'To get an abortion.'

'What?!'

'You have to get an abortion.'

'Why do I *have* to get an abortion?'

'We can't have kids now! We can think about these things later.'

Refusing to pay heed to any of my objections he dragged me to a clinic in Gulshan and forced me to get an abortion. I understood quite well why he needed me to do this. He was convinced that the sperm that had made the baby was not his own, I had procured it from somewhere else. I could feel nothing but pity for him and the corrosive jealousy that had forced him to take the life of his own child and which was threatening to destroy me too. Where was I going, who was I talking to, who had given me what gifts on my birthday, why—he was so suspicious about everything that it was slowly turning him into an animal. The animal was in turn stalking me. I felt sorry for NM. He was so far gone in this downward spiral that he failed to grasp the only truth in all of this: that he was the only one with whom I had a physical and emotional relationship. Assuming that I was trying to fool him, he had fooled me to try and teach me a lesson. It did not take long for me to push NM out of my heart entirely.

The repercussions of his overconfidence were soon felt in the offices of *Khabarer Kagaj*. NM had misused a blank cheque issued by Kazi Sahid Ahmed and when this information came to light Kazi summarily dismissed NM from his services and took over the editorial duties himself. Earlier NM would not stop singing praises of the man but after his dismissal Kazi became the worst person in the world. Angry at having been deposed from his position of luxury and authority NM's quest for vengeance manifested in slander and gossip. NM was nothing if not intelligent. After cementing the popularity of *Khabarer Kagaj* he had branched off and started the newspaper *Ajker Kagaj* and made that the second most popular newspaper in the country almost overnight. Doubtless he was smart. However, more often than not, his smartness was tempered with an edge of villainy. He was not the sort who could be restrained easily.

Instead of going into a depressed state over losing his job he soon gathered his resources and launched another newspaper, *Bhorer Kagaj*, coaxing many writers of *Ajker Kagaj* to break rank and join him. Soon *Bhorer Kagaj* too began to grow popular. When he realized that I was not going to fall for his self-aggrandizing, his rancour grew manyfold. All his politeness, his civility and the many other masks crumbled, leaving behind the true face for all to see—all fiery eyes, gnashing teeth and raging screams. He was no longer concerned if his behaviour was going to hurt me or make me angry. He began approaching my friends and acquaintances to grumble about how much he had done for me and how little I had done for him in return. The endgame was simple—to prove how a faithful, perfect and wonderful boy like him had been cruelly wronged by someone like me and to establish what an indecent, uncaring and insensitive woman I was.

When NM figured I could leave him without batting an eyelid he tried clinging to me like a leech. When he realized I had no interest in putting up with his suspicious nature any longer all he could do was explode with rage. And when he understood that I did not care about his anger any more, always the adept organizer, he set himself to planning how best to humiliate me.

~

I had taken a house on rent in Armanitola, very close to Mitford Hospital. One day there was a sudden knock on my door. It was NM. He should not have known where I was but he had always been like a hawk, able to scent his prey. He was banging on the door so loudly that people in the locality were beginning to gather. At the end of my tether I went out and told him in no uncertain terms that there was no way I was letting him inside the house. I did not want to let him in because I did not want to hear him insult R. After a while, realizing his ploy was not going to work, NM left quietly. What I did not know was that by then he had already concocted two new plans: the first to force me out of the house, and the second to get married again, this time for real.

A Happy Life

I was posted at the blood bank at Mitford Hospital. Many poor people used to come to the bank to sell blood. Rather than the doctors it was the laboratory technicians who were more aware of how to extract blood and how to label and store the bags in the freezer. From eight in the morning till two in the afternoon, except for signing a few documents, I had nothing to do but sit around. Soon I grew tired of being utterly jobless. The obstetrics and paediatrics ward was right beside the blood bank and throughout the day the doctors there could be seen constantly running about, so busy that it seemed they barely had time to exhale. Seeing them I would desperately wish for a similar schedule, to be able to work day and night. One day I wrote an application to the head of the gynaecology department, Dr Bayesh Bhuiyan: 'I wish to work in the gynaecology department. I would be grateful if you would consider taking me on.' To my utter delight, Dr Bhuiyan readily agreed to consider my request.

My new house was in Armanitola, quite close to the hospital. Mujibur Rahman Khoka, the owner of Vidyaprakash, had helped me in getting it on rent. My books of poetry were doing fantastic business for Khoka's publishing house and he was constantly providing me with inspiration to keep writing. During the jobless hours at the blood bank I would often visit his office in Banglabazar to inquire about how my books were doing. On one such occasion I had asked him to help me find a place, having exhausted myself trying to look for one on my own, scrambling to wherever I noticed a 'To let' sign. Almost on all such occasions after the initial general conversation the landlord would invariably ask me: 'How many of you will be staying?'

'It's only me.'

'Of course, but where is the man who'll be staying?'

'There is no man. I will be staying alone.'

The landlord would be unable to suppress his outrage. 'How can a woman live alone anywhere? Don't you have a husband?'

'No.'

'We don't take in single women.'

The doors would then shut on my face with a loud bang. I did not give up hope despite this happening over and over again. When Khoka agreed to help, both of us set out together to look for a place. Every house we went to, since Khoka was there with me, the landlord routinely turned to him to ask him how many people were going to be staying. He usually answered, 'She is the tenant. She's a doctor working in Mitford.'

'Doesn't she have a husband?'

Khoka would meekly reply, 'No, she does not. She has just been transferred to Mitford and it'll be best if she gets a place near the hospital. Don't worry about rent. Since she's a doctor you can surely imagine that she would have no trouble meeting the monthly rent.'

To give him his due credit Khoka did try to convince these people to the best of his ability. Nonetheless, irrespective of how pleading a tone he used it amounted to very little in the end. No one was willing to give their place out to a single woman. We did manage to find some unassuming and cordial landlords who did not shut the door on our faces immediately or bluntly say, 'Go away. We won't rent to you.' Even when these people agreed to Khoka's earnest pleas it usually came with a caveat: the girl had to bring her father or brother along. In simpler terms, as sad as it was that a woman did not have a husband in order to rent a house, some male relative or the other had to live with her. Although none of them could explain why a single woman was not a suitable candidate for a tenant, they did make it clear that I had to bring a guardian along and they refused to even entertain the possibility that as an adult I could be considered my own guardian.

I informed Khoka quite unequivocally that it would not be possible for me to make anyone uproot their life to come stay with me, be it my father, brothers or uncles. The only person I could think of was Mother. I could have asked her, but then that was neither here nor there. Mother was not a man and the landlords were adamant that I needed one of those. We did try to inquire if anyone was willing to rent out their place to a female doctor living with her mother but came up empty-handed on that front too. Tired and harangued from searching we were on the cusp of giving up hope when we chanced upon the Armanitola house. Khoka had to sit for a two-hour interview with the landlord where he put his most docile face forward to finally emerge unscathed from the ordeal with flying colours and a seal of approval for two women to rent the house.

The owner of the enormous battleship of a house was an uneducated man who had made a ton of money from iron. With that enormous wealth he had done what most men with enormous wealth usually do—he had kept a beard, worn a fez and married four times in the name of Allah. Three of the wives were kept in three different houses while he lived on the first floor of the Armanitola house with the fourth. The rent was 3000 taka; by then my salary had crawled its way up to 2500. Despite the discrepancy I agreed to take the apartment on the fourth floor of the building— all of two rooms and a long balcony. Positively trembling with joy and anticipation at finally being able to live on my own without being at someone else's mercy, I was determined to live my life on my own terms.

I went about making the place habitable for the time being, buying a cheap bed, some cheap mattresses, a steel almirah and a few necessary utensils. I also brought Mother and Lily over from Mymensingh to stay with me. I could tell how happy Mother was over the prospect of a house of one's own and a measure of independence. No sooner did she reach the apartment than she set Lily to the task of cooking and cleaning and setting everything in order, while wandering off to the balcony to stand and stare outside—the boys playing football in the Armanitola grounds, the cars and buses on the road, and the sky. Soon I bought curtains for the windows and a large red carpet with red-and-green diamond motifs that I bought after a tense stand-off over discounts. I also got a couple of matching cushions since I had no money to buy sofas, tables or chairs. Not that I was terribly unhappy that I could not purchase a sofa; it was my first attempt at building my own life and though I wanted to make it as pretty as possible with the nicest things in the world, most such things were too expensive for me to even look at. I was prepared to simply look away and search for cheaper things that were just as pretty. Is there any way to describe the sheer elation of being able to buy something with one's own money and bringing it back to one's own home, even if it's something quite inexpensive? The month the carpet was bought there was nothing else I could buy, but even waiting till the next month for money was suffused with a feeling of joy.

Since my salary was not enough to meet the rent I had to depend on the columns I wrote for extra cash. I wrote for the weekly *Purbabhash*, bimonthly *Ananya*, and even for *Khabarer Kagaj* and *Ajker Kagaj* after they parted ways with NM. Another collection of poetry was brought out by Vidyaprakash, *Atale Antareen* (Deep Within). Though this one did just as well as the previous ones I could never ask Khoka for my royalties; I was too embarrassed to bring up the topic of money. Besides, Khoka had been instrumental in helping me begin an independent life. He had assisted me in getting around when required—to the market to buy groceries or to buy furniture and utensils—and even helped me get the best deals. Often when I was too broke to afford anything more than rice and dal he would drop off some chicken or something. Towards the end of the month when finances were in dire straits Mother would simply go off to Mymensingh to stock up on rice, groceries and vegetables from Abakash. I was poor, but I was very happy because I could not remember another time in my life when I had actually dealt with poverty and lived on a budget; neither could I remember a time when I had been as happy. Khoka was always there, like a brother and a friend, to lend a helping hand. Mother was there with her boundless love, and Lily too was there, happy at last to have gotten away from being driven like a slave in Abakash. The house ran on a tight budget but love we had a surfeit of.

In the hospital I had a full schedule in the gynaecology department which was always teeming with patients. The energy reminded me of back when I used to be an intern in the gynaecology department at Mymensingh Hospital. There was so much work that I barely had time to breathe. I was doing deliveries, performing episiotomies, treating eclampsia, removing retained placentas, doing forceps deliveries, or running off to the OT to do a caesarean while putting on my gloves and mask at lightning speed. The longest part of the day, however, was spent in the outdoor ward treating the hundreds of patients arriving in a steady stream. Sometimes, after all this through the day, there would be a night shift to run. In the little free time left after everything I wrote my columns, without which I would not have been able to eat, let alone pay the entire rent.

Meanwhile, I found out that many of the young interns of the hospital were my fans for some unfathomable reason and we all came to be on rather friendly terms despite the age gap between us. Everyone knew who I was, I did not have to introduce myself to anyone. Of course the flip side to this was the unfortunate tendency to overlook my work and assume that I was more focused on poetry than on being a doctor. For instance, I would be writing a prescription and someone would see that from a distance and assume I was writing a column. Other doctors my age, having passed their FCPS, or at least having passed the first part, were all working as registrars or clinical assistants. Others like me, working as medical officers in various departments, were also planning to quickly appear for the exam. I was the only one without any such plans. To me there was nothing to be gained from poring over tomes of information which often took years to process. There were so many people around me who had been trying to crack the exam for ten years, diligently sitting for it year after year and failing every time. Those with rich fathers usually skipped the FCPS exam and flew off to London to return with an FRCS degree. That the latter was a simpler degree to get than the FCPS of Bangladesh was a well-known fact, no matter how incredible it might sound.

Possibly this was one of the primary reasons why I decided to forgo the FCPS exam, even though many of my colleagues at Mitford were working and studying simultaneously. Many of them asked me if I was going to sit for the exam and appeared quite shocked when I informed them that I did not wish to. If they could have, they probably would have asked me what I was doing in the hospital in the first place if I did not wish to get ahead in life. Or perhaps they silently congratulated themselves over the knowledge that I was soon going to learn my lesson—I was going to get transferred to a far-off village somewhere and be replaced by a young doctor with an FCPS degree or on track to getting one.

The would-be FCPS doctors had their heads in their books all the time, even at the cost of their duties in the department, while the other doctors like me were working like interns. I did not mind the work, but nothing was more hurtful than when people alleged that I was indifferent to my profession just because I was known as a poet. If not anyone else Professor Rashida Begum used to point it out to me repeatedly that I was an indifferent doctor. She had disapproved of me from the very first day when I had reached the department two minutes too late; for the rest of our time together those two minutes were etched into her memory. Besides, she was usually irritable by nature. Of the three branches in gynaecology, she used to be a professor in the third and quite expectedly there was nothing going for her except her temper tantrums. Handling patients was an ordeal for her and lest someone notice she was floundering she would try to cover it up by screaming at others. There was a two-fold purpose to this—everyone would get to hear her voice and, she hoped, everyone would learn to respect her, just like they respected the head of the department, Professor Bhuiyan.

Bhuiyan was a wonderful person. He did not have to shout at anyone, his work spoke for itself. Every time we ran into each other he would ask me how I was doing and I would say something evasive to try and get away as fast as possible. As it is I was a tad embarrassed that I had no interest in completing my postgraduation; most of the other doctors usually surrounding him were either postgraduates or on the verge of finishing their degrees. It was perhaps this awkwardness that was instrumental in renewing my interest in finishing my own degree. Hearing that I was contemplating further studies Mother could not hide her excitement. 'Take Allah's name and just start. I know your father will be happy too.' Bhuiyan, despite being the head of the department, was always extra gracious towards me, more because of my writing than my skills as a doctor. He was a regular reader of my columns and often told me about the ones he had particularly liked. I was uncomfortable whenever my writing career came up for discussion at work but there was nothing I could do to avoid it altogether. I was a doctor first and foremost; like any other doctor in the hospital I did not wish for anything to take away from that.

Mother was especially proud of me and I could sense her joy when I left for work in the morning with my apron and stethoscope. She fed me with her own hands and was always bustling about attending to whatever I needed. I had saved up a bit of money and one day I bought a small red refrigerator from the Stadium Market. She would clean the thing twice a day with the pleat of her sari and not let Lily anywhere near it, afraid she might put a scratch somewhere. She would bring me cold water from the fridge after a hot and maddening working day and keep a lot of cooked food in it so I could eat good food without having to run to the market every other day.

Our happy family was doing quite well by itself in sickness and in health. The interns would come over often and we would have raucous evenings replete with food and medical humour. Everyone expressed their appreciation for the life I had built for myself. Initially we would all sit on the carpet and eat. As more guests started coming over I bought a small table and two chairs for the kitchen. A small television and a simple cassette player too joined the roster. Whenever I asked Mother if there was anything else she wanted, she would immediately shake her head and say no. She did not want me to waste money. In fact, she would have preferred it if the table and the chairs had been brought from Abakash. She would argue that a daughter had as much right to a father's property but my own father was hardly doing anything to help.

No, Father did not help me while I was settling down, but that did not diminish my love for him in any way. I could only go home on holidays, only to see him, and I remember buying a shirt and a pair of shoes for him off the Baitul Mukarram sidewalk before my visit. I did not want his help; rather I wanted to be the one helping him. I had so many wishes although I did not possess adequate resources to fulfil all of them immediately. Desperate to change my financial circumstances I put up a signboard at the main gate one day, with the words 'Dr Taslima Nasrin, MBBS' and my visiting hours, among other things. My salary, the consultation fees from the patients coming to see me at home and the paltry earnings from the columns—everything was carefully tallied and kept in the steel almirah. Father's shirt, shoes and things like that were outside the purview of this budget and rightly so. I had to live frugally for that extra bit of expense, but it was all worth it in the end.

Relatives from Mymensingh, whenever they were in Dhaka for work, would stay over at my place. Chotku visited and had to sleep on the carpet; it was only a minor inconvenience when compared to the love between us. He confessed that he had never felt the ease and warmth that he had found in my house at anyone else's, be it Boromama's, my eldest maternal uncle, or Fakrul mama's, Jhunu khala's or even Chotda's for that matter. He assured me that despite the lack of material comfort in my house there was a lot of freedom there—freedom to sing out loud, to be and do what one wished to, and to generally feel at home.

Fortunately I was not spending all my time shuttling between Mitford and my various columns. I was also often attending literary meets and events. Zachariah Swapan of Mymensingh, a foster brother to Yasmin, organized a cultural programme at Bangladesh University of Engineering where I was invited to a debate—my first time attending an event in the capacity of a judge. I did my best to put on my most sombre and judge-like bearing to rise to the occasion. MF invited me to his NGO, Ubinig. Ubinig used to get handsome grants from the US, quite ironic considering MF used to be a prominent socialist back in the day. I had heard his musical programme at TSC;[22] he wrote, composed and sang his own songs. Playing the harmonium himself he would regale the audience with his songs, of which I fondly remember 'Sattaratari jacchi bari' (I have to hurry home). A leftist all his life, he gave up music and published a volume of poetry. And they were such beautiful poems! I remember how deeply moved I had been after reading his poems the first time.

Thus, when MF invited me I did not hesitate. Reaching his office I was greeted at the door by a gaunt woman named Farida Akhtar who seemed to have just gotten out of bed. She sat me down and went inside to give him word of my arrival. It took him some time to appear; he too seemed to have just gotten out of bed and wrapped clothes around himself. Tea and biscuits were called for and we talked, by which I mean he talked. He talked about his poems and explained to me the meanings of a few Arabic words I had not understood. Before I could ask him why he had used such incomprehensible Arabic words in poetry he furnished an outrageous reason: 'Our Bengali is Islamic Bengali and in West Bengal they use Hindu Bengali. Our culture is Islamic too, so we should use a lot of Arabic and Urdu words in our Bengali.'

I could scarcely wrap my head around what he was saying. My first instinct was suspicion that he was trying to indoctrinate me into his madness. Why had he summoned me otherwise? It soon became clear that my suspicions were not unfounded. He wished to start a journal called *Chinta* (Thoughts) filled with these bizarre thoughts of his and he wanted me to write for it. Quite obviously MF had undergone a startling transformation. While Islamic fundamentalism was slowly spreading its tendrils across the country, only a handful of people were fighting against its incursions and trying to foreground how Bengali culture was fundamentally inclusive, be it for Hindus, Muslims, Christians or Buddhists. People like MF were actively trying to decry that. While the partition may have been an unforgivable mistake, at least no rational individual could have denied that the language and the culture of both East and West Bengal were essentially similar. But intellectuals like MF were too far gone in their delusions. He had transformed from a socialist to a sycophant of the capitalists running his NGO and the latest virus he had caught was religion!

He made me listen to this apparently stirring song by some fakir: 'Diner nobi Mustafa . . . harin ekta bandha chhilo gachheri tolai' (Mustafa, the prophet of the deprived . . . a deer was tied under the tree). Arabian deserts do not birth trees, nor do they have deer, so I could not help but marvel at the sheer imaginative reach of the song! He was convinced this was a true song for Bangladesh. Rabindrasangeet was for Hindus, not for Muslims! I later wrote a column contradicting MF's preposterous claims which also included my critique of Shamsur Rahman's use of Urdu words in his poetry and AZ's comments disparaging Rabindranath. A debate over my column and the responses to it raged on in the magazine for quite a while. Even MF wrote a rejoinder although there was very little difference between his arguments and those of any fundamentalist writing for *Inquilab*. I wrote more columns in response to his debate. Around this time Purabi Basu[23] came back to Bangladesh from the US for good and wrote one of her first articles against MF. It soon became evident that it was impossible to continue to disregard MF's questionable affiliations.

After the publication of my column on language Shamsur Rahman wrote a long piece in response. Starting off with a salute to me, the article was written in defence of his position on the question of language. While commenting on the excessive intrusion of Arabic, Farsi and Urdu words in Bengali I had accused him of an unwarranted usage of Urdu words in his poetry. I had questioned his use of Urdu words in place of equally suitable words from the Bengali lexicon and that too words which were prevalent in common parlance.

He wrote in reply:

> There are loan words in every language. They are like guests and it is against the tenets of hospitality to turn a guest away. Doors must be kept open. It is true that not all guests will be welcome or desirous; the unwelcome ones will fall by the wayside on their own . . . Annada Shankar Ray keeps using many Urdu and Hindi words quite naturally. I have never found them difficult or not-pleasant. There is this one instance where he uses the Urdu words 'jaan pehchaan' for acquaintance, instead of the more readily available Bengali counterpart. Or for instance the sentence 'Kamli nahi chhorti' (Kamli won't let me be). I have not gone so far, Taslima Nasrin. So would you accuse the revered Annada Shankar Ray of producing Islamic Bengali in West Bengal?

In my initial article I had contended:

> I don't believe that the Bengali language has become such a pauper that it has to steal or loan words from other languages in order to grow. Why can't we ever be satisfied with what we already possess? The focus of all our writers should be the elevation of the quality of our literature rather than expanding vocabulary.

To that he wrote:

> No, Taslima, such a statement is not something I would have expected from a progressive individual such as you. Just because

our society is at one particular place does it mean we have to be
satisfied with remaining stagnant? Should we not continue to strive
for change? Why should we not import ideas and expressions from
the outside world which can help us change our social conditions?
No language, no matter how expansive or advanced, can shy away
from interaction and exchange with other languages. Surely you of
all people are aware of that!

Even if I had not been aware, Rahman's rejoinder certainly opened my
eyes to a startling realization. Rahman was not in favour of dragging
in terms like Hindu and Muslim within the domain of the Bengali
language. A man of secular ideals through and through, he did not
wish to fan the flames of a dominant Islamic Bengali in Bangladesh.
His words made me take a step back and reassess my position. In
the end I could not help but acknowledge my own complicity in the
blunder and agree with Rahman's opinion. There was nothing called
Islamic Bengali! There was no religion to language; calling Arabic an
Islamic language was in itself a grave error. There were many Arabic
speakers of dissimilar faiths and even more among them who did
not have faith in religion at all. A language had to be allowed to
progress of its own accord, not forced to conform to a particular set
of beliefs. To be fair, there was enough reason behind my anxiety
over the Islamization of Bengali at the time—the conservatives were
in the process of turning the country into an Islamic state. These
people, who had once been against the Liberation War, were trying
to eradicate the Bengali language and culture from independent
Bengal and forcing a new Islamized version of the language upon us
instead. I had written against loan words from this anxious vantage
point. But the problem lay with a few religious fanatics who were
trying to neuter the language to raise the flag of Islam over the state,
bad men trying to serve their own bad ends. Not just in language,
religion was being forced into the realm of politics too. If the nation
was to unalterably take a turn towards radical Islam, simply purging
foreign words from Bengali would be inadequate in the long run. At
my wits' end, nothing could allay my apprehensions.

~

I could never fully comprehend the public appreciation for my columns. Besides, I was always acutely aware of how little I truly knew about literature. I had once nurtured aspirations of studying Bengali literature but Father had forced me into medicine. Consequently, there was not much I knew about the field. I did write poetry but whenever it came to prose I could never be confident about the final outcome of my labours. Even if my prose was appreciated and discussed I was never able to discard the doubts gnawing inside me. Nevertheless, whether I wrote prose or poetry it all came from the heart. I could never concoct something imaginary, something that did not make me think or cry or feel, only for the sake of producing something that would go down well with people.

One day Khoka suggested that we compile my columns into a book. I was justifiably taken aback by his proposal. Could these newspaper articles be even considered literature that he wanted to make a book out of them? Mortified, I replied, 'That's absurd! These articles are about everyday experiences and sensations! What happened yesterday, what's happening today and stuff like that! A few days later these slight things will hardly be of any relevance.' Shaking his head in disagreement, Khoka persisted. 'Be that as it may, not all of them are the same! A few of them will always be topical.' I tried demonstrating my point with the few magazines I had at hand to show that the columns did not work as serious literature. I could not convince myself that my articles—either linguistically weak or more often than not thematically lacking—were suitable for a book. Instead I tried reasoning with Khoka, even offering him another volume of poetry to publish instead of the articles written for daily newspapers and weekly magazines. As a final nail in the coffin I opined that even if the book was published it would not work because everyone had already read all the articles. Nonetheless, Khoka's enthusiasm for the project did not reduce one bit and he applied himself to shortlisting a set of columns from old journals. He asked me to suggest a suitable name for the collection but try as I might I could not come up with one.

It was around this time that I ran into SHA one day. As soon as he heard the idea of a collection of columns he suggested *Nirbachito Kolam* (Selected Columns). '*Nirbachito Kolam*? What sort of a name is that? A column is for a newspaper or a journal. If it's put in a book it can't be called a column any more. It should be called an essay or a paper,' I reasoned. However, calling my columns essays was an even more daunting thought, especially since such essays were expected to be very well researched and quite detailed. My columns were light, mostly irreverent and could never be passed off as serious research. Ultimately, it was SHA's suggestion that ended my reservations. Khoka liked the name *Nirbachito Kolam* too, probably because he wished to retain the word 'column' in keeping with the origin of the writings.

Despite my lack of interest the book was finally published and, as he had expected, it did exceedingly well. The entire first edition was sold out within the span of one book fair and a second edition had to be commissioned immediately. Khoka could not stop smiling; he was happy about the sales but also quite surprised. Even though he had believed in the book he had not expected such a response to a collection of old columns. He requested me to sit at the stall in the fair, where many people wished to get their copies of the book autographed by me. Even the books of poetry were selling well and once his entire stock was exhausted Khoka had to order fresh ones. He informed me that no volume of poetry had ever sold at the fair as well as mine had. Not just from Dhaka, people were turning up from all over to meet me, to queue up and buy signed copies of the book. To me the entire thing was nothing short of strange and frankly quite incredible.

When there was no work at the hospital or I had a sudden free afternoon to myself I would drop in at the discussions of Asim Saha's literary club Ityadi in Nilkhet. It was there that I ran into R one day. We stared at each other for a long moment, the many unsaid words between us hanging like tangible entities, reminding us that despite going back a long way we did not know anything about each other or each other's lives any more. Emerging from the club I asked him, 'Want to come with me?' Without asking anything he simply replied, 'Yes.' We took a rickshaw to Armanitola and on the way R informed me that his prawn farm had folded up. During his long stay in Mithekhali he had written new poems and a new song and he told me about those too. He sang the song to me while we were on the

rickshaw—'Bhalo achi, bhalo theko, akasher thikanai chithi likho'—
and every word touched my heart. It was that very afternoon, after I
returned to Armanitola with R, when NM came and made that scene
at my door.

R could only stand and stare in disbelief at my happy life. 'What
do you think?' I had asked with a touch of arrogance in my tone. 'Only
you can,' he had conceded. 'What's there not to? You have to want it
enough! I should have done this a long time ago. My own house, my
own money, no one to interfere or to order me around, no excuses or
explanations required—is there anything happier than that?'

Later that evening, while R was still there, MM came by with an
offer. Having managed a car from somewhere, he was on his way to
Mymensingh and wanted to know if I wished to accompany him. A
short story writer, MM was also the editor of a weekly magazine called
Bichinta. He had somehow found out where I worked and dropped by
at the hospital one day to meet me. During night shifts—when the
doctors were forbidden from sleeping or dozing off even if there were
no patients—he used to call and we would speak at length. It felt nice
to talk to him. MM never veered towards society or politics; he would
only talk about funny things and it seemed he had the book *Hashir
Golpo* (Funny Stories) memorized! He had dropped by my place at
Armanitola too. He would regale me with his old stories of running
away to Brazil and his subsequent long stay there. He had since
broken up with his maddeningly beautiful wife Kabita, moved back
to Bangladesh to settle in Iskaton and shortened his name. Except for
some obvious fat on the bones and a healthy glow on the skin nothing
much had changed for him since.

'It's been a long time. How are you?' I inquired. Sitting on the
carpet and sipping tea he nodded. 'Yes, it's been many years. I am
doing quite well. This place of yours, you have done it up quite nicely!'
I looked around and could not help but silently agree. Yes, I had done
it up nicely. I remembered that old rhyme about the sparrow and the
tailorbird, the latter proudly declaring how it lived in its own nest and
not in someone else's. The news of MM's break-up with Kabita had
been very upsetting. It had been nice seeing the two of them together,
high on their youth and swimming against the tide. On asking him
why they had broken up, if there was a way to resolve their differences

and if he had tried to resolve them at all, I received mostly evasive answers. I advised him to sort things out with her and start afresh. It was doubtful how much of that advice actually managed to reach him.

I took MM up on his Mymensingh offer quite readily and so did R. The two of them were meeting after a long time. With them in the front seat and me in the back we set off for Mymensingh. Jhunu khala joined us en route; we picked her up from Bhooter Gully. She too was meeting R after a long time. R told us that he wanted to go and meet Yasmin once we reached Mymensingh. The car sped past Jaidevpur and then Bhaluka. Just as we were passing Trishal the tyres suddenly skidded and the car swerved dangerously on the road. By some fortuitous turn of events, just as we were about to be plunged deep into the ravine the car swerved at the last minute and wedged itself along the edge. Inside the car the four of us had just stared death in the face. We simply sat there for a long there, to calm ourselves down and gather our bearings.

After dropping Jhunu khala at Nani's we reached the large black gates of Abakash only to find them locked from the inside. It was already quite late in the night. We did not dare wake Father up at such an hour. He was only going to let loose a volley of questions at me: how did I come at such an hour, with whom, and so on. Besides, if he noticed R in the car there was going to be hell to pay. Swallowing our pride and with no other choice in front of us, we spent the night at Yasmin's and returned to Abakash the next morning. We had decided that MM was going to pick us up on his way back to Dhaka. In the evening when the car came and we were about to leave, R suddenly said, 'I want to talk to Yasmin.' Yasmin had been staying at Abakash. I pulled her to a corner and whispered, 'R wants to meet you.'

'Why?'

'What do you mean why? He's near the gate. Go and see him.'

'No.'

'Why do you say no? What harm will you come to if you speak to him?'

'No, I won't go.'

'So strange! On our way here he kept saying he wanted to meet Yasmin. And now you don't want to meet him? He's waiting right there. Just a few words and we'll be off. What's your problem?'

No matter how hard I tried I was unable to send Yasmin to see R. I went back to him and informed him that Yasmin did not want to talk.

'She isn't coming? Did you tell her I wanted to see her?'

'I did. She still doesn't want to.'

I could sense he was disappointed and I was sad to see him so. Instead of telling him she did not wish to see him perhaps I should have lied and said she was not at Abakash or something to that effect. Perhaps he would not have been so sad had he known she was not home. We did not talk too much on our way back. R had to roll down the window twice to throw up. Apparently both of them had gotten drunk at Mymensingh. MM dropped us off at Armanitola and left.

I asked R to stay over that night. Deep in the night when I felt his arms around me, when he brought his face near mine to kiss me, I let him. When he dragged me closer to his body I let myself get close to him again. It was as if I was with the old R, I was still the old me, and our separation had never happened at all. It seemed as if we were still meeting every day, still in love, our bodies still attuned to each other's touch. The warmth of his breath and the feverish glow on his skin seemed to drive away the cold that had nested within me for long. I knew his body, his every touch and I knew when he was going to yawn, when he was going to get up and stretch his arms behind his head before lighting a cigarette. I remembered which side he preferred sleeping on, how many pillows he required, which hand or finger he was going to gesticulate with while speaking—there was nothing about him I did not know. Try as I might I could never think of R as a stranger. And the more I thought about it the more I was convinced that it was the bizarreness of marriage that was behind all our problems. Did marriage truly bring people together? Then could divorce drive them apart just as easily? I wanted to tell him that he could live with me as long as he wished to, like it was his own house. Instead I told him simply, 'If you ever wish to come over don't hesitate.' Staring at me impassively, R did not respond.

'Are you still seeing that girl?'

'Yes, I am,' he replied in a dry tone.

'Aren't you planning to get married?'

'Yes, we are.' A slight smile appeared on the corner of his lips before vanishing just as fast.

I examined his right thumb that night; it was black and had begun to rot. The next morning I took him to a doctor I knew, got the thumb cleaned of pus and infected blood and had it dressed. The finger was showing signs of gangrene and there was a chance that the infection was going to spread until the only course of action left would be to amputate the entire hand or risk problems in peripheral circulation. His blood could clot and obstruct a blood vessel to the heart or the brain! I could not think of what to tell him. He looked so much more peaceful than before that I felt sorry to have to tell him anything. He was not being able to use his right hand so I had to feed him and help him clean up afterwards.

As he was about to leave I held his bandaged hand in mine and said, 'If there's any trouble, go to the doctor. Or come here and I will make arrangements for your care. This infection is not a good sign.' The doctor had written a prescription for him and I reminded him to take his medicines regularly. 'You have money with you?' He nodded. If he did have money he would have said so and not merely nodded. I extended 500 taka towards him but he was too awkward to take it from me. Instead he looked at me and said, 'You will need it.'

'I will take care of that. You keep this.' There was no response. I could see that he was embarrassed. 'You have given me so much. This time let me help you.' I tucked the money inside his pocket and he turned around and left. I stood there watching him leave, tears streaming down my cheeks. Neither of us knew where, or if at all, we were going to run into each other again.

~

A few days later a notice arrived from the landlord asking me to vacate the house. I was already anticipating something of this nature ever since the day NM had made a scene at the front gate. The notice arrived long before my anxieties had had time to grow to their full potential. I had spoken to Khoka about it and he was already looking for a new house. However, everywhere he searched it was the same old story again. A single woman, alone, without a husband! How could a woman stay alone? She was a doctor. So what? There had to be a husband. It made no difference if an unmarried woman was a doctor, an engineer, a scientist or a prostitute—they were all the same. In fact, women were nothing but trouble! While looking for a house for me Khoka experienced it all: the ridicule, the astonishment, the sky falling on one's head, the scrunched eyebrows and the pursed lips, lines of anxiety on every forehead, the pitiful clucking of the tongue and the helpless expressions of astonishment. However, before he could find another house the incident happened.

Mother had gone to Mymensingh for the night. I had invited MM over for dinner to thank him for his earlier generosity in taking us to Mymensingh by car. He brought three cans of beer with him to have before dinner. He sat finishing his drink and since I was not much of a drinker I was sipping tea and listening to his stories. He seemed so different from the person I used to know so long ago. It was as if he was an entirely new person, more courteous and soft-spoken, more lively and much more profound. The beer was not yet over when there was a sudden knock.

I opened the door to find Father and Dada standing there. As soon as he saw MM, Father gave him such a dirty look that I was forced to ask the poor boy to leave. MM left without even having dinner. I was still happy seeing the two of them—it was their first visit to my new house and the first chance for me to show Father that I could be self-reliant. Were they in Dhaka for some work? Had they gotten late and could not return to Mymensingh? Or were they there only to see me, to see how I was doing, how my work was going and how I had done up my own place? Perhaps they wanted to see if I was studying for my FCPS, or perhaps they had dropped by simply to check on me, to see how I was coping financially and perhaps to lend a helping hand if required. Father said nothing despite my obvious curiosity about their visit. I instructed Lily to make some rice and soon dinner was served but neither of them wanted to eat anything. They simply sat there, their faces long, not saying anything in response to my numerous questions.

'The man who was here, who's he?' The question was directed at my brother.

Dada looked at me and I replied, 'MM, he is the editor of *Bichinta*.'

Father's questioning gaze was fixed on Dada who softly repeated, 'His name is MM. He is the editor of the journal *Bichinta*.'

'Why was he here?' Yet again, it was directed at Dada who repeated the question to me.

'Why was that man here?'

I turned towards Father and said, 'Just like that.'

Dada relayed the answer again. 'Just like that.'

'How is she related to him?' Meant for Dada again, who turned to me on cue. 'How are you two related?'

I jerked my shoulder and replied, 'Just friends.'

'Just friends,' he repeated to Father like before.

The dinner on the table was getting cold. Father walked up and down the balcony for a while. He called Dada a number of times and they spoke in whispers. I had no way of knowing what the big secret was all about. They did not have clothes for the night and I offered them my saris if they wished to use those as lungis. Father looked at Dada again and shook his head in refusal; he did not wish to change for the night. I spread a new bedsheet on the bed I shared with Mother and asked them to use it for the night. Father refused that too. When I asked where they were planning to sleep I was told it was none of my business. No matter how hard I tried I could not convince him to take the bed. So unbending were they, physically and otherwise, that I had no way of forcing their hand. I did not have an extra mattress I could give them and the only thing I could do was to give them a bedsheet to spread on the floor. But Father did not want to sleep; he wanted to stay up the entire night with my brother beside him. I noticed him holding a copy of *Sugandha* and I could imagine someone like him reading such a disgusting piece of trash. *Sugandha* was a right-wing mouthpiece that thrived on abusing people, sexual gossip, and fake news, rumours and rubbish op-eds— basically anything that reeked of yellow journalism. Unable to change their mind till late in the night I finally went to sleep.

The next morning as I was getting ready to leave for work I noticed the two of them were also ready and raring to go. They were planning to return to Mymensingh. 'Can't you stay back one more day?' When they tersely informed me they could not stay back all I could do was nod in agreement. Then to my utter shock I was told that I was going to return to Mymensingh with them! No reasons were furnished, except that I had to. All I could do was laugh at the preposterous suggestion. I had duties in the gynaecology ward that I had to attend to urgently. Besides, some patients were waiting to see me so it was imperative for me to get to work.

Father informed me that I was not going to go back to the hospital any more. Instead, I had to go back to Mymensingh with them. Barely had I turned around to leave after firmly refusing to do as they were asking than Father let out a feral roar and lunged at me. The first slap seemed to dislodge my head from my body. The next series of fierce blows fell on me like the stones pelted at the Jamaraat in Mina during Hajj. He pushed me to the floor and the blows were replaced by kicks aimed at my back and my stomach. He ran and picked up the beer cans and threw them at me. One of them hit me on the forehead, another on the lips; instantly there was blood everywhere. Lunging at me again he picked me up by the hair and hurled me at the almirah, my head banging against the mirror. I remember seeing my reflection in the mirror, my face and mouth caked with blood. Unable to understand his rage, all I could do was stare at him helplessly. The trembling stopped, to be replaced by an overwhelming lethargy as if I was going to faint.

Father threw the copy of *Sugandha* at me. Dada picked it up, opened it and spread it out before me. 'They've published your tales. Everything you have been doing.' Uninterested in whatever anyone might have written I mustered the last ounce of my willpower and stood up. Picking up the apron I started walking towards the door. Father ran to the door and blocked it so I could not pass. Hardening my voice I said, 'I have to go to the hospital. I am getting late.'

With double the force he replied, 'You don't have to go anywhere.'

'I have to,' I screamed, realizing that my voice was choking with tears. I could not look at Father's bloodshot eyes any more, so intense was the savagery in them. He cared nothing for what I wanted, despite my earnest pleas. I had never imagined he was going to stop me from going to the hospital one day, nor in my wildest dreams had I thought he was ever going to tell me I could no longer work. An unbelievable set of things was happening and all I could think was that it could not possibly be true. I told myself it was a nightmare, that I was asleep and imagining the most improbable of things. Any moment I was going to wake up to find myself on my pristine white bed, the full moon flooding in through the window and covering me like a blanket.

None of my protests amounted to anything. Every time I tried explaining that whatever they had read in *Sugandha* was a lie, Father shut me up. He had caught a man red-handed in my room at night and that was all the proof he required. Although they did not really require proof since the plans had been made before they had set off from Mymensingh. They dragged me downstairs, Lily following close at our heels, and Father locked the door and put the key in his pocket. I was dragged into a big car waiting outside and we set off for Mymensingh. My soul was left behind in Dhaka, with my happy little life and my job, where undoubtedly there would be chaos because of my absence. All the doctors of the department would notice my absence and a red mark would appear beside my name, along with another shade of doubt about my abilities. The energy I was putting in at the hospital, taking care of so many patients and learning on the go, was meant to help me for the FCPS. It was very contagious, this examination. The sight of someone else engrossed in the preparations made one want to study. Had Father been serious about destroying all my future hopes that day? I could not even begin to think about it.

I was locked up in my old room at Abakash. Father hung a big lock at the gate and screamed from the other side, 'This is how you must live from now on. You are not allowed to leave the house any more. No more jobs. You don't have to be a doctor either. You've sprouted wings, is it? I'm going to burn them off.' The headline of the article on me in *Sugandha* was 'Taslima Nasrin is now flying around'. I was flying from one man to another every other day, a bee perennially in search of honey. I had been seen with a tall, dark man on a rickshaw one day, then with a fair, chubby one on another occasion. Who would have thought that a yellow-stained hack article in a dirty rag like *Sugandha* had the power to destroy my happy life! Father had tremendous faith in the written word. He was inclined to believe whatever he saw in print, irrespective of where it was.

That very day Father sent movers to the Armanitola house to bring all my things piled on a truck back to Mymensingh. From the window I saw all my prized possessions, remnants of my beloved independent life, scattered in the dirt of the courtyard. The key to the locked room stayed in Father's pocket. If Mother had to bring me food she had to borrow the key from him, push the plate of food inside the room and leave, remembering to lock the door behind her. These were the new rules of the house. A bucket had been placed inside the room and whatever I had to do—shit, piss, vomit, spit—had to be done in that. Mother had to follow the rules whether she liked it or not. Often they would shout at me from the other side and she too would join in with the chorus. 'Things were going well. Why did you have to go fool around with those men and mess everything up! Why do they write about you in magazines? There are so many girls out there who are doctors. They are living decently too. And see what you have done to your life. You don't want to get married? Fine, that's all right. So many women who have lost their husbands or who have never gotten married, don't they live alone? Is there ever such a scandal about any of them? You write so much about women and malign men so much in your articles, so why can't you live without them?'

Gollachhut

There was no escape for me from my life of captivity. I was never going to be allowed to leave and there was no one to understand my anguish—the pain of being an alien in one's own home. My sorrows were my own to nurture in loneliness. I was sure the other doctors at Mitford were undeniably astonished and annoyed at my unexpected absence, but there was hardly anything I could do about it. I had lost the reins of my own life to someone else and my inadequacies were chasing after me, hounding me, crushing me and making me feel tiny and insignificant. I wanted to cry, I wanted to talk to someone, but I could do neither. I could only groan like a wounded animal throughout the day.

I was beginning to feel like Bakuli, the girl from Tikatuli who could not speak. She had come to the hospital once with her mother, obviously their first time since neither of them knew where to go, whom to ask for help or where to seek treatment. On my way to work I had noticed them sitting in the corridor of the outpatient ward—a sixteen- or seventeen-year-old girl with a woman of around thirty. Such people could be found a dime a dozen in hospitals but as soon as I glanced at them my eyes had strayed to the young girl staring at me with her big eyes. Did she know me from before? I had simply assumed they were old patients and had gone about my business attending patients waiting in the outdoor gynaecology ward. In the afternoon, on my way out, I was surprised to find them still sitting there. Unable to help myself I had gone up to them and asked, 'Who's the patient?'

'Bakuli.'

'Is that her name?'

'Yes, she's my daughter. Bakuli.' The woman had placed a hand on the girl's back.

'What's happened to her?'

'She doesn't speak.'

'What's her disease? Isn't that why you are here?'

'Bakuli doesn't speak.'

'I understand that. I'm asking what ails her. Stomach issues or breathing trouble perhaps? What have you come to get her treated for?'

'Please get her voice back. So that she can speak like she used to.'

'Since how long has she not spoken?'

'It's been nearly a month.'

The girl was still staring at me, her big round eyes unblinking and so very beautiful! All I could think of was if I had had eyes like her! Her hair was all over the place, a few strands sticking to her sweaty forehead. She was wearing a plain blue sari, slightly dishevelled.

'Why doesn't she speak?'

'I don't know why,' the woman had said in anguish and turning to her daughter continued, 'Bakuli, say something. Tell us what happened. Please speak, please say something. Only once, just once, please say something, Bakuli.'

'What happened to make her stop speaking? Did something happen a month ago?'

Glancing sideways, the woman had got up, come close and leaned in to whisper. 'She was found by the river. They came and informed me and I rushed to bring her back.'

'Why was she lying there?'

'Who knows! Some people had abducted her. She had gone to work at the factory in Jinjiria but did not come back home for two days. Then some people brought me the news.'

'When she was found was she conscious?'

'Yes, she was. She got up and came home with me. I asked her so many times to tell me what had happened. But she didn't speak. She hasn't spoken since.'

'Did something bad happen?'

'They said those men raped her.'

The woman had been crying by then. 'She was born in autumn and her father passed away the next . . .' I did not have time to listen to her story so I had stopped her midway and told her, 'Bring her to the ENT specialist tomorrow. Maybe there's something wrong with her throat.' Having said that I had turned to leave. Suffering people came to the hospital every day and she had been one among many. A question addressed to my departing back had stopped me in my tracks.

'Aapa, will Bakuli never speak again?'

'I really can't say.'

'Aapa, wait a moment, please. You are very kind. Please help me so Bakuli can speak again. Where will I go with her, what will I do?'

While walking away, I had replied, 'Come and see the doctor tomorrow. See what he says.' I had come out of the main gate of the hospital and found a rickshaw. Bakuli was still sitting like before and her mother was staring after me. The entire way back her words had kept echoing in my head. 'Bakuli, please say something.' The next day I had checked the outdoor corridor again but there was no sign of them at all. There were so many patients, but neither mother nor daughter could be seen anywhere. Neither were they there the day after. Perhaps they had come back to the hospital, perhaps they had consulted the doctor as per my advice and perhaps the doctor had informed them there was nothing wrong with the girl's throat. Surely the mother must have kept on imploring, 'Bakuli, please say something.' From that day I always searched for Bakuli in the hospital. I would try and locate her face among the crowd of people in the hospital every day. All I wished to know was if Bakuli had indeed spoken again.

Nirbachito Kolam was selling better than ever, one edition after another was being commissioned, but I remained in my prison like a convicted criminal. Even the vilest criminals were perhaps not abused as much as I. Guests who came to Abakash would peek in to see how I was doing and so would the dogs and the cats. I would stare out of the window at the hens and ducks in the courtyard, wishing I could walk freely in the open like them. During my captivity I also learnt the true meaning of enslavement. Racked with despair I would scream and keep screaming out loud—everyone listened but no one came to help.

I had nothing except what I was wearing: the sari I had arrived in. Unable to bathe I soon began to stink. There was not a single book I could read, no television I could watch, nor a machine I could play music on. There was not a single person I could talk to. The only thing I could do, indefinitely, was lie on my back and count the beams on the roof. The tears had stopped long ago, leaving behind a dry trail on my cheeks. The only things to accompany me were the new anxieties that soon began to plague me—they latched on to my smallest blood vessels and spread to every part of my body till I was enveloped in their blackness. My unannounced absence had surely cost me my job. How was I supposed to rebuild my life after something like that? The edifice of my happy life was crumbling right in front of my eyes and I was staring at a future that looked even darker.

As I lay there, a corpse and nothing else, I could barely recognize the person I had become. Who was I? I had barely managed to stand on my own feet, barely begun to make a life for myself when they had consigned me to the same quagmire of bias, repression and violence I had crawled out of. Father did not understand the extent of his own misdeeds, the extent of the damage he had done to my life. Besides, I was aware that someone like him would perhaps never know. He would never come sit by my side, ask if I had a problem, or inquire if I was happy. How long was I going to be kept a prisoner? Months? Years? What were my crimes? Had I even committed any? My writings always got their fair share of appreciation and criticism. I was used to the tenuousness of it all. The gossip rags too used to write about me quite a bit, where my character was regularly dissected for public consumption. They were not interested in what I wrote. I was a woman, so they were interested in my private life. And for the same reason it was easy to malign my character, since anything could be said. Gossip about women always found a wide audience, but just because a few people were saying things about me how fair was it that I had to live my life as a criminal! Who was this benefiting—my family, my parents, my siblings or me?

Father did not know the real reason behind the yellow piece about me in *Sugandha*. He did not know that such magazines wrote salacious gossip to boost sales. If he wanted to know about my life he should have asked me directly. Surely the good people of *Sugandha* did not know more about my private affairs than I did. I was terribly angry with him and in my lonely prison there was nothing I could do but quake with useless rage. The room had been mine once, but locked inside, it began to resemble a coffin to me. I was surprised to find how much of a screaming, stomping child I could be instead of the strong and self-assured woman I was. I had been *flying* so Father had caught me and put me in a cage to teach me a lesson. Since he was my father he was convinced he had the right to do whatever he pleased. I languished in my prison and wondered how much longer I would have to tolerate his rule over my life, his cruelty and his stupidity. Can debts owed to parents only be repaid at death? Did I not have the right to chart the course of my own life? Gradually my last reserve crumbled and left me feeling the most helpless I had ever been in my entire life. So many people used to read my writings and tell me how brave I was, how my words provided courage to numerous women. If only they could have witnessed for themselves how powerless I was, how vulnerable, in chains that someone else had put on me.

Abakash—a part of my soul, an archive of my most precious memories, my beloved—had turned into hell, and so I fled. One morning Mother had just brought me breakfast. All of a sudden, hearing Sufi screaming and the sound of clattering utensils, she ran to the kitchen with the door left ajar behind her. There was no one posted in the drawing room, Father was not home and Dada was in the pharmacy. I ran out of the house in the same sari I was in. I took a circuitous route, the sort no one would have expected me to take; I could not take the main road for fear of rousing suspicions. Neither did I wish to turn around and find someone chasing after me to drag me by my hair back to my prison.

What I wanted the most was a rickshaw, and when I did manage to get one I asked the man to take me towards Sutiakhali House via the road behind Abakash which none of us usually frequented. I knew if anyone had run after me then they would either go towards Serpurkur Paar or Golpukur Paar. As the rickshaw crossed Sutiakhali to take the road adjacent to Rajbari School I directed the man to take me to the bus stand for Tangail. There was a possibility Father would head straight to the bus stand for Dhaka on hearing about my daring escape. Except the local ones there were no other buses at the stand. I immediately boarded one of the buses but it did very little to ease the pounding in my chest. It was not completely safe since a local bus would stop at every bus stand on its way to Tangail. I could have waited for the express bus that went directly to Tangail, but waiting alone at the bus stand would not have been the wisest thing to do. Besides, I could not be sure when the express bus would make an appearance. Father could turn up any moment after failing to find me at the bus stop for Dhaka, or someone might recognize me and send him word. That was the reason I had avoided taking the train too.

Inside the flimsy tin can that was the local bus, I sat and fiercely wished for us to leave the city behind as fast as possible. Unable to stay still, my eyes strayed to the window time and again; the pounding in my heart had not stopped. When the bus finally set off not a soul could have known about the terrible war raging inside me. The bus found its usual route—people getting off and new people getting on, the conductor beating on the tin side with his palms to signal the driver accordingly. Being a girl I was not allowed to sit in any of the normal seats. I was ushered to the 'exclusive' seat beside the driver, right by the scalding hot engine. There was no place to put my feet so I had to fold them up to my chest and sit still. It took nearly eight hours to reach Tangail. Once there I got off and went in search of buses bound for Dhaka.

By the time I reached Dhaka it was almost eleven in the night. There were no relatives whom I considered family any more; I wanted to get away from all of them. They had declared me an outcast. I did not wish to see them and neither did I wish for my presence to cause them discomfort. I was hungry and I knew if I went to a restaurant they would also let me use their phone. More than the food I was anxious about who I could ask for a place to stay. Unable to think for too long, once I did get to that phone I dialled the first number that came to my mind.

MM was astounded by what I told him. I learnt from him that he had called the hospital asking about me and they had informed him that I was on leave. How could I describe to him what sort of leave I had been on! The only thing I could do was to ask him if I could stay the night at his place. He agreed at once, and even came to pick me up on his motorcycle to take me back to his place. I was given the extra bed meant for guests in their drawing room. I cannot recall how the entire next day passed, except for the fact that I slept for what seemed like an eternity. I could have slept more, should have slept the entire week given the ordeal I had been through, but MM came with fresh news the day after. His mother was not very happy that an unknown woman was staying in the house without reason because it could potentially become fodder for gossip. If MM and I were to get married then my stay at their house would make sense. That very day a man arrived with a heavy green book, which MM spread out in front of me for a signature. Again someone wanted my signature! Like a complete halfwit I signed the document sealing my fate.

Not for a moment did I pause to consider the significance of the signature. Why did I sign? Because I was angry with Father and I had nowhere to go either. So many years later when I reflect on that moment I cannot help but berate myself for signing that piece of paper that day. I might have been angry with Father but was it really necessary to take such a step? I could have channelled that rage into proving to him once and for all that I had the guts and means to live the sort of independent life I wanted. I did not have a place to go to so I should have looked for one! There were no hostels for doctors but I could have eaten humble pie and sought refuge with a relative. I could have even tolerated Geeta's misbehaviour and gone to Chotda's house, or found a place on the floor at Boromama's. It would have only been for a night! I could have waited for Khoka to find me another place. Why did I call MM instead of him? Khoka's shop had been closed and I did not have his personal number, but I could have waited till the next morning and called him for help!

Had I lost all faith in myself? Had I secretly begun to regret my husbandless life? Perhaps I was overcome by a sudden desire to marry and have children like most other women! Had I fallen for MM? No, how could I have loved someone I had known for perhaps two days! Was it because I simply wanted a man, to feel a man's touch and the heat of his body, something I could get only through a simple signature? Perhaps I had not realized how much I was craving such a touch, to feel complete after spending so much time pitying and deriding myself, a broken cretin baser than even insects. So I guess it did not matter to me who I was with, given how I was unsure if life amounted to anything at all. The signature was imperative for us to be able to stay in the same house and sleep on the same bed. Obviously, men and women sleep together without signatures all the time. But men are not judged for it while for women it becomes a grievous sin. Such a transgression earns women monikers like slut, whore, hussy and demon. It was after sleeping with MM that I understood that a signature was hardly a barrier to intimacy between two people. As expected, the signature failed to provide me the security of marriage I had hoped for. MM's new congenial persona began to show cracks before long, to reveal the old MM who was still Kabita's ex-husband. The desolate husband would sit and cry for her, weep pitifully on hearing the news of her impending marriage and I could sense my life getting more tangled with every passing day. All I wanted was to turn time back to when MM and Kabita used to be together and happy and very much in love.

No one at the hospital was too surprised by my spell of absence and I soon found out why. The day Father had abducted me from Armanitola he had apparently sent a letter to the department with a request for leave. From the hospital I finally managed to contact Khoka and learnt that he had found another house for me in Shantibag. The landlord had been told that Khoka's sister was going to rent the place, a doctor who was going to live alone. The landlord, an educated gentleman, had agreed without fuss. MM was also looking for other places nearby, preferably a big one where his relatives too could move in. Since I was quite impressed by the Shantibag house I convinced MM to give up his search and move in there with me. In that pretty two-storey house the two of us embarked on our new adventure.

I would leave for Mitford early in the morning. MM and I would not run into each other the entire day; he usually left after me and returned late in the night. When he returned he was either already drunk, or had a bottle of alcohol with him so he could be. If not the entire bottle then he finished at least half, and while drinking he wrote editorials for *Bichitra*. MM was a fast writer, no corrections were required, no pausing to think of a suitable turn of phrase. Alcohol did wonders to his mind and whatever he wrote, he wrote well. If he had tried he could have written beautiful stories but despite having started on it, for some unknown reason he never got around to finishing it.

One day, during his usual routine of drinking and writing, he asked me to stop contributing columns for *Purbabhash*. Taken aback, I could not find any credible reason why he wanted me to do so all of a sudden. Gradually, certain recurring criticisms from his end—a certain article was not good enough or I should avoid a particular journal—convinced me that MM was deliberately trying to tear me down so he could maintain control over me. Perhaps outsiders were lucky enough to meet the sober MM because I could only ever get an audience with the drunk one. He had to drink every night without fail and he would not listen to any of my protests when he did. Roaring drunk, he usually came to bed a little before dawn. Except for sex there was no other perceivable relationship between us. Not that the sex could have been taken lightly, given how unfailingly regular it became for us every night. The one bit of information I had not been privy to, and which I soon found out, was MM's long-term relationship with a rich married woman. The house in Iskaton where MM lived was apparently her property. They had broken up for some time and it was around then that MM and I had gotten close. But the break-up did not last long and MM soon resumed his relationship with her. Consequently, the drinking too continued unabated every night and he did not waste time slipping back to his old self. If only I had known earlier that when he used to call me at the hospital at night it was usually because he was drunk beyond measure by then and that I was just one of the many calls he made in such a state. Instead, I had built up an image of a passionate and sensitive man in my head! Alas, the vagaries of an alcoholic! He would be laughing his head off one moment and screaming his lungs out the next. He would get angry and curse at me like a sailor or take off his belt and beat me black and blue. None of this had any reason for happening, it happened because he wanted to do these things.

The first floor of the house had been partitioned into two halves; in one Shoma and her family lived. Shoma, in her early twenties, would come over often to chat with me. On nights when MM's alcohol-induced rampage got out of hand, I often sought refuge with Shoma to save myself from the crazy man. Who knew what the senseless drunkard would do. One night MM came back home, dragged my sleeping form off the bed and began to beat me. There was no reason for this sudden outburst and none of my pleas and anguished queries seemed to make a difference. A series of slaps on my cheeks, a punch to my face that resulted in a bleeding eye, and soon he was choking me and I could not unclench his tightening fingers from my neck. Just as suddenly he let go and began to laugh hysterically. Still laughing, he dragged me by the hair and threw me out of the room, locking me out and forcing me to spend the rest of the night sitting on the stairs. The same scene played out again the next night. On the third night when he tried to drag my bleeding form back to the room for a second round I was forced to run to the landlord to save my life. I cannot recall another time in my life when I was as embarrassed, as helplessly trapped and struggling under the collective weight of shame, fear, disgust, anxiety and my brutally battered self-esteem. All I could do was berate myself. I had been alone before and I was still alone. The only difference was that earlier I did not have any superfluous troubles while with MM I was co-habiting with trouble personified.

What had I done! Who had I chosen as my refuge! I had been enough for myself, I had never wanted for anything else. The more I thought about my actions the more I felt like sinking into the earth under the ignominy of it all. My self-loathing was telling me loud and clear that I had brought this upon myself; I had allowed myself repeatedly to be so debased and derided. What need did I have of a security blanket in the form of a husband? Why had I felt the need to conform to what society was telling me to do? It had led me into a quagmire populated by husbands, families and babies, and the more I tried extricating myself from its grasp the deeper I seemed to be sinking. The customs I had tried embracing because of social pressure were wrapped around my neck like a noose around cattle. All I had gained from it was a sham marriage.

I realized I had slipped back into the old social conditioning despite having always actively resisted it. I also realized that whether I was married or not made no difference whatsoever—if there was going to be gossip and slander about me, there was no way for me to avoid it. So why endure one evil in order to avoid another? Not that this was a new realization. I had no illusions left regarding men, had lost them long ago. So why had I gone and done the same thing again? Why had I placed my trust in a man again? Why had I dreamt that this man would not hurt me like the others had? I was a foolish girl and I should have been aware that the only thing that ever changed was the nature of the pain inflicted. I should have known I could never depend on a man and neither could I expect that a man was going to make me happy. I had been married more than once, I had slept with more than one man—these stigmas were branded on to my skin so much so that a glance at me made people decide that I must be easy.

Even R had come to that conclusion. I met R twice during this interval, the first time at Ityadi. While returning from Ityadi one night amidst torrential rain, we could not find a single rickshaw or a baby taxi. After waiting for a long time when we did manage to get hold of a baby taxi there was no choice for us but to share the ride; it was decided he would drop me off at Shantibag on the way to Indira Road. In the confines of the cab, with the storm raging outside, the half-drunk R wrapped his arm around my waist and murmured to me, 'I want you.' I asked him in what way and he simply raised his eyebrows in response. He only desired my body and on reaching that conclusion I stopped the car near Malibag and got off despite the steady downpour, hoping the rain would wash away my tears. With a suppressed sigh I said my goodbyes to R, silently reminding myself that I could have slept with him if I wanted to. I had wanted to in Armanitola, but I did not want to any more. Till date I had done what others wanted me to do. Going forward, I decided I only wanted to do things my way.

The next time I met R was at Sakura. We had arranged to meet there to discuss the publication of R's collected works. He wanted to compile all of his writings into one book and had asked me to help him out with the publication by arranging for him to speak to my publisher. Just because my books were doing well it did not mean my publisher was going to listen to all of my demands. I did approach Khoka with the proposal, telling him how keen R was about the collection, but Khoka informed me that being keen was not enough to get the book published. A publisher always had to consider the business aspect of such a deal first. If he did not want the collection I suggested he consider some of R's political poems or even his love poems. This last offer was at least something Khoka was interested in pursuing. So I had arranged for them to meet at Sakura to talk it out.

As R and Khoka sat discussing the former's proposal for the collection, I could not help but repeat what I had said to R when he had first told me about it. 'Why do you want a collected volume at all?

Don't people bring out collected works after authors have died?' R, however, was adamant. Even after hours of discussion the deadlock could not be resolved. Khoka was firm that the publishing house was not interested in a collected volume. I tried explaining this to R. 'Of course Vidyaprakash wants to publish your books. Just not the collected volume right away. Try something else.' R was unyielding in his desire and so I persisted. 'How strange! Are you dead that you want to do that? At least if you were old one had reason to consider. You are barely thirty-five! Why do you want a collected volume so early?'

Unable to resolve the stalemate, Khoka left. As we were walking out of Sakura, R was clearly upset and seeing him so only served to trouble me further. The road and our endless journey was perhaps the perfect metaphor for our relationship as it had mutated from the domestic illusions we had once had. R still had difficulty walking and had to stop often to catch his breath. All I wanted was to take a rickshaw and set off on a ride through the city with him like we used to, or sit in the TSC grounds and talk in impromptu verse over tea and jhaalmuri. All I desired was to revisit the time when we were madly in love and to clear the slate of all the despair, hurt and devastation we had caused each other and the differences between us. Placing my hand on his, I looked into his sad mossy eyes and tried to reassure him. 'Don't worry. I will talk to Khoka again about the book.'

'He did not seem too interested,' he sighed and said in response.

'Let's see if I can make him agree on the condition that I will give him more of my books to publish. He's a good guy. I will explain to him that your book too will do well. It's not as if you are any less popular. Everyone is reciting your poems all the time. Publishers don't just look for sales. Sometimes they do want to publish good literature, even if it does not fly off the shelves immediately. Khoka is not as commerce-driven as most other publishers. If not right away he will surely come around.' After he was a bit soothed we walked a bit further and took two rickshaws to our respective destinations.

The night I had sought refuge at my landlord's to flee from MM's wrath, the landlord's wife Parul, shivering in fear alongside me, had asked me many questions. How did MM and I get together, why, and so on. I was unable to answer a single one of them and kept staring blankly at the white wall of the room instead. Even after Parul offered me the bed in the living room reserved for their guests, I spent the rest of the night staring at the wall. I could not sleep a wink; all I could do was reflect on what was happening to me. Was I losing the ability to talk? Why was I not resisting? Why was I not being able to cry? Had I turned to stone so that even in anguish I could not scream? Why was I not breaking down the walls closing in on me and abusing the people who were responsible for it?

All I could think of was Bakuli. Was I becoming like her? Had the shock rendered me speechless? It seemed to me that I had been mute for far longer, ever since that fateful day when Father had destroyed my happy little life at Armanitola and shattered my spine in the process. I could not accuse anyone neither could I have a conversation with myself. My voice was choked from fear and shame; I had failed myself again and again as if that was my only lot. Society was not allowing me to live my life on my own terms and I too had seemingly given up my strength, courage, pride and anger. The walls were gradually trying to crush me. Something in my head wanted out, it was going to burst out if I didn't let it. I kept telling myself over and over again—this time think about yourself, say what you wish to and don't sacrifice your happiness for the sake of someone else's. Take care of yourself, find love for yourself and end this cycle of self-inflicted misery! The blank white wall had a pair of eyes on it that were watching me while closing in on me from all four sides. I was tossing and turning on the bed, twisting my head as if in a daze, and muttering to myself, 'Bakuli, please say something. Bakuli, please talk . . .'

I finally spoke when the fitful night had been dispelled by the first light of dawn. I told Parul that I was leaving and I was only going to come back if they made MM leave. Parul tried telling me to sort it out with him, that men were going to be men and I should not take an irrational emotional decision. I firmly refused to entertain the suggestion and informed her that for the first time in my life at least this one decision I had not taken emotionally.

I left the troubles of Shantibag behind and took refuge at Pakhi's house. She set up a room for me in her apartment, complete with a writing table for my work. I would come back to her place from the hospital and spend the rest of the time chatting with her; I was more interested in hearing about people's lives than writing anyway. We had originally met when Pakhi had come over to the house in Shantibag one day as an admirer keen on meeting me. Since then our interactions had gradually developed into a great friendship. A divorcee herself, Pakhi used to live alone in an apartment on the tenth floor. Her ex-husband was in America. She was very beautiful and always so well turned out that it was nearly impossible to tell how old she was. Somewhat a mother, a lot like a sister, she candidly shared many of her life's stories with me.

She had a daughter who was married and lived somewhere in the Arab world while Pakhi lived on her own in Dhaka. She did not work, just did some occasional sewing and embroidery work that she tried to supply to shops that were interested. While still married, her husband had bought a house in her name in Pallabi in Dhaka. After the divorce she had sold the house, bought a smaller apartment, and put the rest of the money in the bank. Her strength of will that enabled her to live alone was what had first amazed me. Much to my astonishment she confessed to have drawn that strength from my writing, something I had never even considered possible!

Pakhi's older sister came to Dhaka from Kustia and she too turned out to be an equally avid reader of my work. In fact, when we first met she could not believe her eyes. When she was finally convinced and overcame her initial surprise, she gave me a tight, long hug. Justifiably I could only react to such limitless admiration with awkward bafflement. Perhaps from my writing they had all built up a particular image of me in their heads: terribly brave, completely intolerant of men and ready to bust balls. Thus, meeting me in person was probably equally surprising and managed to reduce some of their exaggerated expectations. Would they have fainted had they known how I had endured domestic violence day in and day out?

Pakhi was an ardent admirer of mine but even in her house my sense of abandonment did not lessen. Neither did Pakhi offer me her shelter indefinitely, or even till I had made my own arrangements. Besides, I did not wish to take advantage of her generosity, so my time under her roof soon came to an end. I had many friends in Dhaka, many more relatives, or at least people I could go to for help. I also knew that not one of them would be too pleased to see me. Practically homeless after leaving Pakhi's house, I decided to put up at a hotel.

A new chapter of my life commenced at the hotel in Gulistan—eating in restaurants, spending the entire day at Mitford and returning to the hotel at night only to sleep. The hotel too was not an easy place to get used to. Most such cheap hotels in the busier and more congested parts of the city were not the kind of place a man would usually take his family to. Even the manager of the hotel I was in had been flabbergasted, to say the least, on seeing me. It was Khoka again who had come to my rescue. There had been so many people around me during the good times, but not one of them was to be found when the going got tough. During one of the lowest moments of my life only Khoka had been there beside me like a brother, a father and a friend. Not once did he try to take advantage of my sorry situation, like so many others had before.

He took the manager of the hotel aside and chatted him up. 'Don't we all have our sisters and mothers, hey! We have to look out for each other, don't we? She's a doctor, you know, works at Mitford. Till we sort out the living arrangements she has no choice but to stay at a hotel.' The manager had thankfully been convinced enough to let me take up a room. In fact, he even went so far as to keep an eye out for me henceforth, to make sure no one ever turned up to cause any trouble. Despite all the precaution, inside the room I was still spending sleepless nights. Anyone could have just kicked down the door and entered the room. Since the hotel was populated primarily by drunkards and scoundrels there was no way I could be at peace. Fortunately, this itinerant life came to end when I received word from my landlord at Shantibag that they had served MM a notice and evicted him from the house. It was only after returning to the Shantibag house that I finally breathed a sigh of relief—I could try and build another life for myself, just like I had done at the old house in Armanitola.

The first night back, I fell into a peaceful sleep on the floor of the empty house. Just as silently, even without me realizing it, the self-confidence that I had lost had come back. I was no longer weighed down by the feeling that I was a wretched, despised creature, the lowest of the low.

The One I Yearn for, Night and Day

Asim Saha called me one afternoon with the news that R was ill and had been admitted to Holy Family Hospital, cabin number 231. Without wasting a moment I took a rickshaw and rushed to see him. R loved tuberoses and I bought some from a flower vendor near the main gate of the hospital. Walking up to the nurses' room I requested a nurse to send word to 231 about me. Not everyone was allowed inside, so I wanted to enter only if R was feeling up to it. I was also not sure if I was going to be allowed, since there was a possibility that there were other people in the cabin who would rather not have me there. The nurse told me to simply go up without bothering to wait but I insisted on the permission. I was certain that whether someone liked it or not R would not turn me away and I was soon proven right. In the cabin three of his sisters were already there, but I hardly exchanged a word with any of them. As I walked up to the bed and stood by him, he asked me to sit. Let alone being able to smell the tuberoses, he had tubes running into his nostrils. Keeping the flowers on the table I pulled a chair near his head and asked, 'What has happened?'

'The doctors are saying it's an ulcer.' He did not move his head, only his eyes indicated that he was trying to look around. His face was pale.

'A stomach ulcer is not something very severe. You will get well soon.'

'I will?'

'Of course! Nearly 80 per cent of the population gets stomach ulcers. It's not even a proper disease.' With a half-smirk I continued, 'Do you know how you look with those tubes in your nose?' I was stroking his hair softly with my right hand, the left on his chest. 'Does it hurt?'

'It does quite a bit.'

'Don't worry. You will get well very soon.'

'Who knows! Maybe this is it.'

'Don't say such things.'

In a faint voice he told me about all the people who had come to see him, the writers and poets, and all that they had said to him. He also told me about Shimul.

'She was here today. She just sat there quietly, her face glum.'

'Why?'

'Maybe looking at me made her sad. She didn't say.'

'When are the two of you tying the knot?'

'Let's see, if I get well . . .'

'Of course you will get well.'

His face had lit up at the mention of Shimul and I could see how much he was in love with her. He continued. 'She was sitting far away. I asked her to come closer but she didn't.'

'Why?'

'She is angry. She is angry that I'm ill.'

'That's great. She'll make you toe the line then.'

His face was alight with joy and I tried to pull a smile on mine too. As if it was not hurting me one bit to have to give him up to someone else. R and I never spoke about my personal life. Whatever he knew he had probably heard from someone else. Neither did he ask me if I was living with someone, or how I was for that matter. He spoke about himself, about his relationship, his poetry, his disease and his happiness.

'Have you written anything about Shimul, a new poem perhaps?'

'Yes.' He nodded weakly.

'Do you have it here?'

'Here! In the hospital!' He gave me a feeble smile.

'Why not! Isn't your notebook of poems always with you wherever you go?'

'Oh, that's another thing. Another reason why I can't wait to get out of this place.'

'Calm down. Get well first and then you can go home. The doctor will give you some medicines to have before and after meals. Have those regularly. If you go out keep an antacid with you at all times and have it whenever you think you are uncomfortable.'

'The doctor tells me I have high blood pressure.'

'High blood pressure? Really! Why would you have high blood pressure at this age? Did the doctor check properly?'

'He told me.'

'Then you have to be even more careful. Has he given you medicines for it?'

'Yes, he has.'

'What did he say? To keep drinking and smoking like before?'

'I think I will have to quit this time.'

'Yes, quit. Quit it all. Eat at regular intervals and you will never have to suffer from stomach trouble ever again.'

I gave him my word before leaving that I was going to visit him soon but I could not keep my promise. A few days later Yasmin and Milan came to stay at the Shantibag house. Milan had got a job in Dhaka and they had put up at his sister's house in Basabo. I asked them to come and stay at my place instead. I had been living in exile, trying to scrub the ignominy of my previous marriage off my skin. I had not returned to Abakash and neither had I met or socialized with any of my relatives in the city. In response to an article I had written for *Purbabhash* someone had responded caustically, 'A person missing an ear tries to walk on one side of the road to avoid being seen, someone missing both ears walks down the middle of the road since they have nothing to hide.' True to the wise assessment I decided I was going to start walking down the middle of the road with both my ears missing. I was shameless, which is why I wrote shameless columns. The review was less a critique and more a hateful tirade against me. Since there was no end to these kinds of reactions I firmly resolved that I was going to do exactly what they were accusing me of—be shameless when negotiating their civilized world. Although the stigma of having married multiple times and facing threats to one's reputation were compelling reasons for many women to hide their faces in shame and stay in the shadows, such entrenched and naturalized misogyny did nothing for me.

A few days later I was visiting Chotda's house with Yasmin to meet Suhrid when I received an unexpected telephone call. A call for me at his house was indeed a rare occurrence and I had to make sure whether it was meant for me at all. It was meant for me all right—

it was a call from Caroline Wright, an American poet who was in Bangladesh on a Fulbright scholarship to do research on Bengali women poets. My poems were among the ones she was studying and she had already translated some into English. I had met her twice at the Bangla Academy while she had been working on the translations with Muhammad Nurul Huda. I cannot say that I liked her too much; she had this annoying air about her as if she was a leading authority on the politics, socio-economic relations, literature and culture of Bangladesh after having lived there for only a short while.

Meanwhile, she had fallen in love with Syed Manjarul Islam, a university professor who had also assisted her with the translation. Caroline had an indomitable curiosity regarding other people's private lives. How many times had I married, who had I married— she was overly enthusiastic about any and every personal detail. One would naturally assume that being a foreigner she would have been least interested in other people's affairs. But I soon found out that she was more concerned about the poets themselves than their poetry, remarkably similar to the gossipy old crones from the fairy tales we were brought up on. Since she spoke beautiful Bengali, I had arranged for her to recite a poem at a programme that was to be televised. The channel had only asked me initially but I had convinced the producer to bring Caroline on board too. Caroline had been delighted. She had said glasses made her look unattractive and had taken them off before the shoot. It had made reading from the paper that much more difficult but she had stubbornly refused to put them back on. As a child I used to be fascinated with glasses, would stare into the sun at noon for hours, or poke myself in the eye wishing something would go wrong with them so that Father would be forced to take me to the optometrist and get me glasses.

Caroline's voice drifted down the line as she spoke in her beautiful broken Bengali. 'Do you know R has passed away?'

'What did you say?'

'R is dead.'

'What rubbish. Why will he die?'

'He passed away this morning.'

'Don't be crazy. I went and met him the other day at Holy Family. He was not so sick that he would die.'

'But I heard he's dead.'

'Who told you?'

'Someone did. A poet did.'

'Who? Whoever it is, it's a lie.'

'But this poet won't lie. Why don't you check once?'

'Listen, Caroline, maybe they said R was in the hospital and you misheard.'

'I heard quite clearly that he was dead.'

'Then whoever has informed you doesn't know anything. They must have heard from someone that R is sick and made that into something else. So many rumours keep floating around.'

'Anyway, do find out if you can.'

There was no reason for me to believe Caroline's news. Nevertheless, I immediately went to Holy Family with Yasmin. Not finding R in 231 I went up to a nurse who informed me that the concerned patient had been discharged the day before.

'So he got well?'

'Yes, he did.'

'Did he recover completely or did he refuse to stay any longer and simply walked out, pipes in nostrils and all?'

Clearly annoyed at my probing, the nurse snapped back, 'Do doctors discharge patients unless they get well?' She brought out his file for good measure and showed me the relevant part. 'He got well, so the doctor let him go.' Walking out of the hospital we hailed a rickshaw amidst my angry grumbling. 'People simply have no limits. They say whatever they want to. R's fine, he's been discharged, he's home. And these people are saying he's died.' I directed the rickshaw to take us towards Indira Road. 'Why do you want to go to Indira Road?' Yasmin asked. 'I want to see for myself. I just want to confirm that he is safe at home. If he's unwell the nurse would have said so.' I was convinced that the news was not true but I remained distracted the rest of the way. Yasmin probed, 'What are you so worried about? Nothing's happened. It's just a rumour.'

'Yes, that's what it is, a rumour.'

'Why was he in hospital? What did he have?'

'Nothing that serious. He had an ulcer. I went to see him the other day. He was being taken care of fairly well. Why will he die?

There has to be a reason, isn't it? A man who has recovered from an ulcer in a hospital and been discharged and sent home, how am I to believe he is dead? Is there anything more absurd than that? If he had been suffering from something serious I could have still considered the possibility.'

We were headed towards Indira Road but I had no idea where R's house was. I tried replaying that night in my head when he had brought me back to his house from Jhinaidaha, betting on my instinct to help me retrace my steps. I suddenly noticed a few men standing at the entrance to an alleyway, two of whom I knew, including Mainul Ehsan Saber. In an instant a storm rose within me, threatening to unsettle the very foundations of everything I believed in. Trembling, I felt my blood freezing in my veins and darkness descending all around me. Shutting my eyes and gritting my teeth to force myself to stop shivering, I asked Yasmin, 'Why are R's friends here? What's happened? It's true then?'

Yasmin did not speak. As the rickshaw moved forward more people could be seen and many more familiar faces. 'No, it can't be true. Maybe he's gotten more unwell.' Desperate for some reassurance I grabbed Yasmin's hands. 'Tell me, please. That's what it is, isn't it?' But there was nothing Yasmin could say. 'Why are there so many people here today? Is there a poetry recital in this alley somewhere? Or have they come to see R? But why would so many people come?' My voice rang out with suppressed anguish and Yasmin's grasp on my hands tightened in a silent response. We stopped the rickshaw in front of a house that had a crowd of people standing at the gate. I walked past them and ran up the stairs to the first floor. The door was ajar and I could hear someone crying inside. Asim Saha was standing by the door. Barely had I finished my question—'Asimda, what's happened?'—than he burst into tears and howled, 'Nasrin, R is no more.'

'What nonsense!'

My strength seemed to seep away from me like camphor in the wind. I could not keep standing, but leaning against the wall behind me was not helping either. Like a feather I fell, the world spinning around me like a top as everything went black. Except my own cries I could hear no other keening or groaning or distressed voice, not even

Asim's helpless weeping. I could not recognize the faces surrounding me. None of them seemed familiar, shadows floating in the water or perhaps ghostly silvery fish. I was a dead log that had sunk to the bottom and the fish were swimming around me silently. I was not sure how long I was out. Time seemed to have stopped around me; the clock was still ticking, the world was still turning, but in my own little world everything had come to a crashing halt. I could not feel myself within me any more. Rather, I felt absolutely nothing, not even when someone touched my arm or called out my name.

A fish floated towards the dead log and seemed to take on the appearance of Labani as she reached for my arm. Her touch seemed to transport me instantly to a noisy fish market somewhere far away. I was standing there in the melee, sellers and customers shouting over prices amidst a pervasive stench of sweat and dirt, and strangely, in the middle of this chaos, R's prone form was lying on the ground, peacefully asleep. None of the smell or the commotion was making any difference to him. R, my R, the love of my life, the one I yearned for night and day. R was asleep, lying on a striped white sheet spread out on the floor. I knew that sheet well; we had slept on it so many times, made love on it, let it envelop us in its warmth as we found release in each other's embrace, the many nights when R had kissed me, held me tight in his arms and slept soundly on that sheet. And there he was, selfishly taking the entire thing for himself and not once asking me to lie down beside him.

In a whisper, almost leaning in to his ear so only he could listen, I begged, 'R, now isn't the time to sleep. Get up. See, it's me. Let's go somewhere, just the two of us. There are too many people here. Let's just slip away without telling anyone. Just like before when we used to escape crowds and go off on our own somewhere, desperately looking for some solitude. Get up. Even if you don't want to go out, get up and read your poems to me, everything you have recently written. I will lie down with my head in your lap and listen. Come, dazzle everyone with a poem.' No matter what I said R did not get up. The keening cry in the background suddenly turned into a voice. 'What have you come to see? Who have you come to see? Come here! Come, stare at my son to your heart's content. Didn't you hurt him enough? So what have you come to see now?'

I stood there like a stone beside the unmoving body, and the crudest words of the world were being etched on me—*we have to remove the body*. They were not calling R by his name any more! He was just a *body* now! I wanted to scream at R, tell him to open his eyes and see how Mohan Raidan was calling him a *body* now. Did he remember how Raidan had threatened to murder him? Now the man was relentlessly calling R a *body*! Why was R not getting angry? I could not tell who led me to a rickshaw. The rickshaw began following the truck carrying R away, bound for TSC and then Mithekhali for the burial.

The stone finally began to melt. 'What happened?'

'He'd gone to brush his teeth in the morning. He fainted all of a sudden. It was a heart attack.'

'What rubbish,' I snapped at Yasmin and she stopped mid-sentence. A long while later, I asked her again, 'Yasmin, R is truly dead, isn't he?'

Yasmin said nothing.

'Tell me, Yasmin, please tell me he isn't dead. Why should he have a heart attack? He didn't have trouble with his heart. Tell me he isn't dead. That he is just asleep.'

Like before, Yasmin remained quiet.

No, there was nothing wrong! Yasmin and I were simply taking a turn around Dhaka city. We were out together after a long time, like we used to go out back in the day. Nothing was happening at Indira Road, or anywhere else. I used to fall asleep on the rickshaw. Perhaps something like that had happened and I was dreaming! Buoyed by the sudden thought I pushed back the hood of the rickshaw. 'Let's go to Bailey Road and buy saris.'

'No.'

'Why not!'

'Let's go home.'

'What home! We're going out together. Let's go.'

'No, let's go home, Bubu.'

After some more time I directed the rickshaw to take us towards TSC. Yasmin pleaded, 'Let's not go there.' I shouted at her to keep quiet but she refused to listen to me. Instead, wrapping her arms tightly around me she said in a teary voice, 'Bubu, don't be like this.'

'Let's go to TSC. R will be there.'

'No.'

'I want to go see R.'

'Bubu, stop! None of them want you there. Don't go to TSC.'

~

I wanted to believe that R was not alive any more. I tried telling myself the same again and again, that he was gone and all that was left was his corpse. He was a corpse whose heart had stopped pumping blood, had stopped beating. Blood was not flowing to his body parts any more, not even to his lungs which had long fallen silent. R was not breathing. R was never going to wake up. R was never going to write poetry or read poetry on stage. He was never going to laugh again, or live his life like others were going to continue living their. I wanted to believe this but something would not let me. Whenever I tried telling myself that R was gone forever I felt a vast emptiness in my chest, like a carcass with a gaping ribcage left half-eaten by vultures and abandoned in the dump. There was nothing inside me except desolation and emptiness. When I tried breathing I could feel my lungs straining as if the last bit of air had been sucked out of the earth. The scavengers were circling around me, pecking at the empty sockets of my eyes and my cracked skull through which they could reach into my brain. The feeling of being fed upon spread though my body like a contagion so rapidly that I did not notice when I reached Shantibag, how I got upstairs or how I ended up alone in my room propped up against the wall. I did not realize how long I sat there until the spell was broken by a hand falling lightly on my shoulder. Waking up from a daze I looked up to find NM in front of me. The waves that had been looming in the horizon crashed upon the shore with a mighty roar and swept away the silence of the seaboard.

It was impossible for me to stay in Dhaka. The city resembled a giant crematorium to me, devoid of life except for the smell of burning flesh permeating the air. Chotda came over, packed my things and took all of us, including his family, to Mymensingh. On the way as I stared out of the window of the car at the trees and farms speeding past, everything seemed the same as before—everything except R. He was not going to walk these roads any more or stop to smell a flower. He was never going to admire the river or sway to the beats of *bhatiyali* songs. Try as I might I could not accept he was never going to do these things again. I kept telling myself R was going to come back suddenly one day and claim, 'I was at Mithekhali. I've just come back.' Just like he used to. I was never a big believer in the supernatural but it gave me joy to think that R was going to come back, that he was going to laugh, write, think and love again.

Mymensingh turned out to be an even bigger crematorium than Dhaka. I pulled out the old trunk from under the bed to rifle through my things. I wanted to feel R's presence, wanted his touch at any cost. I did not want him to fade into memory. As I sat and read his old letters, our past seemed to appear right in front of me again, close enough for me to touch my memories, play with them, drown in them again, or tie them in a fishtail with my hair so they would stay with me at all times. But the moment someone would call, the visions would become shadowy and pale at once. Did that mean they were gone for good, those days of love, and everything was consigned to memory alone? Terribly alone all of a sudden, I could do nothing but sit by myself and think of what to do with this useless life. The love of my life, the man of my dreams, was gone. The man I had left but not left altogether, who I had got separated from but who I had never separated from me, was gone. His absence gave my grief a tenor that could not be contained by Abakash or the narrow confines of our locality. I bellowed and wept, uncaring of the many curious eyes trying to see past the black gates and find out what was happening inside. Father was at home, he had heard the news, but he remained largely unconcerned. Instead, he let me cry. Everyone in the house let me cry to my heart's content.

~

Even though I eventually returned to Dhaka, the city remained shrouded in death and impossible to live in. I visited Asim Saha and his grieving wife Anjana hugged me in condolence. We were all looking for shoulders to cry on and friends to share our devastating grief with. So we sat and talked about our lonely apathetic world where R did not live any more. Our loss could not be expressed in words and all our tears and each of our sighs were for him. If he was around us, all I wanted to tell him was that none of us were able to accept his death. A person who had never believed in religion was bid farewell with every possible funeral rite mentioned in Islam. At least if that could have been prevented! But neither did I know a spell that could bring R back, nor could I keep religion away from him after his demise. Instead, all I could do was simply sit and let it all happen, my helplessness and incapacity reminding me repeatedly how stupid I was.

SHA, editor of the literature pages of *Ajker Kagaj*, asked me to write an article on R for the journal. Of course no article could even begin to approximate the pain of his loss; for that I would have had to tear out my heart and show it to people. Who was I going to show it to? There was no one and so I hid my grief deep within me, saving it only for myself. Since R was gone, there was no point in talking about it to anyone else.

Meanwhile, Ishaq Khan, a friend of R, was writing about me and abusing me in public, holding me responsible for R's death. Khan alleged I had killed him, though he failed to clarify exactly how. His accusations hurt me deeply, especially because I had known the man for a long time, since he used to visit R when we were still married. Khan used to have trouble making ends meet and R, always the generous man, would help him out occasionally. Every time we met I had welcomed him with the utmost warmth. Khan was a writer of short stories. Since his stories never made him any money, he was trying to make up for it by writing gossip after R was no more. The newspapers and journals too were always eager to print new gossip about me so Khan had no trouble getting his stuff published. The readers, I was convinced, were reading the columns, making clucking noises about R's miserable fate and generously calling me names like slut, whore and witch. Another one of R's friends snidely told me one day, 'Ishaq's gone crazy because R's not here any more to supply him with free alcohol.' There was a mad race to make profit off R's untimely demise. A poet called Saifullah Mahmud Dulal approached me for the letters R had written to me to publish them in a collection, an offer I refused outright. This was the same Dulal who had flung raw hatred at me from the truck while carrying R's body away.

I did what I felt was the most important thing to do at that point of time. I started the process of finally getting R's collected works published. R had always wanted it but no one had been willing to do it while he was alive. Is that why he died? So his work would get published? All his work was compiled in a single volume and published by Vidyaprakash; the second time Khoka was not as unwilling as he had been before. The collection was edited by Asim Saha and the proceeds from the royalties were arranged to be sent to R's siblings. My responsibility was to proofread the manuscript, but as I sat at home poring over his writings, being printed at the Ityadi press, all I could see in them was R. It was as if he was sitting beside me the entire time, listening to me reading his poems over and over again, every word, every syllable. While working through the night whenever I fell into an exhausted sleep on top of those piles of paper spread across the floor, he was there in my dreams and we held hands, walked and spoke about poetry.

Asim Saha and a few others established the R Committee to organize a fair in his memory. Books and many small-scale handicrafts were sold in the fair which took up the responsibility of celebrating the life and times of the remarkable poet who had passed away at a tragically young age. Many renowned poets and writers who attend the fair now, where they heave many deep sighs and say a great many things about R, could perhaps have gotten him a job in Dhaka when he had needed it most. It was not as if he did not approach enough people for a job! The song 'Bhalo achi, bhalo theko' was used in a teleplay and instantly became immensely popular. If R had been alive it would have delighted him no end. Would anyone have wanted to use the song if he had been alive? There was no way one could say that for sure. As he had asked, I wrote my letters to the sky every day whether they reached him or not.

Licit and Illicit

Iasked Mother to get all my things from Armanitola, things that had been taken to Abakash, to Shantibag. I especially asked her to get all my books kept in the bookshelf in the living room and the shelf too. Mother arranged for everything to be transported in a truck from Mymensingh to Dhaka. It was fairly late by the time the truck reached Shantibag and after everything was brought up I realized the bookshelf was missing.

Mother, sweating profusely, had nearly doubled over with fatigue. I barked at her, 'Why haven't you gotten the bookshelf?'

'I asked so many times. Your father refused to let it go.'

The shelf may not have been mine but I was his daughter. Had it been too much for me to expect that he would let me have it for my new house? Mother started crying. 'What could I have done? I asked him a dozen times. He refused to give it.'

'Why didn't he? The bookshelf had my books. What does he plan to do with the empty shelf, display air in it? All the books are here. Does anyone read at Abakash? Is he planning to eat the shelf?'

Wiping the sweat off her brow Mother replied, 'I asked him to give it to you. I told him you wanted to keep books in it. He made a face and said he'd gotten it made and that if you wanted one you should buy one.'

Her words made my blood boil in my veins. 'He didn't give it, so why didn't you take it anyway? Since you had everything put on the truck why didn't you have that put too? Where am I supposed to keep all these books now? The bookshelf was the most important! What kind of father cannot part with a bookshelf for his own daughter!' My anger with Father had found the closest possible outlet—Mother.

189

Stung by my attack, Mother withdrew to the shadows of the balcony and cried. I could never stand anyone crying!

Since I could not afford fancy things—a new bed with a soft sponge mattress and attached side-tables on either side, writing tables, chairs, wooden sofas—I bought a cane sofa, a dining table with four chairs, a small wooden cupboard for my clothes and a cabinet for storing plates and dishes, intending to do up the place in my own way. Everything I did alone, spending hours trying to locate good but inexpensive things, getting the new things put on a van, accompanying the movers on a rickshaw and getting things taken up to the flat, deciding on how to arrange everything down to the smallest detail. Not a single person helped me with money or assistance. The shelf was going to lie empty in Abakash anyway, so I had asked for it to keep the books strewn about the floor. But Father did not wish to part with it. He was an expert in destroying my life but did not have the time to spare a glance when I was trying to make one for myself. I was fine with his indifference. He did not need to get involved in anything pertaining to my life and I only hoped he would no longer interfere in it either. My life was going to run according to my wishes, I did not need my relations any more. They could need me, but I hoped to never need them for anything.

Nevertheless, concerns about the functioning of my new life occupied all my thoughts. The old bed Mother had brought from Abakash was put in the other room for relatives or guests to use. The carpet was spread out on the living room floor while the pots and pans were dispatched to the kitchen. Mother had brought Lily's older sister Kulsum to Shantibag with her, whom she proceeded to train in every aspect of running the house—cleaning, manning the kitchen, cooking, keeping everything in place.

My kitchen was unlike the one at Abakash—one had to stand while cooking and there was no old earthen oven like the one back in Mymensingh but a smaller modern one that ran on gas. There was no courtyard either where the leftover food could be thrown to the ducks, chickens and crows or where water dripping from washed dishes could be drained on a tree root somewhere. Instead, garbage had to be put in plastic bags or buckets and taken to the garbage dump outside at regular intervals. I was occupied with setting up the house and had scant time for the kitchen, which was mostly left to Mother and Kulsum to manage. They lovingly served me food and while I ate Mother would stand beside me ready to serve me more. She was always at hand, finding me things I required.

Time and again she would go off to Mymensingh to bring back rice, pulses, oil and onions from the kitchen in Abakash without my knowledge. I usually did all my grocery and vegetable shopping from the Shantibag market and took Milan with me whenever there was other work outside. Milan had moved out of his sister's house to come and stay with me. Father had spoken to a friend and arranged for a job for Milan that the latter joined despite the fact that his heart was in Mymensingh where Yasmin was staying and preparing for her master's examination. So he would eagerly wait for the weekend and usually never return home on Thursdays, directly going to Mymensingh instead. On holidays Yasmin too would visit Dhaka for the day. While Mother kept shuttling between Dhaka and Mymensingh I never went back, busy as I was with work, writing and my new life.

One fine day I received a call at the hospital. It was MM calling to tell me that in a few hours he was leaving for America for good and wanted to meet me one last time. He gave me his address and I took a baby taxi from the hospital to go meet him. I found MM drunk out of his mind and unable to even keep his eyes open long enough, a series of swollen love-bites on his neck. I had never asked him about his relationship with the rich woman and neither did I ask him any questions that day. Nonetheless, he informed me that it was she who was sending him to America. He spoke about R, told me how he had gone to the TSC grounds to pay his last respects, touched R's lifeless form and cried, begging for R's forgiveness again and again.

Perhaps there was a kind side to the cruel MM as well, although I could never figure out who exactly was the actual person, which is perhaps why he was never too dear to me. Even on that day I had resolved to leave immediately after saying my goodbyes and would have done so too, had he not tried to put a wrench in my plans by shutting the door abruptly and trying to drag me to his bed to rape me! While my body harboured no desire for MM any more, to him sex was simply a fun game like many other things in his life. For me our relationship was not important because of our personal history and the mess therein; the thing of importance was *Bichinta*. The journal was doing very well but that too had become a game for MM, like castles he had made in the sand—he was ready to step over his own creation and leave without a backward glance.

It was possible the person financing *Bichinta* was not willing to put any more money into it or MM himself had grown tired of running it. It was also possible that he wished for greener pastures and was willing to let go of *Bichinta* and even the country in order to answer such a call. This was exactly how talent was being smuggled out of Bangladesh; doctors, engineers, physicists and mathematicians from Bangladesh were perfectly willing to travel to foreign shores and even work as dishwashers in the kitchens there. The dollars they earned in exchange at the end of the week or the month was a significant amount in our currency. MM, once the editor of a popular weekly journal in Bangladesh, did not take up a dishwasher's job in the US; he chose to become a cabbie instead. We spoke twice after his departure. He called me to discuss how to go about formally dissolving our relationship, a union that had been mostly on paper to begin with. I had completely forgotten about it, so when I signed the divorce papers I remained as impassive as I had been while signing the papers at the registrar's office the first time. He sent a messenger to get my signature on the relevant documents and it was the same person who made all the arrangements to send the documents to MM in the US.

There is one thing I have always noticed about all my relationships. None of them, no matter what the nature of the relationship, has ever ended from my side. I have never been able to stay angry with someone for long and sooner or later the ice has melted and I have looked for a semblance of normalcy. I don't hate anyone and I have always tried to see things from the other's perspective, especially when the person concerned made a mistake. It was the same even when I was the one who had made the mistake. In the case of someone who I was aware wished me malice, I simply removed myself from their orbit rather than let things get bitter. In many ways I learnt to be like this from Mother who was quick to forgive a person's mistakes too. I always detested this aspect of her nature although quite ironically I unknowingly inculcated the same trait in myself.

When MM had called saying he wished to meet I was well aware that I did not feel anything for him any more. We were never going to be together again but he used to be a friend and, even if for a brief spell, had given me a lot of joy and comfort. So I had gone to wish him well. It was always like this, I could never wish for bad things even for my enemies. Even after Father had tried to destroy my life I could not wish him any misfortune. He had taken Mother for granted their entire life, hurt her repeatedly but she too never wished him anything but good things. She would get anxious at the slightest sign of illness and start fussing over him. That she loved him might have been a reason for her anxiety, but even without love things were not altogether different where Mother was concerned. Geeta and Hasina never considered her family, always armed with an unkind jibe or an insult they could throw at her, but Mother was ready to put her life on the line for them too.

She had given a cow to Abdus Salam to take care of. One day he came and informed her that the animal was lost. Even if she was curious as to why no other cows from their house were lost, nevertheless whenever Salam came to the house she would welcome him with lots of warmth and food. She would get angry with Lily's mother one moment, then give her own sari to the woman to wear the very next. Or she would lose her temper and slap Lily or Kulsum, only to forget everything in a few hours and go out to buy them new dresses or new shoes. There was not an ounce of resolve in her character, whatever little was there was extremely fragile. My resolve too was similarly brittle. Was it because we were both lonely? Perhaps. A firm resolve only suited someone who had physical or financial influence, or at least a roof over their heads.

I met and spoke to NM again, the same man who had once done everything in his power to cause me grief and because of whom I was asked to vacate the house at Armanitola. I had even heard of his role in the gossip printed about me in *Sugandha* and how it had reached Father. When he turned up at my house in Shantibag I never turned him away. NM had wished to destroy my desire to live on my own. His schemes had worked as well as he could have hoped, but despite all his machinations he had failed in his objective and had failed to crush my spirit. He would come to the Shantibag house to see for himself how I had recovered and flourished and every time I could tell he was burning with envy within. Other weekly journals were constantly approaching me for columns but NM did not ask me to write for *Bhorer Kagaj*, so afraid was he that I would become even more famous. Not that I was sorry about not being able to write for his newspaper, swamped as I already was with commitments for so many columns in so many different journals.

Nevertheless, it was NM's own fault or perhaps his bad luck that things did not eventually unfold as he had intended. One day his services at *Bhorer Kagaj* were terminated. Undaunted by the setback he started on his own once more, this time not with a journal but an entire news agency. He also had a gala wedding in which he married a girl from Chattagram, a young girl with a BA degree. It was obvious that much careful thought had gone into the marriage and he had managed to locate a girl with all the qualities of a dutiful, obedient wife who would cook, clean, take care of his parents and his siblings, and still have the time to follow his every command.

Even after marrying someone so perfect he still came to my house and he still made passes at me. I did not turn down his offer of a physical relationship, my lonely body thrilled at the prospect of someone else's touch and warmth. My desires refused to be ignored any longer, the compromises I had made with myself finally demanding recompense. These renewed longings were my own, not someone else's. I turned them over in my hand, threaded them through my fingers and said to myself, 'This body is mine and I alone have the right to take any decisions about it.' Perhaps if I had known how to take care of my desires on my own in some other way the routine I developed with NM once or twice a month would never have happened. It happened because I let it happen. Like the thousand other irrational rules driving society, rules that I repeatedly flouted, I defied the unreasonable demand that my body would become dirty or impure if I let a man touch me.

It did not take much for a woman to become fallen or impure. Men have deemed chastity to be a woman's greatest wealth since time immemorial. These rules are fundamentally patriarchal and women are systematically taught that they must guard this wealth at all costs—their virginity before their marriage and chastity after.

Marriage is essentially a social ploy geared towards transforming a woman's body and her desires into a man's private property and most women are trapped in this web of deceit.

On the first page of *Nirbashito Bahire Ontore* I had written, 'I have broken my shackles, I have brought push to shove at last.' Could I really break all my shackles? Or was there only a secret desire to break them and nothing more? When I spoke about breaking shackles I did not want it to just remain talk, I wanted to live it with my own life. This fight against society had started early when I had taken off the burqa at a young age. I had flouted unwritten social dictums, like the one where a woman was supposed to keep the hood of the rickshaw pulled over her head like a quasi-veil. In a crowded town like Mymensingh I had gone on rickshaw rides with the hood rolled back. People stared, said things, and I let them. I had done those things because I wanted to and because I had failed to find any logical explanation for the rules I was asked to follow. A woman was only supposed to marry the man her parents chose for her. She was not supposed to fall in love. She was always supposed to listen to what her husband told her to do. She was not supposed to talk to other men, chat with them or get close to them. None of these dictums I adhered to because I wished to follow my own rules. Only the customs that made sense to me I adopted. The rest, meant to attack the very essence of my being and eradicate all that gave me autonomy, I simply cast aside. It was not within me to live by making a series of compromises with the irrational and the oppressive. I had learnt the hard way that such a life was not meant for me.

It did not take long for me to understand that while our sexual relationship was quite convenient for NM, it was doing absolutely nothing for me. I found no satisfaction in these trysts since I had no love left for NM at all. Once upon a time when I used to like him I used to like his touch too. Those feelings had died a natural death and sex with him was becoming nothing but a painful chore. Even without love there had to be a measure of affection for bodies to react pleasurably to each other. A new resolve took hold of me—to refuse to endure physical pain in the name of intimacy.

In all this there was one thing in particular which was firmly trying to sync with my beliefs—the need to respect my own needs in things that mattered. My body was my own to command and no one else had the right to dictate its course of action. Whatever I chose to do with myself, whether to wade into the mud or rise above everyone else, it was going to happen because I had decided so and not because someone else wanted me to. Because I had slept with more than one man in my life and that was no longer a secret, many men looked at me with a calculative gleam in their eyes as if my body was easy to acquire and all they had to do was lean in a bit. When they realized eventually that I was not as easy as they had made me out to be, their calculative eyes would slowly widen with outrage. I had to navigate more filth and overcome more adversities than most other women around me, under the greedy watchful eyes of men, their tongues hanging out and features swine-like. For them women were objects meant for consumption and this belief was the cornerstone of their existence. I was an alien creature because I had been with many men, because I was single and did not have a family or children, and because my life was unnatural and not at all like that of their aunts, mothers and wives. So they felt no shame in winking suggestively, touching me without my consent, or falling all over me. Not for one moment could they entertain the thought that even men could be viewed as merely objects of consumption by women, that women could want men just as fiercely, and that without rape there was no way any of them could ever have me without my explicit consent.

~

One day CS turned up quite unexpectedly at my house. There had been many upheavals in her life. She had focused on her studies after the breakdown of her relationship with M and her efforts had borne fruit; she got into PG.[24] She was staying at the PG hostel in Dhaka and preparing for her FCPS. M was thankfully out of the picture, but there was someone new in her life. This new man, Haroon, fair, short, a quintessential good student, was studying in PG too. Not exactly a younger man but definitely younger than her; it was not as if they had known each other for long.

In fact, after only a couple of conversations she brought the boy over to my flat in Shantibag. After whispering to each other and cuddling on the sofa for a while she led him straight to my bedroom. Later, she told me Haroon was good in bed too, perhaps not as good as M but good enough for her. Their visits, because of how conveniently available my house was to them, became increasingly frequent. All this was happening in front of Milan. Milan had been witness to CS's torrid relationship with his brother M and had often warned her against putting too much faith in the latter's promises. However, CS had been so obsessed with the man back then that no amount of warnings made any difference to her whatsoever. She was initially quite awkward about conducting her relationship with Haroon in front of Milan but it did not take her long to shake that feeling off. Besides, neither Milan nor I wished to remind CS of her past experience and neither was she interested in remembering it.

Busy as she was with her new life, a new obsession soon reared its ugly head—her concern about Haroon's personal life. Haroon had told her his relationship with his wife was not in a good space at all. So CS would wonder why the two of them were out strolling in the park. Why did he lie to her about leaving the hostel at night frequently to visit his wife? All this was robbing CS of sleep and sending her sixth sense into overdrive regarding Haroon's movements. Why did he visit his wife so often? Was he then in love with his wife? But Haroon had given her his word that he had not had any physical or emotional relationship with his spouse for nearly two years and the only one he wanted was CS! The wife stayed with her parents and Haroon had told CS he only visited them infrequently to see his child. CS could not shake off the feeling that it was all a lie and his primary objective behind visiting his in-laws' was to sleep with his wife. It was a familiar zone—CS's anxieties about a man, her tears and the suspicions eating into her brain like a thousand deadly bugs. I was convinced that her relationship with Haroon too was not meant to last long. She insisted on falling in love with men who were married with children. As it is even bachelors were barely reliable and here she was trying to make a faithful man out of someone who was already married, that too by force!

'Where's Humayun?'

'Don't even talk about him. Just hearing his name makes my skin crawl.'

Humayun lived in Rajshahi and Ananda was with him. CS's mother had left for Rajshahi too. Explaining everything to me as briefly as possible, CS's attention turned back to Haroon. Did he not love her? There was no way I could say for sure and staring at my blank face CS broke down in tears.

'What should I do? Did he lie to me when he said he loved me?'

'How can I tell you if Haroon loves you or not? Wouldn't you know better?'

'I thought he does but it seems he's lied to me.'

'If that is so, why are you still with him?'

'Because I can't stay away! I decided to forget him so many times but I have failed each time I've tried.'

'You've tried?'

'Yes, I have. I have tried concentrating on my studies. But each time I simply sit and stare at an open book and think about Haroon.'

'Married people are tricky. Why don't you try meeting someone who's not married?'

'Which boy my age or thereabouts do you think is still unmarried?'

'Let it be. How does it matter where Haroon goes, what he has to say, if he is lying or not? Why waste your time thinking about these things?'

'I shouldn't?'

'No.'

'So it's only sex?'

'Isn't that what you wanted?'

'But being touched when there is no love does nothing for my body.'

Our eyes met and I gravely said, 'Do you love Haroon?'

CS nodded. She really did love the man. If she were not in love with him why did it hurt her so much whenever he returned to his wife!

I could not help but feel sorry for CS, especially because I had no assurances to provide her. She was not enthusiastic about a physical relationship without love. But there was no one for us to love! We wanted love, we wanted to love in return, but every time we ended up getting deceived by men. The desire to love was eternal and the heart refused to bar its gates despite the repeated hurt. Love was another trap in which men sought to entrap women, in shackles that looked and felt different but served the same purpose: enslavement. I was not seeing anyone, so I might not have related to CS right then, but being single had also provided me an immense sense of freedom. A life without love might lack in variety but it still brought immense relief in its wake. And right then all I wanted was some relief.

A few days later CS came to my house again, this time brimming with joy. Hugging me tightly she informed me with alacrity that for the first time in her life she had experienced an orgasm. When I asked her where exactly Haroon had managed to accomplish such a feat she shook her head in denial and confessed that Haroon had not been responsible for it. Surprised, I asked her if there was someone else in her life. She denied that too and told me that she had taken matters into her own hands, quite literally. In the middle of the night, while tossing and turning in bed, she had gotten aroused and things had followed from there. CS described to me in perfect detail how she had masturbated herself into climax. Masturbation was something that was quintessentially male, at least as far as I knew. It had been so for CS too, until she had turned a definite corner in her life and taken control of her own pleasure. Without any prior experience she had succeeded in giving her own body a taste of an orgasm for the first time.

Unfortunately, CS's discovery of self-love did little to attract me. I was not in love with anyone like she was and I was studiously taking a break from sex too. Whatever little time I had outside Mitford was spent in pursuit of my literary career.

A Maelstrom

Meanwhile, several things happened, especially in the political situation of the country. The people spontaneously came together in an unprecedented popular revolution against autocracy and forced President Ershad to step down. He had never expected the movement to become powerful enough to threaten his rule in any way, confident in his ability to crush any mass movement with weapons and religion. Unconcerned with the conditions and complaints of his people, Ershad had been on a power trip. There were rumours that he often consulted Atroshi Pir[25] for tips on how to run the government.

Most politicians had one religious leader or another they followed who did roaring business thanks to the ministers and bureaucrats of the nation. In fact, these pirs were so influential that their blessings could translate into jobs and even ministry berths. A few years back a certain Hafezzi Hazur had given up being a pir and contested the 1986 general elections. Most pirs were very keen on this neat business switch and many like Atroshi Pir and Sarsuna Pir were living glamorous lives after having renounced the religious trade in favour of politics.

Like Saidabadi Pir for instance, whose domain extended over the entire city of Dhaka. At one point of time the man used to sell second-hand clothes at the Gulistan crossing, before trading up to a palatial residence in Dhaka that also served as his headquarters. Rumour had it he could hold a raw egg in one hand and turn it into a boiled egg. If you wanted kids or a job, or you wanted to make someone go bankrupt, all you had to do was take a raw egg to the pir with your request. And thousands of people did exactly that every day to have their wishes granted.

While the pir's magical abilities were being hotly debated, Ershad too had attempted a magic trick of his own. The superstitious populace had begun to whisper that the President was still childless; the word 'impotence' too had been tossed around. What sort of a man could not manage to sire children? If such a man were to be allowed to govern then the country too would not be able to produce anything. These comments had reached Ershad's ears and in order to keep the situation under control he tried pulling a fast one over the people, much like magically turning a raw egg into a boiled one. One day he produced his wife Roshan in front of the public, put a baby in her lap and declared that at long last he had become a father. Not that it affected the anti-Ershad movement in any way. At the peak of the rebellion the President even ordered his police to shoot at the meetings and processions;[26] the police carried out his orders and numerous people had to die.

Each and every such death was immensely tragic and only added fuel to the fires of dissent already burning everywhere. While there were many martyrs who went unsung, Nur Hussain's death was a significant moment in shaping the nature of the popular rebellion and taking it forward by several leaps. An extraordinarily brave man, Nur Hussain was a baby-taxi driver, a common man who had been at the head of one such anti-Ershad procession. Never one for politics, not too educated either, he had made two placards for the march: 'Free Democracy' on his chest and 'Down with Tyranny' on his back. The bullet had pierced through Democracy and gone straight to his heart. Democracy was freed in the end but Nur Hussain did not live to see the day. Ershad tried his best to arrest this revolution but after a three-year-long united revolution the furious tide of the 1990s swept him off his throne.

A caretaker government was instituted after the change in regime to conduct fresh general elections. This election was primarily a face-off between two big political parties: the Awami League and the Bangladesh Nationalist Party (BNP). In effect it was a face-off between Sheikh Mujibur Rahman's daughter Sheikh Hasina and President Ziaur Rahman's class-eight-educated, beautiful and doll-like wife Khaleda Zia. Although both political leaders had been united under one ideology during the anti-Ershad movement, the moment he was out of the picture and fresh election campaigns were under way, the mud-slinging began in earnest.

While Sheikh Hasina could be seen shedding copious tears about how everyone in her family had been slaughtered on 15 August 1975,[27] Khaleda Zia made it a point to base her campaign on reminding everyone frequently about the extreme misgovernance and corruption during the Awami era after independence. At such a juncture, in a country like Bangladesh where Islam had been formalized as the state religion only a little while back, it was obvious that religion was going to be weaponized. If Khaleda Zia said two things about religion, Sheikh Hasina invariably said four. As it is the Awami League had to deal with their already tarnished reputation of being non-religious, especially since secularism had been one of the four pillars of their original policy of governance. The more Sheikh Hasina tried distancing her party from this bad name the more Khaleda Zia sought to use it to the BNP's advantage.

The initial expectations had predicted a landslide victory for Sheikh Hasina but something altogether different came to pass once the votes were cast. Many voters, reminded of the injustices and anarchy of the Awami League–led government after the Liberation War, deliberately refrained from voting them into power again. The other weapon Khaleda Zia used quite effectively was to highlight the League's long-standing ties with the Government of India. Both strategies worked like a charm in the BNP's favour. Anxiety over the fact that a win for the Awami League would spell doom for Islam in the recently communalized country, and fear that Sheikh Hasina was going to sell us out to India— the ensuing panic worked well with the electorate and was used well by the BNP. The Awami League failed to earn the majority mandate and as a final seal of approval on her successful campaign of terrifying the electorate into voting against Sheikh Hasina, Khaleda Zia was declared the new prime minister of Bangladesh along with a few of her most trusted Razakar lieutenants as ministers.

Another Razakar, Abdur Rahman Biswas, was appointed the new President and the Jamaat-e-Islami took pride of place in Parliament with their eighteen new seats. In order to clear her name of allegations of selling the country out to India, Sheikh Hasina took up an anti-India rhetoric of her own. In the same vein, to clear the misunderstanding regarding her position on religion, she reinvented herself as a devout Muslim overnight. She organized lavish iftar parties, visited the annual Bishwa Ijtema (global gathering) in Tongi, raised her hands in the Akhri Munajat (final prayer) to reaffirm her faith in Allah and even went for Hajj. In the beginning I had been joyous about the prospect of living in the era of a female prime minister where the leader of the opposition too was going to be a woman, but that feeling was gradually replaced by a terrifying dread, like a massive python slowly and fatally encircling its hapless prey.

After Khaleda Zia's ascension to power Ershad was convicted on weapon charges and imprisoned. In the end, one autocracy was replaced by yet another. So many promises had been made to keep the media and all relevant information impartial, but as is the rule of thumb, no one remained too keen on investing in old conversations. Neither did the government show any interest in removing the state religion from the constitution and reinstating the original secular ideals. Their politics was never about the welfare of the people. It was, and remained, solely about amassing power. Every political party was singularly dedicated to devising ways in which power could be concentrated in their hands by hook or by crook, and their primary objective remained the consumption of the ensuing spoils.

~

Since I was not getting any time to pursue my writing after the murderous work hours in gynaecology, I requested for and was granted a transfer to anaesthesia. The situation at gynaecology too was not as it had been before. The old interns were no longer there and had been replaced by a new batch. Bayesh Bhuiyan was transferred to another hospital and a new head was appointed in my unit. The duty hours too were haphazard and left very little time for my writing duties which were considerably more than before and I needed the requisite time to get them done. Not that there was no work in the anaesthesia department or there was no night duty. But at least in the latter case one could get done with one's work with only two hands, instead of praying for ten as we had to in my previous department. In gynaecology unless you were working round the clock with ten hands it was not considered enough and I was always very clear that I had only two. Besides, I was firm in my decision of not pursuing my postgraduate degree any more so there was no need for me to go overboard. I had learnt what I had to learn while on the job and I was confident of being able to make a living as a gynaecology specialist for the rest of my life. The anaesthesia department was not as hectic as gynaecology—simple, clean, laid-back, peppered with tea and samosa during breaks and convivial conversations between doctors. The two professors of the department, Mujibur Rahman and Manas Paul, were both wonderful human beings and very friendly too.

My rapport with the other two doctors, Shamima Begum and B, was firmly established on the first day itself, especially with Shamima. On my first day on the job it did not take me too long to learn the procedure of anaesthesia and from the next day onwards I could do it by myself. My busy schedule did not clear up entirely though, especially when I had to run to the gynaecology operation theatre. It so happened on certain nights that I did not have even two minutes of respite, with one operation lined up after another. Instead of knives and scalpels like before, I had to be ready with the anaesthetic, oxygen tanks and artificial breathing tools.

As simple as it sounded, giving a patient anaesthesia before an operation and then waking the person up after was not an easy task. If the artificial respirators were not used in time after the administration of the anaesthetic and the muscle relaxers, the patient would not start breathing on their own. Each lung had a specific time till which it could remain inactive without it being fatal. Anything beyond that and there was always the risk of losing the patient. After the operation the patient had to be brought out of anaesthesia on the table itself and then sent to the post-operative room to be kept under observation where their breathing and blood pressure had to be monitored.

Not once did I face any trouble with any of my patients; my anaesthesia work usually went smoothly and the waking-up process also never caused me any heartache. Except in one particular case. This one incident happened not because of me, but because of the arrogant Dr M. While he had been prepping for a caesarean I had injected the patient with the anaesthetic and was trying to locate her trachea to put in the artificial respiratory tubes. Having missed it twice I was in the middle of my third attempt when the impatient doctor laid down his operating tools, took his gloves off and, elbowing me aside, took my place to do it himself. Buoyed by the fact that he had finished the first part of FCPS successfully, the doctor was confident that he could do the job better than me. Quite obviously not only did he fail to find the windpipe, he also ended up causing immense damage to the patient. Dr B had to be called immediately.

B might not have finished the entire FCPS either but he had at least completed half. He arrived immediately to take over and managed to solve the issue, although the tube could only be put in after eight or nine attempts and I could tell it had not been easy for him either. As the operation was under way and the patient was under B's observation I did not want to stand one more minute in front of the other arrogant doctor. The next day, in a devastating piece of news, B informed me that he had been unable to wake the girl from the anaesthesia after the operation and the young girl had passed away right after delivering her first child. He had tried to save the girl, had even sent her to PG for emergency care but nothing had worked. Of course, thanks to M who carefully bypassed the incident where he had tried to intervene unnecessarily, the entire blame was put on me. When I pointed it out B accused me.

'Why did you let him touch your patient?'

'But he pushed me aside!'

'Why did you let him! It was your responsibility to administer the anaesthetic. M was just supposed to operate.'

'He wanted to find the trachea on his own, even grabbed the tube from me. He told me he was going to take care of the intubation.'

'Why did you let him? What does he know about endotracheal intubation? Does he have any experience whatsoever? It was extremely difficult locating that patient's trachea. When you couldn't find it, you should have started the oxygen and called for me immediately!'

'How could I start the oxygen? He did not even let me get near her!'

'Why didn't you shove him aside too?'

In all honesty, that was true. Why had I not ignored M's bullying and shoved him aside! For the next few nights I could not sleep, tortured by visions of the dead girl's beautiful face and her beautiful kohl-black eyes. I was never very adept at physical altercations. Why was I always in two minds about saying or doing the right thing, why was I so embarrassed to speak up even against the most obvious wrongdoings! There was nothing I could do but seethe in silent anger at myself, at my habit of letting people ride roughshod over me when it mattered the most.

I noticed the many things I could not do easily. Like when unwanted guests came over to the house and stayed for a long time and I was always unable to tell them that I was busy or unavailable. I would fume on the inside but could never utter a simple 'no'. This used to be the same when I was a child too, this inability to say no. I would notice errant hands advancing towards my body but I would pretend to not see them. I would instead shove a notebook or a pen in the hand and with a silly smile pretend that was what the hand had been after. Astounded by the suddenness of the incident the person in question too would be forced to cover the indiscretion up and pretend as if the proffered items were what he had reached out for. Eventually I would plead an emergency and get away or change the topic to something that never failed to depress the person concerned—for instance, a recently wedded sister who was perhaps not getting along with her new husband.

Let alone slap someone, or take off my shoe and beat someone with it for being disgusting, I could not even manage simple verbal threats—'Is this what you came here for', 'Go away, you bastard', 'You disgusting scoundrel' and the like—though I tried a thousand times. I never tried confronting anyone because I never wanted anyone to get ashamed or, even worse, encouraged to continue. All I ever did was attempt to cure such diseased mentalities with my naive innocence, taking all the shame and recrimination on to myself in the bargain. That is how I navigated the world of men, by not letting them figure out that I could easily sense the covert winks, the unnecessary touching, the disregard for personal space and the attempts at overfamiliar small talk—as if nothing had happened, as if I still held the concerned person in the highest regard, still considered him an all-round gentleman who had never tried making an indecent proposal or taking undue advantage.

My one lesson from this episode was first-hand knowledge of how doctors without an FCPS degree were treated by their colleagues. I was a good doctor, was good in the operation theatre and a good anaesthetist, but none of that mattered in the long run. If I was to make even a single mistake it would be said that I had made the mistake because I was not educated enough and because I knew less. If FCPS doctors made the same mistake then the blame was going to be passed on to someone else. It was indeed a strange system where the knife was blamed instead of the doctor when someone removed a kidney instead of a liver. There was an unwritten hierarchy in the hospital whereby everyone had to lower their heads in front of the FCPS doctors and let them pass if they were walking down the corridor. Whenever one of these FCPS doctors went on a long rant about a medical fact everyone else had to shut up and listen, if they were to go mad everyone had to accept it as a symptom of genius.

I had seen Father behave similarly all his life—a tyrannical feudal lord at home and an oppressed peasant at the medical college. I used to see him rub his palms constantly, hesitation clogging his voice while conversing with the FCPS and FRCS doctors who were his professors. A glow of reverence would light up his face at the sight of them and the biggest shame in his life, even more dishonourable than the fact that he was the son of a poor farmer, was that he had never managed to do his FCPS. Nevertheless, he had studied some courses in jurisprudence and earned an extra diploma after his medical degree. Despite all that he would often express his regret at not being able to pursue his FCPS degree because of his commitments to his family.

In all probability Father would have gotten his FCPS too had he tried back in the day. While I was always an average student Father had been one of the toppers at medical school. Doctors much less talented than him had earned higher degrees and paraded their success deliberately in front of him; in fact the same was true for some of his students too. Was I becoming like him? This was especially troubling because just like him I too was struggling to come to terms with my identity. I hated seeing Father being so subservient to bigger doctors. Once I had made him hold his head high in front of this one particularly arrogant doctor.

Our Poet-President Ershad had organized the Asian Poetry Festival and wishing to extend me an invitation deployed his health secretary, Imran Nur, the latter gentleman a poet too, to get in touch with me. The only bit of information available to them was that I was studying medicine at Mymensingh Medical and based on that they had approached the principal, Dr Mofakhkharul Islam, and tasked him with ensuring that the invitation reached me on an urgent basis. For Mofakhkharul Islam, just another principal of just another medical college, it was such an incredible state of affairs to receive direct orders from both the minister and the secretary of the health department that he had personally got in touch with Father to extend the invitation, and kept following up on it till Father relented. I can imagine Father had been rather testy with the suddenly subservient doctor, and the thought makes me sigh in relief. Father had called me and told me all about it in a rather jubilant tone. Despite knowing that I was not going to accept—from the very beginning I was a staunch supporter of the Nation Poetry Festival which was organized in protest against the Asian Poetry Festival, with those poets in attendance who were vocal activists of democracy—Ershad's invitation had given me an altogether different feeling of joy. The invitation had forced the health secretary to call Mofakhkharul Islam and compel the latter to carry out the orders—the same principal who had called me to his office and said the most insulting things, all on the basis of an anonymous letter. It would have never been in my power to exact vengeance for this abuse, but the emergency calls from his own overlords must have finally convinced him that I was not as expendable as he had tried to make me believe I was. This had been my revenge! An eye for an eye had never been my code and I always firmly believed that no physical harm could be more exacting than mental anguish. The health secretary had taken my phone number from Mofakhkharul Islam and called me up himself to ask that I accept the President's request. I had still turned them down.

~

I was finally through with all the decorations and setting up my Shantibag house. The Armanitola house was nothing in comparison with the second one. The former had been in a slum while the Shantibag house was more modern and upscale. A drawing–dining room, two bathrooms, two bedrooms, a balcony and a modular kitchen—the surrounding area too was as beautiful as the house itself. My life at Shantibag was a tad better than it had been at Armanitola. Of course, this extra bit of material comfort came at a cost.

Since my salary was not enough the columns were an additional source of income as before. Although I was earning more from my writing, I was spending the most time at Mitford. I was convinced that while people were eager to read my writing right then, whether they would remain interested in the future too was not something I was sure of. At least the job was a safety net and there was no way I was going to compromise on that front. If a single column earned me 300 to 500 taka then with ten columns a month I could take care of my house rent and the electricity bill. The salary took care of the groceries, food and commute. Anything more than ten columns ensured a comfortable month, meaning I could go to the theatre, watch plays and buy books. Not that this system was a constant. Often journals closed down, or they changed ownership and the new owners were no longer keen on publishing articles, or there was no money. Sometimes it also happened that I was not paid the amount promised to me. Despite a number of impediments I never backed down or gave up hope, and neither did I wish to be beholden to someone else. Milan too was regularly chipping in at home and whenever Mother was there her management of the kitchen ensured that I did not have to worry on that front. I also knew that most of what she helped me save was at the cost of her own small comforts. Everything was great about the Shantibag house except for the fact that it was a little too far from Mitford. Earlier I could walk to work from Armanitola but from Shantibag a rickshaw was the only way. The rickshaws too would regularly get held up at the traffic snarls near Gulistan and stay immobile at one place for hours.

Many guests would often drop in at the Shantibag residence. Poets, doctors, admirers, relatives, there was someone or the other all the time. Such used to be my attachment to Abakash that no matter where I stayed I would always want to go home. The Shantibag house managed to do the impossible—it went a long way in weaning me off Abakash for the first time in my life.

Of course, there was another challenge to consider too—my quest to become self-reliant, to live alone on my own terms the way I wanted to without a husband or any other man getting in the way. This was what I had always wanted—independence from a life under a husband or even a father. The struggle to be able to live such an unconventional life had been completely worth it and I could finally brush aside dreams of a family with a spouse and children quite effortlessly. Such trivial dreams were not for me and they had caused me nothing but grief thus far. I could finally wish for them to be swept away in the torrents of the Buriganga[28] and not feel a twinge of regret, or bury them six feet under and hope they did not find their way back out. I wanted these dreams off my back and out of my heart so they could no longer work their malice upon me, and all I wanted was new aspirations to replace them, desires of a different nature, dreams of living my life independently and the freedom to make my own choices.

It was as if a burden had been lifted off me, as if I had just woken from a long nightmarish night to be greeted by the joyous morning sun. I had been asleep and a lot of accidents had happened in the meantime. However, I was awake at last and ready to walk out of the dark cavern within which I had been trapped all this while, where the darkness used to regulate my life and all my wishes. In the absence of light I had gone and found it myself and I wanted to share my discovery with others who were suffering similar fates as me. I wanted to stretch out a helping hand to those languishing in obscurity, to lead them into the light. Was my hand strong enough for such a task? Perhaps not, but at least it was something! It was not as if there were too many of those anyway!

~

Incredible things were happening in my life around this time. Bengali publishers were making a beeline for my house wondering if I had made a vow to anyone that I was only going to publish with Vidyaprakash. Of course I had done nothing of the sort; Khoka and I did not have an exclusivity contract whereby I was not allowed to give books to other publishing houses. When I informed them of that I was immediately hounded with demands for new manuscripts that they wished to publish. It was easier said than done, though!

Whatever I had written thus far comprised mostly poetry and had already been published by Vidyaprakash. The columns too had been compiled into a book. The new demand was that I should write novels. How could I even begin to imagine a novel! I tried telling them off for being mad enough to suggest such a thing; I had never written a novel before and neither did I know how to write one. But they would keep insisting that I start one promptly. Even Khoka's friends from the publishing fraternity were approaching him to be put in touch with me. Khoka himself got me the references of three, Shikha Prakashani, Afsar Brothers and his friend Munir of Ananya Prakashani, and requested me to work with them in some capacity or the other—if not a novel then at least short stories or poems! If I could not commit to too many at once then even a small book of ten poems! Some were even happy with five and suggested they would get an artist to draw sketches alongside and make a little poetry-card collection out of them! No matter what, the end result was that publishers began leaving me advances for the books they wished to publish. I was not used to getting royalties.

Khoka was a friend, philosopher and guide rolled into one. There was not one instance when he had come to my house and not brought something with him: fruits, sweets, biscuits, munchies. On occasion when perhaps I had spent too much money on something and gone mostly broke he would leave behind a little money to tide me over. And this was not just during the difficult times. I remember choosing this pretty chair for my writing table once but I did not have the money to buy it. Khoka bought it for me and had it sent over to my house.

He never gave me an account of the royalties of my books and I never asked him. I never asked because I was too embarrassed; my relationship with Khoka was never the kind that was at the mercy of an accounts ledger. I could call him for anything without the slightest hesitation and every time he left everything aside and answered my call. Such compassion cannot be bought with money. In fact, this entire royalty issue itself was too disconcerting. When the good people of Ananya or Shikha Prakashani held out the advance in front of me I could feel my face burning. I was so embarrassed that I kept my hands firmly tucked behind my back and they had to leave the envelope on the table or leave it with Khoka to pass on to me. I told all of them so many times not to pay me in advance because I was yet to write the agreed-upon books. But none of them seemed to care; all they had to say was that I should keep the money and they were going to collect the manuscript once it was done. It did not matter if it took me a year to finish the book or five, if I needed the money or not, none of them were willing to see reason. I tried arguing that they should at least wait for the book to get published and see if it did well before mentioning royalties but the publishers had no patience with anything I had to say. They assured me that I would get my royalties after the book was published and the amount they were leaving behind was just a token advance.

I had never seen so much money before. It was part of public lore that Humayun Ahmed was the only one who used to get his royalties in advance and I could not believe that I was getting it too. I could not help but reflect on how it used to be—about Nausas Prakashani which had the publication rights for my book *Shikore Bipul Khudha* (Hunger in My Roots) but they had shown scant interest in arranging any distribution. After two years of their sitting and gathering dust and getting chewed on by mites I had brought over the entire set of books from their warehouse. Najmul Haque of Anindya Prakashan had been in two minds about publishing my second book; I was certain he too was in the melee of people who wanted me to publish with them. I knew very well that the ones clamouring for me with folded hands were the same people who used to wrinkle their noses in disgust at the mention of my name once upon a time.

It was the publishers who made me write. I wrote sitting in the hospital, in between attending patients. Often guests would come over to my place and I had to entertain them. Besides, there was always something needed in the house. In the middle of a thousand such day-to-day distractions I found time to write. Most of the time before I could even step back and see what I had written, the publisher was there to whisk it away for publication. There was someone or the other at my gate every day asking about something I had promised them, while I struggled with procrastination. Farid from Samay Prakashan had come quite a few times to my house with earnest requests and I finally gave him a novel called *Aparpakkha* (The Other Side) to publish. Similarly, a novel called *Sodh* (Vengeance) went to Ananya Prakashani—a novella or a long story would be a more apt description.

While I had considerable experience in gynaecology after working in the department for so long and was also becoming quite adept at anaesthesia, the same could not be said about my talents as a novelist. I wrote with a lot of trepidation and awkwardness and was never fully happy with the final outcome. Despite the nagging voices in my head regarding my novels there was one thing at least that I could achieve in them. With each woman whose life I laid bare in the pages of my novels I tried to reaffirm that a woman's body and her heart were her own and not someone else's property to treat as they pleased. For Khoka I wrote two new books—a collection of columns, *Noshto Meyer Noshto Godyo* (Profane Writings of a Fallen Woman), and a book of poems, *Balikar Gollachhut* (A Girl at Play). My poems too were about women, their joys and sorrows, the ground beneath their feet, about them breaking chains and overcoming familial and social conventions to emerge as fully realized persons in their own right. Despite the tragic side of life I had stumbled upon through my struggles, despite seeing first-hand how dreams could crash and burn, I had endured and abided. I had learnt to dream again, learnt to stand on my own feet, and whatever experiences I had gathered in life while being battered and bruised were reflected in no matter what I wrote, be it poems, columns or novels. Quite unconsciously the wisdom I had paid such a great price for in life flowed from my pen like blood from an open wound whenever I sat down to write.

My days were changing at a strange and rapid pace. Sometimes I was assailed with doubts as to whether these things were indeed happening to me, the diffident young girl who used to live by the Brahmaputra! For instance, I could not believe that a television producer approached me to write a song and the defiant lyrics were then sung on national television by the popular singer Samina Nabi. This was not the first time that a poem of mine was made into a song. Once previously Yasmin had set one of my poems to her tunes and performed it on stage with her group. But that was back in Mymensingh. In Dhaka, especially in a television industry that was not welcoming to outsiders, could I have even imagined that my song would get airtime? The famous singer Fakir Alamgir came to me for lyrics and I had to oblige him too. A professor from the English department of the university came to ask for poems that they wished

to translate into English and anthologize. I got calls from the British
Council to attend a poetry recital and from the leaders of a women's
rights group also. The magazine *Ananya* published a list of their top
female personalities of the year, of which I was one, and a gala event
was held to felicitate all the women on the list.

Not just Dhaka, invitations to attend literary events and book
fairs were pouring in from all over. Dr Mohit Kamal came to Dhaka
from Teknaf to meet me and express his interest in felicitating his two
favourite poets, MHI and Taslima Nasrin. Kamal was the president
of the fair organized for children and adolescents at Teknaf and the
event was to be at the fair itself. An ardent lover of literature, he was
my age. He and Khoka met and by some strange coincidence the two
of them soon became very close friends. After returning to Teknaf he
contacted Khoka and finalized my visit and the two of us and MHI
set off for the event together. There was still so much left to see in the
country and I had barely visited any new places, so travelling always
managed to excite me no end. Teknaf, the southernmost point in
mainland Bangladesh, was thus an incredible new experience.

We put up at Mohit's house and in due course the felicitation
ceremony took place at the fairgrounds. Not used to being awarded
I was so embarrassed that I could barely glance up throughout the
proceedings. Once the ceremony was over both the recipients were
invited on stage to hand over the annual prizes to the youngsters
present. Afterwards Mohit arranged to take us around St Martin's
Island and Maheshkhali. What a terrifying journey that turned
out to be! We were on a fishing trawler, the sea raging around us
threatening to turn us over one minute and firmly steadying our reins
the next. Tossing and turning, we finally reached the coral shores of
St Martin's. What a gorgeous place! There were only a few people on
the island, living in tall bamboo houses surrounded by unknown flora
and fauna. I walked on the beach with the emerald green seawater,
clear enough that I could see myself in it, lapping at my feet. From
there we went to the island of Maheshkhali, home to a colony of
fishermen. It was the sea that sustained these men and the sea that
often washed them away, and this duel of love and death with the
vast sea was what they called life. We spent a few days there before
returning to Dhaka. I had met MHI in Teknaf but simply as a friend

and fellow writer, no trace of emotion towards him left in my heart. I had a few beautiful memories from Kashmir and those were all I wished to keep, a few cherished memories.

The next invitation was from the Sylhet Book Fair and yet again it was left to Khoka to make all the arrangements for the trip. Khoka, Asim Saha and I set off for Sylhet, accompanied by Farid of Samay Prakashan and his wife. Sylhet was another memorable visit. There was a punishing crowd of autograph-hunters waiting for us at the book fair and I was astonished as well as moved that even so far away so many people were aware of my work. We visited the tea estates of Sylhet and the waterfall along the mountains of Shillong at Tamabil, which merged with the river down in the valley. The river was clear as crystal and I walked barefoot on the tiny rounded pebbles under the water, admiring the quiet magnificence of nature around me.

Just on the other side was India and one could almost stretch out and touch the earth across the border, except for the barbed wire that ran in between as a painful reminder of our limitations. Flowers and leaves from the trees this side were falling across the border all the time, the birds were flying across with ease—it was just the humans who were not allowed to cross over. Are we not children of the earth? Can we not walk anywhere we please, swim in any river or sea in the world? I came back from Sylhet with a stray barb stuck in my heart and the reaffirmation that humans are barbarians who forge their own shackles.

The frequency of invitations was increasing day by day, from bigger cities and more renowned literary organizations. I was felicitated at some of these places, honoured as chief guest at others, my name in big bold letters hanging across the back of the stage. The Natyasabha in Dhaka decided to give awards to Shamsur Rahman and I and the ceremony was held at the National Museum grounds. Sahidul Haque, dramatist, theatre director and head of the Natyasabha, who handed the award to us, was a uniquely talented individual who also had a reputation of being a devious man. I never faced that side of him though and with me he was nothing less than exceedingly hospitable.

Poets and writers came over to my house frequently and we spent long evenings chatting over ginger tea. Of them I grew particularly close to Shamsur Rahman and we spent a lot of time talking about literature and politics. Writer Rashid Karim was a close friend of Rahman and we used to visit his house often for literary discussions. We spoke about literature and religion, me and Rahman arguing decidedly secular viewpoints and Karim countering as a devout believer. But he was also an educated, erudite and talented writer, so the discussions were always rather lively.

These interludes made me confident that there were many renowned authors and litterateurs who were fond of me not because I was a young, perhaps beautiful, girl but because of what I was writing. Possibly, in my poems and my prose, in what I had to say, they found the indications of a new direction of thought and a new generation of writing. They read my work, discussed it and truly believed that what I was writing was indeed important. Rather than with writers my age I was more often seen with senior writers much older than me. Of course, as important as art, literature, society and culture were, what was perhaps most important was to learn how to be truly human.

Suddenly one day I received word from Shamsur Rahman that Rashid Karim was extremely unwell. Rushing to him I got him admitted to Suhrawardy Hospital immediately. The doctors managed to revive Karim but due to internal bleeding in his brain half his body was left paralysed. After being discharged from the hospital both Shamsur Rahman and I went to see Karim to keep him company and cheer him up. Shamsur Rahman was close to writer Panna Kaiser and we went to K's house in Iskaton for drinks and conversations. I even accompanied K to a literary meet in Jessore. The wife of writer Sahidullah K., Panna Kaiser herself was a novelist and was used to giving speeches in political rallies. The speech she delivered at the literary meet in Jessore was fantastic as usual. I was happy seeing a new city and its new people, so one can imagine the level of discomfort I faced when I too was suddenly pushed up to the stage to speak. My speech, devoid of the jargon necessary for such occasions, could scarcely match up to K's in impact.

Often while visiting M.A.R. Akhtar Mukul's bookshop, Sagar Publishers, I would run into renowned author Saukat Osman sitting there. He would catch hold of me and talk to me nineteen to the dozen about everything under the sun. One day he even explained the origin of my name to me. Some days later I found out that he had written a poem about me and was distributing photocopies of it to his readers: 'Nasrin, the wild rose, and so her fragrance endures'. I could not help but feel that I had far exceeded the limits of how much a person was allowed to have in life.

A fine friendship developed with the talented and popular poet Nirmalendu Goon, to the extent that he soon became like a member of my family. One aspect of Goon's character was particularly fascinating. He never hesitated in speaking the truth, no matter how unpleasant, irrespective of who he ended up offending in the process. Goon was the sort of person who lived the truth he spoke in his life. After reading his poem 'Huliya', like many of his other readers I had assumed that he must have been charged with a political case in real life too. I asked him one day how he had managed to evade capture and whether the police had managed to catch up with him in the end. Eager to hear about the banned left politics of his time or some covert operation against the oppressive Pakistani government, you can imagine my surprise when Goon confessed that he had been booked in a robbery case!

Without an iota of hesitation he narrated the story of how in the village of Netrakona he had once joined a gang of robbers. Why had he done it? Because he had needed the money, was Goon's simple reply. That was one constant feature in Goon's life: issues with money. While staying at the Anandamohan Hostel he had been hostel captain and used to regularly steal from the mess fund to buy new shirts. He would run gambling parties in the hostel room at night for which he was eventually expelled. While living in Dhaka the meagre sum he used to earn from his poems was never enough. Broke and racked with hunger, there were many occasions when he would go to a restaurant to eat without even half a cent in his pocket. The play was to run before the owners got wind of his intentions. Accordingly, getting up to wash his hands after the meal, he used to throw the glass and take off on a run with the restaurant people in hot pursuit. But try as they might they could never manage to get their hands on the lanky, Tagore-resembling Goon.

What impressed me the most about his stories was his utter lack of hesitation in talking about past deeds. I had never met anyone who could relinquish pride and self-awareness to this degree and display such an open sense of humour. Once, when I was ten years old and had just been promoted to a new class in school, Father did not buy all the books required for the school year right away. As class started and all the girls began turning up with their new books, I realized most of them had more books than I did. One day after school I noticed Abha R. had left behind her Bengali Rapid Reader by mistake. Since I was the last to leave class, unable to curb my greed I carefully looked around to see if anyone else was watching before quickly slipping the book inside my pyjama bottom. As I walked out of the classroom my heart was beating loudly and I was plagued by an intense anxiety that whoever was looking at me could clearly see the book wedged near my stomach. There were other girls standing at the gate, including Abha R. Seeing her, my first reaction was to take out the book and give it back to her. However, it would have been impossible to take the book out in the middle of the field and so I returned home with it! My anxiety did not lessen one bit even after that and I had to hide the book under the mattress so that no one discovered my ill-gotten gains.

Carrying it around wedged against my stomach, I took it with me everywhere, to the bathroom or to the roof, and finished reading it the very next day. In a couple of days Father brought home all my books, including the Rapid Reader. After returning to school I felt terrible for Abha, seeing her cry for her lost book and asking everyone around if they had seen it. I could not give the book back to her for fear that she would turn around and call me a thief. On the other hand I did feel like a thief and the feeling wreaked havoc on my peace of mind, not letting me sleep at night and forcing me to toss and turn in unease. Neither could I confess my guilt to anyone. Unable to endure this torture for much longer and the reminder of the stolen book weighing like a mountain on my shoulders, I wedged it into my pyjama bottom again one day and, reaching school before everyone else, placed it neatly on Abha's desk, unloading the heavy burden off my chest instantly.

Abha and I became friends later but I could never tell her about the book. In fact, even after I was all grown up I could never tell the story to anyone. Despite secretly returning the book I had failed to get rid of my guilt. Goon could confess to such crimes without batting an eyelid. I might not have liked his habits and his history of robbery and gambling but I must admit that I loved how nonchalantly he accepted his own shortcomings. He even wrote poems about his dissolute lifestyle and his liking for prostitutes.

Goon was once married to Neera Lahiri, a medical student, and they had a happy family with their young daughter, Mrittika. The poet used to be busy earning money and the medical student was busy training to become a doctor. So they had summoned Geeta from Netrakona to look after the little girl. Geeta had no children and she loved Mrittika as her own. One fine day Neera had abruptly declared that she was ending her relationship with Goon and left with their daughter, leaving him behind with Geeta. He moved from Mymensingh to a slum in Dhaka, not just with Geeta but her entire family, all of who he felt responsible for.

Neera married again, this time a doctor, and Mrittika was left to the care of her grandmother. The slum that Goon had moved to was quite close to where Mrittika lived. Not once did I hear him complain about staying in a slum or having so many mouths to feed. He was perennially a happy man; he did not have material comforts but did not feel the lack. Instead he enjoyed life to the fullest, laughed loudly, loved generously and wrote just as much. Not particularly attached to wealth, he was as comfortable eating delicate cuisine laid out on exquisite dinner tables in palatial mansions as he was eating stale dal and rice while swatting flies away in front of his shanty in the slum. To him winning a few thousand dollars in a Las Vegas casino was as exhilarating as earning a few taka in a shabby gambling den in some back alley of Dhaka. He saw the world from a unique vantage point, full of experiences but shorn of illusions. Life, when compared to the universe, was merely a fragile thread whose tenuous hold could snap at any moment—Goon fearlessly walked this tightrope to extract the last bit of joy he could from it.

One night our conversation continued for so long that it got too late for him to return home. Since neither Mother nor Milan was at home I asked him to stay the night at my place since I had an extra bed. Early the next morning we were surprised by Geeta's sudden appearance at my doorstep. Worried that her Dada had not returned the night before, the dutiful Geeta had combed the city in search of him before finally getting hold of my address and turning up there to look for him! As soon as she saw him she got right to the point. 'Dada, what sort of behaviour is this? Here I am dying of worry. You should have left me word!'

'How did you find out I'm here with Nasrin?' Goon asked with a laugh.

A calm slowly descending on her anxious face, Geeta quipped, 'Asimda suggested I try here.'

'Did you walk here or you came in a rickshaw?'

'How could I walk so far? I took a rickshaw.'

'Did you pay?'

'No, he's waiting at the gate.'

'Don't you have school today?'

'Yes, I do. Let's get home soon or I'll be late.' They had tea and breakfast and left soon after.

Goon had dedicated the first volume of his collected poems to Shamsur Rahman and the second to Geeta, short for Geeta Gandiba Dasi. Geeta worked at a school in Azimpur where she rang the bells. She was no longer a domestic help, her body was healthier, and she had learnt to hold her head high. Her little sisters were with her too and she intended to get them jobs soon. Goon had suggested one of them come work for me. After Kulsum ran away Geeta's youngest sister Baby was sent over to work in her stead but she did not last long. She later joined a garments factory where she threaded needles for 300 taka. These were the people who comprised Nirmalendu Goon's family and I had heard a lot about them from him.

Once I asked him why he did not consider moving from the slum to a better place and he explained to me how for them the slum was the best place they could ever live in. The slum gave them the freedom to be the way they wished to be, abuse, scream and shout if they had to, behaviour which they would never get away with in a regular middle-class neighbourhood. Besides, every landlord would have uncomfortable probing questions to ask about his relationship with Geeta and her sisters, questions that no one cared about in the slum. Social shame, the fear of losing one's social standing—these were decidedly middle-class preoccupations and Goon's life cut across class boundaries. He was a man who had moved out of the framework of class; I used to think of him like the mythical swan, with neither the dirt of the slum in Azimpur nor the glitter of the palaces of Gulshan managing to have any effect on him.

Goon never won when he gambled; it was a losing game for him from the get-go. Despite that he was a gambling aficionado. I had once said to him, 'Just let it be. Why do you go? Waste of time and waste of money!'

'What do I do? There's no other way,' he had morosely replied.

'Why?'

Blaming his cohorts he had told me, 'If I don't play they call me a bastard.' He used to go and gamble with them because he did not like them calling him a bastard!

No matter how dismissive and playful he was about life, about politics he was never anything but serious. However, in the 1991 elections he did do something outrageous. He had always been keen on contesting the general elections and since he was a staunch Awami League supporter he was convinced that he was going to get a ticket for the election as a League candidate. Although it did not go quite as he had planned, it failed to deter him from his firm resolve to fight the election. In the absence of the boat[29] he had wished for, he adopted the symbol of a crocodile and registered himself as an independent candidate. Soon, Netrakona was covered in posters and Goon earnestly threw himself into the campaigning. The voice used to reciting poetry could suddenly be heard across Netrakona shouting slogans and speaking to his electorate in a door-to-door campaign. With his crocodile symbol adorning the background of the rickshaw, independent political leader Nirmalendu Goon waved at his supporters and well-wishers throughout his tour of Netrakona. He gained considerable electoral knowledge from this exercise but unfortunately that did not translate into victory for him. In the end, five votes was all he got.

Goon wrote the most evocative and the most number of poems about Sheikh Mujib. The same Awami League that used to include his poems in almost all their special events and programmes, the party that had given election tickets to so many rank idiots over the years, never gave Goon a shot at contesting the polls. At a time when no one dared say anything about Sheikh Mujib, let alone write against

him, Goon was the only one writing such poems and reading them
out fearlessly in public gatherings.

> Mujib meant nothing else,
> nothing more than freedom,
> and the unwritten love
> between father and son.
> Mujib meant nothing else,
> nothing more than might,
> and the brave Bengali's timeless devotion.

His poetry was an asset to the Awami League. Dubbing the 7 March
1971 address delivered at the Race Course grounds a 'poem' and calling
Mujib a 'poet', Goon had written the poem 'Swadhinota Sobdoti
Kibhabe Amader Holo' (How Did We Learn the Word Freedom).
Whenever the BNP tried claiming that Ziaur Rahman was the one who
had called for independence, the Awami League set itself the task of
reminding everyone of Sheikh Mujib's contributions back in 1971 and
Goon was the one who was summoned. Seeing the ardent Mujib-loving
poet extol the great man's virtues through his poems in public gatherings
and meetings must have made Sheikh Hasina considerably proud. In the
pin-drop silence of the congregation Goon read his poems out aloud.

> Like everyone gathered here I too love roses.
> While zooming past the race course yesterday,
> One of the roses whispered to me
> To write a poem on Sheikh Mujib;
> And here I am today.
> While walking past Samakal yesterday
> A freshly blossomed flame-of-the-forest whispered to me,
> To write a poem on Sheikh Mujib;
> And here I am today.
> Yesterday, the fountain at Shahbag Square
> Begged me in a choked cry
> To write a poem on Sheikh Mujib;
> And here I am today.
> A bloodstained brick from the Sahid Minar

Whispered to me yesterday,
To write a poem on Sheikh Mujib;
And here I am today.
Like everyone here I too favour dreams,
And Love. The heroic dream I had last night
Whispered in my ears,
To write a poem on Sheikh Mujib;
And here I am today.
Let the people gathered under this vast oak bear witness,
Let the buds in the fiery flamboyant tree,
Poised at the edge of new life, lend me their ear,
Let the cuckoo in this forlorn spring afternoon know,
In the name of this pious earth under my feet,
I have kept my word to the rose
And the fiery flames-of-the-forest,
I have not come to ask for blood,
I have come instead to sing about love.

Despite his refusal to play by the rules the Awami League never broke off its ties with Goon, and his relationship with Sheikh Hasina too remained as before. After moving to the government quarters on Minto Road, residence of the leader of the opposition, Sheikh Hasina organized a lavish iftar party to rival a similar event organized by the ruling party some time back. Both Goon and I received invitations for the evening and we were more than interested at the prospect of a lavish spread. Goon was carrying a jar of Dove cream in his pocket bought from America as a gift for Sheikh Hasina. Both my hands and my pockets were empty, except for my eyes that were brimming with curiosity about a political iftar. A huge canopy had been erected on the grounds of the house at Minto Road and chairs and tables had been arranged underneath. The Quran was being recited over loudspeakers and as the sirens blared the fasting Awami politicians drank water with chants of 'Bismillah' to signal the end of yet another day of Ramzan. Sheikh Hasina herself was moving from one table to another, greeting guests and informing them that the League too was a religious party just like the BNP and the Jamaat. This unholy congregation of religion and politics was both painful and terrifying to witness.

Communal politics, so long prohibited in Bangladesh, was finally legitimate. The same Jamaat leaders who had gone into hiding after independence were now proud parliamentarians of the nation. Things were so different! The Jamaat would never have come this far had it not enjoyed the tacit encouragement of many established leaders. Golam Azam, the chief figure behind the genocide carried out in 1971, was living in the country with impunity and leading the Jamaat, and many other treacherous agents were roaming about with their heads held high.[30] A few individuals still standing by the ideals of the Liberation War instituted an organization called Ekattorer Ghatak Dalal Nirmul Committee (Committee for Resisting Killers and Collaborators of Bangladesh Liberation War of 1971) in January 1992, led my Jahanara Imam. She also published her memoirs titled *Ekattorer Dinguli* (The Days of the Liberation War), an account of the tumultuous time of 1971 and how she had lost her husband and her son to the war.

One day Khoka took me to Jahanara Imam's house, around the time when she was busy with a signature campaign demanding punishment for Golam Azam for war crimes. I was tasked with helping with the campaign, and when a huge people's court was organized at the Suhrawardy Udyan to try Golam Azam under the leadership of the Nirmul Committee, I was among the thousands of people who marched there. The judgement was unanimous: Golam Azam had to be hanged for his crimes. But there was no one to carry out the sentence, especially in the face of the police forces that the government deployed to stop the people's court. The police came and disrupted the peaceful crowd gathered at the protest, disconnected the mikes and destroyed the stage. Golam Azam was put in prison but that too was merely for show. The slight charge levelled against him—staying on in Bangladesh with a Pakistani passport even after his visa had expired—was nothing in comparison to the crimes committed in 1971 when he had murdered thousands of Bengalis on behalf of the Pakistani military junta, crimes the government had nothing to say about. I was concerned that after things settled down Golam Azam was again going to be set free, and the citizenship he had applied for was also going to be granted to him. What was the country going to look like? Was it going to be habitable at all? The way religion was increasingly spreading its influence over politics,

I was troubled that some day soon state power was going to pass on to the Jamaat-e-Islami.

~

Meanwhile, Kulsum was back in my employment. She had not been able to run far, although she had only resolved to run to her home in Mymensingh and live with her mother and her sister. That dream had been short-lived; she had taken up housework elsewhere in Shantibag where the issues had been too many for her to handle and she had quietly returned to me again. She was barely thirteen or fourteen, but even at such a young age she prayed five times a day, fasted on every day of Ramzan, and refused to take off her headscarf ever. Having worked for a long time in a pir's house it was not difficult to fathom where she had filled her head with all this rubbish. I asked her once, 'All this namaz and roza, what purpose will it serve?' She was mopping the floor. Dipping the dirty wiping cloth in the bucket, she gave it a good rinse, wrung the extra water out and replied, resuming her mopping, 'To go to Paradise.'

'What's in Paradise?'

Stopping her work she looked up with a sweet smile, her eyes sparkling. 'In Paradise Allah will give me fish hearts to eat.'

'Fish hearts! You want to eat fish hearts? I will get you some, tomorrow I will get you some from Shantinagar market.'

Her face twisted in response, the nose wrinkled, the lips pursed and the brows drew together at my suggestion of buying fish hearts from the market.

'You want to eat fish hearts, isn't it? Stop all this praying and fasting. Remove your headscarf. In this heat, don't you feel even warmer? Fish hearts!'

Drawing her headscarf tighter around her head, Kulsum shot back, 'Fish hearts here are bitter! In Paradise the hearts will be sweet.'

I laughed hysterically at that. Annoyed at my laughter, Kulsum threw an irritated glance at me and walked out of the room, certain at last that I was either crazy or stupid.

Suppression

There was an attack on the offices of the journal *Purbabhash*. In the dead of the night a group of unknown assailants broke into the office and ransacked the place, all because they were upset about my writing. They did not like what I had to say and some religious fundamentalists lodged a case against the editors of the journal. I visited the office a few days after the incident; it had left a sour taste in my mouth. In fact, I was so upset that for a moment I genuinely considered ending my writing career. I was already a doctor, so during the extra time I had after Mitford I could have joined a private clinic and earned handsomely. Having arrived at this conclusion I did stop writing for a while, until Mozammel Babu of *Purbabhash* convinced me otherwise. He insisted I go ahead as planned with the article I had promised him prior to the attacks. Answering his urgent summons when I finally went and met him he repeated the request. 'Aapa, how can you stop writing? Write! You have to give me something by today.' In the middle of the conversation Babu received a call from AZ who wrote columns for the magazine too. On hearing the news that I had stopped writing he told Babu he wished to speak to me. 'Don't stop writing. You are writing so well right now. Go ahead and don't pay any attention to what a few goons are up to,' he told me. Just like AZ a number of other people echoed the sentiment and urged me to take up writing columns for journals again. Others went further and advised me to lay off writing harsh things about religion for the time being.

I started again because I could not stay away from it. After a few days it had begun to seem like a mountain of words and thoughts were piling up inside me waiting to be let out. Meanwhile, AZ had started a new range of columns in *Purbabhash*, different from the political and social satire he was known for. These were about women, not the

derisive misogynistic truisms he used to write before, but appreciative
pieces extolling their virtues. Although I had not managed to read
any of them, one day Goon told me AZ was trying to become popular
by imitating my style. Curious, I looked up some of his pieces in
Purbabhash and could not help but concur with Goon's assessment.
The only difference was that AZ was referring to many books and
texts to make the same points that I had already made long ago,
rewriting the things I had narrated from my own experience.

~

The book fair was about to start and a number of my books were
waiting to be published—a collection of poems and some columns
too and a few new novels. Fazlul Alam had translated my poems
into English and compiled them into a manuscript titled *Light Up
at Midnight*, which Vidyaprakash had agreed to publish. I had first
met Fazlul Alam at my old house in Armanitola. Faridur Reza Sagar
had paid a surprise visit along with his London-based uncle Alam.
Sagar was a man of many talents. The son of writer Rabeya Khatun,
he was an author himself and had written many books for children,
besides being the anchor of a children's television show and running
his own garments factory. Besides, he was also one of the owners of
Ajker Kagaj and *Khabarer Kagaj*. He was not usually seen in literary
events, preferring to stay busy with his business and his popular new
restaurant Khabar-Dabar near the stadium. He read the namaz five
times a day, even had a prayer room especially built for that purpose
in his huge office in Shantinagar and kept thirty rozas every Ramzan.
A busy man, he wrote quietly and published quietly too. Despite that
he had taken time out to personally bring his beloved uncle to meet
me, taking the trouble to locate my house in Armanitola.

After returning to the country Fazlul Alam's first wish had been
to meet me. Evidently he had made up his mind about this even before
leaving London all because of my columns; he had resolved to not go
back without making my acquaintance. A jovial, straightforward and
honest man, Alam never shied away from calling a spade a spade even
at the cost of hurting the sentiments of those around him. A bit oddly
shaped, sort of like a sandbag, and a bit hard of hearing, he talked

loudly and laughed frequently. I knew Sagar from before, had been to his house for dinner; in fact, more than the casual dinner, I used to go to meet him whenever I was feeling the blues for some reason. In his absence I used to talk to his wife and his mother.

Sagar's mother Rabeya Khatun and I usually spoke about literature. When it came to writing I never hesitated to admit that I did not know how to write and I mostly did not consider my stuff as writing at all. When I asked how one wrote a novel the soft-spoken Rabeya had told me that it required immense concentration; I had confessed without hesitation that focus was one thing I severely lacked. Sagar spoke to me as a close friend, telling me about his father leaving his mother, his own efforts in restoring the financial security of his family, and how he had saved a tortured girl from death and then married her. I considered his family my own. Consequently, Alam too had grown close to me over time. He was a regular columnist in Bengali journals in London and had also written for *Khabarer Kagaj*.

One day I suggested that he compile his columns into a book just like mine. Excited at the prospect he set himself to gathering his writing and the two of us put our heads together and soon came up with a name for the book. I was tasked with locating a publisher and quite unsurprisingly who else was I going to approach but Khoka! Despite his reservations about the project since Alam was not a known name, Khoka had agreed. I did the cover myself and Alam's joy had to be seen to be believed. He postponed his return to London—or perhaps he went back for a while and returned soon after—not wishing to miss the approaching book fair where his book was going to be released.

The book fair was soon upon us, set to run through February. An entire month dedicated to writers, a special time we too waited for through the year. Rafiq–Salam–Barkat had become martyrs in February; they had sacrificed themselves for the revolutionary cause of instituting Bengali as the national language of the country. This month was dedicated to the Bengali language, to Bengali literature and Bengali music.

One could chance upon a number of engrossing conversations on myriad topics at the fair. In February 1992, I too had enough reason to be happy. A number of my books were at the fair and most were doing well, with the first editions getting over in no time and the publishers having to step up to get a second edition out at the earliest. News was trickling in that Humayun Ahmed, MHI and Taslima Nasrin were the highest selling authors at the fair. MHI had been a popular writer for a long time. Humayun Ahmed had won the Bangla Academy honours for *Nandito Narake* (In Beautiful Hell) and gone off to America. After returning home he had begun writing again and started right at the top. I remembered seeing him walking alone through the fair only a few book fairs ago, his hands crossed over his chest. That was also when I had met him for the first time.

One day, on hearing my description of how we used to read his books at home—one of us reading aloud and the others sitting around and listening—he was delighted and had confessed to me how it had been the same back where he came from. Having grown up in Mohangunje he had a distinct Mymensingh twang when he spoke. He would come to the fair and find me and tell me tales of the old days. He used to call me by the name 'poet'. 'How is the poet today? Would the poet like to go have some tea?'

Such an amazing storyteller was he that one could spend hours sitting and simply listening to him. I loved his stories, stories of very recognizable lives as they were, his own stories, those of his siblings, his neighbours, all simple middle-class people of the suburbs. Listening to their tales of everyday joys and sorrows I could almost visualize them in front of me, they were my own relatives and loved ones. When his drama serials began to be televised he used to invite his friends over to his home to watch them together with him. In his small apartment in Azimpur, Goon and I had seen Ahmed's *Eka* (Alone). Before the telecast he had been nervous, pacing about his room; he had admitted to us that this happened every time a play of his was to be televised.

Despite having lived in America for so many years, Ahmed had a very simple life; it would often seem that he had arrived at the city from the village just the other day. An everyman in the best sense of the term, impassive and erudite, he loved to chat and was rarely concerned about others' opinions, besides being fiercely self-reliant. Just like an everyman, so much had changed with Ahmed since then. Courtesy his immense popularity we rarely ever met and his drama serials had made him so famous that neither was he seen on strolls through the book fair any more. As long as he stayed in the fairgrounds he remained surrounded by autograph-hunters. When I was initially writing columns for newspapers Ahmed had confessed to me that reading them had made him more anxious about his three daughters; my columns had made him recognize the serious lack of security that defined women's lives. I was always a fan of his writing. Many used to say his work would not withstand the test of time, that his novels were slight and their characters even slighter. However, I believed that his words had managed to forge a fundamental connect with the people and that could not easily be written off. His keen sense of observation made him understand what the readers wanted and he catered to that, making sure that even those who never read books still made it a point to read his. His biggest achievement was perhaps the legion of readers he had created over the years.

Khoka asked me to sit at the Vidyaprakash stall in the fair every day in the afternoon. Other publishers too followed suit and made similar requests even though it was just not in my nature to sit still in one place for too long. All I wanted to do was stroll through the fair, watch people, and chat and have tea with my friends. But I had to honour Khoka's request and sit at the stall, signing copies of books for people. Many of them would enter, take the book in their hands to turn it over and examine it, and then leave because they did not have money to buy it. I wanted to give the books away for free and did so with a few, only to be stopped by Khoka's incredulous 'what-do-you-think-you-are-doing' glances. Unable to skirt the issue he would simply tell me, 'I'm giving this one from my complimentary copies.'

This nexus between books and money made me deeply uncomfortable, while Khoka tried to make me understand this basic connection repeatedly. 'You can't be so large-hearted! You are a professional writer now!'

'What are you saying! I am a doctor, and that is my profession. Writing is my hobby.'

Khoka did not agree with me; selling books was his business. His wife and brother-in-law would often be at the stall assisting him. Fazlul Alam too would be at the stall often to check how his books were doing and bringing people he knew along to show them. One such person was AZ, who flipped through *Light Up at Midnight* and said, 'That one isn't there is it? "Saat shokale khor kurote giye, amar jhuri upche geche phule!"' (While out gathering hay at dawn, my basket runneth over with flowers.)

'No, it isn't here,' Alam replied.

Immediately AZ countered, 'Of course! Why should the good ones be here!'

Laughing, I asked him, 'So my poems are good, are they?'

His smile stretching from ear to ear AZ nodded. 'Of course! I love many of your poems.'

'But just the other day you gave an interview to a magazine claiming I wasn't even a poet! That you didn't read my columns because they were meant for kids.'

The grin on his face did not hold up for long and AZ left without a word. This was the person who had gotten annoyed because my columns in *Khabarer Kagaj* had become popular. This was also the person who had spoken to me when we were at the office of *Purbabhash* and told me he liked reading my columns. I could only think of AZ as a child. He was a university professor, a research scholar, a learned man and a good writer who wrote both good poetry and prose. Despite so many talents he was still known for doing silly things and many people mercilessly called out his predilection for pulling stunts to stay in the public eye. He went around abusing other writers and poets, his lackeys surrounding him whenever he was at the book fair and sucking up to him ceaselessly; of course, he too enjoyed the attention.

Used to the London way of life, adjusting to the book fair was nearly impossible for Fazlul Alam. He wanted to stick to me the entire day, sit if I sat, stand if I stood, and have tea if I was having some. Annoyed, I had to tell him to find his own thing to do and left with no choice he had to stop following me around eventually. Besides, neither was his book doing well that that could cheer him up. He did not have a single friend or acquaintance to talk to during the fair and I was too busy to be with him all the time. Since he couldn't hear very well it was too annoying for people to always have to scream in order to speak to him.

Before the fair started Alam had taken me to a party at Inayatullah Khan's house which I had deeply disliked. None of the guests had come across as welcoming, comprising only rich men and their heavily decked-up wives. The women were drinking and introducing each other as Mrs Sahabuddin, Mrs Khan and so on, and there had not been one person with an identity of her own. To me, the entire evening had been too strange for words with the only accepted topics of discussion being wealth, property, the number of houses one had plus the number of cars. Unable to stand it for too long, I had left the glittering gathering early. More things had happened after that to further put me off. I was supposed to go to Mymensingh and Alam had offered to drop me in Sagar's car. Throughout the journey he had driven at such speed—probably the speed he drove at in London—that there could have been a serious accident at any moment. I had screamed at him to slow down, although it had seemed he did not know how to drive slow or had forgotten since moving to London. In the end he had been left perplexed and out of sorts, nearly avoiding collisions with trucks, cars, rickshaws, buses, bullock carts and even people throughout the journey.

~

It was the evening of 17 February 1992. A sense of urgency permeated the air, although I had no way of knowing what it could have been. A procession wound its way past the Vidyaprakash stall with a huge banner at its head. If a march with a banner at the book fair was not incredible enough, no one seemed to know what it was all about or who the organizers were. All of a sudden Khoka got up in a hurry and began to remove all my books that were on display on the table, while his brother-in-law proceeded to pack up the ones on the shelves. Before I could react Muhammad Nurul Huda and Rafiq Azad appeared and I was whisked away from the stall to the main pavilion of the Bangla Academy, right up to the office of the director general. What was this all about?

As I learnt from the director general, the procession I had witnessed had been organized against me by the Taslima Nasrin Suppression Committee, to quash the nefarious 'sex writer' Taslima Nasrin. The committee had issued warnings to the booksellers against selling my books in the fair and anyone who was going to be found not complying had been warned that their stalls were going to be ransacked or burnt down. The booksellers had obviously complied and removed all my books from display. I sat there, stunned by the news, unseeing of the other writers who were already present in the room. Alam had followed us to the office and his face betrayed his anxiety. The ensuing discussion focused entirely on these new developments—why the protest, who was behind it, how could the unrest be tackled and whispered conversations about what was on that banner. Abruptly the director general turned to me.

'Why are they marching? What are their complaints against you?'

'I have no clue what complaints they have.'

In a grave tone the director-general continued. 'Very dirty things are written on that banner. What do you think? Why are they doing this?'

'Probably because of my writing.'

'So many people write. Look around you, all these writers, all of them write books. There are never processions against them. Why against you?'

Alam intervened loudly. 'What do you mean why? How would she know? Ask the ones marching. And why should everyone have to like Taslima Nasrin's writings? She doesn't write compromised pieces like most others.'

There were murmurs among the writers present. Were they being called sell-outs, the ones who compromised on their views? Stopping the chatter the director general raised his eyebrows and turned to me again. 'Despite being a woman why do you try and write like a man? All this is because of that.'

'Why should I write like a man? I write what I feel,' I countered immediately.

The other writers in the room stirred in their seats. 'Not everything is meant for everyone. Don't you understand that?' continued the director general with a smirk. Some of the glitter of that smirk had found its way to the lips of the other authors as well. 'I have read your writing. Can a woman ever write in the sort of language you write in?'

I had nothing to say to that.

'No, they don't,' he supplied the answer. The others nodded in agreement; other women really did not write the way I wrote.

My jaw tightened.

'Your writing is very obscene.'

Gritting my teeth I replied, 'It's my writing. Some find it obscene, some don't.'

Meanwhile, Muhammad Nurul Huda went outside and announced over the mike that no one was supposed to take out protest marches through the fairground and disrupt the atmosphere of the place. Asking the protesters to calm down he informed them that if anyone had complaints or grievances they should get hold of the organizers. Suddenly, a loud din could be heard from afar. 'Fire! Fire!' The people sitting in the room rushed to the window to see what was happening. A fire could be seen raging in the middle of the fairground. The protesters had gathered whichever of my books they could get their hands on, collected them in a heap in the middle of the field and set the entire pile on fire.

Khoka was standing on the balcony of director general Harunur Rashid's office. I got up and walked up to him. He was stunned by the proceedings, perspiration dotting his forehead, his jaws tight.

'Khoka bhai, do you know who these people are? What is happening?'

Khoka shook his head in response. He had no idea either.

The director general conferred with the other organizers, his deputies at the Bangla Academy, and passed his verdict. 'You should stay away from the fair. That'll be best.'

'What does that even mean? Why should I not come?'

Fazlul Alam spoke up. 'Why should she not come? What's her fault?'

'Her presence causes trouble, so she should not come.' He also informed me that should anything happen to me at the fair it would not be their responsibility. So the best recourse for me was to stay away. They did not wish for the spirit and schedule of the fair to be upended because of me.

Outraged, Fazlul Alam asked again. 'You are the organizers. It's you who should be responsible for her safety.' The director general turned towards him with his eyebrows drawn together, the question implicit in his gaze—who was this strange man screaming at him?

'Just because some boys are protesting against me I should stop coming to the fair? There are many who like my writing too, they . . .'

Nothing I had to say was enough to convince the director general otherwise. With no other solution in sight, he remained firm on the judgement he had pronounced. His advice to me was to stay away from the book fair. Since I wrote like a man despite being a woman, since my writing was obscene, since what I wrote hardly had any literary merit, it was not surprising that people were marching in protest against me and neither was it surprising that some of them wanted to crush me entirely. So it was best that I stayed away, more to maintain peace and order at the book fair than because of any concerns over my security. I was packed into a police van and sent home.

The book fair was in full swing but I was prohibited from attending it. I was used to adverse reactions to my writing. The previous year a group of boys, around nineteen or twenty years old, had approached me with a book of poems, showed me one of them called 'Biparit Khela' (Reverse Play) and told me, 'We want to be bought for 10 taka. Please buy us.' At first I had taken it to be a joke. But then their demands had grown more insistent. Flabbergasted, I had gulped and quietly told them it was simply a poem, that I was not going to buy them for real, and moved away. Khoka had been nearby and noticed the entire exchange. He had gone after the boys, called them back and told them, 'It's fine that you want to be bought but are you willing to go along with the other conditions laid out in the poem? Read the entire poem, then come and ask to be bought.'

Nowadays I wish I could buy boys for five or ten bucks.
To buy them and then destroy them,
Throw them to the ground and kick them, and tell them to fuck off.
I will buy boys, kick them in the balls, and tell them to fuck off . . .

I had written the poem after noticing civilized gentlemen picking up destitute girls standing in front of Ramana Park one evening. Where did these men take these girls in their rickshaws? What did they do with them? All these questions had made me very curious. One day while walking past Ramana Park I had stopped at the sight of more of these girls, combing their rough, unoiled hair, holding broken mirrors and rubbing powder on their dirt-crusted faces. I had asked

them, 'Why are you decking up like this?' None of them had replied
at first. On probing further one of them had said, 'For food.'

Ruffled hair, sunburnt skin, old bruises on their faces and hands,
a swollen eye here or a cut forehead there. A young girl, a swollen
red bruise on her forehead, had been standing listlessly leaning on
the railings. I had asked her, 'What happened to your forehead?' She
had looked at me once and then looked away without bothering to
answer, as if I was nothing but an unwanted pest. I had stood there
staring at her hair sticking to the sweat on her forehead. Seeing how
she was not moving the errant lock aside I had felt the insane urge to
do it for her and then take her home, wash her, feed her and give her
a bed to sleep on. She had looked so sleepy, that girl, as if she had not
slept for many nights. Suddenly, she had spoken. 'It's all about what's
written on the forehead, why it bruises and bleeds.' She had looked at
me with vacant eyes and cried, 'Those men, they hit me.'

'Why?'

'Because they wanted to.'

'How much do you get? How much do they pay you?'

'Ten. Five. Some days two. Some days not even that. Only kicks.'

Seeing the police approach, with a bitter smile she had moved
away, and the other girls too had packed up their make-up and left.
The police were men. Did they not exploit these women too? Even if
they did not, they did not hesitate to take money from them, their cut
of the five or ten bucks these women managed to 'earn'. In exchange
the deal was that they were not going to beat up these women or
put them in jail. The men who haggled and picked these women
up in their rickshaws, did the police ever think to arrest them too?
No, they did not. Were these men called dirty? No, they were not. I
had walked away asking myself these questions, the answers all quite
obvious, the heaviness in my heart escalating with every step.

~

The ban imposed on me upset Khoka deeply. Pushing every other
occupation aside, his business, his books, his accounts, even the
book fair, unearthing who was at the root of the Taslima Nasrin
Suppression Committee became his sole obsession. Who were they,

what did they do, what were they after, were they politicians, if so then which party—he wanted to find answers to these and many more questions.

Learning that the chairperson of the committee was a BNP member, he looked up a distant cousin of his from his aunt's side, or perhaps it had been his uncle's—who was also a member of the BNP—to try and broker some sort of an agreement. An agreement, however, did not just come about through word of mouth, such things always required financial investment. I never found out how much Khoka had to spend because of me. Unfortunately, when it soon became clear that despite being paid off my opponents were not going to let go of their grudge, the only alternative left for Khoka was to arrange a meeting between us: the opponent leader versus me.

I agreed after immense persuasion and Khoka warned me repeatedly to not lose my patience and answer everything the leader had to ask me calmly. The meeting was held at Khoka's place. Alam, who had gone into shock after the judgement passed by the director general, was yet to recover. On finding out that I was going to talk to the leader of the Suppression Committee he was insistent that he would come with us. He was suspicious that the leader was going to try and attack me again and he wanted to be the one to leap in at such a moment and rescue me. I had no desire to take him with us but he would simply not listen to reason. Khoka would have none of it; he was firm that the leader only wished to speak with me. Even if there could be a third person in the room it could only be Khoka. He was not allowed to speak, that I had to do myself. Khoka had a cool head and in times of stress he could help in managing things. In such moments, calm heads had to prevail and Alam's was too hot and thus susceptible to cause more harm than good. Alam's hot head was asked to stay put beneath the fan in the other room.

We sat across from the university student leader who had formed the committee that wanted to crush me. He was not exactly imposing—with a moustache, pimples and hatred clearly visible on his face. As he looked up at me I could glimpse flashes of that hatred in his eyes, which was goading him to crush the life out of me. When it came to officially presenting the charges levelled against me the boy, Hafiz, or Haroon, or Hamid, or perhaps Hasan, or whatever his name was, said, 'You are destroying our mothers and our sisters.'

'How?'

'You don't know how!'

'I know that I write for them, about them. Why should I cause them harm?'

'You have asked them to walk out of their homes. You have goaded them to leave their families.'

'I have never said anything like that.'

'In "Balikar Gollachhut" you wrote, "for all of us old girls to run away."'

Hamid, or Hasan, opened a book of my poems to show me the offensive lines.

'Read it, read it again. And tell me why you wrote this poem.' The warning and the command in his voice came at me like a poisoned arrow.

> The afternoon used fall upon the world so us girls could play,
> A game called gollachhut.
> . . . I feel like playing again,
> My feet are restless, they want to feel the dirt underneath
> And they wish
> For all of us old girls to run away.

It was like I was testifying in court. I was standing at the witness stand, having sworn to tell the truth at any cost. I had to because no matter how unimpressive the leader was, even if he could be asked to shut up and sit with a small slap, even if he looked powerless, the truth was that he was immensely powerful. He had the power to form a collective and the power to use that collective to obliterate me.

'You are asking all old girls to run away. Our mothers and sisters should just leave their families. Do you even know what damage you are doing to society?'

'This is a poem about playing gollachhut, about playing tag. The girls who used to play tag when they were young can't play it any more once they grow up. But the desire remains. I have only spoken about my desire to play tag again.'

Hafiz, or Habib, shook his head in disagreement.

'You have spoken about all older women here, not just yourself.'

'All women desire something like that. Everyone wants to turn back, go back to being a child again, isn't it? When I am writing about myself I am also feeling what many other women are feeling. This poem is about their feelings . . .'

'No, all women don't feel like that . . .'

'Many do.'

'No, they don't. Admit it, it's only you.'

I could not think of what to say to that. Habib/Haroon, his eyes rapier sharp, 'By game, you refer to her family, right? Her husband, her children?'

Out of the corner of my eye I could sense Khoka's desperate silent pleas—*I will take you to the book fair come hell or high water. Just tell him that you meant only the game and not the family.* Faced with such earnestness I swallowed the reply I was ready with: 'If you think like that then it can be a family, as well as the chains society puts on women.'

Before I could respond Hasan/Hafiz continued, 'How do you know what other women want?'

Turning the pages of the book, I replied, 'It's what I have felt.'

'Did you ask anyone before writing whether they want to run at all? Or do you judge everyone by your standards?'

There was something in his eyes, a flare of a feeling that would not let me raise my head. Putting the book down, I answered, 'No, I didn't.'

'It's what you think other women want. But you don't know for sure.'

This time, looking directly into his eyes I said to him, 'It's my wish. I will write my own thoughts in my poems. That's not wrong.'

'Yes, it is.'

'What is so wrong about it?'

In a mild voice Khoka intervened. 'Writers write what they think they should. Not everyone finds the works of all authors as good. Not all readers agree with what a writer has to say. I feel she meant the game. It's possible for someone reading it to misunderstand.'

Agreeing with Khoka, I continued, 'Yes, many people misunderstand. For example, take that poem "Biparit Khela". Did I actually want to buy boys in the poem? It was a form of protest.'

'Why don't you explain it to him?' Khoka suggested.

'I'm trying. I'm trying to show how different people react differently to the same piece of writing. The writer may have his own explanations and the reader may have his own.'

The student leader had formed the committee to suppress me, to get his hands on me, parade me naked through the fair and crush me under his feet for all to witness. What was I supposed to explain to him? He had formed his group without understanding a word of what he was protesting against, purely from the suspicion that I was out to destroy society and play with the heads of his mothers and sisters. That sort of thinking was not restricted to only the Hasans and Hamids of the world, there were many other people who believed the same. Looking at his eyes I could not understand if he had accepted my simple explanation for the game in the poem. Khoka's eyes met mine but this time I could not read what was written in them.

The man's next problem was with the poem 'Joy Bangla' (Long Live Bengal). 'Why did you write this poem?'

'Because I believe in the greatness of Bengal,' was my simple reply.

'In the poem you have wished that the unfortunate souls who do not believe in it should die. I don't believe in Joy Bangla. Would you call me unfortunate? Why would you say rubbish about those who don't believe in it?'

'You don't believe in independent Bangladesh?'

'Why won't I? Of course I do!'

Completely agitated, I shot back, 'If you do then there is no reason to not believe in Joy Bangla either. When Bangladesh won its independence what slogan did we all chant? Joy Bangla! All of us sang the same song.' Looking away from the leader's angry face I turned to Khoka. 'Khoka bhai, did you not shout Joy Bangla in 1971? Only the Razakar traitors did not chant Joy Bangla. They are the unfortunate souls I wrote about in the poem.'

'Joy Bangla is the slogan of the Awami League!' The man's voice was hard, his nostrils flaring.

'Why should Joy Bangla be an Awami League slogan? It belongs to everyone. It refers to the victory we won, it refers to our independence. The muktijoddhas, the ones who were never part of the Awami League, did they not use the slogan all the time? Joy Bangla used to give them the energy to face their enemies head on.'

His face lighting up in a smile, Khoka joined in with his bit. 'He wasn't even born then, was he! You were born after the war, isn't it?' The student leader's head froze in indecision between an agreement and a denial. Turning to me, Khoka added, 'Why are you getting angry? They don't know what happened during the Mukti Juddho. Or they don't remember. It's true that the League has co-opted the slogan. They have no right to Joy Bangla . . .'

'Just because the League thinks the slogan is their property it doesn't just become so. Joy Bangla does not belong to any political party. I have been saying it since 1971 and I have never been a member of the Awami League. I have always been neutral and non-partisan. And there are many things about the League too that I don't like.'

Even after the Q&A was over Hasan/Habib/Hafiz/Hamid remained unsatisfied and Khoka had another round of discussions with him. Against his wishes he had to smile and bear the ignominy of it all because at least on the 21st he wanted me to be present at the book fair. Selling books at the fair was not a factor, what was more important for him was to restore my right to attend. Respite, however, is never easy to come by. Is it possible to completely ignore a constant nagging worry that plagues one's mind? The leader of the Suppression Committee promised that for the time being they were willing to back off but with the caveat that in the future I had to be more careful. If I were found writing obscene things again, things meant to incite mothers and sisters and things meant to disrupt society in any way, they warned me of far-reaching consequences.

Only one of the members of the committee had promised these things, were the others going to toe the line too? Khoka assured me they would but his confidence in the matter did not deter him from hiring a set of muscled guards tasked with ferrying me to and fro from the book fair. Flanked by unknown musclemen I did attend the book fair on the 21st but not with the same spontaneous joy as before, though I was immensely grateful for everything Khoka had done for me. No other author had come forward to help and the organizing committee too had shirked all responsibility. In such a scenario if

Khoka had not stepped in and made these arrangements I would have probably had to return home dejected.

The two days I went to the book fair I mostly stayed at the Vidyaprakash stall. Even when I wanted to take a stroll, or go to the tea vendor and have tea, I could not. Not that I could sit at the stall the entire day either; I went back home on both days after a couple of hours. Despite that, I still went and that was all that mattered, even though I could not stop my apprehensions from rearing their ugly heads time and again. Khoka remained visibly on edge the entire time but the joy of our minor victory was evident on his face too. Fazlul Alam was there, pacing a safe distance away from us, both anxious and elated. The members of the organizing committee threw censorious glances my way whenever they saw me, unable to stomach the living embodiment of trouble that I had become for them. Who knew what they had suspected would happen at the fair because of my presence? Had they thought someone would set something on fire? At least if the men had dragged *me* away to some place remote instead and set me on fire it would have gone a long way in allaying their fears. There were very few of my books left in the fair, most having been confiscated or burnt in the public bonfire by the members of the Suppression Committee. Anyone manning a stall which still had some copies left had hidden them away under their tables out of sight. Like every other year there was a poetry recital programme organized by the Bangla Academy. The previous year I had been invited to participate but this time I was not welcome there either.

While conspiracies were afoot to cast me aside and crush me, many readers came to the fair only to catch a glimpse of me. Some approached me with their eyes wide with wonder and said, 'If only we could touch you once and see for ourselves!' Some broke down in tears while speaking about how my books were not merely words but glimpses of life itself. 'You have said what I have always wanted to say but couldn't,' some said. Mothers came with their daughters to make the girls touch my feet in respect. People from far and near, Sylhet, Chattagram, Rajshahi, Bagura and so on, came to the book fair in Dhaka with one objective: to meet me in person, or at least catch a glimpse of me from a distance.

Their love, as well as their hatred, made me cry.

Euphoria

There was usually a steady stream of well-wishers at the Shantibag house. Like many others, Raka and Altaf first came to me as admirers and stayed on as friends. Both were aficionados of Rabindrasangeet while Altaf himself was a poet. They had married at a later age and were living a carefree childless life. They had both been married before too and had children from their previous relationships, but other than meeting the children once or twice a year they did not have too many other parental duties. Thus, even after a ten-to-five job, both of them had ample time to spare, especially in the evenings. So they frequently came over to my house and the place would echo with poems and songs of Rabindranath.

One such evening, amidst a haze of Rabindrasangeet I suggested we visit Santiniketan for the annual Basanta Utsab.[31] Despite being such ardent admirers of Rabindranath, Raka and Altaf had never been to Santiniketan and jumped at the suggestion. Besides, thanks to my publishers who were keeping my pockets full, I did not even have to borrow money from anyone this time. Within two days Raka and Altaf were packed and ready, an extra 2000 taka over and above our estimated expenses safely tucked away with them.

As the leader of the expedition I had the most important jobs. I approached Bilal Chowdhury, the editor of the Indian embassy's magazine *Bharat Bichitra*, for three Indian visas. He had published my poems in the magazine before and used to ask me for new work every time we met. And we did meet quite often; especially while staying at Armanitola whenever I used to head to his office and wile my time away listening to his stories. Even during the bad times at Shantibag I often visited the *Bharat Bichitra* office. Chowdhury loved addas and had a treasure trove of stories which he used to unload on anyone he took a shine to—stories of the old literary circles and small humorous personal anecdotes of many renowned authors of Calcutta which he presented with his own characteristic wit and flourish. Oh, such stories he used to tell! Having lived in Calcutta for so long he knew many of the well-known writers of the city and hearing him talk about the mad, the stupid, the generous, and the miserable, and about the roads and streets and bylanes of the city, it often seemed to me as if I had been transported there. Chowdhury was a poet too but his greatest gift was his storytelling, an ability that made him the life of any party. He was a very solitary man, kind-hearted to a fault, very welcoming, decidedly unfazed and too much of a poet.

In a very short span of time he had become a brother and a friend rolled into one. He had told me about Girindra Shekhar Basu's book *Laal Kaalo* (The Red and the Black), one of the greatest books of children's literature ever written. His voice heavy with regret, he had rued how the book was no longer available and no publisher was ready to bring out a new edition. Hearing an outline of the plot from him I had expressed my wish to read the book and he showed me his own tattered copy. I had borrowed it from him and was so impressed that I had decided then and there to take up the responsibility of getting a new edition of the book published.

I had gone to Khoka with the proposal and he had not turned me down. I proofread the book and had Chowdhury write an introduction, which he kept postponing and took an inordinate amount of time to hand over in the end. Seeing the coloured images of the ants in the book Khoka did wonder if it was necessary to print the photographs too but I had insisted that in a book meant primarily for children images were a must. In the end Khoka had relented and reprinted the book with photos and all. It was a job well done and the end result had given me immense satisfaction, much more than my own books had ever managed to. My own publications usually brought on a severe attack of nerves that managed to spoil any sense of joy whatsoever. The moment I would catch hold of a book I usually started flipping through the pages to find errors and tabulate the number of such errors on various pages. The more the number, the greater would be my unhappiness. I was certain of one thing: regardless of anything else I could never write if I was unhappy.

On hearing that we wished to attend the Basanta Utsab in Santiniketan, Chowdhury narrated to us a vivid description of the festival of colours as he had witnessed it many years ago. He also requested me to take a copy of *Laal Kaalo* for Sripantha who was going to put a notice about the book in the *Kolkatar Korcha* supplement of *Anandabazar Patrika*. He gave me the writer Sripantha's name and address: Nikhil Sarkar, alias Sripantha, Anandabazar Patrika, 6 Prafulla Sarkar Street. He also asked me to meet Indranath Majumdar—Chowdhury kept mentioning how he was a remarkable person—who owned a bookshop called Subarnarekha in Santiniketan. I gave him my word that I would meet both of them.

The three of us reached Calcutta in high spirits and the first person I contacted was Soumitra Mitra of the Information Centre of West Bengal. SHA had once told me that in Calcutta Mitra's reach was nearly godlike. He could solve any complex problem in the blink of an eye. Mitra helped us find accommodation in the government guest house on Kyd Street. Not for free, but definitely for a daily food and lodging expense that was nearly a quarter of what we would have had to pay in a hotel.

While explaining to him the reason for our visit we discovered that he too was headed towards Santiniketan with his own group for the Basanta Utsab; he arranged for both the groups to travel together. Our ride was in a magnificent coach of the Shantiniketan Express, with curtains on the windows, cushioned seats and beautifully carved wooden furniture. I had never known that train compartments could be so beautiful; I was informed that it was the same compartment once used by Rabindranath himself whenever he used to travel between Bolpur and Calcutta. I could scarcely contain my wonder at such an astounding revelation and Tagore's aura remained a pervasive presence around us throughout the journey.

Mitra's team comprised Ashesh, Mona and the danseuse Rekha Maitra. Ashesh and Mona were closer to my age while Rekha was a little older. In our team Altaf was the shy, meditative and unfazed type while Raka was more proactive, intelligent, brave and cautious. Raka was from Rajshahi and a smart speaker while Altaf walked slowly, could never stand straight, spoke softly and as little as possible, although when he did speak, he usually had many interesting things to say. Both of them were older than me by nearly a decade, although age was hardly a concern in such matters; people with vast differences in age frequently end up becoming close friends.

I had thought the seven of us were going to have a great time travelling to Santiniketan together but somehow in the end we split into two groups through no conscious choice of our own: the *bangals*[32] on one side and the *ghotis* on the other. The three of us, the clueless bangals, had no choice but to sit and watch the ghotis at their raucous best. Besides, it was not easy for us bangals to get used to ghoti ways immediately. After getting off at Dumdum we did try getting rid of our accents, shifting to more ghoti-centric vowels than our traditional ones, but the tongue usually has its own story to tell and even without us noticing the vowels would get interchanged while speaking. With our accents, our lack of knowledge about the ways of the big city and our provincial tendencies, chances were slim that we could ever fit in with the ultra-modern Calcuttans reared in a cosmopolitan city. Everything from our stiffness to our hesitation became fodder for amusement for our bangal co-passengers. As opening our mouths meant becoming a laughing stock it seemed best to keep quiet, or even if we had to talk, to keep the conversation restricted among the three of us.

Since I had been to Santiniketan before I was the undeclared guide of our group and took Raka and Altaf on my expert tour of the most iconic places connected to Rabindranath. We roamed around Tagore's house in Santiniketan and visited the famous mango orchard. Mitra was in charge of the arrangements for our stay. Four rooms were allotted in the guest house for us to share—Raka and Altaf in one, Mona and Ashesh in another, me and Rekha Maitra in the third, and Mitra in the last.

The next morning I woke up to the strains of 'O re grihabasi'[33] and found my heart swelling with joy almost immediately. Getting out of bed with a leap I quickly put on a yellow sari. Raka was already dressed and raring to go but the ghotis were still asleep. They had been drinking till late on the rooftop of the guest house so it was expected they would oversleep, but for us bangals who wanted to leave no aspect of the Basanta Utsab undiscovered the wait was excruciating. I began pacing the porch of the guest house impatiently. Finally, after much effort, we managed to wake Mitra up. Even the little time it took for him to take a shower, change and have breakfast was unbearable! Once out on the streets the festivities swept us up in their tide in no time. Girls in yellow saris busy celebrating Basanta Utsab, makeshift stages all over the place from where someone or the other was singing Rabindrasangeet or reciting poetry, Tagore's dance dramas being enacted somewhere—it was impossible to decide which direction I wanted to run in first. So many people were singing on the streets, putting colour on each other, and my eyes did not miss even a single one of them.

I had never experienced spring so intimately before, never felt its wildness excite me so much, never been so in love with the earth, its light and its wind, and its people as well. People were allowing others to put colour on them without a thought. The grounds, the mango orchard, Kala Bhavan, Sangeet Bhavan—every nook and corner was reverberating with music and there was a swing in each and every person's step. Santiniketan always had a smell of its own and on that particular day the heady aroma reached right into my soul, immersing me in colours and Rabindranath. It was an incredible sensation to feel the presence of Tagore so closely, my senses colouring me in the brightest of hues.

I was not used to playing with colours. Even though I did not venture to put colour on anyone, completely unknown people did sprinkle colour on me. On any other day I would have been livid but on that day I let them do it. There were numerous other poets around me, all similarly engrossed in the revelries, even Sunil Gangopadhyay. At some point I had got separated from Altaf and Raka in the crowd. However, I was not alone at all and many people came up to talk to me on their own and wonderful new connections were forged. That night at the musical programme I met three young poets: Sharif, Goutam Ghosh Dastidar and Chaitali Chattopadhyay. Years ago I used to publish Chaitali's poems in *Senjuti*. Till late in the night we roamed around Santiniketan in rickshaws. We even went to the banks of the Kopai to sit and soak in the magnificent full-moon night; living in Dhaka one never got to know when it was the full moon. In Bolpur, miles away from Dhaka, I seemed to have rediscovered my childhood.

While Sharif, Gautam, his girlfriend Urmila and I were doing the rounds of Santiniketan, Mitra had gone to visit the Tarapith temple with his group. It amazed me to discover that he was such a devout believer, primarily because I had assumed for some reason that none of my friends in Calcutta were. Not that you could not visit a holy site without believing in the divine. There were so many temples and mosques I had visited simply to witness the inner workings of such places. Besides, one could never tell for sure why and with what purpose a person went to a place of worship. Who knew what secrets lay hidden in people's hearts! Even in Dhaka I used to frequently discover, to my utter dismay, people I knew to reveal immense faith in organized religion. A powerful poet like Al Mahmud was an acutely religious man. Panna Kaiser, renowned for her tireless movement against authoritarianism, was a regular and devout reader of the Quran. Scholar Muntasir Mamun visited the mosque every Friday for Jumu'ah prayers.

In the middle of the night I was woken up by a sound in my room. Listening carefully I realized it was a male voice speaking to Rekha Maitra in a hushed tone. I could also hear a scuffling sound coming from the other bed in the room. Keeping my eyes shut I lay there unmoving, not willing to let anyone know that I was awake lest it disturb whatever they were doing. Eventually I sensed two people leaving the room. Getting up quietly I went to the door that had been left slightly ajar and locked it from the inside. Sleep was the farthest thing from my mind for the rest of the night and the only thing I could think of was how mysterious the world around us could be. Daylight managed to dispel some of the mystery, though, and the people too appeared more familiar, my new-found friends appearing even more dynamic.

I met Sharif a number of times after returning to Calcutta. He had accepted me as a friend so instinctively that it almost seemed we had known each other for ages. Perhaps it was also because of the easy leap of faith my Calcutta friends could take to 'tumi', the Bengali informal 'you', a shift that enabled one to chart even a 200 kilometre distance in the blink of an eye. Sharif lived fairly close to Kyd Street, in a small room on the top floor of a multi-storey shopping complex where he worked as the security officer. One day we went out together to take a stroll round the Maidan. He took me to his brother's house, a congested locality in Park Circus I had never visited before which showed me an entirely different side of Calcutta. Sharif was Muslim perhaps only by name. He told me tragic stories of the ignominies he and many of his relatives had to face because of their Muslim names.

Syed Mustafa Siraj was a great writer but the way he had been exalted once was also how he had been pulled down to earth. For the leading publishing house of Bengal it did not matter who it was as long as they had one Muslim writer in their roster. So Syed Siraj had been replaced with Abul Bashar, who was being given the same royal treatment the former used to receive. Bashar's novel *Phoolbou* too was being heavily publicized. Sharif told me that Bashar was being pulled up simply to replace Syed Siraj and if he did not fit the bill then he too was going to be replaced by someone new in no time. The authorities at the upper echelons of the publishing house were the ones in charge of deciding who were going to be the bright stars of the Bengali literary world and whose star had to be snuffed out.

It was not difficult for me to sense the discontent pouring out of Sharif's bleak admissions. I had been to renowned poet Shamser Anwar's house once and had sensed his anger with the Hindu intelligentsia of West Bengal too. Neither the Hindu nor the Muslim authors of Calcutta were religious in any way and yet the latter could not help but feel pushed to the margins by the clout enjoyed by their Hindu counterparts. And this attitude was not restricted to the world of literature, it pervaded the entire socio-cultural matrix. The majoritarian Hindus did not consider the Muslim minority as civilized people and Sharif's descriptions could not help but remind me of the similar plight plaguing the Hindus of Bangladesh. In effect, the Muslims of India and the Hindus of Bangladesh had similar lives!

To me it hardly mattered who was what. A newborn child has no religion. They are forced to adopt their parents' religion as their own. In my understanding, centuries ago some stupid and nefarious people created religion because they were afraid of death and uncertainty and also to quench their thirst for power over others. That was how religion had spread from one creed to another, from one society to another, from one nation to another. Most do not accept religion of their own free will, it is forced on them by extraneous circumstances. Religion has caused wars and the death of millions over the years.

In West Bengal some groups of Bengali Muslims claim they are Ashraf and not Atraf. The Atraf are lower castes while the former are upper-caste Muslims tracing their lineage to forefathers who had migrated from Central Asia. That is one reason why Ashraf Muslims usually try and speak in Urdu and Farsi. I have no shame in admitting that I am not an upper-caste Muslim; I am Atraf and at some point in history one of my forefathers or foremothers had converted to Islam to escape some tyrannical Hindu king or zamindar. Bengali is my language, my culture, and I am proud of my Bengali identity. Most people do not bother with history. If they had, communal tension, caste-based discrimination and violence would have ended long back. Haven't we always been taught that humanity is the biggest truth, above all else? Two hundred years ago an uneducated seer like Lalan Fakir sang songs of humanity and denounced caste divisions, and people today who have graduated from colleges and universities are preoccupied with caste! It is indeed so strange! Are people not meant to march forward, towards the light? What joy does it bring them to regress and embrace darkness, stupidity and the lack of knowledge and awareness?

Sharif's admissions rang with the resentment of anyone who has ever been dispossessed. Sitting on the balcony of the Kyd Street guest house I sat gazing at nocturnal Calcutta, a sleeping city about to stretch itself out of slumber with the first light of dawn. Such a beautiful city, such warm people, such life in every nook and corner, and I loved it dearly. But one fact could not help but cast a pall over my happy thoughts about Calcutta—that in most parts of the city Hindus and Muslims did not cohabit in the same locality. There were specific Muslim-only areas and Hindu householders usually refused to rent to Muslim tenants.

Such rules did not exist in Bangladesh and there were no restrictions as to who could be allowed to live where. Anyone had the right to live anywhere and there were high-rises in Dhaka with Hindus on the first floor, Muslims on the second, Buddhists on the third, Christians on the fourth and no one raising objections to such an arrangement. Hindus in Bangladesh were not unaware of Muslim festivals and rituals, neither were the Muslims ignorant of the plethora of events over the twelve months of the Hindu almanac. This was because they were neighbours. In Calcutta, although most Muslims knew about Hindu religious events, most Hindus were hardly aware of the Islamic calendar. There was a question one often had to face in Calcutta: Are you a Muslim or a Bengali? As if being Muslim precluded any chances of being Bengali, and as if being Bengali automatically meant being Hindu.

Of course there were many non-Bengali Muslims in the city but that did not necessarily mean Bengali Muslims were any less in number. It was a noticeable trend especially among the uneducated stratum of the Hindu populace to assume that being Muslim meant being non-Bengali, a classic symptom of segregation. Those who frequently travelled to Bangladesh, Bengali Hindus who had met Bengali Muslims, did not always make this mistake. There was no end to the resentment that most Bengali Muslims harboured and it was not difficult to understand the reasons behind their grouses. There were a thousand problems associated with living as a minority; the Hindu minority in Bangladesh faced no less persecution. In fact, if I were to make a comparison, the Muslims in West Bengal had fared better than the Hindus in Bangladesh. The Left Front government had been in power in West Bengal for a long time and they had made efforts towards the development of their Muslim minorities. There was no state-sponsored oppression of the Muslims in West Bengal, while in Bangladesh the state itself treated the minorities as second-class citizens and no measures were taken for their protection.

Bangladesh could have perhaps become a nation shorn of all communal divisions and politics. There were Hindus and Muslims living side by side everywhere within its borders who did not know how to discriminate against the other, or how to torment and kill the other. Being neighbours taught one to relate to the other, to learn that there could be no separate schools, colleges and universities for Hindus and Muslims, that Hindus and Muslims could get married or be friends simply because they were both Bengali, because they spoke the same language and were part of the same cultural fabric. The culture of the non-Bengali Muslims had not infiltrated the social milieu of the Bengali Muslims.

Besides, in the case of most Bengali Muslims, their forefathers had been lower-caste Hindus, and those left behind in Bangladesh after the partition were not the landowning rich but their poor erstwhile tenants. Subjects always get along better with each other than kings do, and most Hindus in Bangladesh were either very poor or principled citizens who did not believe in the Hindu–Muslim divide. Despite so many reasons for coexistence, time and again Muslims in Bangladesh were known to attack, loot and rape their Hindu neighbours. And there was only one thing to blame for it. A serpent had emerged from the darkness, the venomous serpent called prejudice whose ilk had tried to establish the rule of Pakistan during the Liberation War and whose forefathers had been responsible for the partition. One such serpent was enough to drive back a hundred men. How many of them were there? Not too many for sure, yet. But their ranks were swelling with every passing day and I could almost hear their collective hissing growing louder in the air.

I had not witnessed the partition of India so there was no reason that the pain of the cataclysmic event should find a permanent home in my heart. It still did and I nurtured deep within me an old agony of a country torn apart by something as fundamentally deceitful as religion. The feeling intensified whenever I saw the Bengalis of West Bengal, many of whom had been refugees who had had to abandon home and hearth in East Bengal and build an entirely new life from scratch on this side of the border. Many had crossed over in 1947 and never gone back, and the only things that remained with them were the memories of ponds full of fish, barns overflowing with paddy and orchards laden with mango and jackfruit stretching till the horizon. Living in the congested urban slums of Calcutta, people piled upon more people, these memories were obviously sweet respite.

But how many of them spared even a thought for the ones who had not come to this side, be it because of poverty or because of their principles? How many of them wondered how the others were doing? The responsibility to think lay with the new citizens of a new Bangladesh. Not just thinking, there was a lot to accomplish too. Right after my first trip to India, still bursting with emotions, I had written a poem about the treachery of the partition, the cruelty of borders marked with barbed wires and how the two Bengals were essentially completely alike. India was partitioned in the name of religion—a two-part nation called Pakistan was created for the Muslims—but could the Muslims really live together in one country in the end? The separation of Bangladesh from Pakistan in 1971 revealed once and for all that the partition had been a huge mistake.

The moment my poems were published the snakes had branded me a traitor. Articles maligning me too were frequent features in the journals that acted as mouthpieces of religious fundamentalists. I often did manage to read some of these, as often as I did not. It scarcely mattered to me who was writing what because I was determined to keep writing what I felt like. I was going to write with unabashed ease about the pain inside me, the despair, as well as the dreams. Secretly in my heart I nursed visions of a united Bharat, or at least a united Bengal.

In Calcutta I visited friends and acquaintances to give them the gifts I had bought for them. I loved giving gifts to people. When someone like Subhash Mukhopadhyay behaved like a child at the sight of the kurta I had bought him it gave me immense joy. This habit of giving gifts was something I had inherited from Mother. No matter how much I disliked some of her oddities, there was something about sharing blood that ensured parts of her were there in me in some way or the other. Mother loved giving away her things to others and found a lot of joy in the act. As it was she did not have too many things—no money of her own, or jewellery, or saris—but as far back as I could remember my already impoverished mother never hesitated to give away even the little that she did have, and her unseemly generosity never failed to annoy me.

Suppose I was to buy her a sari; she would wear it happily for two days and then on the third I would find the same sari on Gada's mother. Mother, having taken pity on the poor beggar woman in tattered rags, had given it away to her! Yasmin too had developed the same habit but neither she nor I could quite match up to how Mother used to selflessly give things away without a second thought. Dada and Chotda were more like Father, obsessed with keeping meticulous accounts of even the smallest expenses. In fact, they were often worse than him. At least Father used to treat his poor patients for free, primarily because to him being able to cure someone was an achievement in itself and he never refrained from writing out prescriptions for someone in need whether he got his visitation fees or not. Both the rich and the poor of the city were his patients.

But more recently the crowd of people in front of his chamber had begun to thin and mostly comprised poor patients who came from far and wide and waited on the porch outside the chamber, their feet up on the chairs arranged there, the leather of which had worn out from use. After the influx of various specialists into Mymensingh most rich patients preferred to take their ailments elsewhere. While some did still visit an older experienced doctor like Father, they did so only if the specialists failed to help. Experience mattered a lot and Father could tell if someone had tuberculosis even without taking out an X-ray. Even after his job at the medical college and the line of patients outside his chamber till midnight on most days, Father still flipped through his medical books whenever he had some time to spare. The night before a big class he studied and prepared till two or three in the morning.

His busy life never failed to amaze me and the fact that I had adopted this tenet in my life—working and staying busy instead of lazing about brought me a lot of happiness too—was all because of him. It is indeed surprising how much of our parents' habits we imbibe, only for these to be manifested in us quite unconsciously over time. Much of the time I could not even understand my own character. I was a shy girl once, used to hiding at the sight of strangers, and here I was perfectly at home with new people I was meeting every day; even though I was never garrulous, talking came easy to me. There was a chasm of difference between the old me and the new me. The number of people I knew in Calcutta had increased and I was fond of the city just as I was fond of Dhaka. I had met renowned artists and authors in Calcutta but I was more at home with the normal people I had come across in the city, especially if it was someone kind and sensitive.

The guileless smile on Indranath Majumdar's face made him seem like someone very dear to me. He had another bookshop, also called Subarnarekha, on College Street, and what a perfectly wonderful and scattered man he was! It took me a long time to find his shop and when I did chance upon it I discovered it to be so small, especially with the old books stuffed inside from wall to wall, that there was barely any place to stand. Indranath sold old books and published some new books too; but not just any, the books had to be worth it. For him his ideals mattered much more than commerce and if he were to get hold of a good book which others were not willing to place their bets upon, he would publish it regardless of whether it had prospects or not. The afternoon I went to visit him he took me out, the harsh sun beating down upon us relentlessly. 'You have been eating at great places, no doubt. Come, let me take you to some place absolutely wonderful.' He took me to an Odiya picehotel where we had fish and rice served on banana leaves. It hardly cost us anything but the sense of contentment from that humble food was not something I had experienced even in some of the finest restaurants I had been to.

There was no dearth of events in Calcutta. Rabindra Sadan, Sisir Manch, Kala Mandir, the Academy—something was always happening somewhere. There was a poetry recital at Rabindra Sadan one day and Soumitra Mitra pushed me and Altaf Hossain up on stage to participate in the recital alongside local poets. I had read poetry on stage in Calcutta previously so the awkwardness was decidedly less this time around. However, it was the first time for Altaf, and the shy man could barely modulate his voice and neither could he keep his hands still while reciting.

Poets from Bangladesh were usually met with a warm welcome in West Bengal. People with Muslim names, coming from another country and speaking in Bengali, reading poems in Bengali—perhaps it was a source of immense amusement to most people. Perhaps there were a few instances of pity too, which earned a few extra slaps of encouragement on our backs along with cries of 'go on, it's going great'. Some were always excited by anything related to Bangladesh, ready to roll in its water and dirt if they could. Driven by their ardour they would claim there was nothing of value in West Bengal and everything good lay in Bangladesh. For most people, though, bangals were dainty, partly human, simple-minded, warm and welcoming people who loved to spend money and were more often than not reckless, lazy, partial to food and comfort, well-off and mostly half-witted.

Mitra introduced me to many poets and reciters in the event. I managed to have a quick conversation with a talented poet like Joy Goswami. A gaunt, skeletal man, nearly a hermit, Goswami had been writing wonderful poetry for quite a while. Truly, talent did not reside in the physical body, its domain was the mind. If the mind itself was barren it did not matter how much water and compost one put in, it would not yield even a fraction of Joy's poetic flair. Not everyone was meant to be a poet; if it was meant to be only then was it going to happen. If someone had talent it scarcely mattered whether they were fat or thin—a corpulent man like Sunil Gangopadhyay could come across as attractive and a man like Joy did not appear as emaciated as he truly was, all because of their gifts. No matter how much the latter lamented about his urinary troubles, Joy appeared healthiest among the hundred other people surrounding him.

Despite being a ghoti through and through, Soumitra Mitra managed to make enough time for the bangals to show us around. Honestly, without him it would have been impossible for us to travel around Calcutta so freely. Even if he was not with us all the time he made sure that we knew where to go. The only way to truly know a city is to walk alone, lose one's way and then find it again, and not by peering out of the rolled-up windows of a car. I loved walking in the crowd, exploring old narrow lanes to witness the lives of people there, watching people bathing at the street pumps, sipping tea from earthenware cups in roadside tea stalls, walking through College Street in search of books, and buying saris from the pavements off Gariahat.

There was so much to do in Calcutta that I realized the time I had left would never be enough to do everything I wished to do. Besides the Basanta Utsab and sightseeing around Calcutta I had a few important tasks to complete. First and foremost I had to get a copy of *Laal Kaalo* to Sripantha as Bilal Chowdhury had asked me to. I headed towards the offices of *Anandabazar Patrika* on Prafulla Sarkar Street with Raka and Altaf and a two-point agenda: hand over the book to Sripantha and give a copy of *Nirbachito Kolam* to Shankar Lal Bhattacharya. Bhattacharya worked for the magazine *Sananda* and we had met when he was in Dhaka. Besides, we had met a couple of times in Calcutta too.

Sitting on the terrace of the newspaper office he told me numerous things about literature, much of which I could not comprehend. But there was one thing I did understand. He was quite well read in Western literature and a very erudite man. Interestingly, there were more such educated and intellectual people that I came across in Calcutta than in Dhaka. Bengali Hindus were always all for education, leagues ahead of Bengali Muslims. The latter had always taken pride in their refusal to learn the language of the non-believers while the former had never harboured such hang-ups, so the difference was hardly an inexplicable one.

We asked a passer-by in the corridor the way to Sripantha's office and I could not help feel a surge of trepidation while pushing open the door to his room—learned people usually sat inside these air-conditioned rooms with grave expressions on their faces and I did not wish to barge in and disrupt something important. There were three people inside the room: a small man with a round face and two other younger men. All three were writing.

'Is there someone called Sripantha here?'

The middle-aged round-faced man stopped writing and looked up. 'That would be me.'

'I've come from Dhaka. Bilal Chowdhury has sent a book for you.'

'What book?'

'*Laal Kaalo.*'

'*Laal Kaalo?*'

He took the book from my hand and asked me to sit. I had assumed he was simply going to take the book with an 'Okay, thank you' and say goodbye but not only did he not do that, he asked Raka and Altaf to sit too. As he flipped through the book and glanced at the pictures his face broke into a smile; it was obvious he liked what he saw. 'There hasn't been a single reprint of *Laal Kaalo* from Calcutta. It's finally happened from Bangladesh. I will write about this in *Kolkatar Korcha.*' He was in charge of the supplement and also wrote editorials for the main edition of *Anandabazar* frequently. He was in the process of training the talented Anirban Chattopadhyay and Goutam Roy, the two younger men in the room, into hardened journalists like him. We made our introductions—my name, where I was from, what I did—and Raka and Altaf were introduced too. Milk tea arrived and sipping on it Sripantha told us he was from Mymensingh too and had crossed over to this side during the partition.

'Where in Mymensingh?' I failed to hide the note of excitement in my question.

'Dhobauda.'

They had left Dhobauda and never gone back, much like the millions of others who had migrated to India from East Bengal during the partition and never found their way back. He told us he wished to return once to see how everything was, but like most people had never managed to find the right time. Many of those who had immigrated to West Bengal as refugees harboured a soft spot for people from Bangladesh and Sripantha was no different. As we were about to leave he suddenly asked me, 'Do you write too?'

As usual my ears went red at the question. I did write obviously, but it did not seem right to me to make too much out of that, especially in front of a scholarly person such as him. Realizing I was not going to respond, Altaf intervened. 'Of course she does! She's become quite famous in Bangladesh!'

'Really?'

Sripantha looked at me and grinned; I could not look up and meet his eyes in embarrassment. 'Do you have a book with you now?'

'Book?'

'Yes, do you have one of your own books with you now?'

There was a copy of *Nirbachito Kolam* in my bag for Shankar Lal Bhattacharya. Uncertainly, I took the book out and handed it to him. He turned it over in his hands and said, 'Leave this with me.'

'I had gotten this for Shankar Lal Bhattacharya,' I said meekly.

'Shankar of *Sananda*, right? Get one for him later.'

He called a photographer and told the man, 'Take a photograph of her. She's from Bangladesh; I want to write a note about her book in *Korcha*.' I posed for the photograph just as I was—wearing a plain tussar sari, white but not quite, with tiny threadwork red and black flowers, a red bindi on my forehead and a forlorn smile on my face. There was going to be an article about my book in *Kolkatar Korcha* along with my photograph! Let alone express joy I could barely react for the shock. For authors of Bangladesh, *Desh* and *Anandabazar* were always distant dreams and if someone's poem was to ever find its way to the pages of *Desh* it was considered such a matter of pride that it took them years to live it down. And here I was a puny new writer!

If only that had been all! There was a bigger shock waiting for me a few days after returning to Dhaka. I was back to my usual schedule:

my duties at Mitford, a few regular columns in four or five journals during my free time, and occasionally being driven by publishers to get back to working on new novels. One fine day I received a letter from *Anandabazar Patrika* telling me I was being awarded the Ananda Puraskar of 1992 for *Nirbachito Kolam* by the *Desh–Anandabazar* team! For a moment I could not believe my eyes and I had to read the letter repeatedly to confirm whether or not it had been sent to me by some clerical error. My name was on the envelope, though, and there was slim chance that it was an error. Although there were limits to how much one could dream, my dreams had never even dared to aim so high!

I was struck dumb by the news, unable to scream out in joy for the world to hear, my heart pumping too erratically. The Ananda Puraskar was the biggest literary award in Bengal, the most renowned and prestigious, and no one in Bangladesh had ever won it before. I was someone who had started just the other day, an amateur who wrote poetry because she fancied it and wrote columns when she needed to, and I had been considered for the award! Was this even possible? Was it even credible? Unable to decide what I should do, I paced a little, sat down, got up again and went to stand in front of the mirror to take a long look at myself to ascertain if the person I was seeing was indeed me. I wanted to go to the bathroom and I felt dizzy.

Breaking out of the spell all of a sudden I ran to Milan, who was the only person at home, and in between gasps delivered the fantastic news. 'Milan, I have won the Ananda Puraskar.' Milan did not know exactly what that was, but after I explained to him that this was not a local essay competition or literary circle award but a big deal in the literary world, his astonishment had to be seen to be believed. Despite being my younger sister's husband he was more like a younger brother to me than anything else. I told him to get ready at once, the letter still clutched in my fist, and he quickly changed into a pair of pants.

Our first stop was Khoka's house. After much calling and hollering from outside when Khoka emerged from within his house I informed him excitedly, 'Khoka bhai, I have been awarded the Ananda Puraskar.' Strangely enough, he smiled a wan smile in response and for my life I could not comprehend the reason behind his less-than-enthusiastic reception of the news. He was the one who had always been the happiest at my success, so why was he not happy about this too? Why was his smile so pale, so devoid of life? Was he apprehensive that I was becoming too big for my boots, that the higher I climbed the more unreachable I was going to become for him? I could not keep thinking why and his tepid reaction to the news put a momentary dampener on my mood.

I was not willing to wait till the day after to inform Bilal Chowdhury, even though it was already fairly late. We somehow managed to locate his house and the sight of us at his gate gave him quite the surprise as he tried to fathom the reason behind such a sudden and late visit.

'Bilal bhai, I have been awarded the Ananda Puraskar. I just received the letter. I still can't believe it, it feels strange.' I handed the letter over to him and his elation at the news was immediately evident. He sent word to his wife at once to bring us some sweets to celebrate the happy news. I too was finally relieved to have shared my happiness with someone who understood. Truly, certain joys are too heavy for one to carry their burden alone.

'Do I deserve such a huge honour, Bilal bhai?'

'Of course! You are writing so well! Of course you deserve it! They have not given you the award just like that. The Ananda Puraskar is a dream for every Bengali author. It's the Nobel Prize of Bangla.' As much grief as Khoka's indifference had caused, Bilal Chowdhury's excitement managed to dispel the gloom finally. Nonetheless, sleep was hard to come by after we returned home that night. I lay awake till late thinking: If only R was alive! He would have been so proud of me. Once, after reading one of my columns for *Purbabhash* R had written a letter which had also been printed in the correspondence section of the journal. In it he had confessed that whatever had happened between the two us the responsibility of most of it was his, and that I should forgive him and spare the male of the species from my vengeful vendetta. If only R had known that I had not written anything out of anger or because I wanted to wage war against all men. I was only fighting the corrosive customs we adhered to in the name of society, customs that sought to make women into slaves, into commodities, into sex objects, that sought to rob a woman of her dignity as a human being—my war was against all such society-, state- and religion-sponsored injustices.

I cried when I wrote, not for me but for someone like Sufia Khatun who was raped and buried alive, Farida whose face was scalded in the acid thrown by a jilted lover, Sakhina Bano whose husband had broken her hands and feet and then divorced her because her father was unable to pay enough dowry during their wedding, Sharifa Khatun who was hacked to death because she had given birth to a daughter, Kandi Nurjahan who was stoned because she had dared to talk to a man, and Phoolmati who was burnt alive because she had dared to fall in love. I had a good life, I had a good job as a doctor in a leading hospital in the city, I was self-sufficient and could take my own decisions, and I could afford to live my life as I wished. But how many girls were as lucky as I was! So I could never forget that I was just like them, the Sufia Khatuns, the Noorjahans and the Sakhina Banos of the world, and what had happened to each of them could have easily happened to me too.

The invitation to go and receive the prize in Calcutta was quite unlike what had been the case for my previous few visits. Tickets for both ways, my stay at Calcutta, everything was the responsibility of *Anandabazar*. Around that time, while I was floating in a haze of bliss, a feeling of intense self-importance coursing through my veins, something terrible about two particular columns in the book came to my attention and swiftly burst the bubble. While referring to the Vedas, despite having all the copies of the Vedas at my disposal, I had reproduced a few lines from the book *Prachin Bharat o Baidik Samaj* (Ancient India and Society in the Time of the Vedas) by Sukumari Bhattacharya, renowned scholar of the Vedas. In a daze I had taken sentence after sentence, the book had influenced me too much for me to be able to extricate my own arguments from Bhattacharya's and present them separately. I could have taken the translations of the passages of the Vedas from her work but why did I have to lift entire arguments? I had stolen them because her arguments matched mine in their entirety; so beautifully on point were her explanations that had I not read even a single line of the Vedas my fairly simplistic explanations would have still matched hers. She had said before me most of what I wanted to say on the matter.

Thus, even after the two columns had been published, the doubt and the guilt surrounding them had not diminished, like how a single speck of dirt spoils an entire bowl of cream. On first receiving news of the award I did not immediately remember this shameful old incident, but when I finally did my humiliation and remorse would not allow me to live it down. Unable to look at myself, full of self-loathing, I went to the telephone office that very night to make an urgent call to Calcutta. I called Nikhil Sarkar and told him that my book was not fit to receive the prize because of the two offending columns wherein a large chunk had been lifted off Sukumari Bhattacharya's work.

If after my confession he had told me he was going to inform the committee and make sure they changed their decision I would have perhaps felt slightly lighter. Instead, it did not seem he was perturbed by the news in any way. I knew that many people stole stuff from other writers. HSS had himself acknowledged that the first piece he had ever written had been stolen from someone else, punctuation and all. But this was not my first piece! It was written *after* I had made quite a name for myself with my columns. When I could not forgive myself, how could I expect others to forgive me for such a grievous infraction!

Awards were supposed to make people happy but in my case it was about to cause me further embarrassment. Nikhil Sarkar's lack of an appropriate reaction to my confession added an extra dimension to my existing feeling of shame—that of fear. Did I then have to go and accept the award? How was I supposed to face people, how was I supposed to defend myself? My conscience would not let me rest in peace and kept asking me the same question over and over—who was I, a writer of what calibre, that I deserved such a prestigious honour? The previous winners were all renowned authors and well-known scholarly individuals, and there I was, unmatched in knowledge and talent, a droplet of water or a speck of nothing in comparison.

Even if they wished to award someone from Bangladesh, how was I even a contender over and above so many others? There were many renowned novelists, remarkable poets, comparing whose work to mine would have been tantamount to travesty. Shaukat Osman, Rashid Karim, HSS, Hasan Azizul Haque, Akhteruzzaman Elias, Selina Hossain, Rahat Khan, Bashir Al Helal—I was nothing compared to such stalwarts. Shamsur Rahman, Al Mahmud, Mahadev Saha, Nirmalendu Goon, Rafiq Azad, Abu Zafar Obaidullah—any of them were better poets than me on any given day. Then why had I been selected?

I was convinced that the committee had either gone mad or they did not have clear ideas about the litterateurs of Bangladesh, the only two reasons that could explain their nomination of me. Besides, the committee too comprised many renowned individuals. Essayists and columnists like Zillur Rahman Siddiqui, Anisuzzaman, Sirajul Islam Chowdhury, Rafiqul Islam and AZ had failed to win the award and I was supposed to believe I had trumped them all? Thus far I had mostly written about things that had struck my fancy, a few columns in a few newspapers and journals like so many wrote all the time, and I knew many people from the literary world personally—all this did not automatically imply that I had become a writer too. I had never even dared to dream as such! Many celebrated authors in Calcutta too were yet to receive such an award and I was supposed to walk up to the stage with all of them in attendance and accept the honour?

The declaration of the Ananda Puraskar only served to drive home the point that I was insignificant and undeserving of it, a writer of too little worth and too much of an outsider. It was true that I wrote about women's rights but it was not as if I was writing something radically new that others before me had not already written or were not writing about. I had not renounced anything, I had not suffered, I had not marched through the streets in protest or formed organizations like others had to serve battered women, nor formed NGOs, set up schools or staked everything precious to me for the betterment of women. I had done nothing. I had not even managed to cast aside the everyday abuse and violence against our domestic helps that is socialized in us from an early age, the heinous habit of a slap in rebuke, or a blow on the back to teach a firm lesson. I had once twisted the arm of Sufi's one-and-a-half-year-old daughter when Sufi had been away because she used to constantly cry and nag and then smirk in response. My hands were filthy with my own sins and they did not deserve to hold such an award. The ethical concerns that had influenced me thus far, how many of them had I truly managed to inculcate in my own life? Socialist doctrines excited me but that had never spilled over into implementing said principles in my everyday life. Despite being aware that nearly 80 per cent of the population lived under unspeakable conditions I had never compromised with my luxuries. Despite knowing that thousands of people were going to sleep on the roads and pavements my bed had not gotten any less soft. I had not stopped eating three square meals a day even though millions went hungry every day. My preoccupation with socialist ideals was simply middle-class romanticism and I could not help but reflect with disgust that everything I had written about women thus far had been to earn money or fame! I was as hideous a writer as I was a human being.

When I set off for Calcutta I was completely aware of all this and more. I had replied to *Anandabazar* accepting the award almost immediately after receiving the news, not that I could not have done anything about that later. If I had wanted to I could have easily told them I was not deserving of the Puraskar and I was not going to accept it. Why did I not have the audacity required to turn down an award when there were so many things I had done in life because of my audacity? Was it because I was greedy? No matter how much I tried telling myself that was not the case, the stench of a hidden undercurrent of greed in my actions refused to leave me be. Beneath my shame and my fear a very intimate greed had burrowed into my soul. I was running like a felon towards a grievous mistake that was about to be made, my eyes and ears were desperately trying to shut out the raging current I was standing at the edge of and there was no way I could pull myself back.

Powerless and helpless, I took a deep breath, hoping to dislodge the greed from my heart. I wrote obscene words, I wrote about sex, I was an insignificant writer who knew nothing about writing, I was nothing, I was nothing . . . I was tired of hearing these things over and over again, tired of suffering disrespect and abuse and making my relatives suffer in turn. If I had earned a spot to stand my own ground and hold my head high, a head I had been forced to hang in shame time and again to shield myself from reproach and ridicule, if I had found a way to show them, they who had repeatedly attacked and disrespected me, that I too was deserving of respect, how could I let such an opportunity go! A woman has to ensure that the ground beneath her feet is a little firmer than that of a man's; she has to prove her mettle a little more just to be allowed to stand in the queue with a man. I wished to infuse my identity as a *woman* with pride—pride that was going to shield me from someone trying to shove me aside or throw me out or make fun of me out in the world, and in literary circles, a world which still belonged to men mostly, it was going to make sure that I finally belonged. I tried but was unable to vanquish my greed.

A beautiful hotel room had been booked for me in Calcutta. I met Badal Basu of Ananda Publishers and he told me they were going to publish *Nirbachito Kolam*. How was I going to live down so much largesse, so many rewards! Badal Basu resembled a black mountain and one look at his unsmiling serious face was enough to make one's throat go dry! With the characteristic hard expression on his face he instructed me in a hard voice to sign a series of documents regarding the publication. I was hardly used to so much paperwork. Back in Dhaka there was nothing written down in publishing, all dealings were usually informal and verbal, and the exact share of the royalties between the author and the publisher was never mentioned anywhere.

I barely glanced at the figure mentioned as I signed the entire lot. Everything was formal in Calcutta and there were a hundred rules attached to things. My book was going to be published by the biggest publication house of Bengali literature and that was enough; money was not even a factor in such circumstances. The Ananda Puraskar had a cash prize of Rs 50,000, which had been increased to Rs 1 lakh just that year. I had to sign a few more documents for that too and those were brought to me by Subir Mitra of *Anandabazar Patrika*. I was going to be handed a cheque of Rs 1 lakh, a sum I had never seen together ever before. And yet I could not fixate on the money at all, too small as it was when compared to the honour I was being bestowed.

Just as I finished the last signature, news arrived that Satyajit Ray had passed away. Badal Basu had to leave at once and I remained seated in his office numbed by the sudden shocking news. I was addicted to watching films and of all the films I had seen in my life Ray's had been my favourite. Just *Pather Panchali* I had seen nearly fifteen times and there was no chance that I was going to grow tired of it any time soon. Every time I saw the film I cried for Durga, sighed for Apu, and my heart would break into pieces for Indir Thakrun. Many poets and writers from Dhaka used to visit Calcutta to meet Ray; I had never had the courage or nerve to go up to someone famous and make my own introductions. So the only time I managed to see

Ray with my own eyes was when he was laid out on a bed of flowers
in front of Nandan. He was never going to make another film, he
was never going to look into the camera again, he was never going to
sketch or write again. There was nothing more fearsome in the world
than death. What did life measure up to if the end was always meant
to be so inevitable and abrupt? The Ananda Puraskar ceremony was
pushed back by a day to mourn the passing of the great film-maker.

The award ceremony had been organized in the ballroom of the
Grand Hotel. A stage had been decorated with jasmine, on the black
swathes of cloth hanging from the wall a huge quill had been drawn as
if with jasmine too. I had never seen such a beautifully done-up stage
before. The entire room was heady with the fragrance of jasmine as
the invited guests filed in and found their seats. The room was packed
to the rafters with the wise and the intellectual, renowned authors,
poets and artists.

Every year there were three recipients, but this time it was only
the two of us: me and the writer Bimal Kar. The editor and publisher
of *Anandabazar*, Aveek Sarkar, Sagarmoy Ghosh, the editor of *Desh*,
and the poet Nirendranath Chakraborty were on one side of the stage
while Kar and I were on the other side. I could barely manage to look
past my consternation at the audience and those on stage. I had to
make a speech afterwards and I clutched a torn piece of paper in my
fist, wet with sweat and containing the mostly scratched out lines I
had tried to piece together the night before. The big people on stage
were speaking and as we scaled the roster it seemed my pounding
heart was going to leap out of my chest. What if my knees began
shaking once I was in front of the mike? What if my voice shook or
I fainted? When my turn came I went up to the mike and unrolled
the crumpled piece of paper to read out my speech, right down to the
'Namaskar'. In trying to quell the tremble in my voice I could barely
avoid mistakes in pronunciation, and the words kept jostling with
each other as I desperately focused on steadying my wobbly knees. I
read my speech as if I was addressing the dwellers of Paradise on the
Pul-e-Siraat under the orders of Allah.

Many have thought to point out to me that my mind tends to
wander, that I tend to slip away to imaginary landscapes in my own

mind and dream impossible dreams. I feel like going off to Neptune because I cannot stand the heat at all. I sit in my room and imagine that I have sprouted wings which will help me fly away. There are too many such dreams that hover just outside my reach, but the one dream I had never had the courage to dream was that I was going to be awarded the Ananda Puraskar one day. To everyone gathered here today, I confess that I am delighted and moved.

The book that has been awarded the prize is a simple and uncompromising statement against the systematic abuse and violence that women go through under religion, society and the state. Our scriptures and the rules governing our society would like to reinforce one primary fact: that women cannot have independence. But a woman who is not physically and mentally independent cannot claim to be a complete human being either. Freedom is primary and a woman's freedom has now been put under arrest by the state, with religion being the chief impediment to her natural growth. Because religion is there most women are still illiterate, deprived of property, most are married off when they are children and are victims of polygamy, talaq and widowhood. Because men wish to serve only their own ends, they have defined and valourized a woman's femininity, chastity and maternal instincts.

If these can be maintained, a woman is considered more valuable in society, and by value I mean she will not be considered an outcast or an untouchable. In nearly every major religion in the world the preservation of a woman's chastity has been considered a big deal but nowhere has a similar emphasis been placed on a man's chastity too. That implies monogamy is a necessary ideal only for women and not for men. Men have adorned women in numerous foul jewels. To enslave her he has established the family, society and the state, he has invented God who brought forth prophets and religious books besides numerous philosophies, epics and ballads, and he has instituted sociology, psychiatry and many other disciplines.

The primary objective of the drive towards women's education that had swept through Bengal during the second half of the nineteenth century was not freedom and self-rule for women but the production of a superior breed of wife and sexual partner. The education of women was meant to primarily serve the self-interests of men. Marriage is a profession for women; it is still believed that the best recourse for a woman is a married and settled domestic existence. The greatest sign of a successful married life is the gradual transformation of a wife into a fleshy doll for the husband to toy with.

It is believed that woman was created from a man's bent rib. Women are taught that their Paradise is underneath their husband's feet and keeping him happy means keeping Allah happy too. Keeping wives obedient and always waiting on their husbands' needs by fooling them with ideas of Paradise is a classic manoeuvre of religion and society. Bengali women learn to earn their blessings from the leftovers on their husbands' plates. It serves a twofold purpose: to oblige the husband as well as religion. The only thing it does not guarantee is her nourishment. The only thing women are considered good for is being the object of a man's sexual desire.

Almost all major religions have encouraged an idea of ownership of women as property. They have encouraged giving them gifts because they are valuable objects and condoned the rape and violation of the women of those defeated in war. While women are expected to display signs that mark their marital status, men do not have to bear such signs at all. Similarly, widowhood too is a woman's burden; she is the one who has to observe a hundred prohibitions. Since the dawn of civilization, society and religion have controlled man's fate and as the agents of the two, men have ruled since time immemorial. The most abuse that women have had to face, even more than from society and the state, has stemmed from religion and the only way to ensure her freedom, given the systematic social, economic and political repression she has to undergo is the complete overhauling of the social and administrative apparatus. Her freedom will be a distant dream unless she manages to break free of the shackles of religion too. This is what I have mostly written about, the suppressed, tortured and persecuted women in society and it has given me immense inspiration to know that my voice has travelled across the border so far and reached some of you. Usually when women speak, their voices don't reach too many people or even too many other women for that matter. And because of this I am startled and humbled. I do not think of West Bengal as another country. We share the same language and the same culture, we partake of the same air and the same water, and our houses are by the same river. Whenever I come here I feel an acute pain in my heart, the pain of the partition. There are no barbed wires in my heart. We are Bengali, our language is Bengali and we are all related. On such a happy occasion let me sign off with a small poem for you:

While out gathering hay at dawn, my basket has run over with flowers
Had I even dreamt of so much!
Where do I keep them now, where do I sit, where do I go and cry!
When life was empty, at least it was!
And no one had to do anything.
But you have given me so much, beyond measure,
And drawn me close,
Did I truly deserve so much!

Do forgive me if you can.

I asked for forgiveness because I had dared to accept such an exalted award despite being such an insignificant entity, for having shown the audacity even though I was utterly undeserving. Who knew if anyone forgave me in the end! After the event many writers and artists came up to congratulate me and I spoke to people I had never imagined I would have the opportunity to speak to. The day after, the news of the award ceremony was published on the front page of *Anandabazar Patrika* along with the headline 'Taslima and Bhimsen steal the show'. Celebrations were being held all around me.

Soumitra Mitra was very happy with how things had turned out and he was taking me to various places to meet various people. He surprised me with a visit to Rabindrasangeet exponent Kanika Bandyopadhyay. I was an ardent admirer of Kanika and standing in front of her was like a wave of euphoria had swept over my entire world. Ashesh and Mona, my companions during the Basanta Utsab trip, came to see me and took a bunch of photographs. I was suddenly an important person who no longer had to walk hunched along the

corridors of *Anandabazar* and everyone knew who I was. Sagarmoy
Ghosh offered me a chance to write a serialized novel for *Desh*.
Floored by the offer I confessed I did not know how to write a novel.
He smiled but did not rescind his offer. Nikhil Sarkar invited me to
his Salt Lake residence and gave me a bunch of letters with which to
go and meet a number of well-known people.

Dutifully, the small writer with the big award took the letters
with her and hesitantly went to pay a visit to the big guns. Mahasweta
Devi, Meera Mukhopadhyay and many others—stars one was meant
to show respect to when reaching for the sky. Whether I was even
near the sky or I was where I had always been, I could scarcely tell
for sure; I stood in front of the celebrities with all my insecurities and
remonstrations intact. There was a trend in Calcutta to touch the feet
of senior writers and artists to pay them one's respects. Unused to
the custom, I could not help but stand stiffly in front of most people
I met. I had never managed to grasp the Bengali Muslim version of
the same ritual either, the *kadambushi*. Though my heart was full of
respect, I refrained from touching people's feet and this must have
irked many a senior, made them think of me as an upstart. But there
was hardly anything I could do about it. If I was suddenly asked to
till the field was I not supposed to stand there dumbstruck? It was
impossible for me to abruptly start doing something I had never done
before.

Despite not being one for formalities, I loved giving the small
gifts I had brought from Bangladesh to my friends and well-wishers
in Calcutta. Aveek Sarkar had handed the Ananda Puraskar to me
and it was only right that I gift him a small token in return. So I took
the multi-coloured jamdani sari I had worn for the award function,
got its ornate border cut and had it framed in the best golden frame
from a renowned framing shop on Park Street. When I reached the
Anandabazar offices with my gift, Nikhil Sarkar was astounded by
my daring. What I had failed to grasp was that for an art connoisseur
and a man of such refined tastes as Aveek Sarkar, the limits of
what he preferred among Indian art objects was probably defined
by the Maqbool Fida Husain I saw adorning the walls. Otherwise,
everything else was surely works by famous Western artists and
painters. A jamdani sari border, no matter how beautiful, was not

something that could possibly hope to be displayed in his room. I could not help but think to myself that the women behind such exquisite work were no less great artists, but the tasteful and the rich hardly considered them worthy of their attention. It was fortuitous that I had not turned up at Aveek Sarkar's office directly with the framed piece of jamdani. Nikhil Sarkar advised that if I was bent on giving the gift to someone I should give it to Aveek Sarkar's wife. Swallowing my discomfiture I did exactly that and managed to save Sarkar, the giant of *Anandabazar*, from any further embarrassment.

A leading bureaucrat of the Bangladeshi consulate invited me and some authors to his place, primarily in my honour. As soon as I arrived the poets and writers of Calcutta surrounded me and inundated me with questions. So many questions of so many kinds— renaissance, revolution, feminism, backlash, modernism, post-modernism, my literary ideology, political beliefs, class struggle and so on. They waited for me to reply with startling answers while all I could do was stare at them in wide-eyed wonder. The questions appeared incomprehensible to me and seeing my bafflement they too began glancing at each other in surprise. Embarrassed, I wanted to curl up like a snail and disappear from the star-studded gathering, simply vanish without a trace. I did not want to answer any questions because I had no answers to give.

I wished they would rather ask me to tell them about Rahima Begum who had cried from despair, disgust, worry and pain after having given birth to a girl. I could have cried like that for them if they had wanted me to. I was not an intellectual, I had not consumed fat books on the earth's history, geography, politics, society, literature and culture, neither had I amassed unrivalled wisdom. I was not a speaker and I could never make a coherent speech. I could write with some effort, that too because the pain of those like Rahima Begum made me want to weep. I was not suited to speak at such illustrious gatherings; I was a simple girl who had grown up simply in an ordinary household of Mymensingh. Not being particularly intelligent, I had never managed to grasp philosophy either.

Dialectics

While numerous writers and intellectuals sent me their felicitations after winning the Ananda Puraskar, some sent me their hatred too. A radical organization opined that since I usually wrote against Islam the Hindu fundamentalist Anandabazar Group had conferred me with the honour. I had never heard that *Anandabazar Patrika* was a Hindu fundamentalist mouthpiece. In fact, most of the articles and columns I had read in *Anandabazar* and *Desh* were decisively critical of Hindu radicals. Some also alleged that once upon a time the *Patrika*'s role had been decidedly anti-Islam. Since I was not born then it was difficult for me to accept the responsibility of something I had had no role to play in. Editors change, publishers change, new journalists join the team and a newspaper's ideology too undergoes alterations.

In Bangladesh the newspapers that once used to write against the freedom of the country were all pro independence because the old guard had departed, ushering in the new. The names and the addresses remained the same but the opinions were different and so were the ethical concerns. The second allegation levelled against me was that I was a RAW agent. One article in *Inquilab* accused me of colluding with the RAW and by the next day ten others had followed suit.

What was the RAW? Unable to grapple with this question any longer I asked Milan. 'Milan, what is the RAW?'

'Bubu, you don't know what raw is? Raw is . . .'

'Yes?'

'For instance, take raw tea. If you don't pour milk into your tea it becomes raw tea, doesn't it? Or, for example, our company deals in raw material which is later used to make chemical products.'

'But what does it mean, being a RAW agent?'

'I think an agent that imports materials from abroad.'

'But I am not working as an agent to import raw materials!'

'They've just written whatever. Haven't they written all sorts of rubbish about you already?'

'But, Milan, why will they abuse me as a RAW agent? So many people buy things from abroad and get them shipped. They aren't abused!'

'Well, they've abused you. Maybe they think you are importing contraband.'

'Contraband?'

'You don't even know what that is, Bubu?' Milan shook his head sagaciously. 'Not everything can be legally brought into Bangladesh. There's some stuff which comes by way of contraband!'

'Like?'

'Like Phensedyl, the cough syrup. Children use it to get high. Smugglers sneak in Phensedyl from India. Now if you get Phensedyl won't that be a banned good?'

'But Phensedyl isn't raw! It's a medicine. It's kept in bottles!'

'What if you are bringing in the raw materials for making Phensedyl here? Say you want to make it at home.'

'Then they could have called me a smuggler or an illegal businessman. What is a RAW agent?'

'Maybe they think you are running a racket that smuggles in these raw materials. That you are part of an organized ring.'

'But I'm not!'

'Obviously! But it doesn't matter because all they want to do is write against you. They are writing what they know will turn public opinion against you.'

Try as I might I could not set aside the 'raw' conundrum from my mind. I was a *raw* agent! Of everyone I knew there was not a single soul who had a business like that, so why was I being called such names? I stayed morose for a number of days, the unsolved mystery lying heavy on my mind. After nearly a month, one day when Khusro was visiting me I mustered enough courage and asked him, 'Khusro bhai, what is the RAW?' I had met Khusro through CS; Khusro was a businessman and had opened a factory for building a type of generator called an energy pack along with two other engineer friends of his. His office was in Motijheel and he used to come over to my place often, to check up on me.

'Raw? Raw in what way?'

'They have accused me of being a RAW agent.'

Exploding with laughter he told me, 'They are calling you a RAW agent and you don't know what it is? Is that even possible?' I recalled Milan's definition in a flash but before I could tell him all about it he continued. 'RAW is the Indian intelligence agency. Like the USA has the CIA.'

'Really!'

'You must have known!'

'I didn't.'

'What are you saying! Do you know there are Special Branch operatives tailing you all the time? They follow you wherever you go.'

'No! How? But I've never seen any! As in the Special Branch of the police?'

'Go and take a look, there'll be someone strolling past your house. Keeping tabs on who comes here, who goes where from here, and everything in between!'

My body had gone cold. What had I done that they were calling me a RAW agent and the police was shadowing me? Try as I might I could not recall exactly what I had done to deserve this. Politics in Bangladesh had always been heavily reliant on anti-India sentiments. The more the hatred, the more the votes. There were no political strategists left to think about the people of the nation. I noticed the tail pointed out to me soon enough while on my way to an event organized by the Indian embassy. A white car followed my rickshaw the entire way, probably to record my movements for government use. Even if I were to go to the Shantinagar market to buy cauliflowers and *puti* fish, government agents followed me there too. The entire time I could feel someone breathing over my shoulder. I should have been afraid, except that I was not. I knew I was no one particularly important—I was a doctor and I wrote when I had free time. Neither was I that important a doctor, nor was my writing that significant. A good doctor had to have an FCPS degree. A good writer needed to have boundless knowledge about all things pertaining to Bengali literature. I had neither.

Soon I made the headlines of *Bichinta*. 'Stolen from Sukumari!' My writings were not my own, they were someone else's. I was ready to face any punishment for having stolen from Sukumari but the experts went further and argued that I had abused Islam in *Nirbachito Kolam* and I should have been persecuted and not rewarded. Since they were the same people who had pointed out that I had stolen from Sukumari Bhattacharya, I could not help but wonder why I should be punished. They still called for my punishment, that last fact having slipped their mind around that time. They would have called for the original writer's punishment if it had come to that but their objective was to come after me.

Suddenly, struggling to keep afloat in a miasma of self-contempt, a voice spoke to me. It whispered in my ear that the comments about the Vedas may not have been mine but the comments criticizing Islam had definitely been. What was the book about at the end of the day? About the Vedas or about the position of women in Islamic society? In a tired voice I replied, the writing was mine and it was about the world around me. That is why they wish to punish *you*, not Sukumari, the voice whispered again. I also noticed that my previously bright and lively milieu had undergone a massive change. The ones who used to appreciate my writing, who used to say I was writing well, were now finding many faults in it. Obviously, all of this was because I had won a major prize. Writers who won prizes were meant to aim for a particular level of quality; they were busy judging if my writing had been able to reach up to that and obviously I was losing. The Ananda Puraskar transported me to a strange new space where I found myself completely alone, as if someone had put me along with my award inside a safe and locked it, and then thrown away the key. It was becoming increasingly difficult for me to breathe.

At the time when the excitement around me was at its peak in Calcutta, and the new edition of *Nirbachito Kolam* had been published and was doing exceedingly well, the news broke that I had plagiarized. It rose like a dust storm in one nation and did not take long to crash across the border. The report in *Bichinta* was published verbatim in the journals of Calcutta. For the anti-*Anandabazar* brigade this was the time to make hay. Even though not many things happened, there were a few notable repercussions of the 'Stolen from Sukumari!' piece. Feminist writer Maitreyi Chattopadhyay took up the plagiarism issue vocally. She raised questions about why I had stolen from Sukumari and why I had not included the proper citations in the book. Shibnarayan Roy wrote in response to her accusations that columns in the daily newspaper did not require citation and that the question could have been considered valid only if it had been about a scholarly research article. He also wrote a long piece in *Anandabazar* boldly stating that rumours were not going to be effective in taking away the edge and sharpness of my words. At least that was what happened in Calcutta.

In Bangladesh, they continued with the name-calling for a while longer and then applied themselves to finding out exactly in which parts of the book I had insulted the Quran and the hadith. Ultimately, a legal case was lodged against the publishers of the book, and also against the publishers and editors of the journals I used to write for. My books were burnt in public yet again and bookshops received warnings of dire consequences and severe violence if they continued to sell them. Someone wrote in *Inquilab* that I ought to be hanged. Hanged! Well, that was not anything new! Usually people called for corrupt politicians to be hanged during radical political rallies. That did not necessarily translate into an actual hanging, it was usually a manifestation of suppressed anger . . . or so I kept telling myself. Despite everything I could not get rid of the unease that had settled at the pit of my stomach.

When I used to write about the oppression of women everyone was fine with my writing. The moment I had tried to delve down to the root of the oppression and spoken out against religion, the appreciation dried up. And this was not just the fundamentalist faction. I am talking about the ones who did not pray five times a day, did not observe the roza, the men who used to shave and wear suits and call themselves progressive, the women who used to shun the headscarf, mix with other men, dabble in music and culture, and above all else, those who had been women's rights activists for the longest time and had instituted organizations and committees. Even they were shocked beyond measure at my boldness because I had dared to insult their religion. As long as I had been writing about the fanatics it had been fine, but why had I dragged the whole religious angle into it? How was religion to blame? Even my erstwhile supporters turned against me. The only people still left on my side were the ones who did not believe in religion, who were working towards equality between the sexes and actively fighting against superstitions and communal politics.

AS, a writer and intellectual among others, had established a booming business of abuse directed at me. Numerous anti-Taslima articles by him were being published in newspapers. I had met AS through R who had been a big fan of the man. AS had a distinctly spectral appearance; the first time we met I had asked R, 'Why does he look like that?'

'Look like what?'

'Don't you see? He looks ghostly.'

In response to my heedless comment R had told me, 'There are few men in this country as learned as AS.' There had been enough reason for R's admiration; AS had been instrumental in helping R get his first book published, so R had been devoted to him regardless of how he looked. There were rumours galore that AS was being paid by Libyan agents for his vocal pro-Islam stance but R had paid no heed to such discussion. AS had a lot of connections in many different foreign embassies, especially in the German embassy. He had even translated Goethe's *Faust* into Bengali.

I had met AS even after R and I had broken up, primarily at Ityadi, and he had invited me over to his place. One day he suddenly took up translating my poems and praised them so much that it gave me quite a scare. The translator of *Faust* was praising my poetry! He had told me that poetry like mine had not been written in Bengali previously and my poems ought to be translated in many other foreign languages across the globe. His ultimate aim had been to publish a book of his translations of my poems. Such was his ardour that it never ceased to amaze me how much his views about me had changed since then. This enormous leap from praise to abuse was indeed a conundrum to me.

After the Ananda Puraskar was announced the rebukes reached new heights. *Anandabazar* and *Desh* had first offered the prize to the Bangla Academy but the Academy had turned them down. When I was nominated for the award AS wrote: 'Taslima is nothing. Her entire thing is flippant and deceitful. Since she has been writing against Muslim society *Anandabazar* has chosen to turn the spotlight on her . . . In a certain village two elders always contested the elections against each other every year. Once, to tarnish his opponent's image, one of the elders appointed his own maid as the contestant against the other elder. I feel that's what the *Anandabazar* has done. Since the Bangla Academy refused the prize, piqued and upset, they chose Taslima for the prize as a slap on the face of the Academy.'

At a time when I was surrounded on all sides by zealots and scoundrels with their spiteful accusations threatening to engulf me, someone much bigger than them, Shamsur Rahman, the greatest poet in the country, wrote an article in my defence. In a piece called 'Long live Taslima's columns', Rahman argued:

> She has whipped our patriarchal, backward, moth-eaten society time and again, shaken the walls of many a monolith, never backed down in the face of religious conservatism, prejudice and brutality, and never minced her words either. I feel no shame in confessing that I am not as brave as Taslima Nasrin. There are many things I truly believe in which I want to say aloud, but I refrain from doing so because I am afraid of the perpetually blind, privileged feudal oligarchs and their touts. This gnaws at me bit by bit, I feel ashamed because of my weakness . . .

About my poetry he remarked:

> Many women in our society do not allow their own unique personalities to ever fully develop. Censorious howls and admonishments from all around seek to perpetuate this. This society has failed to grasp the reality that women are as much part of the human experience as men. Since Taslima cannot seem to find a way to adjust to this status quo she rebels and threatens to cast off her chains and even calls for others to do the same.

Not just Shamsur Rahman, many veterans like Jahanara Imam, Rashid Karim, Najim Mahmud and Majharul Islam wrote in my favour. From West Bengal, stalwarts like Sankha Ghosh, Bhabatosh Dutta, Ketaki Kusari Dyson, Shibnarayan Roy, Ananda Bagchi, Maitreyi Chattopadhyay, Bijoya Mukhopadhyay and Sutapa Bhattacharya too were discussing my writing in their journals and magazines. They called my writing fantastic, brave and uncompromising, and even went as far as to call me a rare voice of protest.

Sanat Kumar Saha of Rajshahi University wrote:

> Taslima Nasrin is one of our most remarkable contemporary writers and *Nirbachito Kolam* is one of the most remarkable books right now. It's also the book that's left the guards and hit-men and goons that patrol society foaming at the mouth.

All of this support was unexpected. It was too much even for me. Swanan Abritti Sangha, the poetry club of Rajshahi University, had invited me once; Sanat Kumar Saha was one of the authors connected to the group. The club had felicitated me and renowned writer Hasan Azizul Haque had welcomed me with a bouquet of flowers before saying many kind words about me, sweeping me off my feet in a wave of adulation. Afterwards, when they had requested me to say a few words I had racked my brain and come up empty. No words were on my tongue, no smart lines about literature, culture, politics or society, and despite being aware that the audience wished to hear me say something suitably stern and fiery, I had had to disappoint them with my dazed silence.

But the day I had recited poetry on the university grounds in front of the Shabash Bangladesh sculpture of the twin muktijoddhas, my voice rang out loud and clear. Truly, I could have read poetry tirelessly all day if only someone had asked me to do that. There was no dearth of intellectuals in Rajshahi University and neither was there a dearth of Islamic student bodies. The students of the latter were always a threat to others, killing progressive students in cold blood or slicing their veins to debilitate them. There was a constant hissing sound I could hear over my shoulder, new terrors lurking in the shadows and waiting for a chance to pounce.

Sanat Kumar wrote that when I had been on stage reading my poems

> an uncouth feeling of dread settled upon those that had gathered . . .
> I could hear my heart beat in anticipation, as if something horrid could happen any moment . . . I could spy a few pockets where

fanatics lurked, waiting for a chance to regurgitate all the hatred and bile . . . In the faces of such people one could clearly see the ravages of their naked greed and the hatred and rejection in their eyes. It was as if they were waiting for a chance to violently attack any form of dissent and tear it to shreds.

No, I was not violently attacked. I read my poems and got off the stage unharmed. During my stay at Rajshahi I stayed at Nazim Mahmud's house. Mahmud was a lively individual, keenly interested in my work as well as me. Some people never age, always managing to retain their youthful vigour, and Mahmud was one such person. He showed me around the university campus and even invited me to his house for dinner. Despite the wave of support for me Sanat was still not satisfied.

> The just society Taslima dreams of, for which we must all be grateful to her, we have not been able to properly thank her for it. We only show our solidarity and gratitude with immense hesitation and apprehension and then take our leave. We know fully well that is our limit.

Not that I ever got the feeling that there was no love for me among the people! In fact, I was acutely aware that whatever I had was beyond all my expectations, much more than I deserved. It was true that when I was being abused I was ready for that abuse as if it was due to me, but whenever someone praised me I could not help but be surprised. I understood well that praise left me feeling mortified, uncomfortable and uncertain, so unprepared was I for it.

The debate raged on for and against me. The ones against me were decidedly more in number, their pens sharper, more spirited and brimming with discontent. I also noticed that the tag 'popular', which was hitherto associated with my name, had been replaced by 'controversial', because apparently my writing caused controversy the likes of which no other author's did. Whatever I wrote affected people in some way or the other; either it made them laugh, or cry, or it made them think and get angry. Everyone who read it had something or the other to say.

Sometimes the reactions crossed over from the realm of the written word and reached me with teeth and talons bared. Mir

Nurul Islam wrote a column about me titled 'A Different Poet with a Different Point-of-View' in *Banglar Bani.*

> I have never met the person we are quarrelling over. I have only heard the most obscene things against her. Such words ring with derision and ridicule . . . but they lack . . . any actual critique of her literary merits. Such words only seek to produce a spicy mix of personal gossip and information . . . as if the female body has been . . . served on a platter to meat-lovers. Taslima Nasrin has been vocal against exactly this mentality and her pen has relentlessly sought conflict to make the resistance vigilant against such savagery and malice.

As was my habit, I read the columns written against me with more obvious interest than the ones in support of me. *Dainik Sangram, Inquilab, Dinkal, Milaat* and *Banglabazar Patrika* were all up in arms against me, of which *Sangram, Inquilab* and *Milaat* were known fundamentalist papers. While Motiur Rahman Chowdhury, the editor of *Banglabazar Patrika*, was not a bigot, he never hesitated from toeing the fundamentalist line when it came to me. Previously the two of us had never been at odds but the cracks began to show when Chowdhury earnestly began a campaign to ban the Calcutta-based journal *Desh* in Bangladesh.

In an article in *Desh* Nirad C. Chaudhuri had referred to Bangladesh as 'so-called Bangladesh'. Meeting Chaudhuri a few years later I had asked him the reason for his use of the term and he had explained to me with a smile that all four regions of east, west, north and south Bengal together used to be called Bangladesh. East Bengal had no special right to use the entire name especially because the western half had never laid claim to it. I had heard Chaudhuri out.

Just like that I had heard Motiur Rahman out too when the latter alleged that Chaudhuri's phrasing was a direct attack against the sovereignty of independent Bangladesh. I had accepted the logic but what I had not gone along with was what Chowdhury tried doing after that. He started a campaign to prohibit the import of *Desh* from Calcutta, despite the authorities of *Desh* apologizing for the use of the term 'so-called'. Because of his proximity and connections within the government, much to the dismay of the subscribers of *Desh*, one fine day all copies of the magazine were confiscated across the country and an embargo was placed on its import. *Desh* was a superior and well-regarded literary magazine; after this step there was hardly anything left for most of us to read.

Considering how since the partition much of Bangladesh's politics had been premised upon fanning anti-India sentiments, one political party launched an attack against the other accusing the latter of selling the nation out to our influential neighbours. Was this conflict truly for the future of Bangladesh? There were hardly any comparisons between the two nations; it was like making comparisons between the might of an elephant and a fly. Even if the two halves of Bengal could not get along, was it too much to ask that our literary and cultural exchanges remain unchallenged? Was that not beneficial to both Bengals? Because of the so-called offences committed by the word 'so-called', *Desh* was prohibited; I failed to understand whom that would benefit ultimately.

I was so angry by the actions taken by the government that I wrote a column where, while trying to get to the root of Rahman's anger against *Desh*, I unearthed that Chowdhury had asked for advertisements of the Puja special *Desh* for his *Banglabazar Patrika* but had been turned down in favour of *Ittefaq* and *Inquilab*. His so-called annoyance with the *Desh–Anandabazar* people was ultimately because of rejected advertisements and not some so-called insult to the sovereignty of Bangladesh. Ever since that article Chowdhury's watchful gaze remained trained on me, with articles appearing against me in his paper almost twice a day.

The character of the daily took a turn for the better when Motiur Rahman declared bankruptcy and sold the newspaper to Yahya Khan. Thanks to MM I had previously met the literature enthusiast and garments merchant Khan, and our acquaintance had remained premised on sudden meetings. He was an admirer of my work, and as it happened with many admirers, he was always eager to lend me a helping hand. I never asked him for a favour for myself but I had used his offer to get a job for Nirmalendu Goon as the literary editor of *Banglabazar Patrika*. Though the public face of ownership of the newspaper was Zakariah Khan, the real owner was Yahya, and Motiur Rahman Chowdhury was still the editor. In Chowdhury's office we had sat and discussed a salary of 5000 taka for Goon and only after that had I sipped my tea! Goon was a remarkable poet and it was their privilege they had appointed him as their literary editor; I had done nothing unfair. Through Khan I had also managed to get a factory job for another member of the Goon family, one of Geeta's younger sisters—another one of those things for which I could not help but feel a twinge of satisfaction.

The protectors of Islam were relentless in their sustained rebuke. However, they were not interested in producing counter-arguments and resorted directly to the 'fundamental truth' as laid out in the Quran and the hadith. Despite the complete lack of logic in such truth Abu Faisal wrote:

It is not academic honesty on Nasrin's part to expound on Islam's perspective on women by basing her argument on a twisted version of the faith, just to protect her own family. Nasrin has committed this dishonesty almost everywhere, and spread confusion in her wake. Nothing will happen to Islam ultimately because of her writings. Worse attacks have come on our faith from diverse corners which Islamic scholars have always combatted and are still capable of.

Even though he was sure no harm would come of me, the Islamic fundamentalists were not able to keep me out of their concerns. The attacks were such as if I had taken a knife to Islam and if I were not stopped it would spell doom for the faith.

In *Milaat* a diary entry was published:

A female columnist of our country believes that it was cunning men who had instituted religion to protect their own interests in this essentially patriarchal society and consequently God himself was misogynist. Recently she has written an article in this good-for-nothing daily column—by collating a few disjointed and unrelated lines and verses from various religious books like the Bible, the Tripitaka, the Vedas, the Upanishads, and even the holy Quran Sharif—to further add fuel to her macabre and abnormal beliefs and influence other women, in a nefarious plot to break out of the shackles placed around them by their respective religions. Of course this is not the first time that this crazy and petty writer, like an omnivorous crow, has deliberately poked and prodded at the decaying and the wasted bit of society to pollute the air around us. I have long noticed her strong aversion towards religious customs and rituals and her boundless animosity towards men. I have always been told that she is a highly educated woman and a doctor by profession, besides which she is a poet too. A relative of mine drew my attention to a recent so-called poem written by this anti-religious man-hating female poet. In one of the lines of that 'poem', she mentions that holding her hand means certain death. It seemed to me that since her childhood, or perhaps girlhood, she had always wanted someone whose hand she could hold. But her own experiences in the matter have cured her of any further interest in the matter. Who knows! But all I can say is this, till the day her body remains some or the other hand she will have to grab hold of. If she were to fall into the mud or into a ditch wouldn't she have to hold someone's hand to climb out? Seeing the esteemed columnist's state I am firmly convinced that she is at present up to her nose in filth. If she wishes to extricate herself from such a scenario she has to hold someone's extended hand no matter how much she detests it, and if she can hold the right hand it will not only clean the filth off her but might also end up saving her . . . you can contribute majorly to the women's movement if you can find the right hand to hold. I believe you truly feel pain every day when faced with the situation of women in society, you have a unique point of view and your writing too is very attractive. You are a good writer. It would have been so great if you did not have such lopsided views on religious matters.

The Muslim fundamentalists of Calcutta were not to be left behind. Articles attacking me were regularly appearing in journals like *Saptahik Kalam* and *Mijaan*. They were not too keen on the women's liberation issue and taking forward the example of nature one of them wrote that man was like the sun while woman was like the moon.

Allah has granted women gentleness and has bestowed toughness on men. It is in the perfect harmony of the two that society and the family realize their truest and most beautiful potential. If the two are in antagonism it produces discord, unrest, impiety. The Taslimas of the world are against the holy union of man and woman, they crave antagonism, and as a result there is chaos every step of the way. It is easy to write with one's guns trained at the fundamentalists but it is not as easy to maintain an untainted character and an exemplary moral code like them. The fundamentalists are inspired by the philosophy of Islam while the rationalists are driven solely by their nature.

Whatever they wrote against me in Calcutta, their counterparts in Bangladesh proudly reprinted the same in their papers.

People were reading my columns outside India too and the debate raged on outside the country as well. Writer Golam Murshid came down from London with his video camera to interview me. Shafeeq Ahmed and his wife also lived in London, both well versed in literary and cultural artefacts, and they came to meet me as soon as they reached the country. Meghna from Boston came to meet me during her trip to Bangladesh and left behind loads and loads of love. There I was, love on one side, hate on the other, both terribly effective in moving me deeply, but neither had the power to overwhelm me. It was as if I had fashioned my own self to gradually internalize or be free of both emotions. Be it love or hate, such reactions never failed to disconcert me.

A girl from Tangail came to see me once. She was a college graduate and wished to study further in the university but her family was against it. So she ran away from home and came to me as if I was her last recourse, as if I knew what to do next. Because she liked reading my writing she had been slapped around and verbally abused at home but that had failed to change her mind in any way. She boldly declared that there was no one greater in her life than me—not her parents, not her siblings, nor her relatives. To her even Allah, if He existed, was not as significant.

Not just the young, older people too came to meet me, and women, irrespective of their age—from fifteen to seventy-five—profession or class, found their way to my door at some point or the other. They came to tell me about their lives, showing me numerous colours and sides to human grief in the process, and many also came to draw strength and support from me. I was never confident in my ability to provide such support and aid, and while many were turned away from my door empty-handed, there were as many who refused to leave. What did they gain from staying back? This was a question that always baffled me.

A girl called Nahid, a law student at university, came to see me. Once the conversation dried up and it was time for her go I realized she did not wish to leave at all. Even though she did leave ultimately she was back again to see me in a few days. Another girl, Jhunu, a political activist, came to my house, had tea and biscuits, but showed no signs of leaving even after a while. All she wanted was to touch me once and see for herself that it was truly me. Mitun and Neepa, two smart and beautiful girls studying in the Viqarunnisa School, were regular visitors to my Shantibag house. Mamun and Anu, a young needy couple, were frequent visitors too. Anu worked as a saleswoman in a shop while Mamun did not have a job. One day I wrote a letter to the editor of *Bhorer Kagaj* for Mamun recommending a job for the unfortunate boy in their papers. I had read some of the letters Mamun had written and sensed his writing skills. In the end Mamun did get that job at *Bhorer Kagaj*. My life went on as usual, with Mitford, my home, my writing, evening addas and my admirers. Since I was never particularly enamoured of living a guru's life most of my admirers eventually turned into my friends, or even family, and the gates to my house always remained open for them.

The one major repercussion of the public debate was that the very sight of a fez cap was enough to strike terror in my soul. Their posturing in public convinced me that they were going to gobble me up alive if only they could manage to get their hands on me. But surprising things did not stop happening entirely. One day a bearded man in a lungi and a kurta simply barged into my house; someone had probably left the door open on their way out or in. We were all sitting and chatting in my bedroom. Spying a stranger entering my room I was so scared that for a moment I could not even scream out loud. What did the man want? Why was he in my home? Looking at my petrified face the man said, 'Don't be afraid. I have not come here with any evil intentions. I just wanted to see you once. I have always wanted to see you. Today, I finally feel gratified.'

The unwelcome guest was soon shown out of the house. He had crept into my home like a cat simply to see me once!

Go as You Like

Was I ever truly in love, or was it only the idea of love that I had dragged around with me? I began asking myself this strange question over and over again. What had my old relationship with R been? When I sat down to list the number of reasons why it could be called love, and the number of reasons why it could not be, I discovered that although I had been deeply attracted to R and I had never turned from him despite his many misdeeds, none of it had anything to do with love. It had been something else, something that comprised loneliness, a desire to love and the idea of love itself. I had learnt the codes of social behaviour expected of people in love and merely replicated them. They had been received responses, none of them entirely my own.

I had only read a few of R's poems in the weekly journals. Then one day I had received a letter from him with the poems he had sent for *Senjuti*. I had answered his letter and we had kept in touch through letters. I had never seen him, known little about him, but I had fallen in love with him nonetheless. It was not as if R had been a terribly handsome man; in fact, the first time we met I was quite revolted. I loved his poetry, but then there were so many others whose poetry I admired too. In effect, I had fallen in love with the idea of being in love.

Like when we were children, Chandana and I fell in love with the film actor Jafar Iqbal. We were attracted to his beauty. Obviously, there had to be something for one to get attracted—either looks or talent. But even that had not been love; it had been a youthful infatuation. We had managed to write to Jafar Iqbal and become friends with him. In fact, Jafar had proposed marriage to Chandana when he met her! For the longest time I had a secret dream that one day I was going to meet him in person too. While going to Chotda's house in Dhaka one had to pass by Iqbal's house on 5 Nayapaltan, but not once did I ever go in. Instead I hoped to miraculously run into him some day, somewhere. No, we never ran into each other. And we never will either. The most handsome leading man of the country suddenly died one morning at a terribly young age. There was no disease, no foul play. An apparently healthy man had simply died and the astonishing news had numbed me with shock. He had married a girl call Sonia but they never got along and Sonia had left him. Perhaps out of loneliness and despair Jafar Iqbal had drunk himself to death.

~

When I started watching Hindi films I developed an intense crush on Amitabh Bachchan. I loved seeing him and Rekha in love; they looked so good together. I would imagine myself as Rekha and imagine Bachchan was professing his love to me. Of course I was not Rekha, I was me, and there were no handsome men waiting to love me. So all I could do was to wait for one to come along. Later, during my adolescent years, I wanted to be with the actor Afzal Hossain and that desire had never entirely gone away to be honest. Afzal was very handsome. A theatre actor, he was extremely popular both on television and on stage; he was a dramatist himself and wrote beautiful love stories. He also wrote novels that were published by Vidyaprakash and Khoka was instrumental in pushing Afzal to write.

The first time I had met him was ten years ago at the book fair. He was so tall that his readymade trousers did not fit him and ended way above his heels, but he hardly seemed to care and was roaming about the fairground wearing them. R and Afzal knew each other and R had called him over for a quick chat. We met quite a few times after that but only in passing. Afzal was in a relationship with fellow theatre actor Subarna but the relationship did not last and she left him. In time he started an advertising company called Matra in Nayapaltan, just behind Chotda's house, and I would pass by the place often on my way to my brother's house.

While I was still with R my infatuation with Afzal had stayed under check due to social mores and customs, but after R and I broke up there were innumerable instances when my obsession nearly made me barge into the Matra office and confess my undying love to him. I would stand in front of the mirror and imagine Afzal beside me, our combined beauty a thing to behold! Despite everything I could never enter Matra and neither could I ever tell him anything; each time when I wanted to I had to pull back the reins of my own desires.

Many years ago two poets from Mymensingh, Shafiqul Islam Salim and Ataul Karim Shafeeq, had invited Afzal Hossain and MHI to Mahakali School in Mymensingh for a programme. At Salim and Shafeeq's request I had gone to the event to read a short story from among the ones I had been writing for the women's page of the magazine *Sambad*. The story I had chosen, 'Madhabir Jiban Katha' (Madhabi's Story), written in the austere sadhu-bhasha dialect of Bengali, was the best of the bunch, and I was supposed to go up on stage almost at the end right before the invited guests. But the moment I was on stage something terrible had happened. The audience had started shouting as none of them wished to listen to me; unable to continue in the ensuing chaos I was forced to go off the stage after reading only a few lines. I never managed to find out why the crowd had gotten so annoyed—whether it was simply because they disliked me or because they had been more eager to listen to the special guests. Whatever it was, I did not have the guts to meet Afzal or MHI that night.

After that incident whenever I felt the insane urge to barge into Matra and speak to Afzal I would remind myself of the embarrassing fiasco that had transpired. I had gone to Matra on only one occasion— not to meet Afzal but to see MHI. This was just before MHI and I were scheduled to go to India. MHI's afternoons were usually spent at addas in Matra and he had asked me to meet him there. Afzal could have turned me away that day saying MHI was not there but instead he had welcomed me in and invited me to his office. We had tea and spoke at length about advertisements, plays and novels, and he had even gifted me a fat English novel. On my way out he had escorted me to the door and asked me to visit again. I was not expecting this sort of a welcome and for the rest of the day a balmy frisson of joy had kept me enveloped within its embrace.

In the aftermath of the book fair incident and its fallout I ran into Afzal at Khoka's, where both of us had been invited for dinner. I received a sudden call in the evening from Khoka; his wife was going to be cooking and I had to go over to his place for dinner. I simply picked out a sari and took a rickshaw to Khoka's. When I entered his place I was decidedly dishevelled and quite homely since I had assumed I was the only one he had called over. But the biggest surprise was waiting for me in the form of Afzal and his wife! I learnt they had gotten married recently and hence he had brought her along. Despite this new development I found my fascination for him not dimming one bit; I only had to work harder through the evening to conceal it and try and have a normal, courteous conversation. I was not the old Taslima who had had to walk off stage because the public had shouted her off; I was a popular writer and an Ananda Puraskar winner. However, that evening for me was not about my pride—when a person you admire appears in front of you pride can be very difficult to cling on to.

People who inhabit one's dreams are best left right there. They get all ragged and filthy if one tries to reach for them. Rather, dreams ought to forever remain out of reach and thus stay pure and unsullied. That way one can bring one's dreams out on occasion—like a kite one flies in the sky, for instance—without running the risk of losing one's grasp on things. It is a safe way to be, to carefully protect the little joys against the tyranny of reality. It is the most certain way of making sure one's dreams remain eternal. That is what I used to do with my desires, keep them away from all the sorrow and the pain, the darkness that overshadowed my life.

Instead, I let myself get sullied. I slept with other men because bodies have their own demands that need to be fulfilled. The first person I had ever slept with was R, after him there was MHI, NM and MM. The games I had played with them were pleasurable to me, but at the end of the day it was still their pleasure that had been paramount. I had spent three nights in Calcutta with Sharif too in an odd fling. While we were both in Calcutta, one evening he had come over and told me the story of his life. The entire night we had spoken about his love affair, his marriage, the subsequent break-up, and how loneliness was slowly beginning to choke him to death. He had been drinking while speaking and sometime around dawn when the alcohol had run out he had turned to me. I did not turn him down, not because I could not say no, but because I did not see any reason in doing so. Sharif was not in love with me, he had only been making love to another upcoming poet.

Of course the body is crucial, but it cannot be the last word when it comes to desire, can it? It is a little like playing the flute. Unless you are in love with the flute will it be possible to play it for long? Sharif was very happy with my Ananda Puraskar but I had also noticed a flicker of envy in his gaze. After the ceremony he had remarked how I had used the word 'sexual' too much in my speech; he had immediately clarified that it was not his own observation but something he had overheard people discuss. Unless he too had felt the same why had he made it a point to mention it to me?

Sharif wished to keep sex confined to the secrecy of the night, and he was willing to approach a woman with his sad story to have her feel kindly towards him. He was willing to sleep with her but any mention of anything 'sexual' in public, even in a non-personal context, was anathema to him. Most Muslim ghotis hold a special place in their heart for the Muslim metropolis of Dhaka. On his trip to Dhaka, Sharif stayed at my place and though I could not accompany him, he went out to see the city on his own and to visit friends and acquaintances. None of his stories had the same effect on me any more, especially because I hardly had any time for them. He was staying at home, taking showers, eating and going out only to return late. Though there was nothing lacking in hospitality on my side, there was definitely a certain amount of coldness. If Sharif had assumed I was going to be as easily available as before then my firm refusal to resume a physical relationship dealt a hard blow to the notion. Because of my early shift at Mitford there was no way for me to know when he returned to go to sleep in Milan's room, and throughout the day I had no time either. Calcutta and Dhaka were not the same places—in Calcutta I was usually on holiday while in Dhaka I had a clogged schedule.

Besides, even though there were no men in my life that did not mean that I was going to find solace with just about anyone. My body was used to going without a man's touch for years and I was steadfast in my decision to no longer compromise on my emotions for the sake of sex. Letting a few overeager sperms get me pregnant, only for NM to come and assume it was his responsibility and make him help me get an abortion—perhaps it would have been the perfect revenge on NM, but it would have done very little good for my body and heart. Sharif told me I had changed. It was true, I *had* changed a little; it was only fair that it should have happened since I had fallen for K by then.

~

Even though I was convinced that I was never going to fall in love with someone again, nor was I going to link my life with another's, I did end up getting involved with someone and that too quite deliberately. I had assumed I was going to spend the rest of my life with my family, my job, my literary and cultural engagements, and no man needed to be part of that. However, one fine day I met this startlingly beautiful young man who I could not stop staring at, my eyes straying quite involuntarily to his wide frame again and again, to his big beautiful eyes, his aquiline nose, his rosy cheeks and his beguiling smile. The hungry glances that men usually cast at women—that was how I looked at K's beauty.

A beautiful man had been a lifelong dream for me, a dream that was yet to be fulfilled, and I desired K with the force of all my unfulfilled yearnings, albeit in silence. It did not remain a secret for long, though, not especially after a couple of screwdrivers at Sheraton managed to unlatch a floodgate of confessions one night. K was not a doctor or a writer, nor had he ever read any of my books. Baharuddin, a journalist in the Calcutta-based daily *Aajkaal*, had come to my house to see me, with a friend from Jaidevpur. That was when I had first met K, and although Baharuddin had returned to Calcutta, K had kept coming back to see me.

There was nothing common between our worlds, but all I knew was that I had mingled with my kind for long enough and it was time to see how the other half lived. I had applied for a telephone nearly a year back but there was still no sign of a connection. K promised to try and help, although I was going to have to accompany him to the concerned minister's house. Accordingly I went with him to see the telecom minister—by which I mean we went, had tea and biscuits, listened to what the man had to say and then left with a smile. Thanks to K's connections, my connection was soon approved, something I doubt I would have managed to get done on my own.

Back in Mymensingh I had taken the connection by myself and we had never had to run to a minister for help; a simple application had done the trick. But Dhaka was not Mymensingh and applications meant less than nothing there. Corruption was at an all-time high and things were in such a state that a simple application did not move from one table to the next without multiple palms being greased. Or one had to have connections, and K's role in helping me get a phone automatically elevated his status in my house.

During Ershad's reign K had been the chairman of Gazipur district, something he was exceedingly proud of, and the more I learnt about his life the more I realized how much it was premised upon both a thirst for power and complex equations of commerce. Not that K was big fish in this murky pond, he was at most small fry, but he did have aspirations of becoming a big shot. When he declared which ministers he knew, his friends, relatives and also the ones who always listened to him, all in an effort to impress me, it was nothing short of an ugly display. It was at moments like these that I was even more convinced that our lives were entirely too different.

Besides, he was married and had two daughters, Ananya and Sukh. Quite ironically, Sukh was also the name I had picked for my daughter if I was ever going to have one. K's wife H was a short, plump, extremely fair woman. We met only on one occasion, that too because of Nirmalendu Goon. K had asked her to wait in the car while he had come up to meet me. On his way to my apartment Goon noticed the car and asked him whether it was his wife sitting inside. While K had gone pale in an instant, I had shepherded all three of us downstairs to meet her.

K did not like speaking about his wife and he used to change the topic whenever I had a question I wished to ask him about her. In fact, not just H, he did not feel comfortable talking about his two daughters either. Perhaps if he had been able to prove that the only people he had back at home were his mother and brothers, and not a wife and children, he would have been happiest. I had no problems with his family, though, especially when he stared at me with entranced eyes or silently took my hand in his. I did not move my hand away and when his face bent closer to mine it did not take long for our lips to meet; more than K himself, that was something I needed desperately.

The first time he was a little wound up, his fingers trembling in anxiety over my warm flushed skin, but gradually the warmth helped thaw the icy hesitation in him. For me the needs were exclusively physical, while for him they were undeniably emotional; his body gave me pleasure and my vitality gave him satisfaction. There was no bond between us as such except that of a free and open relationship and a mutual understanding that our respective personal lives were not up for discussion. It was a relationship of convenience and need, or perhaps not even that. It was not meant to be anything per se, and even if it was anything neither of us dwelled on that aspect too intently—it lasted because there was no harm in it at the end of the day. I could do without K and at the same time I could not. For instance, if he did not come by on a certain day after visiting a couple of days in a row, I would invariably end up missing him, much like one misses a habit. Once he did not come by for two weeks. After two weeks when he suddenly turned up one day it was astonishing to say the least.

'What is it, K bhai! You were missing in action! Did you forget the way to this house? Or has the *kharaj*[34] been low recently!'

'Milan, don't be crazy!' K replied to Milan's jibes, attempting to maintain a serious facade.

K was no longer chairman. He travelled to Dhaka from Jaidevpur every day to drop in at the various offices at Motijheel. I had no way of surmising what his source of income was though he told me he had businesses which were mostly run by partners and the primary reason behind his trips to Dhaka was to meet them. When questions arose in my mind about K's profession Milan clarified them for me.

'Bubu, don't you get it? He gets kharaj.'

'Kharaj?'

'Yes, kharaj.'

This was a new word for me and when I asked him what it meant Milan tried explaining. 'Oh, it's nothing. Say you have an industry in my area, so you give me some money and I will try and manage your business so that someone with nefarious plans does not cause your business any harm. While he had been chairman he must have used his influence to help someone in their business. Now he gets money from them.'

I asked K about it too. 'They say you get kharaj from people!' Our interactions had become decidedly informal and the jump from the polite formal ways to the distinctly informal ones had been rather quick. K only smiled at my question. I was thinking about him; even if it was nothing too significant, because of the 'kharaj' I was curious about him at least. This little bit of information was good enough for him and the grin refused to slip from his face.

Our relationship was in no way that of a couple, though that was probably what K wanted ultimately. But it was impossible for me to think of K as a partner. He was a friend, almost like a family member. Kulsum was away and my flat was not getting cleaned. One day he took off his shirt and shoes and cleaned my house. He followed every one of my orders to the letter. K was aware that I was not in love with him and in time he grew desperate with the need to change that. If I were to call him beautiful, his face would shine with joy and he would admit freely that a few months or years back he had been even more beautiful. At times he came across as a two-year-old, such was his behaviour, and on other occasions he would be like a jealous lover. He was suspicious of everyone who came to my house, assuming I had a secret relationship with them and his suspicions amused me as much as they annoyed me.

I did not particularly care about his issues with inferiority. When I paid him attention it made him happy and when I did not he would go mad with rage thinking I was about to cast him aside. I had no intention of doing that but I did not want him to disrupt my peace either. I did not let myself get disturbed and whenever he tried pulling something on those lines I asked him to leave immediately. I was certain that I did not need another person to think they were in control of my life. Who was Khusro? Why did he visit me? What did he want? Why was I letting Alamgir into my house? What did I have to do with Rashid? Whenever he tried asking such questions he learnt quickly enough that I had no patience with such pot-stirring. His arrogance was welcome everywhere but with me. Who was allowed in my house and who was not, or how my life was going to pan out—these were my concerns and mine alone.

K often spoke about his wealth. He had a lot of money, a lot of property, a new house under construction in Dhaka, a new car, and so on and so forth. Once, Milan, Yasmin and I were invited to his house. His mother and other family members were at home but neither his wife H nor his daughters were there. It was not difficult to guess that he had taken me home probably because they were not there. A small two-storey place in Jaidevpur, the house had been built by his father and there were not too many signs of the wealth he usually spoke about. Despite his fussing over where to make us sit and what to give us to eat, Milan came away disappointed with the experience. 'Bubu, hadn't K bhai said so many things? I was expecting a palace! And we got a house with the paint peeling off, plus the broken, rundown furniture. The only thing he has to show off is that car. He must have bought it with all that kharaj money.'

The more K tried to impress us with his efforts to prove he was a tycoon, the less we respected him. In time he became like a laughing stock, his words and his actions like munchies with our afternoon tea, or a constantly performing joker in a circus. But whenever I took him to my bedroom and closed the door behind us I loved him and he gave me joy and profound pleasure. I was done with being a piece of meat trapped under a heaving man, my presence there solely for his pleasure. No man had ever bothered to find out if I was satisfied, they had only dived in for their own; K would have done that too because men are not used to being concerned. But I asked him to be concerned, told him to be the moon and bring me my tide, made him arouse me and touch every trembling pore, and made him lose himself in loving me. K never disappointed.

In fact, giving me pleasure brought him pleasure too and eventually it so happened that my pleasure became the top priority, the reason for all of it to begin with. I was the one who *had* K, whenever I wanted, however I wanted, and the fact that I needed him made him swell with pride. His desire to bring me joy was an ever-increasing urge and he took me away on trips, brought me gifts and did everything else that he thought would make me happy. Of course he could afford to do many things, but even those things that were beyond his reach he tried to do for me.

When I was suddenly transferred from Mitford to Jamalpur without any prior notice we decided to drive to Jamalpur in his car. I was going to go and join my new post at the civil surgeon's office in Jamalpur and then come back with him the next day after putting in a leave of absence. The drive to Jamalpur was wonderful and we stopped at Mymensingh to stay the night at Abakash before carrying on the next morning. It was on rare occasions that I had the chance to get away from the humdrum of Dhaka and while driving K told me many things about his life.

He told me stories from his childhood, about his friends and their games. Our childhoods were so alike that despite K being older than me by nearly ten years we appeared to be of the same age. Besides, he looked young and his liveliness ensured that he stayed that way. Gradually we left the brick and concrete city behind us along with the shrieks of the trucks and buses on the road, the metropolis giving way to a sea of green dotted with small mud houses in the distance and miles of agricultural land and peaceful hamlets. Travelling never failed to excite me.

Arrangements for my stay had been made at the Jamalpur Circuit House. The civil surgeon had offered to book two separate rooms but I had insisted on one. 'Is he your husband?' the surgeon had asked.

'No.'

'Then two rooms . . .'

'No, one will be fine.'

That night it seemed we were back to our sixteen-year-old selves, our excited and ecstatic bodies writhing in seventh heaven the entire night. I had never seen K so happy before. He did not have me all to himself too often and the two of us being able to spend some time together alone, far away from our busy lives in Dhaka, was akin to divine providence for him. I had barely any time to spare for K in Dhaka and although the time I did get to spend with him was usually enough for me, it clearly was not enough for him. In Dhaka we met frequently, and then again we would end up not meeting for days. I always missed him during such times.

K was important to me as much for the little playful games we liked playing as for the serious discussions we often used to have. 'You know anything about a job? Help my cousin get one!' K never said no to anything. Even if it was not possible for him he would promise to try. And he did try, like many other things he tried to do, even if he failed to keep his word in the end. My cousin Motaleb had been looking for a job for the longest time and used to come to me often to ask for my help in getting him one. In our unruly and poverty-stricken country even a university degree did not guarantee a job for someone. Thus if someone in the family was successful or financially well-off it was common for a lot of other relatives to gravitate towards them. Some came for financial assistance and some in search of employment.

Since I did not have the necessary clout to get anyone jobs K had to step in; he managed to talk to a friend of his, the owner of a bread factory, about a job for my BSc cousin Motaleb. Irrespective of the nature of the job, for an unemployed young man it was as good as any other. On my part, I could not help feeling even more grateful to K for all his help. Obviously that was what he wanted anyway, to prove to me once and for all that he was not someone to be trifled with, that he too had power and influence. He often took me along with him to his rich friends' houses or offices in his shiny red car, all in his vain effort to impress me.

Once at the Kankrail crossing his car collided with a rickshaw. In a fit of rage K got off and began to beat up the rickshaw-puller mercilessly. When my screams from the car failed to stop him I had to get off and drag him back to the car in front of the gathered crowd, with K growling about the dent on his car. I was so incensed by his inhuman reaction that day that I did not allow him to enter my house for days after the incident. In time K realized that I was not reacting to his physical strength and bureaucratic clout the way he wished I would and he switched his strategy to telling me touching stories of his humanitarian side—the many deprived and unfortunate souls in Jaidevpur who approached him for aid and how he helped them.

I never knew how he was when he was away from me but at least in front of me he had to be what he claimed he was. Very soon, driven by his emotions, he took to writing poetry, most of it about me. While I would be busy speaking to journalists or other authors he would wait for me for hours on end, sitting and writing poems. If ever I was to offhandedly remark that his poetry was good he would immediately flush with embarrassment and pride and start putting in more effort. In effect he wanted to prove to me that he could write too. A person who had never read a book in his life suddenly started reading one fine day.

My simple, straightforward, undefined but stable relationship with K survived the test of time. It did not bring me pain and neither did it waste my time. I did not have to feed it constantly to help it grow. Neither did I have to lose sleep over where it was headed. The relationship took care of both my worries and my loneliness. K was sometimes a young man, sometimes a baby, sometimes visible and sometimes not. But as long as he remained in front of me he was mine and absolutely so. Whether he was a human being or a monster, a friend or a foe, he was mine and I could rain my anger, sorrow, pain and all my joy upon him. If I was angry I could tear at him and draw blood, cry on his shoulder if I was sad or raise hell if I was happy, and yet he tolerated everything silently. I could be drawing him close and showering him with love one minute, or shouting at him to get out the next, but nothing I did or said, or any number of kicks, slaps and punches failed to drive him to anger. He knew I was going to pull him towards me again and possibly he also knew that I felt a certain kind of love for him.

I did love him. I also loved my favourite doll. After a long tiring day out in the world everyone wants something that is their own, be it an object or a person. K was a bit like that for me. The fact that he loved me, this knowledge gave me relief, it gave me happiness, it gave me security, it gave me freedom and it helped me stay busy. Even if I did not acknowledge it, I knew I needed him in my life. I could take him anywhere without feeling even an iota of hesitation. He accompanied me to the houses of my author friends, or they met him at my place whenever they came over, and during our addas he would simply sit quietly in one corner and listen. No one asked me who he was or what was our relationship and I simply assumed that they drew their own conclusions. Perhaps this raised a few eyebrows too. However, I was not too worried about raised eyebrows and having failed to garner my attention the eyebrows too returned to their natural shape in due course.

With my sister, her husband, Kulsum and even Mother at home, I would take K to my bedroom and shut the door behind us. Not a single person ever said anything to me about it, especially Mother, and often after I came out of my room it was she who stayed hidden somewhere inside so as not to embarrass me. Mother never wished to come in the way of my joy; she wanted me to have everything that brought me happiness and satisfaction. In fact she worried about me so much that she worried about my expenses of her own accord even though I was not going through any financial crisis. Sometimes she would worry that more food had to be bought if she stayed over and off she would go to Mymensingh to get rice, pulses, vegetables and anything else she could get her hands on from Abakash. Unwilling to sit and rake up my bills she would then head back to Mymensingh again, but not before giving Kulsum various tips on how to take care of me.

Was I becoming like Father? My temper at least was like his. Everything ran on my money and according to my orders. While people in Shantibag respected me and were always at hand to get me whatever I required, people at Abakash too were wary of how they spoke to me. Father no longer spoke to me with rage in eyes and gnashing teeth. Rather his voice was mellower and more placatory when he made requests. 'Do you have anyone connected who can help with jobs? See if you can do something for Manju.' Manju, Uncle Iman's son, had not studied too far. Just like Father had always been responsible for the education and employment of his family in Nandail, I had to be a little responsible too. I spoke to Khusro and managed to get a job for Manju in the former's generator factory in Savar, a worker's post with basic pay.

We did not have friends in high places who we could approach for help in times of need. In the entire extended family the only person with some degree of fame and affluence was Father. If there was anyone after that, it was me. Having managed to get jobs for both Motaleb and Manju through K and Khusro respectively, my status within the family was suddenly elevated to Father's level. I visited Abakash with K but not once did Father inquire about who he was or why we were together. Evidently I was beyond such questions. Was it solely because I was self-reliant? That could not be the only reason because I had been self-reliant back in Armanitola too. Then was it because I was more responsible? Because I had assumed responsibility of Yasmin and Milan, at the very least ensured a roof over their heads and food on the table? Or was it because I was older? But I was not that old, I was not even thirty. So was this changed attitude because I was financially better off than before? Or because it made no sense trying to talk me out of things since I did not care about people's opinions? Or perhaps because I was famous! But I had been famous back then too when Father had torn down my happy life and dragged me back to Mymensingh by the throat to lock me up. Perhaps it was because I was more famous! Whatever the reason, it nonetheless made me happy that there was no one to forbid me from doing what I pleased. For the first time in my life I could truly taste independence.

Friends, well-wishers, poets and authors—someone or the other was always at home and raucous addas would happen where everything, from literature to culture and politics to society, was up for discussion. There would be frequent rounds of tea and during lunch or dinner-time food would be laid out on the table for each person to serve themselves at their own convenience. Even in welcoming and taking care of guests I was following in Mother's footsteps. Sunil Gangopadhyay came to see me from Calcutta. Sarat and Bijoya Mukhopadhyay, on their trip to Dhaka, dropped by as well. So serene and safe was the place I had gradually made for myself that I could welcome anyone to my home and any of my friends could stay over for a couple of days. I had done up my home, my world and my life in exactly the way I had wanted it. My friends were much more precious to me than my relatives and whatever leisure I had was exclusively reserved for them.

Badal Basu, the dark mountain of a man whom I had never seen smiling, visited me from Ananda with the newly published *Noshto Meyer Noshto Godyo*. If one made the effort to get to know Basu it quickly became apparent that he did not lack a sense of humour at all. He could smile too and it was a pleasant sight when he did. All the humour was lost, however, when I opened the book and immediately began to notice a plethora of horrifying mistakes. 'What is this? Was

this not proofread properly?' Flipping through the book for a closer
inspection Basu's face betrayed his despair. 'This is a catastrophe! It
was not proofread at all.'

'Then stop selling them immediately!'

I did not think twice before asking someone as forbidding as
Badal Basu to stop the sale of the 5000 copies already printed. Instead
of being delighted at the sight of a freshly printed new volume, the
book only made me feel depressed. Basu suggested, 'Since it's been
printed already let these be. We can correct all the mistakes in the
second edition.' But the readers who were going to buy the book were
being cheated; they were not going to get to read even a single correct
sentence! They were going to assume that I had deliberately written
all that nonsense! A formidable publication house such as Ananda
failed to make amends for a mistake they had made and refused to
recall the book despite my request. Publication houses in Bangladesh
were far less influential than Ananda Publishers but I was sure that
if I had asked one of them to hold back a book that had not been
proofread properly they would have honoured my request. The fracas
with Ananda left me in despair for a long time.

But then how long can one wallow in misery? There is no end to
regrets, wretchedness, anguish, pain and misfortunes in life. Despite
all that one has to deliberately make an effort to move past regrets
and launch into new endeavours. I was well aware that I had to keep
my spine straight against the quagmire of gossip, harassment, cruelty
and jealousy around me, or risk losing my footing and falling and
shattering to bits. There were people perpetually ready to wreak
havoc in my life; fame had as many downsides as it had perks. As for
the perks I no longer had to go to the newspaper offices to submit
my articles, the offices usually had people who came by to pick them
up from me. Whatever I wrote, however I wrote it, was published.
Publishers dutifully left my share of the profits at home and the sums
of money I had never even imagined in my life became like spare
change for me.

However, the downsides too were considerable. The most
intrusive, of course, was the undue interest in my personal life.
Since I had been married more than once it was assumed I had slept
with numerous men too and the list of my purported husbands had

names which I had never heard in my life. I was shameless and of low moral character. Since I was well acquainted with Sunil he had 'managed' the Ananda Puraskar for me (Sunil Gangopadhyay used to be on the committee that decided the Ananda Puraskar and from the information I had he was the only one who had been opposed to the award being conferred on me). I was anti-men and anti-Islam. I was a RAW agent. What I wrote was not literature but pure pornography, and so on and so forth. As my friends increased in number, so did my enemies.

Despite the growing number of enemies a plethora of people still came to see me! Girls of various ages came to tell me about their problems—some did not like the husbands they had been married off to, some husbands were having affairs or had the habit of beating their wives up, some women had been divorced summarily by their husbands, or their fathers were not allowing them to study, or their husbands were not letting them work, or their bosses were making passes at them. Things most of these women could not confess to someone else I noticed they could easily say to me and it seemed to lift a stone off their hearts.

A short novel of mine called *Niyantran* (Control) was published, about a young girl, Sheela, of about sixteen or seventeen who falls in love with a handsome boy. However, the boy does not love her back. One day he takes advantage of her naive love and, using the ruse of an invitation, lures her to an abandoned house where he rapes her along with his friends. Such a tragic and heart-rending story was immediately deemed offensive by people. Apparently it was not fit to be read or even touched, and because I had given a visceral description of the brutal rape it was so obscene as to be almost pornographic. It was fine as long as things like this were happening in society but writing about such incidents was not acceptable. It immediately caused scandal and I was threatened with excommunication and social ridicule.

Of course, the ridicule was a foregone conclusion, and while I was being spat at in public, one afternoon I received a visit from a stranger who wished to talk to me about the book. She had read it more than once and had even made her daughters read it. Imagine my surprise on hearing that she had *made* her adolescent daughters read the book, a book that was so dirty that one had to wash one's hands after touching it, whose words were so vile that it nauseated people! The woman told me that the book was a must-read for all women and also informed me that she believed her daughters were going to be far more careful henceforth so that no one could succeed in luring them anywhere. She thanked me profusely for writing such a book and also earnestly requested me to continue the way I was writing. One tattered piece of praise washed away the ignominy of the hundred people rebuking me outside.

~

What had been the real reason behind transferring me from Dhaka? Many suspected that it was my writing. A few government officials did not like what I was writing. In the BNP's own newspaper, *Dainik Dinkal*, articles criticizing me, beautifully garnished with perfectly imaginary details, appeared regularly, accusing me of overreaching and speaking nonsense under the influence of hedonism and debauchery. So the smartest thing to do had been to move me from one place to somewhere far away where I would be too busy trying to save myself and fending off snakes to give any thought to writing.

I wrote an application to the health department, signed by the health secretary, Manjurul Karim, stating that it would be impossible for me to work in a remote village in Jamalpur and requesting an immediate transfer, if not to Dhaka, then at least to a nearer hospital. Manjurul Karim was a poet too, under the nom-de-plume Imran Noor, and he had perhaps signed my application precisely for that reason. As per Noor's advice Nirmalendu Goon took me to meet Sheikh Hasina, hoping something could be done. Even though I was not sure, Goon was certain Sheikh Hasina would be able to overturn my transfer. Sheikh Hasina and Goon went back a long way, right back to when they used to be classmates in Dhaka University; Goon had probably even written a few love poems back in the day dedicated to her, just as he had written 'Beauty Queen' for Purabi Basu.

I had been to Sheikh Hasina's residence on Minto Road on two previous occasions, the first time for the grand iftar she had hosted when Goon had also introduced me to her. Then I had met her at 32 Dhanmandi for Sheikh Mujibur Rahman's birthday celebrations.

That had been my first time at 32 and Sheikh Hasina was there welcoming all the guests. It was a devastating moment to stand at the exact spot on the stairs where Sheikh Mujib had been riddled with the assassin's bullets on that horrific day of 15 August 1975 when sixteen members of his family were also murdered. Sheikh Hasina and her sister Rehana had thankfully been away from the country that day, or else they would have been similarly killed.

Around the time of our second meeting Sheikh Mujib's murderers were all free citizens and were at complete liberty to go wherever they pleased. In fact they had formed the Freedom Party and its student wing Yuva Command, and were terrorizing the country just like the Jamaat-e-Islami. For many of us Sheikh Hasina represented the ideals that Sheikh Mujib had stood for, a ray of hope that allowed us to dream even when beset with darkness.

I met Sheikh Hasina only one other time at Minto Road when she had called a few poets over for lunch: Shamsur Rahman, Sunil Gangopadhyay, HSS, Bilal Chowdhury and me. Sheikh Hasina had spoken at length about her husband, a neat description of what a downright rascal he was, and how Wazed Mian was always calling Khaleda Zia at the slightest pretext to have racy conversations with her. Not once had she gotten into any serious discussions about politics or literature and after lunch, while we sat and listened, she had spoken mostly about her home and her family.

I had simply sat and watched her talk, nothing she was saying the least bit impressive to me. I was not a member of the Awami League so I did not have League-tinted glasses on when it came to her. After returning from Hajj she had put on a black scarf to cover her hair, taking care to ensure that not a single wisp was visible. There was nothing more obscene and dirty than a woman's hair, hence the desperation to hide it, and I had been truly angry with her for making these compromises. That day Sheikh Hasina had not uttered a single word about religion, though; that she usually reserved for the outside audience. Despite that I remained acutely aware that progressive individuals of the country all had high hopes for her; that she was finally going to deliver us from the clutches of the fundamentalists and the outright communal, the enemies of independence.

As soon as Sheikh Hasina came and sat down, Goon began. 'They have transferred Taslima. Please do something to bring her back to Dhaka.'

'But I am no longer in power. If I had been I could have done something. Now I don't think anything is possible.'

'Still, if you can do *anything*! The Khaleda Zia administration is after her. They are not giving her a passport. Plus, the transfer to such a place . . . they are doing this because they don't like her writing.'

'That even I don't like.' There was a hint of disdain in the tone.

My eyes met Goon's and he responded in a meek tone, 'Why? Why don't you like it?'

'She writes without knowing anything about religion. Men and women have equal rights in Islam, women have more honour in Islam—she keeps denying these things.'

Sheikh Hasina was the leader of the opposition and was usually very busy all day. After our stipulated time she left citing her busy schedule, or perhaps it was due to some other reason. Before leaving she instructed a League member to handle my request, who in turn noted down where I used to work and where I had been transferred to. No one at Minto Road seemed interested in 'handling' my problem.

~

I kept visiting the health department every day for fresh news about my transfer. MA, a doctor and leader of the Bangladesh Medical Association who had been entrusted with the authority of deciding which doctor stayed in Dhaka and who had to leave, bore a striking resemblance to a fierce bandit. The way the man looked at me made me certain that he knew who I was and was familiar with my work too, although I had no way of knowing what he thought about it. The afternoon he was supposed to finalize the list he asked me to visit him and I turned up as instructed without questioning even once if the meeting was at all required. He was alone in his room and he showed the list to me. There was a vacant post at Dhaka Medical College and he was considering recommending me for it.

He was sitting in his chair and I was standing beside it. The beginnings of a blush of delight seeped away and I could feel my face turn ashen in fright when he got up from the chair and slowly began advancing towards me, telling me my posting there depended solely on him. I kept walking backwards till my back hit the wall. He had managed to get me into a corner and it did not take an ingenious mind to guess what his intentions were. He wanted to take advantage of his empty office and have his way with me by enticing me with a good posting. By then fear had frozen my insides and I could barely restrain myself from spitting at the loathsome man's face. But what would that have achieved? He would have gotten his way somehow in the end. He was four times my size and there was no way I was going to win in a physical struggle. There was only one way left for me to save myself from a grisly fate, to get away from him somehow. Thankfully the door was near that corner. Leaving the angry man wrathfully gnashing his teeth I sidled out and escaped. I ran down the corridor, ran downstairs and out into the road and somehow managed to make my way to a rickshaw. Gradually my beating heart settled but the hurt and tears would not go away. I did not care if I had lost a chance of working near Dhaka. Neither did I care about a good posting any more.

I was the queen of sexuality, I wanted independence for the vagina—there was no dearth of such publicity around my name. This probably made many think that I was easy. Even if they did not believe so at least they were confident that if they managed to corner a woman somewhere they could get away with anything. After the incident, dread settled within me like numerous tiny tormenting ticks constantly pricking me; I was perennially anxious about the dense and unforgiving forest I was surely going to get reassigned to.

And then one day a transfer order arrived for the marooned doctor on a raft hewn out of wonder and setting her adrift on a sea of joy—the letter declared that she had been posted to Dhaka Medical College!

The Hour of the Headless

6 December 1992, around noon. In the operation theatre of Dhaka Medical College I was in the middle of putting a patient under, but my mind was racing. Since morning I had been trying to hand over my duties to someone in the department and leave, but it was past noon and all my efforts had come up in vain. I was new to the college and not very close to anyone yet. Since the first day at work the schedule had been unchanging and relentless—reaching on the dot, heading straight for the OT, administering anaesthesia to one patient after another, and then waking them up. The days blurred into the afternoons and the afternoons limped to the evenings, but my duties hardly showed any signs of letting up. Even if I were to start work exactly on time it was next to impossible to finish on the hour too; in fact, on most days we were not sure when the duty hours would end.

There were regular patients, as well as sudden ones, emergency patients and near-fatal cases that required immediate surgery. There was also no chance of getting off at two after beginning at eight in the morning, since on most days duty hours stretched till the evening and even the night. I barely had time to breathe unlike back at Mitford where not many operations used to happen and things were far less hectic. Dhaka Medical was in the heart of the city and there was no concept of off-time there. Besides, I was even more conscious of my job because I was aware that not all doctors had the good fortune of being posted there.

I had to be careful about reaching sharp at eight in the morning, even if there was no guarantee that I would get to leave sharp at five. And since I was also a 'known' face I had to be more alert than the other doctors; as it is the number of enemies I had rivalled that of my friends. Since the first day I had been extra careful to avoid getting typecast as a writer who had to be a negligent doctor, like it had happened before. In order to prove my diligence I had to work twice or thrice as hard than the others. I knew that if my colleagues did not care about timings there would not be any talk against them but if I were to attempt something similar then I was never going to hear the end of it. These experiences I had had back at Mitford and I decided to be extra careful while working at Dhaka Medical.

On this particular day I simply had to break the rules, and my heart was about to burst out of my chest. But who was I going to ask? Who was I going to approach for permission? My earnest imploring eyes failed to have any impact on the stone-faced doctor present. I glanced at my watch from time to time but that hardly mattered because the moment one patient was done there was someone new to take their place. Having spoken to the doctor with the diploma in anaesthesiology, the one with the bushy moustache and thick black curly hair, I had felt that despite being part of the league of hard-faced doctors his heart was not as implacable.

Taking a chance I approached him cautiously and told him about my predicament. I had to leave, I had to break the rules for one day. I told him Yasmin was in the hospital about to have a baby. Not that it was sufficient reason for leaving! Kids were conceived and delivered without incident with alarming regularity and it was not sufficient reason to be allowed to leave one's post at the OT. Driven by anxiety I could not help exaggerate a few of the details, my voice trembling as I did. Dr Rashid asked me where Yasmin was and afraid that he was not going to agree to let me go if he knew she was at Mymensingh I told him she was at PG. Gulping to get rid of the tremor in my voice I added, 'I'll go and come back in a blink. It won't even be an hour.' Seeing that Dr Rashid was still not convinced I piled it on thicker. 'It's a caesarean and apparently she isn't doing too well.' The tremor was back in my voice.

My eyes were pleading with him to take over my duties only for a while. I knew if Dr Rashid was to refuse there would be no way left for me to leave. Just then a tiny half-sentence emanated from under the bushy moustache. 'Fine, you can go.' No sooner did the words spring forth than I was away, running down the corridor, out of the main gate of Dhaka Medical, on to a rickshaw bound for Shantibag. K was not there yet; I had asked him to come to my house in the morning but he must have waited for me and left. I began to contemplate how to go to Mymensingh in such a situation. I could not wait for him, I had to leave immediately and take a bus or a train. Thankfully, on my way downstairs I ran into K. I grabbed him by the arm, literally dragged him to the car and we set off for Mymensingh, heading straight for the hospital and the paediatric ward.

Reaching the ward I found out that Yasmin was no longer there, she had been shifted to the post-operative room. A shiver ran down my spine at the news. I had thought she was going to have her baby in the labour room and I was going to be right by her side, holding her hand if she wished me to and giving her strength and comfort. But the baby had been delivered nearly an hour before my arrival, that too by caesarean section. Yasmin was actually not doing well. The doctors had tried their best for a normal delivery but failed, and the forceps had been tried too till it had become clear that the baby was in critical condition. After that an operation had been the only recourse.

The caesarean had taken a long time and the fifteen-pound infant was placed in an incubator after it was over. Yasmin was still unconscious; she lay there with a channel of blood running through one arm and saline in another. I spoke to Milan who was standing miserably outside the post-operative room and got all the updates. I went inside and stood by Yasmin's side, the room heavy with the gloom that had also settled within me. How did it matter in the end when I had not been there by her side? It would have been better perhaps had I not come. I was not a distant relative of Yasmin's. I had given her my word that I was going to be by her throughout the entire thing and Yasmin too had been keen on it. But I had failed to keep my promise.

I could have dared to take the day off if not for the strict rules and regulations of Dhaka Medical. I also could not help but get angry with myself for not having taken that leave regardless. I was angry that I had put on such a performance in front of Dr Rashid, something I could never admit to, when it had all been in vain. It had all been so unnecessary. I should have been with Yasmin. Instead I had arrived there as a relative visiting her newborn and not as her sister. What a sister indeed!

I returned to Dhaka. The city appeared disconsolate at night, the melancholy punctured by sudden groups of people huddled together at various places on the road. We were stopped at Magbazar by a group of radicals who were marching in protest for some unknown reason and the traffic sergeant told us to take a detour. Cars were forbidden on the main roads. Sticking my head out of the window I asked the sergeant what had happened and why the men were marching but was met with silence. I asked K too but he was as confused as I. It wasn't until the second procession that we finally understood what exactly the matter was. Out of the earth-shattering cries of the protesters I could manage to single out two words: Babri Masjid. What was wrong?

Back in 1990 a rumour about the destruction of the Babri Masjid had resulted in attacks and destruction of Hindu property. Were they trying to do the same again? K dropped me off at home and left. As soon as I switched on CNN the devastating image appeared in front of me: a group of saffron-clad Hindu extremists lunging at the Babri Masjid and tearing it down. The newsreader was saying that the Babri Masjid had been completely razed to the ground. It was as if someone had taken a hammer to my heart and ruptured the walls and like a raging flood my blood was threatening to rush out of me in waves. What was going to happen now? There was no way I could have known.

7 December. 8 December. Then 9 and 10. What were those days like? Had I been a good storyteller I would perhaps have been able to write a perfect description of the days after the demolition of Babri Masjid. But I am not one, I can only feel and more often than not I fail to translate my feelings into words. The morning of 7 December arrived with confirmation of the tragic news in headlines emblazoned across all the major newspapers of the country—Babri Masjid. Back in October 1990 when there had been another attempt on the contentious mosque a single wrong article in *Inquilab* had sparked a violent attack on the Hindu inhabitants of old Dhaka in which their temples had been destroyed and their homes and businesses robbed and burnt down.

That day too I had returned to Dhaka from Mymensingh late in the night. I was at Armanitola then, and the entire night I had stood on my balcony listening to the noise of the rioters and the screams and cries of the victims. I had witnessed the fire slowly engulfing people's homes, temples and shops and finally reach the sky. I had seen all of it and suffered in silence with my anger, pain, despair and outrage. There was nothing I could have done; it was not a tragedy I could have averted on my own.

The day after, on my way to Mitford I had to pass by the burnt remnants of the violence from the night before. Later in the day I had gone to Shankhari Bazar, Sutrapur, Nababpur, Nayabazar, Babu Bazar, Islampur, Thathari Bazar, Sadarghat and had been left stunned by the devastation and debris everywhere. I could barely stand to glance at the burnt remains of the Dhakeshwari temple and I did not know by which name to call such barbarism. How could people set fire to the houses of the very same neighbours they had lived beside since birth? How could they take part in such carnage, how could they loot, plunder and burn shops that they knew sustained multiple lives? There was a limit to brutality and people in my country were beginning to forget that. Something had gotten into them! Hindus in Bangladesh did not know where the Babri Masjid was, let alone what it looked like, but they were being accused of being complicit in conspiring to destroy it. That day I had only seen the tears of the broken people sitting amidst the ash and debris of their homes but I had been unable to do anything about it. What could I have done? What resources or influence did I have? I had only shed my tears in secret.

If a piece of fake news could spark something of that nature, what was going to happen when Hindu fundamentalists had actually demolished the Babri Masjid? This anxiety would not let me be. On my way to work in the morning I got the first inkling of things to come at Malibazar. Jalkhabar was burning and tables and chairs from the restaurant lay littered on the road. I had eaten at Jalkhabar on many occasions. On days when there was no food at home or I was in a happy mood and wanted to eat something nice, I would often come to Jalkhabar for puris and halvas. Many other shops on the road had been set on fire too and it was not difficult to guess that the looted and burnt shops belonged to Hindus. Although I had never bothered to note which shops were Muslim owned and which were Hindu owned, someone clearly had. Reaching the hospital I silently went up to the OT and began my work but the apprehension would not go away. Who knew what was going to happen. Was the government taking any steps to ensure the safety of Hindu citizens? What if they were not? Standing in the air-conditioned OT I broke into a sweat at these thoughts.

While having tea at the doctors' canteen in the afternoon I overheard a few doctors discussing how difficult it was getting to manage the influx of so many casualty patients in the Emergency ward. In a flash, a stab of worry like a fierce gust of wind shook my hand holding the cup, scalding my tongue with hot tea. Throwing the cup I ran to the Emergency and was greeted by the sight of numerous patients with shattered hands, injured legs and broken backs, and more being brought in every minute on stretchers. There was not enough space in the ward and some were being laid out in the corridor. I went up to some of them and asked their names— Vishwanath, Sudhir, Gopal, Karuna, Parvati.

Finding three attending doctors in the Emergency I caught hold of one and said, 'You will need more hands. How will you manage so many patients?'

'What can we do?' he replied in desperation. 'There are no extra doctors here today. Everyone is on duty elsewhere.'

'I have two patients left in the OT. I'll be here as soon as I'm done with them.'

I ran upstairs to finish work with the two patients I had at the OT. By the time I woke the last patient up new patients had begun to arrive at the OT via the Emergency and the surgery wards. The anaesthetist of the evening shift was there too and it was time for my shift to end. I informed my replacement that I was going to be in the Emergency and told him to call me if he could not handle things alone. The Emergency was even more crowded and I joined in as an additional doctor to help the patients, running around handing out saline or bottles of blood. Someone had been hacked with an axe, someone had a bleeding head wound, some were unconscious after being hit by a stick or a similar blunt object, some had been shot or beaten so mercilessly that it had broken their spine. Evening stretched to night but the wave of patients showed no signs of abating and the doctors barely had time to breathe let alone glance at the clock. I had not eaten the entire day but even a small break to go down to the canteen for tea and samosas seemed like a distant dream. Since patients were simultaneously being sent up to surgery I went back to the OT to join as an additional anaesthetist. 'This will go on the whole night. More riot victims will be coming in,' the surgeon suddenly said.

'Riot? There has been a riot?' I croaked.

'Don't you see them? These are all riot victims.'

'But they are all Hindu! During a riot shouldn't there be victims from both sides? The Hindus aren't fighting amongst each other. It's the Muslims beating the Hindus.'

The surgeon did not reply.

By the time I left the hospital it was almost ten. Reaching home, completely exhausted, all I could manage was to barely glance at the headlines of the newspaper.

Babri Masjid demolished by fanatic Hindu fundamentalists; The Uttar Pradesh government and State Assembly dissolved; Tide of protests across India; Security measures hiked up across the country; Extra security deployed in front of mosques; Twenty-four-hour bandh called across West Bengal by CPI(M); Bangladesh expresses concern over Babri Masjid; The Prime Minister deeply concerned; Sheikh Hasina expresses her outrage and condemnation; Five political parties issue joint statement of protest; CPB condemns the incident; Hindu sadhus attempt to build temple at contentious spot, lands the Narasimha Rao government in a fresh political row.

8 December. Early in the morning while sipping tea I again glanced at the newspaper.

Bloody riots reported in India after the demolition of the Babri Masjid; More than two hundred feared dead, thousands injured; Fundamentalist organisations RSS and Shivsena and the like banned; Advani resigns as Leader of Opposition; Mosque to be rebuilt on the exact spot; Twenty-four-hour strike in the country called by the coordination committee to protest the Babri Masjid incident and four stages of demands; Attempts to disrupt peace will not be tolerated; Protests, clashes, and violence in Dhaka and other places in the aftermath of Babri Masjid; More than three hundred

*reportedly injured; Twenty-five people shot; Sheikh Hasina calls for peace
and communal harmony at any cost; Special cabinet meeting; call to the
citizens to remain calm; Jamaat supporters destroy, pillage and set fire
to various temples in Chattagram in reaction to Babri Masjid, situation
grave; Left parties implore citizens to maintain communal harmony.*

There was no time to read the news in detail as I had to rush
to the hospital as soon as possible. There was a strike across the
country in protest of the Babri Masjid incident and there were very
few rickshaws. I walked till Malibag for a rickshaw and since it was
too early for the picketers it did not take me long to reach Dhaka
Medical. There was an even bigger crowd than the day before at the
hospital—people who had been beaten, shot, hacked, stabbed or
burnt. The strike had no effect on the influx of patients, some of
whom were strong enough to walk while others had to be carried in.
Just like the day before I finished my immediate duties at the OT and
joined the Emergency.

Each person, each life, was a story unto itself. I asked the ones
who could talk how they had been attacked, how the terrorists
had lunged at innocent people out of nowhere, armed with sticks,
axes and knives. One man, Subodh Mandal, was barely conscious
and was moaning occasionally. Blood was coming out in spurts
from a wound on his head where the axe had cleaved his skull. I
wiped his wound with antiseptic and wrapped a bandage around it.
Giving him an emergency shot of anti-tetanus I started the blood
and saline channels on either arm; while putting the oxygen mask
on his face as he was being transferred to a stretcher, I asked him,
'Who? Who did this to you?' Subodh's wife Gayatri was standing
beside us. 'Who were they? Do you know them?' I could feel the
beads of sweat on my forehead.

'Of course I know them! They were boys from our locality, Abul,
Rafiq, Halim, Sahidul.'

'Why did they attack you? What did they say?'

'They said we had broken a mosque,' Gayatri replied in a hushed
whisper and burst into tears. Grabbing my hand pleadingly she
continued, 'Didi, trust me, we haven't done it. Didi, I swear by Ma
Kali, we didn't destroy that mosque.'

'Do you know which mosque they were talking about?'

'Who knows which mosque! I don't! While I was coming here by rickshaw with Sita's father we passed by so many mosques. None of them were broken.'

'Haven't you heard of the Babri Masjid?'

Gayatri did not know where the Babri Masjid was. She had only one concern, that I save her husband. Subodh was a vegetable vendor in Babubazar. If he were to die she would have to starve to death with her two daughters. Despite their best efforts the doctors were unable to save her husband. In front of my eyes I saw her sitting like a stone in the corridor with his lifeless body. Not that she could sit for long. There were so many other patients coming in that she had to vacate her spot eventually.

I let some patients go for basic first-aid while transferring others to medicine or surgery. I also had to run to the blood bank to get fresh blood supplies. Not all the medicines were available at the hospital and neither did the relatives of the poor victims have enough money to buy them from elsewhere. Whatever money I had on me I gave to some of the patients to buy medicines. I also went to Sandhani to buy medicines in bulk for some of the others. I had no time to listen to the patients talk about how they had been attacked, though, I knew whatever I had to know. I did not need to know what wonderful things the ministers had said at the cabinet meeting, or what Khaleda Zia or Sheikh Hasina and their parties had said. All I wanted to do was smear some of the blood around me on their politics.

My night duty started at eight. On the days I had night duty I usually went home in the afternoon to freshen up before returning to the hospital but on this day that was impossible. I started work at eight in the morning and for the rest of the day there was hardly a moment to take stock of the hours I had worked. The entire night the injured kept arriving in waves and the doctors in the Emergency ward could barely manage to keep afloat in the tide. Towards dawn one of the unknown doctors asked me, 'Are you a Hindu?' I did not have duty in Emergency but I was still working extra hours and trying to save patients, so the doctor had assumed that I was a Hindu, working extra because I was devastated by the plight of my own community.

I did not reply but when it became apparent that he would not leave without an answer I gritted my teeth and replied, 'I'm a human being.'

Usually after a night duty I had a day off. I returned home early in the morning, exhausted physically as well as mentally. There were protest events being organized throughout the country, alongside repeated calls for maintaining communal accord. The left-wing parties were issuing statements for people to come together to maintain peace. Even the Awami League had issued a statement saying there was no place for fanatic communal politics in Bangladesh and that the country should run on the principles set by the Liberation War. The pro-freedom parties were being asked to band together and student federations were organizing a peace rally to call for communal harmony. Despite that the persecution of Hindus showed no signs of ceasing.

After some food and a shut-eye, I decided to go out to assess the situation. The rickshaw wound its way past Shantinagar towards Paltan and from there to Motijheel. On the way I came across the office of the Communist Party burnt to the ground and, a little ahead near Sapla, the Indian Airlines office too in a similar state. The streets were littered with bricks, stones, burnt bits of wood and broken and charred remnants of what used to be shops. I was certain that if I made my way to old Dhaka I would be greeted by many more such sights and I was not sure if I wanted to see them. What would have been the point. I knew what was happening across the country and I did not wish to go and gawk at injured and dead people or their broken and burnt houses and temples.

A huge procession of fez caps marched past shouting: 'Why the Babri Masjid! India must answer!' I was certain these were the same people who were destroying property, setting things on fire and attacking Hindus on the roads. To me these people were not human beings but feral animals in human skin. I asked the rickshaw-puller to take me towards Palasi. Reaching the slum I let the rickshaw go and walked up to the shanty in which Nirmalendu Goon used to live. The rickety door of his shed looked so worn out that anyone could kick it in without much effort. The shanty was also right on the road and I was terrified that someone was going to set it on fire and one of the most renowned poets of the country would burn to death in his own home.

Goon was at home, sitting on the bed. I sat in front of him for the longest time but did not know what to say. Why was I there? To comfort him? What was I even supposed to say? A group of boys were shouting on the road 'Ekta duita Hindu dhor, shokal bikal nasta kor' (Grab a Hindu or two and feast on them night and day). Once the shouting had died down Goon spoke. 'I'm afraid of getting out of the bed. What if they grab me immediately?' Even in the face of mortal danger Goon's sense of humour had lost none of its sharpness and he was still trying to make people laugh. But was it only a joke, or was it also what he was anticipating? Was he truly afraid? Even in the eyes of someone as strong, resilient and dauntless as him I could see dark swirling masses of terror and uncertainty, despite his best efforts to hide it from me. Women had no security in this country and yet I felt safer than him simply because of my Muslim name. And despite being a renowned poet, a brave man and a clever political theorist, Nirmalendu Goon was not feeling safe. He appeared more helpless than I.

'You have to come to my house with me.' My words came out with a sigh.

But Goon refused. He had a family of dependants—Geeta and her sisters. He was not going to leave them alone to find security. I asked him how Asim Saha and Mahadev Saha were doing but he had no news of them. He only knew that he was still alive and that was probably only because he physically resembled a Muslim maulvi. With his long beard and the kurta and pyjama he always wore, his neighbours in the slum had been convinced that he could not be anything but a Muslim. Such an unintentional deception perhaps worked with a few people but chances were slim it was going to work with everyone.

On the floor a little boy of about four was playing, the son of Geeta's sister Kalyani. Suman was Kalyani's son from her marriage to a Muslim man. Goon pointed at the boy and said, 'He is half-Muslim. We have hope because of him. I have asked him to sit here. If someone comes to attack us we will simply tell them that this house has a Muslim so they ought to be careful before they attack.' I laughed at that but Goon did not. He was clearly convinced that he was going to be saved along with Geeta and her sisters by a four-year-old Muslim boy. Goon continued. 'They are feeding Suman well and taking a lot of care. He is our protector and even he understands that. He keeps scolding me!' I laughed louder at that but Goon remained serious. 'I was wondering if I should go to Asim's place to see how he is doing. I will take Suman with me. Suman will walk ahead and I will walk behind him. I'll be a lot less scared with at least someone Muslim with me.'

This time I did not laugh. Instead I could feel pain ring through my head. Helplessness was beginning to bite at me like a pest and I tried reassuring Goon as well as myself by changing the topic to the human chain being formed from Bahadur Shah Park to the Jatiya Sangsad Bhaban to protest against communal violence. Both the Awami League and the BNP were going to bring out peace marches; the student union peace march was happening already. Everyone was trying to hold back the Jamaat. Goon listened to me, his face betraying no reaction. He was always eager to discuss politics but that day all his natural exuberance had deserted him. I asked him if he was reading the newspaper and he told me he was neither reading anything nor watching television. He was sitting on the bed all day, eating his meals there, running to the bathroom whenever he had to and then running back to the bed again. Not that we were sleeping either, too afraid as he was that he was going to be killed in his sleep. Even Suman's half-Muslim identity would not be able to save him then. A naked boy, covered in dirt and with a runny nose, was the most powerful person in their house. Suddenly even I could not help but feel Suman indeed was the strongest and the most intelligent person in the house, much more than all the other adults. Suman was their most valuable asset.

I walked out of Goon's house enveloped in despair and decided to visit Asim Saha and Mahadev Saha. Neither of them lived in a ramshackle shanty like Goon but the fears were identical. They were confined to their houses, limp with terror, their doors and windows bolted shut and their grown-up children huddling around them. Neither of them knew when they would be able to venture out, if at all. Asim Saha's Ityadi press was shut. Mahadev Saha, an employee of

Ittefaq, was not going to office any more. I had no fresh assurances to give them and the news of the human chain being organized the day after did little to allay their fears.

While returning home I could not help but think that if well-known poets of the country were being forced to cower inside their houses, then how were the ordinary Hindu minorities doing? Nirmalendu Goon, Asim Saha, Mahadev Saha, each and every one of them was an atheist. But because of their Hindu names they were being compelled to cower in front of religion. I could have been a Hindu too and I could have been born in a Hindu family. What would have happened to me in such a scenario? Would I have been able to go out? Perhaps they would have caught and raped me. Or perhaps they would have destroyed my home and left me a destitute, or even burnt me to death.

~

10 December. I reached the hospital quite early. There were no patients in the OT yet. While having tea and samosas in the canteen I noticed a two-day-old copy of *Inquilab* with the headline: 'Hindu Temple to be Built In Place of the Babri Masjid, Right-wing Hindus Rejoice, 1000 injured, More than 200 Dead'. I turned the newspaper over and pushed it away. I was assured that the paper was doing its job 'admirably' in paving the way for more violence on Hindus in this country. Snatches of a conversation drifted towards me from a group of doctors at the next table.

Eight members of the Bharatiya Janata Party (BJP) including L.K. Advani and party president Murli Manohar Joshi had been arrested and protests were being held demanding punishment for Kalyan Singh, the chief minister of Uttar Pradesh. Seven Hindu terrorists had also been apprehended. The Lok Sabha was suspended and the Vishwa Hindu Parishad (VHP), RSS, Bajrang Dal and Jamaat-e-Islami had been banned. And what was happening in our country? Hindu houses and temples were being looted and torched in broad daylight. Land was being taken away and some Hindus had even been arrested by the police. Section 144 had been imposed. The left parties, the Awami League and the student unions were issuing statements and holding meetings and marching to drive back communal forces. The forces that had been in favour of the Liberation War were being asked to come together in solidarity to preserve peace and harmony. And the Jamaat was at the centre of it all, inciting communal tension. The television channels were thankfully no longer showing footage of the Babri demolition and the leaders of the opposition along with government representatives were out on surveys to assess the violence-ridden areas. Despite all the things being done the Hindus were still not safe and the communal violence continued.

I had no time to go join the human chain as my entire day passed at the hospital. The number of casualties in the Emergency ward was showing no signs of decreasing. News arrived that Mitford in Old Dhaka was full past capacity and many patients were being transferred to Dhaka Medical. That night I made a phone call to Abakash to ask if our neighbours were all right. Amlapara, our locality, was a Hindu-majority area and our household in fact had been the first Muslim family to move there. Gradually more had settled, and before 1971 there used to be many more Hindu families too, but many had left for India for good and Muslim families had moved in. Hindus still outnumbered Muslims, though.

Mother informed me that while a number of Hindu families had abandoned their houses, many had chosen to stay back. But she had not heard of an attack yet. The atmosphere was tense and few people were out. I requested Mother that should someone come asking for shelter she must not turn them away. Mother gave me more news that upset me and relieved me in equal measure. Chotku's friend Bhulan, a goon who was probably even capable of murder, was planning to contest the municipal elections for the post of commissioner. Hoping for votes he had arranged for the safety of the Hindu inhabitants of the locality, who had pledged their support for him in the upcoming elections in exchange. The fate of the helpless residents of Amlapara rested on a terrorist like Bhulan! For a moment it seemed to me as if I was a Dolly Pal, a Gayatri Mandal or a Gautam Biswas—a Hindu—and a slow-burning fear crawled down my spine and spread across my body. Almost immediately a sudden flash of anger made me clench my fists, made me wish I could breathe fire, and I began to pace from one room to the other. When I finally went to bed I had an insane

urge to fold my feet and huddle like I had seen Nirmalendu Goon
doing, and an irrational fear took hold that they were going to come
and kill me because I was a Hindu.

News arrived at the hospital the next day that 700 houses had
been set on fire in Chattagram. I got news of Bhola where the Hindu
localities were in ruins, with thousands of houses completely gutted
and nearly 10,000 families homeless and living under the sky. Tofayel
Ahmed, the Awami League MP from Bhola, was in Dhaka. Was it
not his responsibility to be in his area and take pre-emptive initiatives
to combat communal forces? It seemed to me as if the Awami League
was fine with the violence being rained upon Hindus to pave the
way for their future campaigns against the BNP. This issue could
become a potential trump card for the opposition and the thought
made me even more angry and disgusted with political parties and the
machinations of their leaders.

The communal violence could have been easily avoided with
proper precautions. The Indian government had managed to prevent
many riots in the past with their timely intervention. Riots did
happen in India, and even the minority Muslim community was at
times responsible for violence committed during such riots. But in
Bangladesh what usually happened was not a riot but a terror attack
in which Muslims tortured Hindus.

After finishing my shift I headed towards Old Dhaka. A group
of protesters from the Jamaat-e-Islami was marching to the Indian
embassy with a deposition. At the same time students were marching
together shouting: 'Golam Azam–Advani bhai-bhai, ek dorite phansi
chai' (Golam Azam and Advani are brothers-in-arms, hang them by
the same rope). Truly, fundamentalist bigots of all countries were
fundamentally similar. But was hanging both the leaders the perfect
solution to every problem? I knew it was not. Because sooner or later
someone new would grow and replace them; religious pedagogy
and a decaying social order were the perfect grounds for breeding
intolerance. When fundamentalists pushed their way out of the earth
a few peace marches and speeches on fraternity and camaraderie could
hardly be enough to combat them. Thus human chains were being
formed while human rights violations were being simultaneously
perpetrated.

I roamed around various places in Old Dhaka. I had once brought writer Tarapada Roy and his wife to the Dhakeshwari temple when they had come to Bangladesh—I found the temple broken and burnt to cinders, and a few policemen sitting beside the ruins. If police had indeed been posted then why were they not posted on the night of 6 December itself? Obviously there was no one who had any answer to my question. None of the other temples in the locality had been left unscathed and neither had the Hindu shops and business establishments been spared. The same went for the houses too. I got off at Tantibazar and started walking. I walked into a narrow lane and reached a burnt house, on the ruins of which a man was sitting. Burnt wood, burnt books and burnt clothes were scattered across the yard. When I approached the man and asked his name he did not answer. Neither was he interested in who I was or why I was there. He simply sat there, like a charred piece of log himself, staring fixedly at his burnt house. Even the blank look of someone who has lost everything had deserted his eyes and I stood there amidst the ruins for a long time watching him. Walking out of the lane I met a man who seemed curious on seeing me. I asked him, 'That man sitting there, do you know his name?'

'Oh, that's Satipada. Satipada Das.'

It was dusk. I walked past the lane and kept walking till I reached the main road. I wished I could place a hand on Satipada's shoulder and tell him, 'Human chains are being formed, protest marches are being organized and peace brigades are being constituted in various localities. Intellectuals are writing harsh columns against communal forces and Bangladesh is not going to tolerate religious terrorism. Don't worry, no one will ever harm you.' I was unable to say any of it though and I could feel shame engulfing me. I was ashamed of my Muslim name and I was ashamed of the violence people were committing on their fellow humans. It was nearly the end of the twentieth century. Human civilization was in the middle of unprecedented advances in knowledge, science, technology and humanity. At such a juncture men were attacking each other like vicious, heartless butchers because one of them was of a different faith.

I could barely sleep a wink that night. I lay awake with my thoughts and close to dawn I sat up and wrote about my shame, about the shame of not being able to touch Satipada.

My shame refused to leave me; it accompanied me both times when I went to check up on Goon. I found him with his face buried among the tattered blankets and when I asked him why he was hiding his face he replied, 'So I don't have to see anything.' I hated seeing him like that. I wanted him to roam the city like before, sit in his office in Azimpur and finish his writing, play chess during leisure or chat at Ityadi in the evening. I wanted to see him standing upright on stage and reading poems in recitals he was going to be invited to again. Instead, I heard him say what I had never expected to hear from him, that he was considering sending Mrittika off to Calcutta. 'What are you thinking? If Mrittika goes away how will you live here all by yourself?' I said to him.

Mrittika, Goon's daughter with his ex-wife Neera Lahiri, lived with her grandmother but he was the one who took care of her. She was his life and he loved her dearly. Even a day away from her unsettled him and he used to take her to school and bring her back home regularly. Neera worked at Komilla and only managed to come down to meet her daughter once in a blue moon. Goon lived nearer and was the one to manage all her demands. Despite not living under the same roof father and daughter were very close and the largest share of whatever he earned was spent on Mrittika, leaving only a pittance for himself and his dependants. His only aim in life was to bring Mrittika up with care and love and inculcate the right education and culture in her. And here he was contemplating sending her away! I was shocked and could not speak for a while.

'No, you can't send her away! Why should you? This is your country, hers too. Why should she have to leave?' The words collided with his obvious anguish and lost some of their urgency.

My shame refused to leave me. I heard that fanatics had burnt down Sri Chaitanya's house in Sylhet and even the 400-year-old library had not been spared. I wanted to scream and cry; my identity as a human being had begun to mock me in the face of the inhumanity of my fellow countrymen. Many acquaintances came back from Bhola and described the vicious barbaric acts unleashed upon the people, the desperate cries of the persecuted and their anguished wails. I felt as if I was one among the homeless sitting on an open field in Bhola, a wretched soul who had been robbed and left penniless and whose house too was now a pile of ash.

Even after the communal unrest died down in a few days this feeling refused to abandon me. We were hearing news of the mass exodus of Hindus from the country. Some were heard saying, 'They should not have done that. They should have stayed and fought.' Trying to place myself in a Hindu citizen's shoes I tried to understand how strong the feeling of insecurity had to be for someone to arrive at such a devastating decision of leaving one's home. I imagined myself to be a young man from Tantibazar with a Hindu name— Suranjan Dutta, atheist, a member of a progressive organization and most of whose friends were atheists too—who loved his country and was concerned day and night about the well-being of the nation, but whose life was being torn apart by communal violence, whose ideals were gradually eroding along with his love for his country, so much so that he was beginning to look at everyone with suspicion. He was afraid that Muslims were going to come for him any moment. His feelings of insecurity were not lessening despite the gradual easing of communal tensions and he was so afraid that any day there could be an attack on him for the flimsiest of reasons; that in the end, despite his own misgivings, he was losing a battle with himself and was being forced to decide to leave the country. I closed my eyes and visualized the small two-room house in Tantibazar, Suranjan's family, his parents and his little sister . . . before I could finish sketching the image in my head I turned over on my bed and started writing.

> Suranjan is lying on his bed. An agitated Maya is telling him to hurry up again and again. 'Dada, get up and do something!'

Suranjan's days from 7 to 13 December were sending my thoughts in disarray. I had no time to sit at home and write either because I had to get to the hospital soon.

In the OT I injected sodium thiopental and suxamethonium chloride in the spine of the patient, induced sleep using oxygen and nitrous oxide masks, checked the blood pressure and pulse rate and then gave the surgeon the go-ahead. The OT at Mitford did not have modern machines for artificial respiration and one had to sit near the head of the patient and manually supply oxygen to the lungs using a mechanical balloon. At Dhaka Medical none of that was necessary and the machine did all the work. So I did not have to wait beside the unconscious patient, other than checking the pulse rate, blood pressure and breathing from time to time and, in case of a lengthy operation, re-administering anaesthesia. Sitting near the patient I continued writing Suranjan's story. When the surgeon indicated the end of the operation I had to get up and resume my duties. The conscious patient was taken away and a new one brought in his or her place. The paper and the pen remained in the pocket of my apron and I began to spend the time between putting someone under and bringing them back out working on Suranjan's story.

One day Purabi Basu told me over the telephone, 'Everyone is writing columns against communal politics. Why aren't you writing too?' I felt a tad disconcerted because I had truly not written any columns. Immersed in despair I had been unable to decide what to write and whatever I wished to write had already been written by someone or the other. 'Purabidi, I haven't written one. But I am trying to write something a little bigger, something more factual.' I wanted it to be factual but where was I supposed to find facts! I went to Old Dhaka and somehow managed to find my way to the offices of the newspaper *Ekata* (Unity) where I found a detailed investigative report on the places communal violence had affected Hindus. *Ekata* was a paper of the Communist Party and they had published detailed reports of such incidents across Bangladesh. *Sambad*, *Ajker Kagaj*, *Bhorer Kagaj* too had published extensive reports and these were my sources, besides all the violence I had seen with my own eyes in Dhaka and its neighbouring areas.

In not too many words and with scant descriptions what I finally wrote was a factual account of the state of the Hindu population in Bangladesh. It could not be called a story, nor could it be called a novel. I named it *Lajja* (Shame). It was almost February and Bengali publishers were all busy printing new books. Altaf Hossain Minu of Pearl Publications had left me an advance and he was certain about getting a book in February. With a lot of hesitation and embarrassment I gave the manuscript of *Lajja* to the excited Minu who was hoping for another bestseller from me. His face brightened as soon as he got his hands on the manuscript. 'What is this? A novel, is it?'

'No, not exactly.'

'Then? A collection of stories?'

'No. Not that either.'

'Then what is it?'

'It's a book written against communal politics.'

'A book of essays?'

'No, not exactly essays either.'

'Then what is it?'

'It's nothing great. It's something I wrote in a lot of hurry. It's about the persecution of Hindus that happened last December.'

Minu's bright face immediately became dark. He was quite obviously disappointed. 'This won't work.'

'I know it won't,' I replied self-consciously, 'but print it for the moment since I have nothing else that I am working on right now. I promise you that I will give you a proper novel soon.'

The promise of a novel managed to mollify Minu. His drooling red tongue sticking out a little he asked, 'When?'

'As soon as possible.'

'Can I expect it by the book fair?'

'I'll try.'

'You promise?'

'Yes, I do.'

As he was about to leave with the manuscript of *Lajja* I could not help but feel sorry for all the losses he was going to suffer because of me. In a desolate voice I said to him again, 'Don't place your hopes on this book. This is not the kind of book that does well. Don't print too many copies either. Print a limited number so that you don't incur too much loss.'

Trying to placate me Minu shot back, 'Be that as it may, since you have written it, I am going to print it. Later I can publish a novel written by you and make up for all the losses.'

A Forbidden Scent

Ireceived an invitation to go to Calcutta to read my poems at a convention organized by Abrittilok. Soumitra Mitra came down to Dhaka to personally invite some of the other poets they wanted. It was in my house that he finalized the list of people he wished to call and he went and invited some of them himself. Since he had to leave before he could finish, he left the rest of the invitations with me, giving me the responsibility of making sure it reached the poets concerned. He parted with a provocative admission. 'You're the main attraction this time by the way.' More than being the main attraction anywhere what I was genuinely excited about was the prospect of visiting Calcutta again. I could barely contain my excitement and made secret plans for quick visits to Darjeeling and Santiniketan afterwards, a two-week trip in all. It was not possible to get two weeks of casual leave. As per Dr Rashid's advice I put in an application for earned leave.

Goon was not in the country. Kayesh, a disciple of his, had taken him on a trip to America. Asim Saha initially agreed to go, only to back out later for unknown reasons. I went to Shamsur Rahman to get his signatures on the documents for the passport and visa and got his visa and tickets done along with mine. Over an entire week I shopped for my favourite people, jamdani sari and silk kurtas from Bailey Road, books, dried fish from Shantinagar market, sweets from Muktagacha, beautifully hand-embroidered *kantha* blankets, lovingly packed jars of mango pickle, besides loads and loads of love for Calcutta, much of which I could not stuff into my luggage.

On the day of the departure I picked up Shamsur Rahman in K's car on the way to the airport. Such was my excitement that Soumitra Mitra and Abrittilok were merely pretexts; it was as if I was the one who had organized the convention; as if Calcutta was my city and I was taking Rahman there on a visit. At the airport Bilal Chowdhury and the poet Rabiul Hossain were waiting for us. I checked in with my luggage, collected the boarding passes and eagerly went ahead. With the same zeal I extended my passport towards the person at immigration, Shamsur Rahman in front with me and the other poets behind us. We were all looking forward to landing at Dumdum and then heading out to see the city, to Chowringhee, Park Street, College Street, Gariahat or Chitpur, and we could barely wait to meet and catch up with our friends and fellow poets on the other side.

The person at the counter looked up from my passport and stared at my face for a while. He looked down again at the document, then back up again, before taking out a piece of paper from his pocket and comparing it with the passport he was holding. Abruptly, my passport still in his hand, he turned around and sped off towards the room of a senior immigration officer. He and the senior officer stood at the door of the latter's office and discussed something under their breath for a while. It was impossible to guess what they were talking about and neither could I understand what problem there had been with my passport. The photo on the passport was mine, the name and address were mine too. What was it they had to be so furtive about?

The man came back to the counter and asked me, 'Do you work?'
'Yes, I do.'
'Where?'
'At Dhaka Medical.'
'Do you have permission to go abroad?'
'Since when does one need permission to go abroad?'
The man could not tell me whose permission I needed. The only thing he kept repeating ad nauseam was, 'You can't go if you don't have permission.' We went to the senior officer's chamber and asked what the matter was but even he could not explain it to us. There were three chairs in front of him on which Shamsur Rahman, Bilal Chowdhury and I were sitting. Rabiul Hossain was standing behind us and the other poets were outside the room. Perhaps the senior officer felt a surge of pity on seeing us; given how many thieves and crimelords he had to allow every day he had been given the thankless task of stopping a group of poets flying to a convention. He pushed the telephone towards us and said if someone from the upper levels of the government

was to call and recommend he could allow me to go. There were two phones on the table, one of which was repeatedly ringing and which the man kept picking up and speaking into from time to time. 'Yes sir, she's here. Yes sir, she's sitting right in front of me. Yes sir, we aren't letting her go. Yes sir.' Was he speaking about me with the sir at the other end of the line? I was convinced that whoever was on the other end must have given prior orders to stop me.

Chowdhury and Shamsur Rahman were busy trying to locate a name big enough to get me reprieve. After a tense moment Chowdhury said, 'The health secretary is my friend. If we can get in touch with him we won't have to worry.' But repeated calls to the man went unanswered. Chowdhury tried calling the inspector general but he was indisposed. Shamsur Rahman tried calling a minister friend of his but discovered that the man was not in Dhaka. There was hardly any time and most passengers except for the delegation of poets had boarded the flight. I was telling myself to calm down and that everything was going to be all right, although I could not quash the uneasiness in my heart. Time was ticking past in its own cruel way, uncaring of our plight. After repeatedly calling a number of people we managed to get hold of the health secretary Imran Noor, who was a poet himself. He was of a suitably high rank and we finally managed to breathe a sigh of relief; the smile that had disappeared from my face reappeared in a flash. Shamsur Rahman explained everything to Noor. 'We are on our way to Calcutta but they are not letting Taslima go. Please tell them to allow her. If you tell them they will listen.'

Noor asked to speak to the senior officer. I could not tell if they were talking in code but none of us could make sense of the ensuing conversation. The officer finished speaking and handed the receiver back to Rahman. Imran Noor informed us unequivocally that Taslima Nasrin was not going to be allowed to leave.

'But why not?'

'She needs government permission to leave the country.'

'Can't you make arrangements for that? If you tell them now won't it work?'

'No, it won't.'

Shamsur Rahman's face was pale while Chowdhury was sitting with his head lowered on his hands. For a moment the immigration officer's room seemed to sway ever so slightly in front of my eyes, the walls, the airport and even my hopes feeling the tremors. I was not to be allowed any further. The plane was about to leave and the last call for boarding was urging stray passengers to quickly get to their seats. Lines of despair clearly etched on his face, Chowdhury suggested, 'Let me stay back. Taslima and I will come in a while.' Shamsur Rahman would hear none of it and suggested he would stay back with me instead, promising to take the afternoon flight with me after taking care of things. Close to tears at their words I managed to choke out in a tear-soaked voice, 'Why will any of you wait here for me? Go ahead. I will come in some time.'

The other poets were getting impatient; some were clearly saddened by the turn of events while others were visibly pleased. None of the other poets with government jobs were being asked for permission; clearly none of them required it except me. Rafiq Azad grabbed hold of Rahman's hand with a 'We have to go, the plane's about to leave' and dragged him towards boarding. Chowdhury followed them with a 'Go to Imran Noor's office right now and see what he wants you to do. Try and come by the afternoon flight, or if that isn't possible, by an early morning flight tomorrow'.

Leaving me behind, everyone made their way towards the plane. Shamsur Rahman kept glancing back at me, regret clearly etched on his face. I stood there helplessly by myself and when the last person in the group had gone out of sight I broke down in tears in the middle of the airport. Till then I had not realized that seeing them go away was going to cause me so much pain. A storm arose within me, my carefully laid-out plans shattering like a fragile house of glass. The entire airport heard the sound along with my anguished cry of pain.

My passport was not returned to me and I was handed a piece of paper and instructed, 'Go to the Special Branch office with this for your passport.'

'When will they give it back?'

'If you go today you will get it back by the afternoon. If not, definitely by tomorrow morning.'

My two tagged suitcases had been extracted from the belly of the airplane before departure. Tucking them near my feet I sat in the airport for the longest time. How suddenly all of it had happened; I could not shake off the feeling that it was a nightmare, that such a terrible thing had not just happened with me.

K went to a friend's office in Bijoynagar on most mornings. I called and managed to get through to him and asked him to come to the airport. Instead of returning home we went straight to the secretariat to meet Imran Noor. Noor took me to a separate room, sat across from me and told me quite clearly that it was not within his power to help me. Although he could not clearly say why that was so. Instead he suggested that I apply for an ex-Bangladesh leave in order to be allowed to go to Calcutta. I was not even aware that such a stipulation existed; I had always seen doctors go out of the country without any hitches and none of them had ever had to apply for such a leave. These legal hoops were obviously uniquely for my benefit. I had no problems with following laws, however, and I rushed to Dhaka Medical immediately to get an application attested by the authorities, and then to the health department to submit it. The director of the department took a look at the application, read it and asked me to come back the next day. When asked if he could sign it the very same day he refused and said he could not. Despite my best efforts to explain to him how important it was for me he said it was not possible.

I returned home. Soumitra Mitra called to check if I was taking the afternoon flight and I told him I was not.

'Tomorrow then?'

'I'll try.'

The next morning I went back to the special passport office in Malibag but they refused to hand my passport back to me again. At the health department too I was informed that there had been no movement on the ex-Bangladesh leave application and I had to return home exhausted and dejected. Soumitra Mitra was calling repeatedly from Calcutta to find out what was happening with my trip. He told me everyone was looking forward to seeing me and there would be a scandal if I was absent. Obviously it was going to be a scandal but what was I supposed to do? They were not returning my passport! This continued the next day, and the day after; neither was my passport returned to me, nor was I granted leave. Eventually I was forced to cancel my trip to Calcutta. After the poets came back I asked them how the convention had gone, which poets had read poems, everything about Calcutta and how

things were in Nandan, Rabindra Sadan and Sisir Mancha. They
answered all my questions but no matter what they said it failed to
soothe the ache in my heart.

~

The book fair started in due course. The previous year the Taslima
Nasrin Suppression Committee had taken out a protest march and
burnt my books, so the organizers asked me to stay away. Many poets
and writers were scheduled to make an appearance and I was the only
one asked to sit at home alone. I did not want to stay away and in
my lively imagination I kept floating off to the fair on an imaginary
magic carpet. In the end my overpowering desire forced me to break
out of my self-imposed exile; I resolve to head out to the fair come
what may. There was nothing for me to be scared of, I had not done
anything wrong and if every other person had the right to go to the
fair so did I. Why did I have to sacrifice my basic freedoms to appease
the draconian demands of the authorities?

When I informed Khusro of my decision he said he was also going
to invite two of his friends. Going alone was out of the question and
we decided to go in a large group. Sahidul Haque Khan, bald, lanky,
bespectacled and with the distinct air of a philosopher around him,
stepped forward and volunteered to take care of my security. Khan
worked in television and as a result spoke a lot, but he always spoke
beautifully. He had once invited me to his programme and though I
had turned down the offer to appear on television I had accepted the
Natyasabha prize they had conferred upon me. Eventually we had
developed a warm friendship. After meeting at my house, Khusro
and Sahidul too had developed a rapport. Khusro had a noble heart
and he was already ready to go the extra mile for his friends. He had
met Alamgir, a journalist at *Ittefaq*, at my house and in only a few
days he had taken the young man on as a partner in his business. If I
ever needed a car to go somewhere, even if he was too busy to come
himself, he always made sure to have a car sent over for me. One day
he had sprung a surprise and brought me a new computer.

Khusro was a rich man but he was not like most other rich men
in Bangladesh. I had seen many a muktijoddha living a life of luxury,
having made decent profits for themselves, with scant concern about

the jackals and vultures preying on the majority of the people. Khusro had been a muktijoddha too and he had never sold his ideals to anyone. He was always ready to contribute to the cause of those still fighting in favour of a liberated Bangladesh; leaders of the Awami League used to visit him and sit for hours for contributions to the party fund and he never turned anyone away empty-handed.

Flanked by Khusro and Sahidul Haque on either side I set off for the book fair, elated and terrified in equal measure. There was going to be no roaming around the fairgrounds. My well-wishers decided that I was going to sit in one stall for some time, soak in as much of the fair as possible and then return with my guards. No sooner did I enter the Pearl Publications stall than Minu yelled in delight. Many people were apparently buying my book and many were returning again and again hoping to get my autograph. For an instant, faced with the brightly lit fairground, the festive air generated by the meeting of writers and their readers, the music drifting in the air and the strains of poetry being recited, I almost forgot that I was not safe there. Instead, it felt as if I had as much freedom as any other writer to stay and roam the grounds.

If the place where the most civilized, the most educated, the nicest, the most honest, the most decent and the most free-spirited literary and cultural personalities assembled was not safe enough then where else would I have been safe? A mosque was not safe for me, nor was the home of someone staunchly conservative, nor a dark alley, an empty road, a terrorist's hideout, a den of drunks, some religious event, a Jamaat congregation or literally a villain's lair. Except the confines of my own home, if there was one other safe place for me to be in, it was the book fair. It was a familiar place, close to my heart, something that was in my blood and in every beat of my heart, a balm after a long spell of pain and a refuge that welcomed me with open arms to rest in its embrace after every gruelling year.

Minu informed me that *Lajja* was doing very well, the first edition had been exhausted in no time and he was confident that very soon the second edition too would be over and he would have to commission a third. I was astonished to learn that in only a few days of the book fair a few thousand copies of *Lajja* had been sold. Why would someone want to buy *Lajja*? What was in that book? It was not a love story, nor did it have a fantastic and intriguing plot. It was a fact-laden, simply written account of something everyone was aware of. Usually readers never favoured such books.

No sooner did I take a seat at the Pearl Publications stall than a line of people eager to buy the book formed out of nowhere. Not that everyone wanted to buy *Lajja* specifically because they knew about it. Many bought the book simply because they wished to buy a new book. Many came to the stall to ask if there was a new Taslima Nasrin book and, when informed about *Lajja*, they bought it immediately, some even going so far as to buy multiple copies. Even vendors from other stalls were coming for fifty to a hundred copies at a time to take to their own stalls. At first I assumed it was mostly Hindus who were buying the book but when many of them approached me for autographs I heard their names and realized that many were not.

The more the book sold the more anxious I got, thinking that after reading a couple of pages people were going to hate it. Were they buying the book because they were admirers of my work or were they buying the book specifically because they knew what it was about? I had no way of knowing which of these was true and neither could I ask any of them. As the crowd for the book increased so did the crowd for those hoping to get an autograph and I could not put my pen down for even a breather. Sahidul was sitting beside me, Khusro was standing at the door and his strong friends were scattered about here and there. So many people loved me, so many read my books and I was supposed to feel unsafe in the book fair? Perhaps Khusro thought the same too. He excused himself and went off on a stroll for a little while.

It happened some time later. No one could have anticipated something like it. There was a group of people surrounding the open area in front of the stall. All of us inside the hall noticed much to our surprise that in only a few minutes a few hundred people had gathered behind this huddled group. There was a colossal crowd around the stall, none of whom wanted to buy books. None of them were moving either. Someone from the stall called out to them and asked what they wanted and why they were blocking others if they did not wish to come in themselves. No answer came from the crowd except for a collective holler that went on for a while. The sound was not a pleasant one and under his breath Minu asked me to pull my chair back further inside the stall. There was a nearly two-foot-wide gap between the crowd and us, where a long table had been placed. As requested I pushed my chair further back inside. Almost immediately the crowd started making an odd sound that slowly morphed into slogans: 'Get her, beat her'; 'Break her head, tear off her clothes, break her hands'.

Someone inside the stall was crying for the police and Minu asked them to run to the police and get help. There was no way out, though, because the mouth of the stall was completely blocked and not even an insect could have slipped past. Suddenly, someone threw a stone and in a flash there was a shower of stones aimed at me by the crowd outside. Some whizzed past my ears while most hit me. By then both Sahidul and Minu were in front of me shielding me from the stone-pelters, while I sat there pale and numb from the shock. Big rocks were being thrown at the stall, aimed at the shelves, some of which collapsed. Books fell out and scattered everywhere. A stone hit the bulb, which exploded and showered me with shards of glass while plunging the stall into darkness.

Those inside the stall had a moment's furtive discussion among themselves; most were perspiring profusely. The crowd of nearly three hundred had begun to push the stall with all their might and the barrier of the long table at the entrance crashed under the weight. The police were standing like silent witnesses not too far away and they had not raised a finger yet. There was no time left to wait for them to do anything either. The people gathered outside were going to finish me and those inside the stall knew they had to do something immediately if they hoped to save me. Within moments they had picked up whatever they could get their hands on: large broken pieces of wood, bamboo, leftover material from the construction of the stall that had been stacked inside.

Leaping over the broken table, they charged fiercely at the mob outside. The moment the startled mob retreated a few steps to shield themselves from the abrupt attack, two of the waiting policemen swooped in, grabbed me by both my arms, and took me out of the stall. Another group of policemen were behind us providing us cover as we began running. My handbag was missing and so were my shoes, the sari had almost unravelled, and in such a state they somehow managed to take me up to the first floor of the Academy. They pushed me inside and closed the iron gate behind me. By then everyone in the fair had gathered to watch the spectacle of me being dragged from the stall to the Academy. It must have indeed been a spectacle! I stood on the first floor trembling while the police spoke to the director general of the Academy. Afterwards the director general called me and told me in no uncertain terms that I could never come back to the book fair ever again. I was banned from the book fair of the Bangla Academy for life.

The police dropped me off at my house in Shantibag in the kind of black van they usually used to transport thieves and criminals. On the way one of the police officers said to me, 'Why do you write about religion? Of course these things will happen if you write about religion.' Another chimed in, 'If we hadn't saved you that would have been the end of you today.'

A little while later Khusro arrived at Shantibag with Sahidul and Minu. All three were still shell-shocked and once they had had cold water from the fridge Minu informed me that his entire stall had been destroyed and all the books had been looted. Sahidul paced up and down the room and confessed that while the carnage had been playing out he had seen AZ and a few other writers standing a little further away, sipping tea and watching the drama unfold. The crowd had made it impossible for Khusro to come back to the stall and he had urged the police to do something but none of them had been too keen on intervening.

Through it all I sat quietly. All I could do was replay those terrifying moments in my head again and again; the chill in my bones simply would not leave. I asked them what would have happened if they had not charged at the crowd but none of them had any answer to that. All of us could speculate quite accurately what would have happened.

~

On the eve of 21 February, the Sahid Minar in Dhaka is swathed in a cloth with a giant red sun at its centre. A few hours before the attack on me unknown assailants had set fire to the red sun. Were the men who had done it the same ones who had surrounded the stall at the book fair and cut off the lights? Were they the ones who had plunged my free world into darkness all of a sudden?

Shamelessness

TASLIMA NASRIN'S NOVEL 'LAJJA' SEIZED!

In a news report issued last Saturday it was communicated that Taslima Nasrin's *Lajja* (First publication February 93, Pearl Publications, 38/2, Banglabazar, Dhaka-1100) has been confiscated by the government as per Article 99-A for spreading misinformation among the people, causing troubles among various communities, inciting communal tension, anti-state rhetoric, and any sale, distribution or preservation of any copy of said book is strictly prohibited.

—11 JULY 1993

This appeared on the front page of the Sunday newspaper and it managed to astonish, shock and unnerve me in equal measure. That *Lajja* had disrupted communal harmony was an accusation I had never heard before. The prose was not good, it was not a good book, the plethora of facts was too distracting, I had heard all of those things and I acknowledged them too; the book had its faults. I had spent too little time on it and had been unable to consider the quality of the book due to constant pressure from my publisher. But whatever the honourable government could say against my book, it could not accuse me of jeopardizing communal harmony. The book was written precisely because there was a lack of communal harmony in the nation, it was written to help inspire concord so that no person ever had to feel persecuted by another because of a difference in their respective faiths. There was a festering wound on the corpus of the country and the book was written to reveal that wound to all so that proper cure could then be arranged. Did that automatically mean I had insulted the body by talking about the wound?

If *Nirbachito Kolam* had been banned I would not have been surprised, neither would I have been surprised if *Noshto Meyer Noshto Godyo* had been banned. In these books I had expressed my personal views on religion that most people in the country did not agree with. But in *Lajja* there were no opinions on religion. Instead, the book wanted to foreground how everyone had an equal right to their own religion and that was how it ought to be. Why the Hindus were being persecuted, how and where it was happening, why they were suffering from so much insecurity that they were considering abandoning their own country for another—this was what I wanted to examine. I wanted to understand everything about their pain and misery.

A few days after the ban I received a long letter with the words 'Secret and Confidential' emblazoned across it. The letter had been sent to the secretaries of the home ministry and the information ministry from the army barracks of Dhaka, written by Brigadier M.A. Halim on behalf of the chief of staff of the army. I had heard that there were two factions within the army, one extremist and the other moderate. It was the former who had sent the order to the government. Even if it did not come across as an order in the strictest sense of the term, ultimately that was what it was. I had no doubts regarding the limitless power that the army enjoyed. It was they who had been in power for the longest time in the history of independent Bangladesh. Some of the non-military governments too had had a gun to their head the entire time. The army was aware that they could march with their guns to seize power, to rule and exploit the country any moment they wished. The prime minister who was in power was an army wife and her convoy used to travel from the barracks too. When the people had no respite from the army how could I expect to be spared? The army had decided *Lajja* needed to be banned and so that was what had happened. Every decision-maker in the country was subservient to the barrel of the gun.

The letter began with a short synopsis of the novel and a few excerpts from it. Towards the end, right on the last page, it was written:

In the subcontinent it is Bangladesh which has the strongest communal ties among its citizens. If religious feelings are hurt and a few stray incidents of communal violence occur, it does not necessarily mean a disruption of this harmonious fabric. When it comes to employment minority Hindus are being given their fair share of opportunities, sometimes more than that. The same goes for businesses. But Madam Taslima Nasrin has etched a fictional portrait of violence on Hindu minorities in her book, provided wrong information regarding opportunities in employment, and has tried to incite the Hindus in the process. Based on such a book by a Muslim writer the international community will simply assume that all the misinformation provided regarding the persecution of Hindu minorities and the suspension of their rights in Bangladesh are true. Besides, this will also create tension between the various communities living in Bangladesh and disturb the existing temperament of peaceful coexistence.

If someone's book has the potential to unsettle the communal harmony of a country and incite tension between communities then it is only right that the book is not allowed for public consumption. Madam Taslima Nasrin has ridiculed the communal harmony of the country in her *Lajja* and has attempted to rile up people of various communities against each other, and for that reason the prohibition of her book and confiscation of all copies from the market is justified.

This is being sent to you for your knowledge and to ensure appropriate steps are taken.

Where was it from?

The Detective Department of the Defence Ministry. 1300/164/D/CIB. Asad 1400/3 July, 1993.

~

Lajja was banned within seven days of this letter. As soon as the ban was declared the police went ahead and confiscated every single copy of the book from booksellers in Dhaka. Besides, a team from the Special Branch raided Banglabazar and seized all the copies they could get their hands on and carried them away in trucks, even the half-bound or unbound printed pages they found in the printing press on 6 Walter Street. Not just in Dhaka, these sudden raids were carried out all over the country in every bookshop, and wherever the police found the book it was immediately impounded. Published in February, it was banned five months after its release, within which time nearly 60,000 copies had already been sold and the seventh edition was under way. And yet the book was banned! Who did the government wish to prevent from reading the book? Sick of the tortures and crimes perpetrated by an authoritarian government, the people had waged a bloody war for a number of years to drive them out and earn democracy and this was what that hard-earned democracy looked like!

Shamsur Rahman protested against the ban, not simply by making a statement about it in the newspapers, but via an article he wrote in *Bhorer Kagaj*:

> I have read the novel. Except for a few aesthetic concerns I have found nothing objectionable in the entire narrative. Taslima has unhesitatingly written the truth and a writer's greatest responsibility is to do exactly that. Taslima Nasrin is a freethinking and secular individual and it is impossible to accuse her of wishing to incite communal conflict; neither has she ever been one to mislead her readers . . . A young man informed me the other day that after reading *Lajja* he had felt as if he was Suranjan, the protagonist of the novel. What was the justification behind banning such a book?
>
> A democratically elected government always maintains that it wants to set up a democratic framework of governance. Everyone knows that freedom of speech and expression is one of the pillars of such a framework. The government is trying to disrupt freedom of speech by banning such a progressive author's book. However, another book that is boldly inciting its readers to kill Taslima Nasrin is selling freely in the market . . . Personally I am never in favour of prohibiting any book because I don't believe that a book can bring harm to society. But it is a different matter altogether when a book encourages and provokes someone to commit murder or is a mouthpiece of fascist ideology. All of us who are advocates of a writer's

freedom are demanding the immediate lifting of the embargo
on Nasrin's *Lajja*. We hope the government will honour our
request and prove that they are indeed in favour of democracy
and the freedom of speech.

Rahman's article appeared in *Bhorer Kagaj* on 19 July. Another
article, by former judge K.M. Sobhan, appeared the very next day.
Referring to the vast police force deployed by the government to
confiscate copies of *Lajja* from the markets, Sobhan noted:

> . . . if this show of spontaneity by the police had been demonstrated
> against the communal terrorists who were running amok in
> December then perhaps there would not have been any need to
> write *Lajja*. No reader will consider what has been said in the book
> as responsible for inciting tension between communities unless
> they are themselves a part of communal terrorist outfits, or are
> sympathizers at the very least.

Sobhan wrote another column titled 'Religious fanatics are a source
of shame for the government' where he foregrounded the stark
similarities between the autocratic Ershad government and the
nationalists who had usurped his power.

> In the case of the autocratic government the influence and
> provocation of religious fundamentalists had been crucial in
> paving the way for communal violence. Even though the present
> government has expressed its disapproval for many of the previous
> government's policies it holds remarkably similar views on this
> one matter. This explains the ban on the collection *Glaani* and the
> embargo on *Lajja*.

The government was beginning to foam at the mouth trying to
assert that it was pro-democracy. But as K.M. Sobhan pointed out
a democratically elected government did not automatically guarantee
actual adherence to the tenets of democracy.

The government banned *Lajja* with much fanfare. Barely a month later, the foreign minister, while attending the International Human Rights Conference, had this to say about it:

> Our nation professes its allegiance to the charter of the United Nations and for the very same reason we are also deeply invested in upholding the human rights policies that are its component. This is part of our culture and our constitution. We are a democratic nation and we believe in complete transparency in our dealings. The government is beholden to the people and the Parliament, the press is free, and the Opposition is firm in its political stance. We are ethically invested in upholding human rights . . .

What a wonderful way of upholding human rights the government had chanced upon. Was there even an iota of resemblance between their promises and their actions? The constitution unequivocally guaranteed the freedom of speech and expression for every citizen but these people hardly cared about anything, let alone the constitution. They had taken over the state as if it was just another branch of their political party, with the assumption that they could play fast and loose with state policy whenever they wished to. And if they wished to they could strip the constitution bare and parade it naked on the road for all to see.

K.M. Sobhan expressed his outrage over the violations:

> Despite provisions to the contrary in the highest legal document of our country, the constitution, a certain fundamentalist and extremist faction of the government has succeeded in banning the book . . . Every nation in the world is taking steps to uproot such radical and ultra-conservative elements; even the Muslim nations too are a part of this progressive movement . . . It's only in Bangladesh that the official party in power, grateful to such elements for helping them win the elections, is toeing the line showed by them. These fundamentalist factions are using the democratic process to undermine democracy itself. The government must understand what is happening and not only prohibit such groups but also summarily separate religion from influencing politics.

Although I did receive some bouquets for the book, what I mostly received were brickbats. And there was no end to that list. I was causing harm to the Muslim community, I was a traitor to my own people, there was no communalism in Bangladesh so whatever I had written was untrue, the Hindus were responsible for their own condition, they ran to India at the slightest provocation, I had no sense and I was a puppet of the Hindus, I had been awarded by Hindu fundamentalists, they were the ones who had made me write *Lajja*—and so on and so forth. Of course, this was understandable when coming from fundamentalists. But when liberal intellectuals chimed in too—one of them called *Lajja* 'trashy and low-class' and expressed serious concerns that the novel was going to cause much harm to his Muslim brethren in India while a colleague of his accused me of dishonest reiterations and writing with only the market in my mind—there was hardly anything left to say.

Despite the attack from all sides the only thing that brought a measure of relief was the fact that many writers protested the ban imposed on the book. I had never met Abdul Gaffar Chowdhury. He lived in London and wrote his columns from there. He once wrote a column for *Bhorer Kagaj* titled 'Not her work, her point-of-view, or her opinions, but the person Taslima has become an object of critique', touching upon my life, the Ananda Puraskar and the controversy around *Lajja*.

... what has started in the name of a debate around her work is not a debate at all, but an Inquisition. Her self-proclaimed Inquisitors are vicious and murderous fundamentalists who are being egged on by the government in turn. Our secular and progressive intellectuals who are the jury at this trial are themselves conflicted and confused. Some of their writings reveal their not-so-subtle personal vendetta against her, or their unspoken outrage at having been passed over for the Ananda Puraskar in favour of her; for others this is a cunning attempt to undermine her in order to show themselves up in better light ... The *Anandabazar Patrika* is not a communal mouthpiece, its scope concerns both democratic as well as commercial. Being a government institution that is a beneficiary of the government of Bangladesh it was perfectly justified that the Bangla Academy of Dhaka had turned down an honour conferred on them by a private publishing house. But it is foolish to expect all writers and artists in Dhaka should do the same. One can accuse the awarding of the Ananda Puraskar of partiality, but it is most definitely not communal. Taslima's *Nirbachito Kolam* has critical evaluations of both Hinduism and Islam when it comes to questions of women's rights and honour. The Ananda Puraskar has perhaps awarded the book's brave stance against communal bias, and not simply its literary merit.

The sort of literature that wishes to drive forward a movement, an amendment or a revolution does not always possess a conventional literary artistry that everyone aspires for. The Nazim Hiqmet or Vladimir Mayakovsky that we celebrate today, does much of their political poetry contain exceptional literary merit? Taslima Nasrin's *Lajja* is a brave, topical and relevant work reflecting on a particular moment in Bangladesh. How do our intellectuals expect the extant conventions of a traditional work of literature in it? How is it Taslima's fault that the BJP has picked up the novel for their political campaigning? Recently I managed to get my hands on one of the BJP's publicity booklets in London, titled 'Minority Repression in Bangladesh'. It contained nothing that could be attributed to the BJP. All it had was twenty-five news reports of various lengths on repression of minorities and demolition of temples in Bangladesh, culled from daily newspapers of Dhaka and Chattagram and reprinted verbatim. One of the source newspapers is Maulana Mannan's *Inquilab*. So should one assume that all these newspapers are mouthpieces for the BJP or the party has paid them handsomely for printing such news?

A collection called *Glaani* (Disgrace) was published from Chattagram in August 1992, comprising a few images from the communal violence in 1990, pictures of demolished temples and some information on the torture of Hindu minorities by Muslim fundamentalists. The government had banned the collection, just like it banned my book. Selina Hossain wrote about the bans placed on the two books:

In the case of both books it has been said that they will incite communal tensions among the readers so the best recourse is to remove both books completely from the public eye. It is as if the nation's unstable communal situation will become immediately normalized if the two books are hidden away from the public eye.

The slogan for the National Poetry Festival 1989 was a call for poetry against communal politics. The declaration stated that we believed poetry was born out of harmony and humanity, and communal identities had no place in it . . . It is the epoch of humanity and secularism. All our lines and verses, every metaphor and every symbol, our poetic imagination and our voice, and all our collections are dedicated to those secular individuals who are going to stand guard as sentinels of humanity against state-sponsored communalism . . . Such a humanist and secular worldview is the true wealth of the people of this landmass.

Some of my feelings of shame and disgrace about *Lajja*, and the fact that it was lacking as a novel, were mollified when intellectuals took up the task of writing in favour of it. Dr Muhammad Anisul Haque wrote:

Taslima Nasrin's *Lajja* is a bold instance of dissent against the recently engineered communal violence in our country . . . it is possible the book will raise the hackles of some people in our country; especially the ones who have the most nefarious roles to play in disrupting communal peace are bound to get very upset. What is true is true and trying to suppress the truth does not make it a lie.

Haque himself came and gave me a copy of *Tritiya Dhara* where the column was published and on his way out said to me, 'Today the Serbs are demolishing mosques in Bosnia, so will our zealots go and attack churches next? No, they won't because the government won't let them, because if that happens then the British and American imperialists will be displeased.'

Hasan Firdaus, a fearless journalist, lived in the US and wrote regularly for Bangladeshi newspapers. He wrote:

Books can't be strangled to death. But they can be banned and burnt. When the truth that emerges from a book terrorizes the powers that be, they try their utmost to prohibit it . . . Powerful people and their

societies have done this since the dawn of time. At least they have
tried, but they have not succeeded. They killed Socrates but could
they hide the truth he had uttered? Hitler had bonfires of books
only to be relegated to the trashcan of history in the end. *Lajja* is not
simply a story of the communal riots of 1992, it is a testimony of the
insidious communalism that plagues Bangladesh today.

Jatin Sarkar wrote a long column in *Ajker Kagaj* on the ban on *Lajja*.

This is a law they have inherited as a legacy of their colonial past.
So many people died fighting the colonial state, they sacrificed
their honour and their lives to gain independence, and when that
independence was threatened by totalitarianism they went and did it
all over again in the name of freedom. But in the newly freed country
the new powers that were democratically elected used the same laws as
used by the despots before them to rule and control the masses. In fact,
I should rather say they misused these laws. This is our shame, but the
people sitting over our heads as our rulers do not feel any shame at all.

Shame, hatred, fear are useless investments and our rulers were well
versed in the axiom, a fact Sarkar did not fail to point out. *Lajja* was
not the source of my shame, it was an account of our collective disgrace,
and Sarkar had no qualms in making such a huge claim. He was clear in
his stance that he did not consider Bengalis to be inherently communal.

Bengalis have made secularism an inextricable component of their
national identity by their heroic struggle against the communal
state of Pakistan. But just like every other race even among Bengalis
there were always these few scurrilous elements, like dark craters on
the surface of the moon. These deceitful elements had opposed
the Mukti Juddho too and even after the independence they have
always been active in devising new ways to embarrass the people.

I began to deliberate how much of this shame I had managed to address
by writing *Lajja*. The story I had written was not something people were
unaware of. I had written about certain oft-discussed and oft-repeated
issues, things I thought of every day, things I spoke about regularly with

friends and relatives, protests I was trying to articulate or indignations I was accumulating every day, the dissent that was waiting to burst out of me—only a fraction of these things had found space in *Lajja*. I knew and so did my progressive friends that the path ahead of us was littered with thorns, but we were doubly aware that if we were to stop the thorns would only pile up and the way would only get more difficult. We had to walk the road less travelled, the one most were afraid to take, and compromises were out of the question. There were clearly two camps: one reactionary and the other progressive. The former wished to push society back by millennia and infest the human mind with blindness, superstition, jealousy, hate and fear. And our democratically elected government was aiding the reactionaries in their project. Although their hands were full of money and weapons and ours were empty, our hearts were emboldened by our faith in the ideals of equality and equity.

Every day I was being abused and called names—traitor, heretic, etc.—in the fundamentalist newspapers. I expected as much from them, but through this ordeal I also got to take a closer look at some familiar faces who always claimed to be secular and who were always perfectly progressive in their public interactions. One of them alleged that the BJP, a right-wing political party of India, was trying to 'use certain Bangladeshis to produce an exaggerated narrative of the consequences of the demolition of the mosque to spread fiction and gossip'. This was the latest false charge against me, that the BJP had paid me to write *Lajja*.

In reaction to such statements Shibnarayan Roy observed:

> We are all communal and god-fearing behind our masks. The educated Bengalis may call themselves modern but their life and history do not justify such a title. Till date the Bengali has been unable to overcome his Hindu or Muslim identity and truly become human.

It was an observation Safi Ahmed agreed with and he did not back out from making an unhesitant confession.

> The fault of communalism is something we are all infected with to varying degrees and simply covering up or denying the wound does not make it any less real. One has to be brave enough to make such an

admission, identify the disease, and then work towards the cure. We were all born with communal tendencies and we have been nurtured in its atmosphere for the past forty-six years. It flows in our veins consciously or unconsciously. Not just as tools of exploitation for the powerful overlords, behind our masks all of us nurture and nourish this ideology . . . It is only by revealing that we can absolve ourselves of our shame. Shame will not cause riots, shame will bring us together.

When the government was out gunning for me it was not easy for anyone to write in favour of the book or me. Despite such apprehensions many people wrote to me in support and the ones who did not either did not like me, or did not prefer my writing in general, or did not agree with my observations in *Lajja*. That was perfectly understandable; I did not like most of my own work. Even though I liked what I had tried to say with *Lajja*, I did not like how I had said it. The same story could have formed the basis of a touching novel and the characters too could have been more humanized. I was aware that the book possessed none of the depth and scope required of a novel, and being aware of this I was deeply embarrassed whenever someone effusively praised the book, although secretly it also gave me inspiration to write something great without losing my courage and strength.

Even if pride had made me inconsiderate, or self-importance had rendered me blind, I don't think I would have been able to claim that someone some day was going to look up my book while writing a history of literature, or this book was going to rescue the honour of our race. Instead I firmly believed that many were rather hyperbolic in their assessment of the book, and me too, perhaps because the book had been banned and reactionary factions were out to get me.

I had never met Bashir Al Helal, a renowned novelist of the country, and one of his columns startled me no end.

Isn't it natural that Hindus will write about Muslims and vice-versa? Does the government believe this harms the state? No, it does not. Rather it benefits the state. If communal tensions are to rise in India we will be able to proudly say that one of our writers has written a novel about our Hindu minorities. Isn't this a thing of pride, a mark of humanity? The truth cannot remain hidden for

long. While writing the history of our literature people will single
out such books and that day *Lajja* will defend our honour . . . I
consider Taslima Nasrin's *Lajja* to be an outstanding novel, the kind
that has hitherto not been written in Bangladesh. It is profound and
it packs quite the punch, but whatever she has written is the truth
and some may not take kindly to such harsh unadorned honesty.

Even in West Bengal *Lajja* managed to create enormous controversy.
Pirated copies were out and these were being rampantly sold in markets,
thoroughfares, trains, buses, basically everywhere, and various debates
regarding the novel were on. Maitreyi Chattopadhyay questioned the
narratives that existed around similar oppression of Indian Muslims by
the Hindu right and asked why a book like *Lajja* was yet to be written
about the plight of minorities in India. According to her this was a
source of shame not for Taslima Nasrin but for the people of India.

A minister of the state government of West Bengal remarked, 'It
will be wrong to take Taslima Nasrin's *Lajja* as an accurate depiction
of the actual conditions prevalent in Bangladesh at this moment.' The
communists of West Bengal were vigilant so that no attacks were carried
out on the Muslim minorities of the state. This vigilance was less because
of their love for their Muslim citizens and more because of a desire to
conserve their Muslim vote bank. I was clear about one thing: I was fine
with *Lajja* being called a false account if that ensured the safety of the
minorities of West Bengal. I was not upset by what the communists had
to say, but what did make me sad was when they alleged that either the
Anandabazar Group or the BJP had made me write anti-Islamic things.

I had dedicated the book to Buddhadev Guha and this too was
used to criticize me. According to them Buddhadev Guha was a BJP
spokesperson and he had even written the manifesto for the party. I
had met Guha at the Ananda Puraskar ceremony. A lively, fun-loving
man with a remarkable sense of humour, such bold and quick-witted
people were hard to come by. Wherever he was, whichever city or
distant forest, he never failed to write to me about his adventures and
his love for Bangladesh and its people. I was not aware if he was a BJP
or CPI(M) supporter, if he was a staunch believer or an utter atheist.
He had dedicated one of his books to me. If someone were to do that
it did not necessarily mean I had to return the favour in kind. I was

an avid reader of his work, I respected him, and which is why I had dedicated the book to him.

The publisher of *Lajja* dropped by to see me. The book was not on sale any more and his business had taken a massive hit. Before the ban the seventh edition had been in circulation and nearly 60,000 copies had been sold. However, nothing could make Altaf Hossain aka Minu any less unhappy. He was not being able to sell the book in Bangladesh and neither could he export the book to West Bengal. When I had handed him the manuscript he had been less than thrilled. His long face had broken into a wide smile only after seeing the sales at the book fair. That smile was nowhere visible any more. 'They've banned the book. My business has taken a hit. Give me something new to print.'

What new book was I supposed to give him? I was rewriting *Lajja*, keeping the incidents and the facts the same but correcting errors in language and style and making the characters more flexible and real. Not one of the novels I had written thus far was any good. They had been printed but when I sat down and flipped through one all I noticed were the spelling and syntactical errors, and the problems with language or plot. It never failed to get me down and whenever a publisher came to me with a freshly printed copy of a novel their joy usually disappeared as soon as I got a chance to glance through the first few pages. Invariably, seeing my anxiety they would ask me to correct the mistakes so they could incorporate the corrections in the subsequent editions.

Minu was talking from time to time. 'I received word that *Lajja* is being sold at a bookshop in New Market. Not just that, it's being sold at the science fair, on the streets, in newspaper stalls and in the flower markets. Eighty taka without the cover and hundred otherwise.'

'A 40 taka book is being sold for 100! The readers are paying 60 taka more for it? Then the ban has only harmed the reading public!'

'You are worried about the readers but you are not thinking about how much harm it has done to me! There was an order from Calcutta for 10,000 copies but I could not send it.'

'You just told me the book is being sold here. How did they get the book? Since you are not selling it.'

'How can I sell it? The police are coming to my shop twice a day. They have taken all the books already, even the ones in the godown and the unfinished ones at the binder's. Pirated copies of the book are out.'

'I heard about pirated copies being sold in Calcutta, but it's happening here too? So how did the ban help the government?'

'The pirated copies flooded the market within two days of the ban. There are some in Banglabazar too who deal in pirated books. Maybe it was one of them. I have no news as yet.'

'What is the police saying? The government has banned the book, so why does it not ensure the book is not sold?'

'They are not selling the book out in the open. They keep it hidden away. Only when you ask them secretly do they bring out a copy for you. They wrap it in newspaper. My guy went and bought three!'

'Some are asking why the publishers of *Lajja* are not challenging the ban in a court of law.'

'A court case?' Minu's face fell and he looked around him in discomfort. It was clear to me he did not possess the guts required to challenge such a draconian law in court. 'Will a court case make a difference?' he wondered in a barely audible whine.

'It might. And even if it does not, it will still show them that we have not given in to the government's bullying. What they are trying to do is against the freedom of speech and expression.'

Minu stayed quiet for a long while. He sipped his tea with an audible slurp and pushed it aside; it had gone cold. Then in a soft voice he said, 'Write a new book for me.'

'New book? Now? I am busy with the corrections of *Lajja*. It'll be done in a couple of days.'

'How much time does it even take to write a book? Sit, finish and get up, in one go. Humayun Ahmed has written so many books overnight.'

'Minu bhai, I can't write like Humayun Ahmed. How can one write a book overnight? Besides, the corrections of *Lajja* should be done very soon. I'll think about a new book after that.'

'How many times will you write the same book? That too a banned one! You are rewriting it, but I can't print it any more. You must know that I am leaving the import and export of books and opening my own publishing house. Don't leave me high and dry now!'

I did not wish to do that to him, so I gave him my word that I was going to write a new book for him. And it was not just Minu who was after me with such a request! Things were so stressed that even the sight of a publisher was enough to terrify me. Moinul Ahsan Saber, a good writer, had started a publishing house called Divyaprakash and had also come over to my place on a number of occasions to ask for a book. 'Nasrin, if you don't write a novel for me in a few days I am going to die.'

How was I supposed to watch out for so many people? The line of publishers wanting to work with me was increasing daily. Writing was not my only vocation. I had a full-time job, myriad issues pertaining to the household to take care of, a number of magazine columns to write, besides our weekly meetings. This last bit was not technically strictly weekly; it could be called on any day and any time. These meetings were open for everyone irrespective of gender, age, profession; neither did it matter if the attendee was a writer or not. Allegiance to a particular political creed was not an issue for us either, or faith in a particular religion, although none of those who attended our meetings were religious in any way. The only thing we ensured was that everyone in attendance was on the same page regarding certain fundamental issues that concerned all of us—establishment of social democracy, secularism, freedom of speech and expression, freedom of thought, a free press, equal opportunities for all vis-à-vis food, education and health care, a secular pedagogy, ensuring women's rights and equity between the sexes, equality of law, eradication of poverty, strict actions against criminal and terrorist activities, security for all, preservation of Bengali culture and identity, a just political and socio-economic system, purging superstitions, fundamentalism and bigotry from the social body and the complete obliteration of communal politics.

We discussed everything: politics, the economy, society, religion and sometimes literature and culture. We never fixed a prior date for a meeting, neither did we ever fix an agenda of what we wished to discuss. Anyone could call a meeting on any issue they wished to discuss with the group. There was no fixed place where the meetings were held either. Since I did not have a husband or children my house was usually the most ideal place. There was no dearth of enthusiasm and dreams on our part and we were all equally perturbed by the growing tide of fundamentalist ideology around us. We were aware that these reprehensible elements were mustering their forces to launch an all-out attack on us and we had to be prepared to withstand the assault.

Purabi Basu had left her high-profile job in the US to come back to Bangladesh to join Beximco as a scientist. In her free time she was also writing short stories. In such a time of anarchy when everyone, be it a poet, a novelist or a writer of short stories, was writing political columns, she too was not far behind. Since our Bengali identity was in jeopardy she brought out an edited volume of essays called *Bengali*, along with journalist Haroon Habib. Then she began work on editing a huge book titled *Ekhono Gelona Adhar* (The Darkness Hasn't Left) with Professor Safi Ahmed of Jahangirnagar University, a collection of news reports and essays on the communal violence in the aftermath of the demolition of the Babri Masjid.

Safi Ahmed was like her shadow and seeing them together reminded me of Jean-Paul Sartre and Simone de Beauvoir—a truly remarkable philosophical camaraderie. When someone like MF, who was known as an intellectual, refused to call whatever had been done to the Hindu minorities as violence and went on to claim that the culture of Bangladesh was fundamentally Islamic in nature and needed to be preserved, it alarmed us no end. We were not as apprehensive of the stupid as we were of the cunning and it only intensified our desire to unite and protest and marshal our forces to fight a common enemy. One day I received urgent summons from Purabi Basu to discuss our plan of action, the programme for the protest, the work we had to do, who was going to write and when. None of us had any time to waste and we went ahead as we planned, but despite everything I could not get rid of the feeling that not enough was being done. All of us could see that our country was beginning to decay but no was doing anything to prevent it. There were not too many of us and the ones who were willing to stay silent and let things be were far too many in number compared to us.

~

The work on *Lajja* got over rather fast. I had to finish the entire edit lying down, not on the bed but on the floor. I had been suffering from a terrible backache and the orthopaedic took an X-ray of my spine and asked me to stay off my feet entirely; I was not allowed to go to the bathroom by myself either and was asked to spend three months lying on the floor on my back, without turning on my side. This was the prescription, and when I inquired about the disease I was informed that my spine was too straight. It was something I had been born with, a too-straight spine, which meant that whenever I tried lying face down or tried to bend over there was a risk of dislodging the vertebrae.

The spinal column is not straight; it bends in a wave near the lower back. But my spine did not possess that undulating shape, hence all the trouble. There was a treatment for it but it could never be turned into a spine like what most others had. The best course of action was to lie down on one's back to realign the vertebrae. Even after three months of this treatment I was told never to lie face down again. I was also asked to not carry anything heavy and always sleep on a hard bed for the rest of my life if I wanted to keep my straight spine intact.

I knew three months of bed rest was never going to work for me, but I did take a two-week leave from the hospital to rest and lie on my back on the bedroom floor. I had the computer moved to the floor too and, switching between lying face down while working and lying on my back otherwise, I typed in the comfort of the knowledge that my spine was being taken care of in the way the doctors had asked me to.

Once the work was done I took a printout of the new version of *Lajja* from my computer, this one nearly twice the size of the previous version. I never read any of my books after finishing them because invariably a hundred errors popped up, especially in the construction of sentences, and it made me want to rewrite the entire thing all over again. I knew that way I was never going to finish a book in my lifetime. The one good thing in reworking *Lajja* was that it helped me flesh out some of the information.

However, the next big hurdle was to figure out how to get the manuscript to Calcutta. Officers from the Special Branch were always posted in front of my house and if I attempted to go to the post office with it they were surely going to follow me and arrest me for smuggling contraband. Since I could not leave the country—my passport had still not been returned to me—the only recourse was to have someone who was going to Calcutta take it along with them. However, none of the people who I found out were scheduled to go to Calcutta around the time were brave enough to attempt such a daring mission.

At such a moment of crisis Mostafa Kamal came to my rescue. A straightforward but garrulous man, Kamal was the brother of renowned singer Firdaus Wahid. While the latter had made quite a name for himself, Kamal had never attained that level of success. The first time I met Kamal was in Calcutta during a post-event dinner organized by Abrittilok at Kenilworth Hotel. Sunil Gangopadhyay had introduced us. The man I had met in a suit had suddenly turned up at my place one day in a T-shirt and sandals and immediately launched into a boisterous conversation without even bothering to pause for formalities. 'I came to see how you are. Tell me, how is everything! I arrived from Calcutta the day before. I usually stay at Sunil's whenever I'm in Calcutta, you know; Sunil and Swati don't let me stay anywhere else. Sunil was telling me about you. So I said to him, I'll visit Taslima one day. Do you know Nabanita? Nabanita Dev Sen! Of course you know her! She asked me to go see her but I couldn't manage this time. Tell me all about you. When are you going to Calcutta? Everyone knows you by name there! I had thought I would pick up one of your books from Badal but I didn't get the time.'

Mostafa Kamal was quite an old hand at talking all by himself for a length of time. 'Sunil has written a book about me, do you know? Have you read it? He recorded everything I said. And then he wrote an entire book out of it . . . Firdaus and I don't talk any more. So what if he's my brother, I don't care.' Kamal would turn up at my place suddenly and as long as he stayed the house reverberated with his liveliness. He would tell me all about his relatives, his neighbours and his friends, almost as if we had known each other for ages and I knew everyone around him.

Similarly, he would tell me about his own misadventures and the ensuing repercussions. 'I got married, took my wife to Canada, and then Dora left me. It's all my rotten luck I tell you. Every business I try, it fails. Right now I'm thinking of another one. Supplying maids to Malaysia. It's in high demand . . . I don't have a house or a car. Even money, there's some today and there won't be any tomorrow . . . All my brothers are doing well. That's fine, let them. You know what, no one likes me, it's because I'm a little crazy.' On the one hand he would casually drop names of famous people he was well acquainted with while on the other he also freely admitted that he was nobody.

Mostafa Kamal came to my rescue at such a trying time and boldly offered, 'You want to send the manuscript to Calcutta? Fine, I'll take it.'

'Really?'

'Yes.'

'It won't be a problem?'

'Why? What can happen? Who will do what?'

Dr Rashid was there and he pointed out that the Special Branch officers usually followed anyone who entered or left this house. If he was to get caught with the manuscript it would be a disaster. Not just sale, even the possession and conservation of *Lajja* was forbidden. Kamal's face went pale in an instant. He had magnanimously declared he was going to get the manuscript to Badal Basu in Calcutta so he could not back out of his promise. But he put in a condition that he was not going to leave with the manuscript. Someone was going to have to hand it over to him on the way to the airport. Who was going to take the responsibility of taking the manuscript out of the house? Dr Rashid volunteered and the two of them worked out the logistics of the exchange in a furtive conversation—which road, which turn, in what clothes, which car, left or right, black briefcase, dark shades, so on and so forth. All in whispers since even walls had ears. The title page with the name of the book and the author was expunged from the manuscript.

In the middle of the night—with pounding heart and trembling legs, soaked in nervous sweat and the incriminating manuscript in his possession—Dr Rashid left my house. If he had been religious he would have perhaps prayed to Allah too. With the manuscript under his pillow he spent a sleepless night and left home at five in the morning. At the previously designated spot just past the Mahakali seven-point crossing a man in dark shades suddenly materialized in front of him as if by magic, or like an alien from another planet. Almost on the same beat a brown packet from his sling bag made its way to the other man's black briefcase like a packet of toast biscuits or a new garment sample. Silently the man with the sling bag turned and headed south while the one in the dark shades headed north. Perhaps keeping each other in mind both walked away as swiftly as possible to disappear before anyone could even catch a whiff of them.

Lajja managed to cross the border and reach West Bengal.

~

I did not write *Lajja* because I wanted to have it published from West Bengal. I wrote *Lajja* for Bangladesh. The book had caught the attention of Ananda Publishers only after the pirated copies reached West Bengal. The authorities at the publishing house took the help of the police and got some of the counterfeiters jailed eventually. I did not ask them what had dictated their actions— ethics or business. The manuscript taken by Mostafa Kamal was the first official manuscript I sent to Calcutta and Ananda Publishers published *Lajja* in West Bengal.

A ban was perhaps a contagious thing. News arrived that *Lajja* had also been banned in Sri Lanka though there was not one reason I could think of why the book should be banned there. There was no end to the debate over the book either. The conversations went on everywhere, on the road, in trains and buses, at homes and offices, courts and markets and public grounds . . .

One day Shamsur Rahman, Nirmalendu Goon and Bilal Chowdhury were at my house when the talk invariably veered towards *Lajja*.

Pushing a copy of *Inquilab* in my direction Chowdhury said, 'The BJP has apparently published *Lajja*. They have gotten it translated too.'

'The mullahs are blaming Taslima for the fact that the BJP has published or translated the book,' Goon interjected, 'but how is this her fault? If Golam Azam loves my poetry will that be my fault too?'

I intervened. 'How can the BJP translate the entire book? There are many things in the book against them.'

The only criticism Shamsur Rahman had against *Lajja* was that despite everything the book failed to provide a complete picture of the movements that were continuously battling the forces of communalism and the fact that there were secular individuals too in the country. I accepted his point and told him that my wish had been

to narrate the story from the point of view of an angry Hindu boy
to whom none of the secular and non-communal movements were
of any help. On the BJP, Rahman remarked, 'Just see how they are
trying to turn something completely non-communal into a communal
issue. Debesh Roy of Calcutta has written a novel from the point of
view of their Muslim minorities, does no one here notice that?'

Goon burst out laughing. 'The mullahs are saying the BJP has
paid Taslima Rs 45 lakh to write *Lajja*. So, Taslima, aren't we getting
a cut too? Or do you want it all?' Laughing, I replied, '*Inquilab* is
writing this, isn't it? Now even the common people believe that the
BJP has actually paid me money!'

Shamsur Rahman was having none of it. 'It's so easy, is it? Just saying
you've been paid off? Why aren't they proving it then? Before the elections
the BNP had accused India of paying Rs 500 crore to Sheikh Hasina.
The Awami League had shot back with a 600 crore offer from Pakistan
for Khaleda Zia. Neither has been able to prove these accusations yet.'

I could not help but agree with him. 'And they will not be able
to prove their accusations against me either, that I was paid to write
Lajja. But what I am wondering is why are they out trying to slander
me? Have the political parties paid them off?'

Throwing the copy of *Inquilab* aside with a curse Chowdhury
burst out, 'More than the Hindus it is the Muslims who have benefited
from Taslima's *Lajja*. The book is an example of how compassionate
Muslims can be. To speak on behalf of the minority despite belonging
to the majority, that too so boldly and insistently, is not something
you get to see too often. Muslims can probably use this when the time
is right, to show how open-minded they can be.'

Laughing at his suggestion I countered, 'Bilal bhai, so easily you
have turned an atheist like me into a Muslim!'

'Aren't we all atheists? Since you have a Muslim name they will
slot you as a Muslim. That way no one is an atheist here. You're a
Muslim or a Hindu, a Christian or a Buddhist. Religion is a must.'

I turned to Shamsur Rahman. 'Religion is the culture of the
uneducated, and for the educated culture is religion. Isn't that so,
Rahman bhai?'

'Who do we call educated?' Rahman replied. 'Golam Azam is an
educated man, so is MF. Both have university degrees.'

'No, no, I'm not talking about academic education,' I hastily added. 'Even a person who has never gone to school can be educated. Take for instance Araj Ali Matubbar.' Chowdhury, who was a great admirer of the self-taught philosopher and rationalist, excitedly joined in at once. 'Araj Ali was a poor farmer. But look at the beautiful books he wrote. His books should be taught at school.' Shamsur Rahman nodded at the suggestion and added, 'Not just schools, they should be part of the syllabus in colleges and universities too. Reading his books will help people raise pertinent questions about religion and many will find inspiration in them to embrace atheism.'

Kulsum came in with tea and everyone picked up a cup. Meanwhile, Dr Rashid had come in and silently taken a seat. He used to be an active member of the JASAD[35] but recently his role had taken a more passive turn. A sharp and rational individual, Dr Rashid was staunchly against any form of communalism, superstitions and religious dogma. While sipping tea I pondered on a more immediate question: Were all our problems going to disappear if the Muslims were to turn atheists? Somehow I was not convinced by such a quick fix. I was convinced that someone like Golam Azam was an atheist too and the same went for all the leaders of the Jamaat. It was their followers, the foolish gullible disciples, who were the true believers. These were the people who were being led by the noose of religion around their necks, for people like Golam Azam to play their political games. Keeping the tea aside I turned to Shamsur Rahman. 'I believe Golam Azam is an atheist. Take Ershad for instance. Do you think he believed in religion? The way he suddenly amended the constitution and made Islam the state religion, do you think he did it out of his love for Islam? Of course not. It was a clever use of religion to serve the needs of power.'

'Yes, this is what political Islam is all about. I too believe that the people who use religion for politics know very well how effective it is in keeping people stupid and docile. It is highly unlikely that people who use religion for their own benefit believe in it themselves.'

'Even if we assume they do believe, it should be noted that ultimately they are adhering to the tenets of Islam. In Islam the world is divided into two: Dar al-Islam and Dar al-Harb, the land of the Muslims and the land of the non-believing others. The sacred duty of Muslims is to invade the Dar al-Harb and convert the people to Islam by whatever means necessary. So the ultimate target is to transform the entire world into Dar al-Islam. Then whatever the Bangladeshi Muslims are doing is perfectly according to the principles of Islam. Islam condones such acts.'

'That's not exclusive to Islam. Even Christians had the same principles. Just see where they started and how far they have spread!'

'True. Most monotheistic faiths have a horrifying history. But Rahman bhai, why even now? Why are we being subjected to acts of cruelty that can only be termed medieval even at the fag end of the twentieth century?'

'Because we still haven't managed to become human.'

'But the Christians no longer rabidly pursue a policy of slaughtering the other. Why have the Muslims held on to it?'

'Because most Muslim nations are yet to embrace secularism, like most Christian nations have.'

'But there were movements on that front too. Consider the pan-Arabism movement for that matter. It was a secular movement. Almost everyone concerned from the Arab countries were Muslims.'

'The derailing of the secular movement in the Arab countries is squarely the responsibility of a few evil Arab leaders, although even they are puppets of imperial powers. None of the imperial powers could tolerate a big movement in any of their colonies, especially the ones that directly challenged their power and authority.'

'But, Rahman bhai, the pan-Arabism movement came into being after the colonial powers had left.'

At this juncture, Dr Rashid intervened. 'How far did the imperialist go? Somehow or the other their greed for oil made sure they stayed in the Middle East in some form or the other. Who controls the oil reserves? It was always the British, before the Americans replaced them. Did the leaders of pan-nationalism fight any less to nationalize the oil reserves?'

'Fundamentalist movements like the Islamic Brotherhood grew out of a rebellion against such imperialist forces. They too have a role in destroying any chance at a secular uprising,' I added.

'The Arab leaders could not unite because they were busy fighting each other. Nasser of Egypt had wanted to unite all the Arab countries but the other nationalists rejected the idea. If the Arab countries had united, could an American or British have dared to try and put a puppet in power and pull all the strings from the shadows?' Dr Rashid was agitated and gulped down the cold tea in front of him.

'This growing tide of Islamic fundamentalism in the Middle East, is it because of the Israel–Palestine issue? Or is it because of the Berlin Wall? The Wall has fallen, the irreligious Soviet Union has fallen too. Does that imply ideals of secularism have fallen too? Hence, awake and arise religion! O great Islam . . .'

Chowdhury interrupted and said, 'The history of the subcontinent is different, here fundamentalism has been strengthened primarily by state complicity.'

I agreed with him. 'Of course. But fundamentalism is contagious. It spreads from one place to another . . .'

'These Jamaatis in Bangladesh are pandering to . . .' Shamsur Rahman had angrily just begun when his words were interrupted by a sudden knock on the door. His unfinished sentence hanging in mid-air, Rahman turned to look at the door as Dr Rashid got up to answer. All our senses had zoomed in on the door. Everyone was aware that it was not a good idea for a stranger to casually walk into my house. Every Friday there were meetings in the mosque where people were abusing me and protest marches were held demanding the noose for me. Such was the time that any devout Muslim could barge into my house any time and murder me. Was it someone like that? Or else why was Dr Rashid hesitating to let them in and guarding the door as he spoke to the strangers beyond the threshold? After talking to the unseen guests a while longer he turned, leaving the door ajar, and said, 'Four boys from Shani's *akhada* are here to see you.'

'Who are they? What do they want?'

'You won't know them. One of them is Shankar Ray.'

Goon immediately said, 'Don't let them in. Close the door. They could just have assumed Hindu names and come here with ulterior motives.' After a pause, he laughed and said, 'But then you can't trust the Hindus either, can you?'

Dr Rashid went back to the door, softly spoke to the men outside again and then turned back to me and said, 'They are perfectly harmless simple men. They have just come to pay their respects. They will go away after that.'

More out of curiosity to know who they were and why they were at my house, or perhaps also out of a sense of security that there were many people present who would rescue me if something untoward happened, I replied, 'Fine, ask them to come in.'

Four young men entered the room, all of them within twenty to twenty-five years of age, in simple clothes and sandals. They took off their sandals near the door, looked around the room once and then lowered their hands towards my feet. I jerked my feet away and stood up. Even before I could say anything the boy called Shankar stood in front of me with folded hands and said, 'Didi, you are like a goddess to us. We feel blessed to meet you. We've looked everywhere for you. We wish to touch your feet once.' But I moved my feet away again when he tried the second time. Shankar pointed to the two other boys and said, 'These are my cousins', and then pointing to the third man in a red shirt, he said, 'He is a friend. We are all in college, didi.' When he tried lowering his head for the third time I said, 'No, you don't have to touch my feet. I don't like these things. Tell me what you want to say.'

'Didi, we have read your book *Lajja*. No one has ever spoken on behalf of us like this before. Didi, what you have done, if only you knew how great . . . you have written what has always been in our hearts.'

'See, it's not a Hindu–Muslim thing at all. As a human being I have written about the pain of other human beings around me. Everyone you see here, all of them are writers and they have all spoken out against social injustices.'

'Didi, the Jamaatis have destroyed the house of my cousins. And my friend here, Samiran, they murdered one of his brothers.' Before I could stop them the four boys fell to their knees, wrapped their arms around my legs and began to weep. I was in a fix. I could not pull them up and neither could I move my legs. I could only stand there helplessly in discomfort. After a while they wiped their tears, said their goodbyes and left. No sooner were they gone than Goon remarked in a deep voice, his words slow and deliberate, 'Taslima's *Lajja* has done more harm than good to the Hindus of Bangladesh.'

'What do you mean?' I was staring in astonishment at Goon's expressionless face and I saw the others were as flabbergasted. 'What kind of harm?' I could not suppress the curiosity in my tone.

Goon continued slowly. 'You have managed to quench the fire that was burning in their hearts all this while. The outrage they had nursed all this while, which could have made it possible for them to do something drastic, has now abated a lot. Now they feel that there are people to speak on their behalf, that they are not alone. If the strong keep speaking up for the weak, the latter forget to fight their own battles. They don't start the fires that they have always wanted to.'

With his words ringing in the air we sat with our empty teacups for a long time in the throes of the desolate silence that had descended around us.

~

I did not stay at the Shantibag house for too long after this. The landlord had started looking at me strangely. He read the namaz five times a day and was a subscriber of *Inquilab*. He also went to the mosque every Friday for the Jumu'ah prayers. There, after the namaz was read, the imam delivered the *khutbah* (sermon), which was mostly his own version of *gheebat* (backbiting or slander). Milan used to often go to the mosque near Shantibag on Fridays, for the namaz as well as the imam's abusive tirades. 'There is a blight called Taslima in this country, my brothers, and this Taslima is against Islam; despite being a Muslim herself she is hell-bent on harming other Muslims. This sinner has taken a bribe from the Hindus to write a book. If you haven't read the book you have done a good thing, a thing to be proud of. In this book she has alleged that Muslims are the worst, that they have slaughtered Hindus and washed the streets with rivers of blood. She is a disgrace to all women. She is encouraging women to sleep with random men and leave their husbands. This woman doesn't believe in religion, she says Allah doesn't exist, and dares to claim that Muhammad sallallahu alaihi wasallam, Allah's beloved prophet, was a lustful and wicked man. Shame! My brothers, you must demand that all her books, not just this one, be incinerated or banned. You must demand that she be hanged. If this sinner is hanged this country will be saved and Islam will be saved too.'

After the sermon they prayed to Allah with their hands raised towards heaven to save Bangladesh and Islam by giving me the death penalty. On some days even leaflets were distributed to that end. My landlord was a witness to all of this. He was a witness to the protest marches against his tenant, or at least he read about them in *Inquilab*. In fact, even I was held up by these marches twice. On one occasion I could take a detour in time, but on another the rickshaw had to stop to let the massive procession pass, with men in fez caps walking past me and demanding my head. Without a headscarf and with only an apron over my salwar kurta there was nothing for me to hide my face with either. Terrified, I had to pretend to cover my face and nose against the swirling dust and stare fixedly at the foot rest of the rickshaw, as if like any good, docile woman I wished to avoid eye contact with a man. I did not have a shadow of doubt that if even one person in the procession managed to recognize me, my flesh and blood and bones would be found littered all over the street. After the procession had passed and the rickshaw had gone a little ahead I asked the rickshaw-puller, 'What was that all about?'

'It's a demonstration against Taslima.'

'As in?'

'As in they want her to be hanged.'

'Why? What has she done?'

'She has demolished a mosque.'

'Which mosque? Do you know?'

'Babri Masjid.'

'How did one woman manage to demolish an entire mosque?'

'That I don't know.'

'Where did you hear this?'

'We hear things. Delwar Hossain Sayeedi's cassettes play everywhere. And there are these processions too.'

'Do you want her to be hanged too?'

'Yes, of course, why wouldn't I! Since everyone does, I do too.'

I got off in front of my house in Shantibag and paid the man for the trip. It was fortunate that I had long removed the signboard with my name from the gate.

The day I was held up by the demonstration Chotda dropped by with a friend. It was lovely to see him. He never came to my house and I too had stopped visiting because I could no longer continue to face Geeta's misbehaviour and witness the unspeakable tortures she put Suhrid through. His friend Shafeeq worked in the airlines like him and he had come with a request. He wanted me to write about the air hostesses that worked in these planes, about how they were usually fired as soon as they were thirty-five, how they were deprived of the mandatory nine-month maternity leave guaranteed to them and in some cases even deprived of their pensions.

During our conversation when I found out that Shafeeq was a car trader who imported cars from Japan and sold them in Bangladesh I suddenly burst out, 'I want to buy a car! Today!'

'If you want Shafeeq can give you a good discount. But you have to put down an advance.' It was decided that I was going to give Shafeeq an advance that very day and the car would be delivered to me in two weeks. I gave him 50,000 taka in cash, the remaining three lakh to be paid after delivery. It was the money that Salim, the owner of Kakali Publishers, had left the day before as an advance for the book I was supposed to write for him, a book I had yet to think about, let alone write. Shafeeq left with the money. I knew that without a car moving around in public was never going to be safe for me; so it was a foregone choice. I did manage to write that column about the air hostesses too and it was published in the magazine *Jai Jai Din*. But I never got my hands on that car and neither did I ever see that money again.

Every time I stepped out of the house it was at the risk of death. But there was no way I could stay at home either. Discontent was brewing both outside and inside the house. I could sense that the landlord had decided he could no longer let me live in his house. His pinched eyebrows and repeated and deliberate attempts at pretending to not notice me was enough to convince me that he was no longer interested in being on good terms with me. I understood the anxiety. Any day the angry agitators might have found their way to the house, doused the building in petrol and let it go up in flames. It was a risk he was trying to avoid and I felt that day and night, so much so that it made me squirm in worry.

I was petrified that the landlord was suddenly going to throw me out one day and I would have nowhere to go. I had no shelter, no security and no guarantees, and no other house owner was going to rent a place to me. My name was dangerous; it made civilized people recoil in fear. Those girls in schools and colleges who spoke dismissively with the boys, who walked with their heads held high and without a care in the world, the shameless and daring ones, they were teased and dubbed 'Taslima'. Even before I could sense what was happening my name had become a symbol of sin, shame, decadence, greed and depravity in society.

So the day I noticed the ten-storey apartment of Eastern Housing under construction at the Shantinagar crossing, just past the Shantibag main road and Malibag, that very day I decided to buy my own place. I went to the offices of Eastern Housing in Motijheel at once without even stopping to check the place or consult anyone. I asked for the rates and was told that one apartment on the ninth floor of the first building was ready for residents. And just like that I bought my own place. I had to take a loan from the bank that the people at Eastern Housing helped me with and the rest had to be paid off in instalments.

Since I was buying the place, the owners did not care who I was going to be living with or if I had a husband or not. They were not concerned with what I did or if there were demonstrations being held against me. All they wanted to know was whether I had the money to buy the house; since I did have the money they could not care less about my husbandless life, my writing, the slander and accusation against me, my banned book, or the protests demanding my hanging. Besides, there was nothing else left for me to do. I had initially intended to deposit the money I had received from my publishers in the bank and use the monthly interest to run my home; my salary from the hospital was hardly enough. Tossing all these careful calculations aside I pooled in all the money I had to buy the place for a total price of 27 lakh taka, of which I gave them twelve lakhs in cash as advance. The longer the duration of the bank loan, the more the amount of interest I had to bear.

On hearing I was buying the house my publishers immediately made arrangements for some more advance royalty. Kakali Prakashani sent me 3 lakh taka and Minu of Pearl Publications sent 5 lakh taka more. It did not take me long to pay off the bank loan. I asked Father for a loan of 1 lakh taka too and he did not turn me away; he was always enthusiastic about buying property. As soon as I got the papers of the house I called a loading van to transport all my things from Shantibag to Shantinagar. It was a sad moment, leaving the Shantibag house. There were so many memories scattered here and there, all over the place. Eventually I let out the sigh I had held back and walked out from the black gates for the very last time.

~

Meanwhile, the controversy over *Lajja* was refusing to die down even after months had passed. Especially in West Bengal, where *Lajja* had landed squarely in the middle of a contentious political arena, the debate raged on. The left parties labelled it a bad book and even a staunchly leftist film-maker like Mrinal Sen gave a statement to the effect that *Lajja* should be called a pile of putrefying garbage instead of a book. On the other hand, right-wing Hindus were celebrating it almost like a holy book.

The scene in India was actually the complete reverse of how it was in Bangladesh. In Bangladesh, the left-liberal secular intellectuals, except Badruddin Umar, were all of the opinion that it was a valuable book. But in India people of similar political and ethical dispositions were calling *Lajja* garbage. Only a handful of people from West Bengal, despite being inclined towards the left, were speaking on behalf of the book. All I could do was sit back and watch in amazement as the book was cleverly turned into a pawn of political games. The only good thing in all this was that I was far away from it all.

One fine day, Baharuddin from the Bengali daily *Aajkaal* turned up at my place. Gone were his ingratiating manner and the beguiling smile. Instead, his sharp eyes lacerated me in a way that made me feel as if Golam Azam's progeny had just walked out of the Baitul Mukarram to come and stand in front of me. *Aajkaal* was a left-wing newspaper. They had been very appreciative of me after the Ananda Puraskar, especially perhaps because I was Muslim. So when they realized that the same Muslim girl had written a book in which she had said not-so-nice things about Muslims, *Aajkaal* felt deeply slighted.

Baharuddin came to me looking for answers, demanding to know why I had written the book. Baharuddin was from Assam and he used to be a teacher of Arabic at a college there. One fine day he had left everything behind and moved to Calcutta, married a Hindu girl called Swati, become father to a son called Lalon, and settled down to live happily or unhappily ever after. He was a writer and poet, had been published too, and I must admit he wrote beautiful prose. He was an atheist through and through and could often be heard loudly abusing religion and those who bothered too much with it. He was also very concerned about the Muslim minorities oppressed by Hindus in West Bengal.

In all, there was no reason why the two of us should have been at odds. We fell apart when Baharuddin realized that right-wing Hindus were using my book to their advantage and he decided I was to blame for it. The one crucial point he missed was who I was writing about and why, and in which country. No matter how left-leaning or how much of an atheist he was, he was still a minority. He had always seen Hindus as oppressors and not the oppressed. When you are not used to something it is difficult to even visualize it in your head. Not because I felt sorry that he had flown all the way over from Calcutta but because I wanted to clear some of the misconceptions he had about *Lajja*, I agreed to talk to Bahar. There was a debate raging in *Aajkaal* over the book and the arguments and counter-arguments were at their peak. Not Muslim fundamentalists but progressive leftist writers and politicians of West Bengal were of the opinion that, firstly, I was writing to incite; secondly, I was consciously or unconsciously floating in the tide of right-wing Hindu fundamentalism, the kind that was on the rise in India, and that I was also a victim of an international conspiracy that was working its way through South East Asia; and thirdly, *Lajja* was a weak novel, shrouded in the fumes of an escapist point of view.

Bahar asked me, 'You must be deeply bothered by *Lajja* right now, isn't it?'

The very first question was successful in putting me off ever so slightly. 'Strange! Why should I be bothered? I am not bothered at all.'

'Are you trying to tell me you are not bothered by *Lajja* or any of your other works?'

'Yes, that's what I want to tell you. I am never troubled by what I write. The only things that bother me are my weak descriptions, my immature use of language and my inability to chart the depths of a character.'

'The book has been made into an issue in Bangladesh by both the mullahs and the government. In West Bengal and in other states of India the BJP is reaping the benefits of your carelessness. Don't you feel you have just handed a dangerous weapon to the Sangh Parivar?'

'My first concern is with your use of the word careless. I was not careless while I was writing *Lajja*. I have accepted that *Lajja* lacks in structure and is majorly deficient in aesthetics, but there is no problem at all with its content and critique. I have written nothing but the truth. While banning the book not once has the government of Bangladesh said that the information in the book is wrong. If the BJP is trying to take advantage of it it's their dishonesty and not my book's fault. The ones who are arguing that I have given a weapon to the Sangh Parivar are simply trying to create confusion in the minds of the people about a book that is only in favour of communal harmony. When they don't criticize the BJP and the Sangh Parivar but choose to criticize the book and its author instead I can't help but wonder if they have read the book at all. Is there even a single word in the book in favour of religious fundamentalists? No. And I will say this again, if the Sangh Parivar is using the book for their benefit, it betrays their dishonesty. That burden is not on *Lajja* or its author. I am also sure they know that *Lajja* is not speaking on their behalf. "Let the other name of religion be humanity" is written on the first page of the book.'

'Specific sections from your novel are being reprinted in the RSS mouthpieces *Panchyajanya* and *Organiser*. The day the BJP and the VHP decided to distribute the novel to as many households as possible, the very next day the book could be found everywhere in Calcutta, on the roads, the pavements and even the local paan shops. Did anyone take permission to print your novel?'

'Of course not! I have not allowed any fundamentalist political party to print *Lajja*; it's out of the question. Not just *Lajja*, they don't have rights to publish any of my books.'

'Then why aren't you suing *Panchyajanya* and *Organiser*?'

'My publishers in Calcutta, the ones who have the rights to the book, should be suing them. It is up to them to have the book translated or to allow it to be reprinted. If there are any violations to that they must take legal action. Haven't they done so already? The police did catch some of the people who were behind the pirated copies, didn't they?'

'We feel your novel is causing trouble both for Hindus here and Muslims there.'

'There are certain problems in what you feel. I have told the story of a progressive, educated, Hindu family of this country in *Lajja*. The family falls victim to communal violence, where a rationalist and atheist young man gradually transforms into a staunch Hindu, becomes a fundamentalist and gets destroyed in the process. The state destroys him, the government destroys him and gradually mushrooming religious fanaticism destroys him. He is defeated. Many young men in this country are transforming from human beings to Hindus. They are being repeatedly victimized by the state, in educational institutions, workplaces, business and trade, all because of religious discrimination. They are being labelled second-class citizens. Why should I not speak the truth? The truth will always be valued. The ones who make a truth controversial, the fault lies with them and not with the truth. And the ones who blame the truth support the actions of the miscreants. The Hindus getting into trouble here is a bad excuse. Those who like to stay silent for the sake of convenience are responsible for eroding human strength and courage. They are cowards and exploiters. They are the biggest threats to all minority communities. They believe if you point out a wrong it will lead to trouble. The same argument works for the Muslims there.'

'In the near future if something unpleasant happens because of your novel, what will you do? Will you accept your responsibility?'

'Why will something unpleasant happen because of *Lajja*? Something unpleasant will happen because some people want bad things to happen. *Lajja* is a humanist appeal so that unpleasant things don't happen any more. So that people can manage to coexist in mutual respect and to help religion truly embrace humanity.'

'Your novel only has a single point of view. You have given detailed descriptions of riots, rapes, murders and demolition of temples.'

'Yes, I have. Because these things happened. I have not made anything up.'

'Why are there no statements made in protest of the riots by rationalist individuals? Is this a conscious omission?'

'The novel is about the memories, dreams, joys and troubles of one family. I have described the events like how the members of the family saw them happening. The few instances of protest they saw, all those instances are mentioned in *Lajja*. About the human chain, about the protest march calling for communal harmony, all of it. There are accounts of Muslim boys coming to Suranjan's aid. Sudhamoy reminds his son Suranjan that the people of the country are coming down to the streets and that they are protesting. So much has been written in the newspapers too and there are so many people vocally resisting injustices. Does every nation possess such strength? Does everyone get the right to protest? Of course there are protests happening here. You know what, the number of secular rational people protesting and voicing their dissent is far lesser in this country than the sheer intensity of communal violence that people had to witness for seven days starting from 7 December. If my account of the dissent had been at par with the level of violence perpetrated I would have been blatantly fabricating facts. You asked me if it was conscious. Yes, I consciously did it. I wish to write the truth. I do not obsess over who will use my words to serve their own ends, who will get it translated, or who will take advantage of it to spread slander about me.'

'We've heard and verified that you have corrected and expanded the novel. Have events and characters changed because of that? Should we expect a more nuanced picture of the resistance towards communal violence?'

'Yes, I have expanded *Lajja* a little. In essence the story remains the same but a few characters have increased, they have more dialogues and there's more information on the riots, the pain and the suffering. Whatever resistance was there, I've written about that too.'

'Why write it again?'

'I had written *Lajja* within a very small window of time. It was a time when the pain and hurt inside me had been threatening to burst out. Once the book was out I realized there were many literary weaknesses in the text. Can everything be expressed in language? While correcting sentences I thought why not add a few more characters.'

'We believe your intentions are noble. Do you never feel that by giving in to pressure and a moment's emotional turmoil you have allowed yourself to be led in the wrong direction? Like how the non-believing Suranjan becomes a fanatic Hindu, abuses Bangladesh, tries to run away from the country and ends up committing a crime like rape. We have never seen such defeatism in your writing before. Are you giving up?'

'I don't believe in tricks. I witnessed the communal violence in December with my own eyes. *Lajja* is not the fruit of a moment's emotional turmoil. It's a history of our defeat, an account of our collective shame and all our disgrace. For any sensible and rational person this defeat is excruciatingly tragic. Whether a human being like Suranjan becomes a Hindu or someone like Haider becomes a Muslim, both incidents are equally disgraceful. When I saw religion taking precedence over human beings I felt a responsibility to protest. I have been protesting since long before *Lajja*. The book is a bold statement against communalism and terrorism. Suranjan abusing Bangladesh in the book is a severe indictment of the gradual transformation of the country from the brave, self-confident, secular nation of the Language Movement and the Liberation War to a communal and Islamic state. Any conscious and thinking individual, be it a K or a Suranjan, has the right to criticize Bangladesh if they find that the foundational ideals of democracy, socialism, equality and Bengali nationalism are slowly eroding from the state machinery. They are criticizing the nation because they have immense love for it.

'Are you saying they can build the nation but if the nation is about to walk down the wrong path they do not have the right to criticize? A country does not go down a destructive path on its own, a few nasty people drive it down such a road. When these few nasty people instigate the majority to follow them down such a path then the entire country is put into jeopardy and the state doesn't remain a state any more. Suranjan loves his country. Which is why such a turn of events pains him, angers him. Since this is his motherland he demands security and respect from it. Do I want his failure and his escape; do I condone his rape of a Hindu woman? No, I don't. Since I don't want these things to happen I protest his fall and the disasters that befall him. Since I don't want these things to happen I have to write a book like *Lajja*.

'Even I want to ask, why are the Suranjans leaving? Many Hindus from Bangladesh are moving to India and becoming Hindu fundamentalists. Why? Why are talented and loyal citizens like Suranjan feeling forced to leave? Why are they losing the strength and confidence to stay on and fight for what they believe in? That is what I want to know and since the government has no answers to these questions the only thing they can do is ban *Lajja*; to try and put out the fire raging just below the surface with ash. I don't believe in defeat, which is why I was forced to write a book like *Lajja*. *Lajja* is not a solution, it's my protest. I was never a defeatist and neither am I one now. I highlight discrimination because I cannot stand to see it. And I won't stand it either.'

'Do Hindus truly have so many grievances against Bangladesh? Do they actually abuse it so much?'

'Suranjan wasn't like the other Hindus. He did not believe in religious dogma. He was an atheist. But people around him, people with communal objectives, marked him as a Hindu. Suranjan had many dreams regarding his country. But all his dreams shattered and it irrevocably poisoned his heart against his own country. He abused Bangladesh because he was unable to live with the discrimination. Just like there are many Hindus who choose to live with discrimination; they do not have the courage to protest it. You might ask me if I support abuses against Bangladesh. Of course I don't! But why does a person like Suranjan, who used to love his country, resort to such an end? There must be reasons behind such a transformation. Instead of discussing these reasons how do the words uttered by someone who has been deceived by his own people, someone who is angry, hurt and mad with grief, become a bigger issue?'

'I believe the entire subcontinent today is suffering from a terrible ailment. Conscience is under erasure. Or it has lost its bearings? And even you are not safe from such confusion, are you?'

'In *Lajja* my conscience is absolutely clear. Pure. Unblemished.'

Around a week before this meeting the Sahaba Sainik Parisad of Sylhet had issued a fatwa in my name and Baharuddin referred to that too. 'Rushdie did not stand by his own writings. He apologized and read the *kalma* to become a Muslim. Your situation is far more tragic than his. Even the government is not by your side and neither is the opposition. Writers too have taken a vow of silence. Why are you so alone? If your loneliness, as well as pressure from both without and within, forces you to apologize what will you do?'

'I am not alone. Thousands of my readers are with me. Whatever I write is as unpalatable for the government as it is for the opposition because neither side is willing to rise above religion. Religion is a potent weapon for them. Besides, it's not true at all that all progressive writers have taken a vow of silence. Many writers as well as a non-partisan cultural coalition have unequivocally condemned the fatwa-loving maulanas of Sylhet. Even after *Lajja* was banned many writers spoke out against the government's communal standpoint. The ones who did not never speak on behalf of anything ever and neither do they ever take any risks. Not everyone has the heart to swim against the tide; most prefer to run in the direction in which the wind is blowing. I will never ask for forgiveness. Rushdie did, that was his foolishness. I would rather die than ask for forgiveness.'

'In case of danger will you leave the country to go and live somewhere else?'

'Am I in any less danger now? No matter how much more danger is heaped upon me I will not run away from my country. The mullahs have joined forces to demand I be hanged. I am still standing my ground, and I will continue to abide by my ideals.'

'Don't you think the hitherto firm ground for resistance in Bangladesh has come under attack? That you have unwittingly provided the Jamaat with a terrible weapon?'

'No, I don't think the ground for resistance has come under attack. Even when all avenues are blocked, resistance can erupt from a single point. The Liberation War of 1971 proves that. We, the ones who believe in free thought, rationalism and humanism, are still fighting and our fight won't stop. The fact that I have provided the Jamaat with a weapon is something even my enemies here are yet to accuse me of. Only you are saying it. Just like that, whatever the fundamentalists are saying about *Lajja* here, your people are saying the same things over there. We are fighting the Jamaatis who have always been enemies of freedom. *Lajja* is not a weapon for them to rule with, it's a weapon against them. Across the country there is a call for the prohibition of the sort of politics that the Jamaat-e-Islami dabbles in. These merchants of faith receive massive wealth and a lot of weapons from the Middle East, all of which they are passing on to our youth in order to lead them astray. Their student wings are terrorizing the various colleges and universities in the country. We are the progeny of the Language Movement of 1952 and the Liberation War of 1971 and we will not let our land be poisoned.'

Despite everything, a few leftist intellectuals in West Bengal persisted in their condemnation of *Lajja*, though much of their rants fell upon deaf ears, especially after E.M.S. Namboodiripad, the grand vizier of the communists in India, publicly acknowledged that *Lajja* was a valuable book. He congratulated me for speaking out on behalf of minorities despite being a Muslim, his words dealing a severe blow to the confidence with which many had dismissed my book for being substandard from an aesthetic point of view. I was sure Namboodiripad understood its literary merit far better that I. To me *Lajja* remained an aesthetically inferior book no matter what anyone said.

Demon

N*irbachito Kolam* was published in February 1991, comprising columns I had written between 1989 and 1990. Instead of the word 'nirbachito' in the title the book should have probably been called 'prapto' (found); Khoka had only included the columns he had managed to find. Many of the columns were lost and I hadn't ever thought to keep a copy; I had never imagined it was all going to be compiled into a book one day.

After the book was published those who did not agree with it had carried on long debates in newspapers and magazines. A few enthusiastic ones had even written entire books in response. Over time, I managed to get my hands on some of these books. In February 1993 the publisher of Gyankosh sent me a book called *Uchit Jabab* (The Right Answers) by a Mohammed Mokaddas Hossain. In his book Hossain had reprinted *Nirbachito Kolam* in its entirety, added his own comments and responses below each column and made it into a new book. While *Nirbachito Kolam* was still selling well, so was *Uchit Jabab*. The second book cost 10 taka less so obviously it was going to sell well!

The readers were getting my book plus something extra by way of his critical commentary! My publisher also informed me that those who were going to buy *Uchit Jabab* would not have to buy my book at all since almost the entire thing had been reprinted in it. He was concerned about the business side of it, while what I could not get over was Mokaddas Hossain's dishonesty. I wanted to find out about the copyright laws related to books in the country and I decided to ask Nahid for help. Nahid was a law student and a frequent visitor to my house; she was an admirer of my work and came over frequently to see me. It was Nahid who enthusiastically suggested one day that I should sue them. There was no one who knew less about legal matters

377

than I did so I was justifiably a little reticent about it, but Nahid assured me that I would hardly have to do anything on my own in the matter and she promised to get Rabiya Bhuiyan to fight the case.

I was still a little unconvinced; I had heard it took a lot of money to fight such cases. Nahid spoke to Rabiya Bhuiyan and the latter agreed to fight my case pro bono. Rabiya Bhuiyan was a well-known lawyer and had been the minister of law at one point of time. Such a renowned barrister was going to fight my case for free against the publishers of *Uchit Jabab* for the copyright of my book, and I had to do nothing! Obviously, there was no longer any reason for me to refuse. Although it was not long after I had agreed to sue that I noticed a spike in Nahid's requests regarding my involvement—from insisting I go meet the legal team at least once, to small payoffs for the clerks to get files to move, to coaxing me to have a meeting with Rabiya Bhuiyan regarding the case.

It was at the meeting that I learnt that no one else had lodged a case regarding the copyright of books in Bangladesh before me. Apparently everything from bricks, wood, mangoes to dried mango candy had a copyright, except for books. Legally, no matter who held the rights to a book the royalty due to the author did not reach the right person unless the copyright was registered. Bhuiyan sent me to Sher-e-Bangla Nagar to the copyright office of the democratic government of Bangladesh to register my copyright. I put in the application on 16 March and received the final documents on 15 May, after which Bhuiyan wrote the petition herself and began proceedings for my case at the sessions judge court in Old Dhaka. The subject of the petition was the prohibition of the publication, distribution, further editions and sale of the fake book. The logic was simple: I had not permitted any author to copy the entire text of *Nirbachito Kolam* verbatim. They could quote from me if they wished to or if they were looking to critique my work then they could write entire critical tomes like what people like AS had done. The abuse directed at me in the name of critique did not really bother me as much. This was nothing new and such offensive pieces appeared in magazines like *Inquilab* quite frequently. Besides, I was perfectly aware of who was abusing me and why they were doing it, so their words barely made a dent any more, not physically and most definitely not mentally. But how could they steal my entire book?

Nahid's excitement with the case was palpable throughout the proceedings and it reached such a crescendo that I had to relent and accompany her to the court on the day of the verdict. A horde of men in fez caps were all over the court premises. Mokaddas Hossain was present too, along with his followers and his lawyer Korban Ali. Barrister Korban Ali had made it his mission to sacrifice his life to battle me. Whenever there was a report against me in the newspapers one could expect to see Ali's name all over it. He was clearly the perfect person for the defence, absorbed as he was in bringing me to justice.

What happened in the end was deeply unfortunate. The judge did not decide in my favour and my plea was rejected. Mokaddas Hossain did not stop at bringing out a fresh new edition of *Uchit Jabab*, he also began distributing pamphlets containing the appeals made by both parties and the responses to each appeal. One of the pamphlets went thus:

> My dear Muslim brothers and sisters. Beware of this demon in human disguise!! Mokaddas Hossain, the author of *Uchit Jabab*, gave such an answer to that Islamophobic man-hater Taslima Nasrin, who was awarded the Ananda Puraskar by those non-believing foreigners, that her sharp pen has lost all its edge . . . it has left her the recourse of resorting to fake legal cases against *Uchit Jabab*. *Uchit Jabab* has been re-edited, updated, extended . . . and published with more irrefutable rational rejoinders—henceforth, below every column of the controversial *Nirbachito Kolam* you will find the most appropriate and jaw-breaking right answers!

In response to my petition, barrister Korban Ali had this to say on behalf of the defence:

> The defence would like to reassert that they in no way have written their own book with any intention of plagiarizing the plaintiff's repulsive, obscene, uncouth, antisocial, filthy, anti-religious, anti-national book that is replete with tasteless sexual scenarios. Rather, they have in a tried and tested manner made every attempt at giving a fitting reply to such an impudent piece of writing through a stringent critique. The plaintiff has confused the copyright office

into granting her the copyright of this distasteful book even though the publication and distribution of such a book is a punishable offence under Bangladesh Penal Code article 292. In the guise of literary production the plaintiff is attempting to push civilised society to barbarism in a despicable ploy to engender anarchy. In comparison the defendant is, first and foremost, a leading writer and publisher who had earned great renown during his student years for his academic performance and whose reputation as a diligent student earned him government scholarships from an early age. In his Madhyamik School Certificate examination he had created a record of sorts by earning five letter marks, besides star marks and scholarships. He passed ISC with a first division from the renowned Dhaka College and while studying in Dhaka University came to be associated with publishing. He started writing in 1987 and at present he is the successful author and publisher of a number of books like the *Niharika Madhyamik Geography Guide* for classes nine and ten, and the *Niharika Madhyamik General Science Guide* papers 1 and 2. His guidebooks for English and Bengali literature for classes six to eight have been certified by the National Syllabus and Textbook Board. He has forever been preoccupied with ensuring the progress of our people by guiding children and young adults down the right path through a constructive and creative literary education. At present as the assistant general secretary of the Creative Writers' Association of Bangladesh he is dedicated to the betterment of many talented and innovative writers of the country.

The other defendants too were quite highly regarded. They opined:

The plaintiff has not shied away from ridiculing Islam in many of her columns and has even gone so far as to give distorted explanations of things that have been said in the holy Quran and the hadith. She has mocked the holy Quran Sharif, claimed that it was composed by a patriarchal man and has called its followers and readers barbarians and stupid. So dangerous is the plaintiff's recklessness that the democratic government of Bangladesh had to recently confiscate her book *Lajja*. What started initially in Sylhet has now brought together all conscious citizens of the nation in a united demand to jail her and put a stop to all her activities within seven days, or risk a strike in various cities of the country.

In her various columns the plaintiff has repeatedly spewed unnecessary insults and obscenities against men in the name of women's liberation, in order to stir up antagonism between the classes. Not just that, she has not even shown any respect for women in any of her columns and has constantly tried to pollute them. She has repeatedly tried to insult and undermine the Muslim family, society and individuals as part of her nefarious plan. The plaintiff has attempted to push her readers to confusion again and again by challenging naturalized laws and social norms, and destabilizing acceptable boundaries of taste and civility through repeated discussions of all manner of lewd and explicit sexual matters. From the very beginning till the end of *Nirbachito Kolam* she has spewed hatred against the social system that Muslims have established over hundreds of years, and without bothering to show people the right direction she has attempted to lead society to a realm of naked shamelessness and dissolution, with some imaginary liberated female figure at the centre of it all.

She has crudely attacked a man's divinely ordained right to marry more than one woman and as an alternative has suggested women be similarly permitted to have multiple husbands. Not only is such an arrangement a sin for a woman, from a sociological perspective such a suggestion will surely jeopardize the paternity of all men and reduce human life and human civilization, congealed over centuries, instantly to rubble. The plaintiff herself is a key player in this conspiracy. In the same book the plaintiff has argued in favour of the independence of the vagina. The vagina is nothing but a body part through which human reproduction, and by extension the fate of human society, is regulated. Her demand for its independence had directly challenged Allah's natural laws. By committing such an act she has fallen from grace and according to the holy light of the Quran she must be executed just like the cursed apostate Salman Rushdie.

There was nothing I could do against *Uchit Jabab* and the book continued to be sold with impunity. The learned men of the court did not rule in my favour and consign the book to the only fate it deserved. I was made into a demon in human guise while the defendants became messengers of Allah, the greatest creatures in the universe. There was no way I could hamper the business of those so blessed by Allah, especially since His blessings had never quite found their way to me.

Despite the continued vendetta against me in *Uchit Jabab*, I had no time to waste on lamenting about what was right and what was not. I wished to spend my time in other, better ways, by doing something for others. Since I could not always manage to do this the way I wished to, I had to write instead to make up for it. Not that I could always successfully express all my tumultuous thoughts and anxieties in writing either! And how could I not be anxious when women were being dishonoured almost every day, when they were being raped or killed. I wrote about things happening in the country that moved me deeply, made me cry, made me think, filled me with outrage or stirred me with pain. I did not write deep philosophical tracts or information-laden essays; most of my writings were immediate emotional responses and not results of intense research. They were printed as columns in daily newspapers, which were made into paper bags for holding nuts the day after, or in the weekly magazines which found their way to the garbage bin after the week was over. There, fragments and stray sentences from my daily columns mingled with rotting old things . . .

A magistrate named Shahida was murdered by another magistrate, Liyaqat, because the former had refused the latter's proposal of marriage. They were friends and Liyaqat had tried to use that as leverage to force her hand. He had simply assumed that since he was a man she was going to listen to every demand he had to make. Shahida had perhaps refused because she had been an educated self-sufficient woman wishing to make her own choices. But Liyaqat the man had not found that to his liking. If he did not show off the strength of his body, his knife and his manhood, how would everyone know that he was a man! If Liyaqat had managed to marry Shahida he would have killed her slowly, bit by bit, and no one would have noticed her gradual erosion. They would have clucked their tongues and remarked on what a stunning couple they had been. Liyaqat was a man among men and he had done what men were supposed to do. He had murdered a woman in cold blood.

The papers had a field day over how magistrate Shahida was having an extramarital affair and her child was not her husband's, as if all of that was enough justification for what Liyaqat had done. She could have been having an affair. It was entirely someone's personal choice who they were going to allow to access their life and their body. When living women barely had any freedom it was too much to ask the same for someone who was dead.

In Basabo a woman named Nilofer was murdered by her husband. The husband had financial strength and, above all, government support, so he was let off. No matter how big a thief, robber, ruffian or murderer, government backing was enough to throw them a lifeline and help them across. The government had constructed a strong bridge of loopholes for all its devotees, a bridge far sturdier than the Pul-e-Siraat of Allah.

Members of the Women's Council were stridently demanding the death penalty for Khuku. Munir had murdered his wife and he was scheduled to be hanged but the Council was demanding that Khuku be hanged too because she had a loose moral character, she had had an affair with Munir despite being a married woman herself. When the Women's Council began protesting at the court demanding death penalty for her, there was nothing left for me to do but hide my face in shame. Why did she have to die? What had been her fault? She had not been involved in the murder. She had a disabled husband who used to abuse her, a lover who had tricked her, and this helpless girl was vilified by the entire nation and put in jail. Khuku had only been in love with Munir, she had not committed a crime. Was love a crime?

A female passenger on a ferry from Patuakhali was raped. Not by robbers or hooligans on the ferry, or drunk co-passengers. She was raped by the five *ansar*s employed to ensure security for all passengers of the ferry. They forced the twenty-year old Musammat Begum to their cabin and raped her. Even a ferry full of passengers did not deter them from carrying out such an act. How could the ansars—the word 'ansar' means volunteer—who had been employed by the government dare to rape the very passenger they were sworn to protect? How could those in charge of security become the biggest impediment to it? None of the men were punished, obviously.

It was amazing that we lived in a country where both the prime minister and the leader of the opposition were women. Did they never receive the reports of rapes being committed everywhere? Or did it not make any difference to them? Was rape something so amusing for them that they never felt incensed by it? Despite there being a female prime minister in charge of the country, incidents like the murder of housewives, rapes, kidnappings, acid attacks, dowry-related violence and child marriage were commonplace. There were still a plethora of laws prevalent all geared towards suppressing women. If a woman failed to understand the plight of other women then how was she going to serve the people? If those in power failed to stand by the oppressed then for whose benefit had they assumed the mantle of authority? For the rich, the despotic, the self-centred and the sinner?

A gang rape committed by five men was not unheard of; such things were happening everywhere, in villages, towns, cities, roads, ferries, trains, boats and ships. No one was punished for such crimes; rape was not a punishable offence in the country. The top brass and their friends would rather issue fatwas against women and celebrate such declarations with pomp and show. In a country where they could confiscate someone's passport for writing on behalf of women, was it any surprise that it was the politics of fatwas that ruled above everything else? Nothing surprised or shocked any more. We were used to noticing, reading and promptly forgetting startling news in the papers. Nothing caused us grief and there was very little of our conscience left to fall like whiplashes on our backs. We were all aware that when protectors took on the mantle of rapists it left us with very little power to bring them to justice.

Faces in power changed periodically but their natures, irrespective of their genders, remained the same. The girl who was raped by the ansars on the ferry in Patuakhali was labelled a prostitute. As if her being a prostitute legitimized the ansars' right to rape her. Since she was a prostitute the perpetrators were declared innocent. If it had been a pavement dweller instead, the same argument would have been repeated; since she lived on the pavement, raping her was perfectly all right. Rape was made into the victim's fault and it was usually alleged that she had provoked the man into committing rape. That her fluttering eyes, her needless smiles and her suggestive clothes were all responsible for it. Such thinking found heavy traction too in society.

A girl should smile when she wishes to, do exactly as she pleases and wear whatever she wants—why should she have to face rape because of these reasons? I believe in sexual independence. Like other kinds of freedom this too is crucial for human existence. Why should one tolerate someone else trying to control one's body? A beggar, a prostitute or a housewife, if a woman says no then no one has the right to touch her. Thanks to our judicial system rapists often get off easily and time and again the state belittles a woman's fundamental rights as a citizen. In this case, I was convinced that despite such incidents if the women of Bangladesh still failed to unite for a mass movement demanding life imprisonment as the minimum punishment for rape, then there was no recourse left for these senseless women other than surrendering to rape when it happened to them.

I had a regular column called 'Aamar Meyebela' (My Girlhood) in *Jai Jai Din*, where I had once written: '. . . even in a bus, a conductor makes a woman travelling on her own sit with another woman, or at least with an old man or a young boy. Being a man himself even a conductor knows how men are. So he wishes to feel safe by seating the woman beside someone who is infirm or not yet an adult.' The reason I was reminded of an old article was a letter. I usually received hundreds of letters every day and never had time to read all of them. But sometimes some letters managed to shock, or make me think, or even make me cry.

Mou, a girl from Komilla, wrote to me, 'In your latest column at one point you have mentioned that old men are infirm. Not that I doubt it but this reminds me of an incident that had happened to me when I was very young which I want to tell you about. Not because I want to redress it—sometimes you just want to share things with someone. I was in class six. An old man came to our suburban town to put up performances of Shakespeare's plays and raise money. I was to sing a song in one of them. One night after the rehearsals he offered to drop all of us off in his jeep. I was the last one he dropped—perhaps because I was the youngest and also because he wanted to take advantage of us being alone to press his hand against my vagina. Anxious that something more was going to happen I kept counting the seconds we spent in his jeep that night and wishing we reach my house faster.

'The next day he came to our house to teach me the song more thoroughly. Thinking that she was only going to disturb us my mother never came to the room to check in on us. After some time the man suddenly said to me, "My dear, there's something I want from you and you can't say no." He forced apart the legs of the terrified young girl I was and planted a kiss on my vagina. For days after this incident all I wanted to do was simply dunk myself in water and stay there. And I never spoke about this incident to anyone, neither my friends, nor my parents, for fear that they were going to think I was tainted. Till date the sight of a white beard makes me want to throw up and I try to stay as far as possible from their touch in case they insist on giving me their blessings and try something that might make me hate them ever more. Deep within I hope I only have a mother-in-law and not an apparently civilized father-in-law. Whenever I travel somewhere by bus I search for a young man to sit beside and not an older one. I have noticed young men try and get a conversation going and then let it go when they realize the futility of it all. Old men on the other hand, whether asleep or awake, make it a point to stick to your body. Please write about those young girls too who never learnt to save themselves from such so-called grandfathers.'

I read the letter and silently apologized to Mou. I should not have called old men infirm. Men were men, whether infant or old. Just like you could not clean a piece of coal by washing it in water, men's characters too did not change even after they turned doddering old.

~

Inheritance laws in Bangladesh were formulated on religious lines. The discrimination in Muslim inheritance laws could give the impression that mothers and fathers were not equal, nor were sons and daughters, or husbands and wives. What was the reason behind such a stark dissimilarity between them? Why could mothers, wives or daughters not get the same due as fathers, husbands and sons? In turn men and women kept such dissimilarities going and told themselves they were happy and satisfied, when in fact they were simply digging their own graves with others watching them in the act and applauding it.

Since I was not too intelligent I could not feel the same happiness and satisfaction at how property was distributed. I was a much reviled, much abused, violated and helpless woman, and I was not ready to accept such draconian laws. I wanted a fair distribution of property and I could not help but ask if the first female prime minister of the country did not feel the burn of such discriminatory practices. If it stung me why did it not sting her? I was convinced that as a human being, as a woman, as someone who was compassionate, intelligent, honest and dedicated, the burden of such an unequal system was something she too was familiar with.

The accepted narrative was that if daughters inherited their father's property it did not 'suit' them. The only one property suited was boys, as if it was only the penis that could do the heavy lifting. The ones that did not have a penis found property to be a heavy burden, sometimes even a fatal one. Cunning men fooled women into believing such things, depriving them of their rights. When it came to the division of property, the fathers thus benefited much more than mothers did. These tricks had been codified in the sharia which held property rights and distribution in a perennial stranglehold. Consequently, women were never inheritors of property; they were only entitled to leftovers. Quite obviously this automatically made them legitimate right-holders but only as second-class citizens. Whatever was left after things had been distributed among men went to them, just like how in many homes whatever was left after the men had eaten was kept aside for women. Wives, daughters, mothers, sisters, sisters-in-law—this rule of leftovers was uniform for all. Besides, there were a thousand social impediments even when it came to staking claim to what was left and often the tried-and-tested argument would be repeated again: property did not suit women.

I was convinced that steps had to be taken to ensure that property suited them; the solution could not lie in giving everything away to men. If wealth was to be distributed *equally* between fathers and mothers, sons and daughters, husbands and wives, everything was going to suit everyone. Otherwise, the government which made all the laws was not going to suit us for long. Hindu inheritance laws were worse. Women did not even feature anywhere in issues of inheritance. The role of women was restricted to being the perennial donors, who could never expect anything in return, with the general assumption being that women had no use for property of their own. She had three caretakers all her life: her father, her husband and finally her son. Society in general was not too keen on independence and self-reliance for women and all its efforts were directed towards keeping women as destitute, helpless and alone as possible.

Hindus in Bangladesh still relied a lot on their scriptures, not that Muslims were any less at the mercy of their own holy treatises. It is an inherently erroneous thing for laws to be premised on religious differences and it only foregrounds how progress and religion have always been antagonistic. If laws cannot rise above its base inclinations then neither can man, and religious differences in the case of laws are a sign of that disgrace. For human beings to truly call themselves civilized their laws have to be civilized too. In Bangladesh's case it was imperative that strict laws be drafted at the earliest for many of its coarse, uncultured, not-so-modern people, to ensure that there remained no differences between men and women in cases of inheritance, marriage, divorce and custody of children. Everyone had to be equal before the law, whether they were Hindu, Muslim, Christian or Buddhist.

Many read my articles on the inheritance laws of the four aforementioned faiths and remarked that it was all too complicated. When I asked some women who held similar views why it was complicated they confessed they did not understand much about these things. Obviously they did not understand! If they had understood they would not have been so content with what they had, which was essentially handouts. In fact, so content were they that I could not figure out if they had sensed my sarcasm. But they did leave with the request that I stop writing about such difficult things as inheritance and write more about how to beat up men. No one wanted to get into complex issues related to inheritance. Neither did they feel it was 'right' to take up a tape to measure percentages, or fight with their own siblings over property. In effect the men were brothers, so what if they got everything!

Besides, if they appeared too keen on their father's property people were going to call them greedy. The father had fed and clothed them and now the husband was performing the same duty; everything was fine. So what was the point in fighting over the father's property like a hussy? This was the mindset of most middle-class and upper-class women around me. Obviously, the lower classes did not possess land to claim, and even if they did, the brothers usually had no qualms beating any desire for inheritance out of a woman. How long were such injustices going to go on? How long were our foolish, gullible, cheated girls going to believe that their fathers' property was only meant for their brothers and not for them, that all they were entitled to were the dregs? When were they going to realize that all children had equal rights to their parents' property? Because women were fullyformed individuals who were in no way less dear, less precious or less deserving than men. The day they were going to realize this truth they were going to step beyond the inheritance laws, go up to their parents and demand they be given their fair share. They were going to assert that they were not born to only give, that they wanted a hundred per cent of what was due to them. It was not as if only half an egg and half a sperm was required to make women, so why the discrimination when it came to property?

Men spearheaded many a progressive movement but not once did any of them utter a peep about inheritance and property laws. It was something they were not comfortable tampering with and I knew many a revolutionary social crusader who had cheated his own sisters in matters pertaining to property. Such men would get agitated over any alterations in the state machinery but when it came to variations in the sharing of land or property they were nothing but calm and never agitated. For them it did not matter if nothing else followed the sharia as long as the inheritance laws did. That and marriage, since the sharia permitted a man multiple wives. Whatever had to be done had to be done by women. Women were going to have to create advantages and opportunities for other women and remove impediments from the path of other women to make their way ahead smoother. In our society it was easy for a Golam Azam to be born, but not so much an Ishwar Chandra Vidyasagar. Hence polygamy persisted and property laws too were inherently discriminatory. Women had to become their own Pritilata Waddedar, Leela Nag and Begum Rokeya, and their water-like calm hearts had to flare up like a hundred flaming powder kegs for any change to happen.

There was a new rule in the works whereby a husband would have to get legal permission from the courts to be able to marry for the second, or third, or fourth time. Earlier, men only had to seek permission from the already existing wives. I failed to grasp how this was supposed to be beneficial for women. Was it so difficult for men to convince the courts to allow them to do something? Neither courts nor court orders were difficult things to acquire if one had the necessary resources. If new laws were being thought of why not rethink the entire custom of allowing men to commit polygamy in the first place? Or was that too bold a step to ask for? Did every law have to be geared towards making men happy in one way or another? If a bill had to be passed then it had to cut out the court permit nonsense and summarily prohibit polygamy right at the outset. We did not want token amendments; we wanted a complete revision of everything that was decayed and crumbling in society. We wanted civilized laws, humane laws and not religious, false and offensive laws any more. If a demand for rice was met with a few paltry crumbs we were prepared to go without in protest. The time of being content with nearly nothing was over and we wanted what was owed to us and all that we deserved.

It was men who had once invented iron chains to protect women's chastity. It was men who had forced women atop burning funeral pyres to prove their purity. Men were still coming up with horrifying plans every day for the same end. By forcing a world of rules and regulation on her they were keeping a woman's chastity for themselves. What used to be done with a suit of armour previously was being achieved by social pressure. Society was telling women to stay indoors, to seek their husbands' permission whenever they wished to step out, not to mingle with other men, and risk talaq or even death if they paid no heed.

No man had the right to put a woman's body in chains and keep the key; a woman had the right to her own body. Just as a woman needed financial independence she also needed sexual independence without which no other kind of freedom—economic, social or political—amounted to anything. The very idea of a woman's sexual freedom was revolting to those who believed a sexually liberated woman was as good as a whore. If earning one's complete freedom meant being called a whore then that was a better fate than remaining a man's slave for life. Sexual autonomy was just like any other kind of autonomy; a woman was going to be called a whore no matter what freedom she wanted to achieve. If women were to extricate themselves from such historical conspiracies they had to pursue complete physical and mental liberation.

~

A new trend was doing the rounds, of randomly using words like 'inshallah', 'mashallah', 'subhanallah' while speaking, words I had stopped using no sooner than I had developed some sense. In fact I never used the traditional greeting 'Asalam walekum' or the traditional goodbye 'Khuda hafiz' either. Instead of such foreign words I used our more familiar Bangla greetings. Allah and Khuda were on everyone's lips but did repeatedly uttering the name ensure His blessings? I did not believe it did. Instead one had to be honest, conscientious, kind-hearted, tolerant and rational. Only then could humanity hope for goodness and benevolence for both themselves and the world in general.

I had nothing but rebuke for the people who called our state a democracy. The first condition of any democracy was its complete separation from religion. Without fulfilling this necessary condition, to call oneself a democracy was surely a way to fool an entire people. There were limits to being despotic but the government was flouting such limits time and again and one was beginning to feel the need for the sort of public awareness and dissent witnessed against similar conditions back in 1990. People needed to come out on to the streets again for the sake of a secular nation. Like locusts to crops, the maulanas were destroying the villages of golden Bengal. If they were not uprooted in time then all of Bangladesh was soon going to be reduced to massive ruin. None of our cries and laments were going to amount to much then and one had to be vigilant while there was still time. The fatwa brigade was already at work in various villages across the country, serving fatwas to women who were trying to become self-reliant and making them outcasts. The new generation had to solemnly swear to ensure the exile of such fatwa-crazy maulanas; I was still alive and still proud of my country probably because I hoped that one day the fatwa brigade was going to be wiped off the face of Bangladesh.

Most progressives were of the opinion that all our problems were going to be solved with the eradication of communalism. They also maintained that there was no problem with religion per se, people were free to follow their own faiths and Islam could remain the state religion, as long as communal politics was no longer at work. I could not place much faith in their deductions because I firmly believed that communalism was a problem that was going to persist as long as there was organized religion. If you let a snake loose in the house and then placate the people inside saying you have asked the snake not to bite can that even make sense? In our case, if the snake was not biting that did not mean it was not going to at some point of time in the future. It was what a snake did and there was no way of changing its nature by 'explaining' things to it. Did pruning the leaves and branches of a poisonous tree ensure its poison had been neutralized too? No, it did not. We could not hope to eradicate communalism by simply cutting down the tree, until and unless the roots were destroyed along with it. Religion was at the root of communalism and unless we managed to deracinate it entirely communalism as a problem was not going away any time soon.

~

Around this time Boromama was a frequent visitor at my house. He no longer had his job at the Soviet embassy. He had been in charge of the international page of *Bhorer Kagaj* for the longest time but that too was over and done with. The newspapers were not keen on the way he wished to talk about international news; it was hardly surprising that they found it difficult to agree with a staunch Marxist and communist like Boromama. He was more like a freelance journalist and all his articles were usually published under a pseudonym. One day he came across a book titled *Taslima Nasrin'er Islam Bidyesh o Opobyakhya* (Taslima Nasrin's Islamophobia and Misinterpretations) in my study, written by two well-known Islamic scholars. The back cover of the book had a description in bold letters of the punishment ordained for a Muslim for insulting Allah and the Prophet—one had to chop off the offender's right hand and left leg with a sword from behind, and then their left hand and right leg. Having read a few pages of the book Boromama expressed interest in reading the entire thing and borrowed it from me.

When he came to return the book he also brought along the latest issue of *Dainik Sambad* where a critical review of the book had been published under his real name. He was a scholar of Islam and had used the tenets of Islam to attack not just other Islamic scholars but all those believers who held the Quran and the hadith in the highest regard but did not follow its tenets when it came to their own lives. About the various politicians in the country he had observed that although such people often preached how Islam was an entire way of life and how in religious gatherings they were always quick to advise people to live by the tenets of the Quran and the hadith, in their own daily lives and ways of thinking and actions none of these teachings were anywhere to be seen. On the one hand they wore shirts and trousers, which were the garments of non-believers, but in an Islamic gathering they were quick to change into more religion-appropriate outfits, right down to the fez cap, despite being clean-shaven! Both the Islamic hadith and the Bukhari hadith clearly stated that it was *wajib*, a pious duty, to keep a beard, and haram, a forbidden sin, to shave it off! If they were so fixed on Islamic ideals why did they commit such sins!

Since they are government officials they go to the religious events of other communities as chief guests and say things in praise of such faiths. But according to the Quran and the hadith all other religions except Islam are unacceptable! According to Islam is it allowed for them to show mercy to other faiths or attend their religious events to get better acquainted with them? The Quran and the hadith say, 'Those who attend suchlike will be counted among them and will face the same *hashr* (exile or banishment).' In the Quran Allah Himself is heard saying, while describing the characteristics of the *mumin* (believer), 'Muhammad is the Prophet of God, those on his side are as firm with the non-believers as they are lenient with each other (48.29).' In another *ayat* (verse) Allah declares, 'They are indulgent with the mumin and severe with the kaffir (5.54).' In yet another verse He instructs the believers, 'Take not the kaffir as your friends (4.144).' Why are the critics silent about these things?

In one section of *Taslima Nasrin'er Islam Bidyesh* the Islamic scholars had opined:

> The word 'namaz' that Taslima Nasrin mentions is a Farsi word. In the entire Quran and the hadith sharif there is no mention of such a word. Instead the word that is used is 'salat'. After the Night Journey, Muhammad decreed that Muslims perform the 'salat' five times a day.

In response Boromama had written:

> The critic has pointed out something extremely valid. Namaz is of course a strange and confusing foreign word. It would not have been wrong to use the word 'Quran' instead of 'namaz' for 'salat', because even in the holy Quran in one particular ayat the word 'Quran' has been used twice to mean salat. In fact in ayat 78 of sura (chapter) 17, the word 'Quran' is used to mean the salat of *fajr* (dawn prayer). But where were the expert critics all this while? For a thousand years the Muslims of the Indian subcontinent, Iran, Afghanistan and Central Asia have mistakenly used the word 'namaz' for salat like Taslima has, and right from the instruction manuals for prayers to the lakhs of books written on Islam the word 'namaz' has been used. Be it on television or radio every day the word 'namaz' is used multiple times before the azan (call to prayer) to declare that He is the Lord of all. Why is the word *sawm* not used, why is 'roza' used instead? The word 'roza' can be found nowhere in the Quran or the hadith. Besides, where did they find words like kulkhani, 'chehlam', 'Fateha Doaz Daham', 'Fateha Yazdaham', 'Akhari Chahar Somba'? Is the word 'Musalman' even in the Quran or the hadith? The word 'Musalman' is a distortion of the word 'Muslim'. The word 'Muslim' means 'one who submits', someone devoted, but what does the word 'Musalman' mean?

There were quotations in the book from prominent scholars and writers of Islam like M.N. Roy, A.G. Arberry, R.O. Nicholson, Dr Maurice Bucaille, all of whom were praised highly in *Taslima Nasrin'er Islam Bidyesh* and whose books I had been asked to read. At this Boromama had observed:

Despite being highly approving of Islam they had not converted and as such remained kaffir. Rather, they said one thing but practised another in their life, and made a ton of profit out of it. Why do Taslima's erudite critics insist on suppressing this point?' The book had also alleged that since I had mentioned certain hadiths in my work without providing any references, or stating if the said hadith was true or fake, they were unable to discuss those particular references in detail. They had then alleged that I did not have a particularly thorough knowledge of the hadith either. Boromama had responded to this too. 'But if the two experts in Islam themselves had been particularly well informed in the matters of the hadith then they would have surely been able to point out exactly which of Taslima's references were fake.

When I had read the book the first time there were minor details I had missed but Boromama had pored over every detail.

If not mentioning the proper references to the hadiths is an instance of Taslima's academic dishonesty, then one wonders if the erudite scholars have thought to protest the broadcast of the hadith every day over radio and television throughout Bangladesh without ever mentioning the source. Or have they thought to protest how right from the time of Pakistan the media has systematically blacked out many a significant ayat of not just the hadith but also the Quran? The radio and the television channels keep broadcasting those ayat which tell people what to do and what not to do, but they never broadcast the ayat which instruct the powerful administrators, lawmakers and judges about their duties. For instance, cutting off the hands of both male and female thieves (5.38); punishing both the adulterer and the adulteress with a hundred lashes; 'Let not your mercy for the two influence your ability to mete out the punishment decreed by Allah, if you believe in Him and the hereafter, and let a group of mumin be witness to the punishment (28.2)'; 'Those who do not obey what Allah has decreed are kaffir' (5.44)—many such ayat are never broadcast and despite being obligatory these decrees by Allah are not implemented in the state or society. Of course, hasn't Allah

Himself said, 'The edicts and the path I have laid out as right for
humans in the Book, despite they being clear beyond doubt, those
who seek to obfuscate, Allah's *lanat* (curse) will fall upon them,
and so will the lanat of other sinners (2.151).'

While critiquing the book Boromama had not stopped at simply
refuting the arguments of the authors and responding to their
questions with more difficult ones of his own. He had gone on to
make a few pertinent observations about the new breed of people who
were trying to pass off as modern by claiming 'I believe in religion,
but I'm not communal', and who were constantly trying to foreground
the many good things said by Allah by quoting some good lines from
the Quran.

These days you are not communal if you believe in and adhere to
some specific parts of the Quran, but if you are to believe in and
implement some other sections of the same Quran you risk falling
prey to communalism. Some self-proclaimed protectors of Islam
do not wish to be seen as communal, they are ashamed of such a
label. However, they feel no shame at all in breeding and fostering
a horde of ills, untruths and contaminants within Islam, because
at least that does not earn one the sobriquet communal. But the
Quran itself decrees that one has to believe in the Quran in its
entirety. 'Do you then believe only a part of the Book and cast aside
the rest? Those who do so must suffer ignominies in this earthly
life and the harshest punishment on the day of Qiyamat (2.85).'
Belittling or ignoring a part of the Quran is as good as belittling
or ignoring the whole book. For such people the Quran decrees,
'They are the ones who through thoughts and deeds wish to say
they believe some parts and reject the rest, and truly these are the
kaffir (4.150, 4.151).'

These arguments about believing in the Quran would have perhaps
made many a fundamentalist very happy with his views. His aim,
however, was not to please the fundamentalists, but to displease the
'I believe in religion, but I'm not communal' brigade, the intellectuals,
political scientists and sociologists who were eulogizing religion while

condemning fundamentalists for communal violence in the same breath. Both Boromama and I were of the same opinion on this—that such people were far more dangerous and harmful than regular fanatics.

According to the basic tenets of Islam the Quran has always been and always will be immaculate, irrefutable and beyond suspicion; it is unchangeable and its clear dictums are unalterable. If someone is to censor sections of the Quran or if someone tries running the administration and the judiciary using modern laws imported from the West instead of the clear laws laid out by Allah in the Quran, such people are not to be considered Muslims according to the holy book itself. It is in the Quran that one finds words like kaffir (5.44), zaalim (5.45) (the oppressor) and fasiq (5.47) (impious or depraved).

His critique had ended with an important observation.

Twenty-four years under Pakistani rule, between 1947 and 1971, and eighteen years since the disavowal of secular ideals, from 1975 till date—for forty-two years Islamic tenets have not been put into action and Muslims in this country have been systematically duped by a state religion and cries of 'Bismillahir Rahamanir Rahim'. Those who have spoken in favour of Islamic laws and Islamic principles have been tagged as fundamentalists. During Ershad's rule while the bill to instate Islam as official state religion was being passed the Prime Minister had said in his closing speech at the Parliament, 'This bill is being tabled as a counter-measure against fundamentalism.' Were these mumin Muslims or merely Muslim name-bearing followers of modern Western thought, disciples of Mohammed Ali Jinnah, Sir Syed Ahmed and Sir Muhammed Iqbal? At the end of the day what these modern merchants of religion were doing was pruning the poison tree of communalism while simultaneously watering its roots, thus helping it to grow and flourish.

I agreed with Boromama absolutely. I had always been aware he was an atheist but I had never known religion was his weapon of choice to combat communal con artists and that his weapon was exceptionally strident. We had never discussed religion prior to this incident and it was only recently that we had managed to read each other's work and develop an interest in each other's ideas. Whenever he came over he would head straight for my study. I was in the middle of writing a new book, *Koraner Naari* (Women in the Quran), about all the ayat in the Quran that were about women along with my own critical commentary on them.

Since Boromama was a scholar of Arabic I showed the piece to him. He had the Quran at the tip of his fingers; he knew its verses by heart as well as their interpretations and could even translate it word for word. He went through my manuscript and pointed out a couple of mistakes. I had used the Bengali translation of the Quran by the Islamic Foundation, the Bengali version of the Quran published from Calcutta by the Islamic Foundation Trust, besides the translation by Maulana Maududi, to help me navigate the Arabic text, but knowing the language always helped in unearthing many more things. Since Boromama knew the language so well he could easily tell which Arabic word had been muted in translation by a particular translator to produce a more moderate interpretation of a particular verse. 'When you beat women beat them gently, and spare the face'— reading something along these lines he laughed and pointed out that nowhere in the Quran was the advice for 'gently' beating present; it must have been an addition by the translator.

The older the Bengali translation, the higher were the chances of accuracy. With the passing of time, with rapid modernization and growing clamour over women's rights, Islamic scholars who were desperate to foreground how women were being given their due dignity in Islam were also the ones trying to suppress Allah's cruelty while translating the Quran. As if Allah would appear more benevolent if it could be shown that He had asked for women to be beaten gently! Unless one knew Arabic such expert interventions by contemporary scholars were not easy to discover. Boromama took the manuscript home with him to check more thoroughly if there were any mistakes in the translations of any of the verses and came back a few days later with more edits. One glance at the manuscript was enough to understand that he had put a fair bit of effort in it.

We spoke about the Satanic verses. The twenty-first and twenty-second verses of the sura An-Najm had been expunged from the

Quran and replaced with new ones, because Muhammad had claimed later that the verses he had originally uttered were words Satan had put on his tongue. Satan had whispered the verse to him in his ear and Muhammad had failed to discern whose voice, Allah's or Satan's, it was; or Satan had taken hold of his tongue or his mind and the Prophet had sat in front of the Kaaba Sharif . . .

I asked Boromama what the Prophet had said. 'Have you thought of Al-Lat and Al-Uzza and Manat, the third?'

'This is in the Quran. So which bit was removed?'

'"These are intermediaries exalted whose intercession is to be hoped for." That's twenty-one, and twenty-two goes, "Such as they do not forget". These two ayat were later rejected as the Satanic verses and replaced with "Are yours the males and His the females?"—the sons for you and the daughters for Him? This is then a fraudulent distribution!'

I could not hide my astonishment.

'Al-Lat, Al-Uzza and Manat were considered the three daughters of Allah by the people of the Quraysh tribe. Their God was called Allah. That's where Muhammad took the name from, from the pre-Islamic polytheists, who believed in a multiplicity of gods.'

'Why did Muhammad wish to show respect to the three daughters of Allah?'

'Back then, according to the Islamic scholars who were writing Muhammad's biography in 800 CE, people like Al-Tabari, Al-Wahidi, Ibn Sa'd, Ibn Ishaq, Muhammad did not have that many followers in Mecca and most had deserted him. Wishing to bring the Quraysh into his fold he sought to mention their three chief goddesses. And truly, the Quraysh people were quite happy with him for that . . .'

'So when did he alter the verse?'

Mother entered the room just as I finished the question and we fell quiet. She looked at both of our faces and asked, 'What are you two talking about?'

Almost on cue Boromama replied, 'We were talking about her studying in PG. She could have become a professor at the medical college!'

Distinctly pleased, Mother asked sweetly, 'Do you want tea?'

'Yes. That would be lovely.'

Mother went off to get tea and the conversation returned to the Satanic verses.

'In the fifty-second and fifty-third verses of the sura Al-Hajj, Satan is mentioned again. Muhammad is informing Allah that all the Prophets and messengers Allah had sent prior to him had fallen prey to Satan.'

Mother suddenly appeared at the door. 'What are you two talking about?'

'Nothing much, just like that,' I responded weakly.

'I heard Allah and Muhammad!' She turned towards Boromama with a snarl. 'What are you teaching Nasrin?'

He got up and headed towards the exit, with me following suit. 'What is he going to teach me? We were just talking!'

'Tell me what you two were talking about? What were you trying to teach my daughter?' Mother's eyes were raining fire on him while he was looking at everything but her—the artwork on the wall, the curtains, the doorknob.

Mother's voice was rising. 'Why are you bent on destroying her? Don't you see what is happening in the country? Don't you see the giant processions? Don't you read the newspapers? Despite that you advise her to write against Allah? Do you not want to stay alive? They can kill her any day! Believe what you will but don't mess with my daughter. You give her these warped ideas and she writes such things. You are influencing her to write against the Quran and against Allah.'

I had to intervene at this point. 'I am already messed up, there's nothing new to mess up further.'

His face pale, Boromama replied, 'I have not said anything bad about Allah. The ones who do business in his name are the ones who say bad things. They are the ones who use Him for their own dishonest motives.'

Boromama did not have tea that day. He was supposed to have lunch with us too, but that did not happen either. Having remembered some urgent work, he left. After that whenever he visited Mother would warn me in advance not to discuss the Quran and the hadith with him. One Friday, Boromama came over again.

Taking off the cap that he was wearing and tucking it into his pocket he said, 'These days mosques are so packed there's hardly any space to read the namaz.'

'Are you coming from the mosque?' Mother's voice was soft.

'Yes, from the Jumu'ah prayer.' Her face brightened instantly and a smile appeared.

I could not help laugh out loud. 'Why are you laughing?' he asked seriously. 'What's there to laugh? I read the namaz five times a day.'

I only laughed harder.

'I don't know what's going to happen with Nasrin,' Mother lamented. 'She's not going to find place even in hell! People change. If a man like him can understand the folly of his ways, ask for forgiveness and read the namaz, why can't you do it already?'

That day Mother affectionately fed Boromama rice and fish. Burping after the heavy meal he peeked inside my study and, quite deliberately, said in a loud voice, 'Why now, you can't spend the entire day only writing! Gynaecology is the best field for you to do your specialization in. Being a doctor you will be able to serve many more people much more effectively.'

'That won't happen any more, I'm afraid.' I was about to ask my next question almost immediately—'The man called Abdullah that Muhammad had executed after winning Mecca, was it the same Abdullah who used to edit the verses uttered by Muhammad? The one who had renounced Islam later because he had begun to wonder why Allah's words required editing at all?' But Mother entered the room just then, her face glowing. 'You must convince Nasrin to start reading the namaz every day.'

Boromama agreed. 'Yes, that she should. Especially now that she is not getting too much movement or physical exercise. The namaz at least guarantees a regular workout.'

Mother did not take kindly to that advice at all.

She wanted me to read the namaz but when I read the Quran it terrified her. I could be reading the Quran sitting at my table, would leave it open and go for a little walk, and on returning I would find the book gone. Or I would fall asleep while reading in bed and wake up to find the book missing. Finally one day I recovered the Quran from Mother's cupboard where she had hidden it.

'Why do you keep hiding the Quran Sharif?'

'Why do you keep reading the Quran Sharif?' Her face betrayed her anxiety.

'It's good to read the Quran Sharif. Brings *sawab* [merit].'

Annoyed, she spat out, 'You are not reading it for sawab.'

I laughed. 'Shush, don't say that to anyone! If Allah finds out you are stopping someone from reading the Quran then He will instantly cast you into the deepest pit of hell.'

'Let me go to hell, you try and get to heaven.' Mother sighed.

'Don't worry about that. I have had contact with Allah. Paradise is guaranteed for me. The other day Allah told me my name is number four on the list bound for Jannat ul Firdaus [the highest point of Paradise].'

'That's good, then. If you are bound for Paradise.'

'Yes. You will burn in the fires of hell and I will be in heaven. I will have to entreat Allah to bring you to Paradise too.'

Unable to continue, Mother burst into tears. 'Nasrin, I beg of you, don't write anything against the Quran. The Quran has done nothing to you. It's all the mullahs, so write against them.'

Unable to see her cry, I turned away.

I often found Mother kneeling on the *janamaz* (prayer rug), hands raised in munajat (supplication), eyes closed, muttering and sobbing. Eavesdropping on her muttered prayers one day I heard: 'Allah, I pray do not turn my daughter into a kaffir. Allah, I pray free my daughter from the company of the kaffir. Allah, I pray grant my daughter Paradise. Allah, I pray grant my daughter good sense and wisdom. Allah, I pray do not turn my daughter's heart into gold coins.'

All I felt was a surge of kindness for Mother.

Resignation

The police had taken my passport away at the airport and told me to retrieve it from the Special Branch office in Malibag. So the very next day I went to the office as instructed, only to discover that none of the officers seemed to know anything about my passport at all. I went back again the day after and then again the next, but each time returned with the same answer—they did not know anything!

'I was asked to collect my passport from here. Give me back my passport.'

'It's up there. When they send it back you can have it back.'

'What do you mean up there? With whom?' I looked up in bewilderment at the stacks of old papers on the ancient wooden racks all around and above us.

'Oh, not there, not *up* there!'

'Then where?'

The kurta pyjama–clad man smiled and replied, 'The home ministry.'

'Oh, the home ministry is *up* there for you, is it? So who will send it back from *up* there?'

'The ones up there.'

Within a couple of days I wore out the soles of my shoes travelling to and fro from the Special Branch office but this was the only answer I ever managed to extract from them. My passport was *up* there somewhere. Unable to devise any other way of getting my passport back down to me I decided to write an application directly to the home minister requesting to have my passport back. Unsurprisingly, I received no response. Besides, what would have been the point of getting my passport back? I had to get an official ex-Bangladesh leave to be able to go anywhere. I had written to the health department about that and was going there myself every day to inquire. However, the director general was either too busy or unavailable every time I asked to see him. So one day I sat in front of his office for hours till he had no choice but to meet me.

'Yes, what do you want?' He was perusing me over his glasses.

'A signature.'

'What signature?'

'It's been some time that I have put in an application for an ex-Bangladesh leave. I want a signature on that.'

'I can't sign that.'

It was as if someone had thrown a stone aimed directly at my heart. The pain travelled from my heart up my throat, threatening to spill over from my eyes. There was no way I was going to be able to attend the programme in Calcutta.

'Why can't you sign?' I had to ask.

'I can sign only when I receive word from up there.'

'From where?'

'From the health ministry.'

'Do other doctors need approval from up there too for you to sign their applications?'

The director general took off his dark glasses. It was clear I had asked an unsettling question and his voice hardened as he replied. 'No, no one else requires permission. But you do.'

'Why do only I need permission?'

He leaned over a piece of paper on his desk and said, 'You know very well why.'

'No, I don't. I want to know why there are separate rules for me.' I kept my gaze fixed on his face hoping for a reply.

His chin rose a fraction. 'Then do one thing. Keep asking yourself that question and you will get an answer at some point of time.'

'Why do I need to look for the answer myself? You have made the rules, so you have to tell me why.'

Pretending to not hear me he looked around at the others sitting in the room and suddenly began a conversation with one of them. 'How have you been? How's everything there? It's so hot isn't it! Ha ha ha!'

The 'Ha ha ha' had not finished when I asked again, 'Why is the health ministry not giving me permission? What's wrong?'

Turning towards me, his slack jaw suddenly tight, he opened the file in front of him, picked up a copy of my application and said, 'Whether I sign it or not how does it matter? Your leave is not just a health ministry issue, it's a mainly a home ministry thing. If we don't receive clearance from there you won't get leave.' The only file on the table was mine and for my life I could not understand why my file should be so important to the department. It was not like he had searched for the file after I entered the room to meet him; it had already been there in front of him. Every doctor of the department had a file to their name which contained papers related to their recruitment and transfer. When he opened the fat file in my name to show me the application, I noticed much to my astonishment copies of some newspapers and magazines inside. Why were they inside my file?

I kept visiting the health department at Mahakali over the course of the next few days, immediately after finishing my shift at the hospital. After returning home late in the afternoon Mother would take a look at my downcast face and ask, 'Why do you return so late these days? You only had a couple of biscuits in the morning. I'm sure you haven't eaten anything today', before running to the kitchen to get food for me. Somehow I would manage to satisfy my hunger and go to bed, to wait for the next day so I could visit the health department again and receive the same disappointing answer as the day before. To get permission one had to go *up* there, but when I tried to do so I was not granted entry into any of the places, neither the health ministry nor the home ministry.

There was a news report in *Inquilab* alleging I had tried to go abroad with a fake passport, accompanied by a picture of my passport. The report demanded that the government take the strictest steps against me. I did not have my passport, so how did *Inquilab* manage to get their hands on a photo of it? It clearly meant the newspaper had clout within the home ministry. The home minister Abdul Matil Chowdhury had been a Razakar in 1971 and used to guard the Kanchpur bridge as a member of the Pakistani army during the Liberation War. He was a minister in the same nation against whose independence he had once fought. The Razakar invasion of the administration had begun during the time of Ziaur Rahman and continued till the situation became such that the brave muktijoddhas of yesteryears were left to languish in hospitals for the disabled, while the Razakars were in charge of the ministries and the wealth.

A sliver of unease crept up my spine and settled right under my skin. *Inquilab* knew very well the passport was not a fake. They could perhaps ask why I had chosen to mention journalism as my profession. But everything else—my name, my father's name, my height, address, age, even the black mole over my left eye—was mentioned in the passport and none of the details were false. In fact my choice of profession was not a lie either. I was a journalist too and since it was something I preferred over being a doctor I had chosen to mention it instead. While demanding punishment for me the people at *Inquilab* did not stop at the fake passport story only; much more space was expended on excerpts from my writing about religion, the two Bengals, and various other things I had written on the communal nature of the government. Since I had a habit of writing disparagingly about such things it was deemed the moral duty of the government to announce exemplary punishment at the earliest and vindicate the nation and its people. The people at *Inquilab* were also helpful enough to suggest what the exemplary punishment ought to be: hanging. *Inquilab* was Maulana Mannan's newspaper, the same Mannan who had been a known Pakistani sympathizer back in 1971 and who had over time reinvented himself as a media mogul. My feelings of uneasiness would not let me rest. They dug inside through my skin and spread to my heart, my lungs, my blood and every cell in my brain.

I could not stop going back to the health department again and again despite there being no news regarding the approval of my ex-Bangladesh leave. On one occasion the director general told me quite decisively: 'You won't get leave.'

'Why won't I?'

'Because things are being written against you in *Inquilab*, that's why.'

I failed to fathom if it was the paper *Inquilab* that was making all the decisions of the ministry. Any decisions pertaining to me could only be taken by the health department. As a doctor if I had failed to adhere to any of the rules of the department then whatever punishment I deserved could only be pronounced by the department and not by *Inquilab*. Nevertheless, I did not need the ex-Bangladesh leave any more. The programme I was scheduled to attend in Calcutta was over and my fellow poets were all back home.

~

In order to get my passport back, in order to earn back my rights as a citizen, I went back to the Special Branch office in Malibag again. I found Abdus Sattar, the official who had informed me about my passport being 'up there', reading a book. He had a red pen in his hand with which he was underlining sentences from the book. In one corner of the table there was a stack of every book I had ever written. Seeing me he did not bother to keep the book he was reading aside. Nonetheless, I pulled up a chair, sat down and asked, 'What about the passport? Has it come back from up there?'

Without getting into the 'up there' business he replied, 'The investigation is on.'

'What investigation?'

'I have received orders to read all your books. And note all the places where you have written offensive things.'

'How are my books related to my passport?'

A ghost of a smile appeared on the corner of his lips before disappearing in a flash. No answer was forthcoming. A while later he said, 'You have gone too far with religion!'

'What do you mean?'

'You have written so much nonsense. Why do you write such things?'

'I write what I believe. But how is my writing related to me not getting my passport back? They can't be related, can they?'

Abdus Sattar did not bother to answer my question but I did receive an answer at the health department. The director general smiled sweetly at me and exclaimed, 'Ah, the great writer is here! Come, sit down!' Ignoring his jibe I took the chair he offered.

He was still smiling. 'I read your columns in the newspapers.'

The only thing I could say to that was a soft 'Oh.'

'So how do you write?'

'As in? Previously I used to write by hand. Now I write on a computer.'

'That's good, you write on a computer now. You don't just write columns, you write books too, right?'

'Yes, I do.'

'Did you take permission from the government?'

'What do you mean?'

'All this writing that you do, these columns in the newspapers, do you write without the government's permission?'

A furrow was beginning to crease my forehead. I could scarcely believe what I was hearing! 'Does one need the government's permission to write?'

'Of course! You are a government employee, how can you write stuff without government permission! You can write if you want to, but at home. You need the government's approval to get anything published.'

'Is this a rule?'

'Yes, it is.'

'But there are so many writers who write in magazines or write books, they aren't taking permission!'

'How do you know they aren't?'

'I know.'

'No, they are.'

As a piece of long-nursed hurt broke off and reached my lips I found myself asking, 'Can you tell me how one can take permission for such things?'

'Whatever you want to publish, you have to first submit it to the government for approval. When the government says, "Yes, we permit you to print this", only then can you get it published. Very simple.'

'Is this rule only for me?'

The director general threw me an unfazed smile and said, 'No, why should it be only for you? This rule is for everyone.'

'If I publish without permission what will happen?'

'Then you are breaking the law. You must know what happens when someone breaks the law.'

I could well understand that he had been instructed to tell me all this from 'up there'. He was merely relaying their decision to me. Light-headed and not wanting to speak to him any longer, I walked out of his office, took a rickshaw from the Mahakali crossing and headed home. Once home I did not wish to speak to anyone. I refused the food Mother brought me and took to the bed, to lie there and stare out of the window. Just beyond the window clouds were floating past, headed to some unknown destination. Wasn't flying around without an address such a wonderful way to be? Or did they too hanker for a home somewhere? Suddenly agitated, I got up from the bed, unable to calm my pounding heart. I began to pace from one room to the other restlessly, went to the balcony to stand and stare, though I barely saw anything. Everything seemed empty, as if there was nothing except the vast sky overhead and me underneath it all by myself. I wanted to scream and cry but the tears would not come. Even though no one else noticed what I was going through, Mother did.

'Nasrin, what's happened?'

'Nothing.'

'Something's definitely happened. Tell me what it is.'

'Don't irritate me. Nothing's happened.' My voice was harsh.

Mother went quiet.

She handed me a glass of lemonade which I drank in one gulp before going back to the bed and curling up like a dog. Mother sat beside me and put a hand on my head. Passing her fingers through my hair, drawing patterns as she went, she asked softly, 'Why are you so restless? If you are sleepy then sleep for a while.'

I sighed and answered in a forlorn voice, 'Ma, I might have to stop writing.'

'Why would you have to do that?'

'They have issued an order. And they have figured out this new rule. I can't write if I wish to keep my job.'

'I have told you so many times to not write about religion. You were writing about oppression of women, wasn't that good enough? Why did you have to criticize religion? You never listen to me. What will you do now? Tell them you will not write against religion any more, or anything against the government.'

I was sleepy. Mother's words seemed like they were coming from far away.

~

I had two clear choices in front of me—writing or my government job. I had to choose any one, so I chose my writing. Without telling a soul, without consulting anyone, while still in the employment of the best medical college hospital in the country, I did something outrageous. I drew a sheet paper and wrote on it:

> Respected Director General,
> Health Department, Bangladesh
> Janaab,
> ~~It is my humble request that~~ I, Taslima Nasrin, consciously and of my own volition, wish to resign from my post as a medical officer in the anaesthesia department of the Dhaka Medical College hospital. ~~Please accept my resignation and oblige.~~ I hope you will accept my resignation at the earliest and free me from ~~stifling~~ government employment.

I finished my resignation letter, signed it and personally delivered it to the health department office. Of course, tendering one's resignation was only half of it; one had to make sure it was accepted too. Despite going to the office again and again I failed to get any piece of paper that certified that my resignation letter had been officially accepted. With the certified acknowledgement I could prove that I was not a government employee any more and demand they give me back my passport.

Father was devastated by the news of my resignation, convinced that his daughter had finally lost her mind and everyone else at home too thought the same. Whoever heard what I had done was shocked into silence, as were most of my friends. And in all fairness, it *was* a ridiculous thing to do! A government job was not easy to come by, and once you were a government employee, losing the job was as difficult. People were willing to pay lakhs as a bribe even for a government job of 500 taka. Even if you were absent for months on end, for years for that matter, no matter how slack you were in your job, a government job was a permanent thing. It was the biggest security anyone could hope for and here I was tossing away such a job, that too of a first-class gazetted officer, on a whim! Without pausing to think twice that was exactly what I did.

Meanwhile, I chanced upon a report in the papers announcing the recruitment of a new doctor in my old post at the Dhaka Medical College hospital. Obviously, it was good news since it meant they had accepted my resignation. They had let me go, which was the only thing that could explain why they had declared my post vacant. If I was not occupying that post, then where was I? I had not been transferred, so the only way a doctor's post could be vacant was if I died. I was dead to them, which could only happen if they had let me go. Then why were they not telling me, 'Here, we release you, you are now free from all our plotting and scheming and the filth, and all the nefarious and devious complications!'

I did not receive any letter to that effect and neither did I get the salary owed to me for my final few months at the hospital. To get the money I went and petitioned at the revenue office, but to no avail. I also sent a copy of my resignation letter submitted to the health department, along with the newspaper report about the new doctor hired to fill my vacant post at Dhaka Medical College, to the home minister, with a fresh application for the return of my passport. I was no longer a government employee, I was a completely non-governmental citizen. At long last my profession was exactly what it said on my passport. So it was only fair they returned it to me. Nevertheless, not a word arrived from the ministry about any of my requests. I wanted my passport back not because I wished to go abroad but because it was my constitutional right as a citizen. I wanted it back because they had violated my right and taken it from me unlawfully and even more unlawfully they were not giving it back even after I had left my job. There was no one to hear my outrage, though. Seeing no other way I went to the passport office to apply for a fresh passport but even that request was turned down.

~

One day, some time before the government banned *Lajja*, Nahid, the law student, told me she knew someone, a supporter of the Jamaat who was also close to the bigwigs in the government, who could arrange for her to meet the home minister at his house at around eight in the evening. Nahid requested him to arrange the meeting for her hoping it would be the perfect opportunity for her to talk to the minister directly about my passport. It all sounded good on paper. Nahid set off for the meeting with a copy of the application I had written, only to come back in about two hours with despair etched all over her face.

'Boss, he tossed aside your application.'

'What?'

'Yes, and he said, this woman writes against religion. She writes horrible things against Allah. Not only will I not give her back her passport, I will also ban *Lajja*.'

'He said that?'

'Yes, he said it, and then he laughed loudly.'

'You didn't say anything?'

'I did! I asked him why he wanted to ban *Lajja*, if there was anything objectionable in it, and he said yes. I argued that it was just facts, facts you didn't make up. But he said, "Be that as it may, even if a few Hindus were slapped around or abused somewhere, or a few fences caught fire, is it right to report such things? These bloody malauns[36] will get encouraged."'

Nahid lit a cigarette and extended one towards me.

'No, I don't want to smoke.'

'Oh boss, take one. You're anxious. This will help.'

No one at home liked Nahid, especially because she smoked. Not that I was very fond of cigarettes myself, but Nahid usually insisted on lighting one up while sitting in my room and then coax me to take a few drags. Even when I hated her calling me 'boss' she insisted on using the term. Nahid was a very brave girl and I have always liked brave girls. She would set off for her house in Narayangunje at odd hours, that too by bus. I would ask her, 'Doesn't it scare you, Nahid?' 'Boss, talking about fear doesn't suit you. Why should I be afraid? If someone tries anything'—her hands would clench into fists—'I will lay them out flat.' The sixth finger on her right hand, unable to fit inside the fist, would usually flail helplessly. Nahid never wore saris, preferring kurta-pyjamas and stoles instead, and sandals. This was a must for her, as was the lack of make-up on her face. Whenever she had time she would come over to my place and say, 'Boss, is there any work? Tell me, I'll do it for you.' If there was work she would help, or else she would simply hang out and start singing loudly.

As promised, *Lajja* was eventually banned. The home minister cackled and declared, 'I'll ban the rest of her books too.' The enemy of our country's freedom was also in charge of our lives and a writer's freedom to write what she wished to and her freedom of expression were being crushed under his corpulent ass.

I had thought a simple resignation from my government job would be enough to free me from government ire too, and give me a chance to write freely and in peace. Obviously, even that was too much to ask! Despite becoming a non-governmental entity the administration maintained a strict watch over my movements and my activities. One day two officers from the Special Branch turned up at my place in Shantinagar. At first I did not want to open the door, but when they began banging on it and shouting, 'Open up, we're from the police', I had to relent. Holding my fear at bay I opened the door and the two men marched in boldly, as if they were at some bosom friend's place. They went from room to room, switched on the fan in the living room, pulled the curtains on the windows aside and settled themselves comfortably on the sofa. One of them had a faint smile on his face while the other's brows were severely crinkled.

Mr Brow spoke first. 'Do you have a copy of *Lajja*?'

It seemed someone had poured a glass of cold water on me. Of course I had a copy of the book! But since it was illegal they could arrest me if I told them I had one. For a moment I was unable to decide whether I should lie or tell them the truth.

Instead I asked, 'Why? Why do you want to know?'

Mr Brow said again, 'I need a copy.'

'It's illegal to possess a copy of the book!' I was facing Mr Brow while Mr Faint Smile was to my right.

'Do you have a copy of the book?'

'No.'

'Are you telling the truth?'

'Yes, I am.'

My answer did not betray what I was feeling inside and my eyes were fixed on their feet. If they were to walk into my study they were obviously going to find the copy of the book. I had answered their question without even pausing to think about what was going to happen if they did. If only Mother had heard our conversation and managed to hide the book somewhere! As I made a move to get up from the chair Mr Brow stopped me, 'Where are you going? Sit.' I had to sit down with a ton of discomfort and distaste weighing on me. A niggling fear too settled somewhere deep inside my gut.

The middle-aged Mr Faint Smile intervened. 'Why is your book still being sold in the market?'

'My publishers are not selling it. Neither do they have any copies any more. The police took away everything.'

'But it's still being sold! Why?'

Gravely, I answered, 'How do I know why or how it's still being sold?'

'You are supposed to know!'

My jaw tightening, I replied, 'I have written the book. I am the author. But I am not responsible for selling it. Go ask the ones who are selling it why they are still selling it.'

The tiny sliver of fear within me vanished entirely, leaving only the discomfort and distaste behind.

Mr Brow began, '*Phera* . . .'

Pouncing upon the word immediately Mr Faint Smile asked, 'Why did you write *Phera*?'

'What do you mean why did I write it? I wrote it because I wanted to.'

Phera (The Return) was a long story I had written recently. Dulendra Bhowmick had asked for a new novel for the special Puja issue of *Patrika* (The Journal), but when I could not develop a novel I had written a long story, actually a novella, which was published as a novel in the journal instead. *Phera* had already been published as a book in Bangladesh but was yet to be published in West Bengal. I could send my books for publication as soon as I finished them because the Bengali font I used for writing on my computer was the one that the publishers in Bangladesh used too. So once I gave them copies of my writing in a diskette they simply had to send it straight off to the press and there was no need to compose and proofread it further. For Ananda Publishers everything had to be done from scratch since they did not use the same font. *Phera* was about a young girl from East Bengal, who had been sent to West Bengal for her own safety, returning to her homeland after three decades. The novella was a description of everything she witnesses during her visit. The police wanted to know why I had written it and I could tell they were not happy with my answer.

Mr Brow continued, 'Who asked you to write *Phera*?'

'What do you mean?'

'Someone must have told you to write such a story. Who was it?'

'My publishers keep telling me to write. But the names, the plot, all of these are solely my decisions. That I write on my own.'

'*Phera* could not have emerged from your head. Someone must have told you.'

'No, no one asked me to write it. As I said, I decide what I want to write.'

'Do you know any of the characters in the book? As in, do you know a woman called Kalyani?'

'No.'

'Then why did you write about a Hindu woman named Kalyani returning from Calcutta to see her old house and land?'

'So strange! It's a story!'

'So you made it up? Nothing like that happened?'

'Authors imagine their plots, don't they?'

'But there has to be a connection to reality. Isn't there one? Or can anyone imagine anything bizarre and write it?'

Mr Faint Smile asked, 'Has the novella been published in Calcutta?'

'Not as a book.'

'Then how?'

'As a long story in a magazine.'

'Which one?'

'*Patrika*.'

'As in, what is the name of the magazine?'

'*Patrika*.'

'What do you mean?'

'I mean the magazine is called *Patrika*.'

'Hmm. Do you have a copy?'

I was burning with rage. All I wished to do was throw the two men out. The loo blowing in from outside was only fanning the flames.

Mr Brow probed, 'Do you have a copy?'

'No.' My reply was rather forceful.

'Why do you write about Hindus despite being a Muslim?'

'I was born in a Muslim family. I don't believe in religion.'

I said this with enough force and the moment I uttered the words I could feel the weight of the remaining distaste and discomfort being lifted off me too. As if I was finally breathing in the fresh air after being inside a locked vault for the longest time.

Mr Brow asked, 'You don't believe in Islam?'

'No.'

'Do you believe in any other religion?'

'No.'

'What about Hinduism?'

'No.'

Mr Faint Smile interrupted, 'Then why do you write on behalf of the Hindus so much?'

'Because they are human beings. I don't see religion, I see human beings. If someone is being oppressed for no reason I try to stand by them. That's it. That's all there is to it.'

Slamming the door on their departing backs I turned around to find Mother standing in one corner, her face pale. 'Why did you tell them you don't believe in religion? Now they will create even more trouble for you.'

'Let them,' I said and walked away.

Mother pulled out my copy of *Lajja* from underneath three layers of mattresses, tore it to bits, and while disposing it in the garbage bin in the kitchen declared, 'There's no need to keep such a book. Who knows when they will arrest us and take us away saying we have the book!'

I had a copy of *Lajja* in my computer so I did not feel too bad about the book being destroyed. It was good in a way. At least I would be safe from attacks. They let me be but not entirely. Mr Faint Smile often called to ask about me and how I was doing. Once, during such a conversation he made sure to let me know that he only wanted the best for me. During that very conversation he asked, 'Did you, in a recent interview to *Aajkaal*, say that religion should be abolished and marriage should be abolished too?'

'Yes, I did. So?' I replied tersely.

'The home ministry has ordered an investigation.'

I sighed and hung up. They were investigating even the statements and interviews I was giving, basically in a quest to create a boundary for whatever I wished to say or write. There was going to be an investigation every time I overstepped. Files were going to be opened in the ministry and they were going to gorge on information and grow fat day by day. The police were constantly keeping a close eye on me in the meantime, so much so that it became impossible for me to try and differentiate between a normal person and a policeman in civil clothes. But even if I failed to grasp their presence I was told by many others that sleuths were always hanging around my house. However, what it was they wanted or what they got was entirely beyond me.

I had assumed moving from Shantibag to Shantinagar would bring me a measure of peace. But the sleuths followed me like shadows wherever I went. If it was only the police it would not have been so difficult, but no sooner than I moved into the new place that an entirely novel set of troubles began. Every few days someone or the other would turn up at my door demanding a donation for some committee. I was not interested in being part of any committees so there was no question of any donation but the other owner members informed me that it was something I had scant choice in.

There were four huge buildings within the complex, each building ten floors tall, comprising forty apartments and 160 families in total. That was quite the number and a committee was necessary in this case to ensure everything required to maintain such a large community was taken care of. So that there were no robberies the committee was supposed to ensure there was round-the-clock security and that all the guards were being paid their salaries regularly. It was also supposed to maintain other services like get the elevator repaired on time, employ a gardener, make sure the guards wrote down the names and addresses of drivers coming from outside or driving them away if required, keep the corridors clean, get someone to take out the garbage, ensure salaries of all monthly employees, install and maintain dish antennas, maintain the apartments and get repairs and paint jobs done as and when required. In fact, there was no end to the amount of work that needed to be done.

Zahirul Islam, the owner of Eastern Housing Estate, was not going to take care of all this; having sold off all the flats in the complex his job was done. The ones who had bought the flats and were going to be living there were the ones responsible for their smooth running. A handful of enthusiastic homeowners had come together to form the committee with elections scheduled every year to elect a new board of members. The aforementioned duties were not the only things the committee had to take care of; there were elaborate future plans too. There was going to be a laundry, a bakery and other shops adjacent to the garage downstairs. What I gathered in the end was that the committee was meant to serve all the needs of the one hundred and sixty families living inside the complex. Silently I accepted their stipulation of a contribution of 1200 taka per month and even went to the committee office one day to get acquainted with the secretary, Shafeeq Ahmed.

Before I could introduce myself he exclaimed, 'I know you!'

'Have you seen me anywhere?' I asked.

'No, I haven't but I keep seeing your photos in the newspapers and all. This is the first time I have seen you up close, though!' Throughout the exchange a congenial smile remained fixed on my lips that held a stray shadow of apprehension at bay. I generally did not have to introduce myself anywhere any more and I was not sure if that was a good thing or not! In my heart I knew very well that it was not a good thing at all.

I had to refuse the next demand of the committee straight away. It was impossible for me to give them money to build a mosque. I told them no one from my house was going to go to the mosque and there was no way I was giving any money for it. However, all my protests fell on deaf ears and Shafeeq Ahmed himself came to talk to me. A simple man of average size in a white shirt, black pants and black shoes, Shafeeq Ahmed was a harmless, decent man. He owned a pen company and, perhaps because he was a business owner, had a lot of time to spare which he gave to the committee. He had been a muktijoddha too and he told me he quite liked some of my writing, especially when I wrote about the country's struggle for independence.

'Everyone is paying for the mosque, you should too. The mosque is being built, it needs money to be completed.'

'What is the need for a mosque inside the complex? There are many mosques in this locality. Those who want to read the namaz can go to those mosques.'

'But there was always a plan to build a mosque inside the premises!'

'You need money to build anything else, you can ask for it. But I will not give any money for construction of a mosque.'

'How will it harm you, paying for it?'

'How does it benefit me?'

'Even if there is none! It's meant for everyone. All of us have to live here together, don't we? Everyone's paid, except you.'

'Your mosque will not get held up if I don't pay. If you want to build it, please go ahead, I can't stop you. But I have no faith in mosques and I will not pay for one either.'

Shafeeq Ahmed finished his tea and left without a word.

Not that this brought me peace. The committee wished to organize a Milaad Mehfil and wanted contributions for it. I told them right at the door that I was not going to go to the Mehfil and neither was I going to pay for it. Then they came with a demand for contributions to an iftar party. I told them I did not want to eat the iftari, so I was not going to pay. A Shab-e-Baraat programme too I similarly refused to pay for. At the same time I did not hesitate to pay whatever sum they asked of me for organizing 21 February and Victory Day celebrations.

~

Two weeks after our conversation about the mosque I received a phone call from Shafeeq Ahmed. He asked me, 'Who is K?'

'K? Why? K is my friend.'

'Does he come over to your place often?'

'Yes, he does. Why, what's happened?'

'There's talk.'

'Where?'

'At the committee.'

'What talk?'

'They are saying you have an illicit relationship with K.'

I laughed out loud. 'What is our relationship, whether it's illicit or not, is this within the committee's jurisdiction? What gives the committee any right to try and enter my bedroom?'

'I am not saying all this. I am simply letting you know as a well-wisher. This is all Zubair Hussain's doing. He is the chief engineer of Eastern Housing, he has an apartment in Building 2. He's also the president of the committee.'

'He can do whatever he wants. He can say whatever he wishes to. I don't care.'

'You might receive a letter.'

'What letter?'

'To ask you to refrain from doing anything illicit in the apartment.'

'Whatever I do in my house is my personal matter.' I hung up. I had no desire to talk about this any more.

A few nights later I received another call. Shafeeq Ahmed informed me that the president was hell-bent on taking action against me. He also had the support of a number of people. Ahmed also informed me that it was within the committee's rights to assess if anything illicit was going on anywhere and take appropriate action.

'What are you implying by illicit?'

'For instance, if the owner of the house uses it for prostitution. It happens quite often. What if an owner is letting a prostitute and her client use the place and making money out of it? The committee then has to evict the person.'

'How will you evict the person? They are the owners of the flat.'

'It's a rule. They are obliged to sell the house and leave.'

'I am not running any prostitution rings in my house. Why does he wish to take action against me?'

'They think you are doing something illicit. I am merely a well-wisher, don't misunderstand me. Tell K not to come over any more.'

I protested immediately. 'No, I will not do that. K is unimportant here. It is entirely my decision who will come to my house, who will stay over, who can come in and who can leave. It's not something the committee can decide. This is my last word on the matter. This is the minimum freedom guaranteed to a human being and I am not going to give this freedom up.'

'They will send a letter.'

'Let them.'

'First warning. Then a second warning. Then a third. And then an eviction notice.'

'Let them do whatever they want. I will also see how they plan to evict me from my own house.'

I hung up with a clank, my breath shallow and rapid. My own house, bought with my own money, and they were plotting to throw me out! Earlier I could not rent houses. If I could not stay in my own house either, where was I supposed to go? They had pushed me against the wall and there was nothing else to do but turn around and resist. Where did they want to push and kick me to now! How much more damage did they want to cause? I paced my balcony restlessly, these thoughts racing through my mind.

I had lovingly decorated the house after buying it, picked the tiles for the kitchen, done it up entirely with modern kitchen cabinets, put in a big slab of marble where all the prep for cooking was to be done, put in heavy floor-length curtains on all the doors and windows, bought a wooden sofa for the living room, a new bed for the bedroom and a big teak cupboard too, had a huge book rack installed all around the study wall and stacked it with books, and put my computer on the table.

I had decorated my house as per my tastes, spent as much as I could afford to spend and invited my friends over for a housewarming. My restless life had finally found certainty, a place where it could rest, having invalidated social dictums that claimed it was impossible for a woman to survive or gain a solid footing in life without a husband. What no one else in my entire clan had managed to do, I had done it and that too as a woman. Just when I was beginning to stand tall with immense self-confidence, they were planning to throw me out! Which gutter were people trying to drag me into next? It seemed they would not rest until I was dead once and for all. If I had to survive in their society I was supposed to choke the life out of my independence; I was not going to be allowed to hold on to my own ethics! Every cell in my body vibrated with rage at the thought and all I could think was how if I had a revolver I would have shot that man named Zubair.

Zubair Hussain continued to keep a silent watch over me. Even though his flat was not in Building 1 whenever I had to get on the elevator there he would be, the neatly dressed white mongrel, his piercing gaze trained on me. One day both K and I were in the elevator and so was he. No sooner did he see us than his nostrils began to flare in anger. That day K had parked his car in the guest parking spot. Zubair Hussain was there and he asked K to move his car somewhere else because, as he put it, it was not in the right place.

'Why? This is an empty spot. What's the problem if I park my car here?'

'There is a problem.' The security guards conveyed Zubair's indication to K.

'Tell me what the problem is.'

Zubair was screaming. 'You cannot park your car here!'

'Why can't I?' K's voice was rising too.

'I will see you . . . Yes, I will see you too.' These heated exchanges went on for a while between the two. In the end K had to park his car on the road. Zubair was far more influential than K, and insulting the latter, who was my guest, was akin to insulting me. Zubair Hussain was desperate to drive me out, but despite whatever he tried neither did I give them money for the mosque nor did I ask K to stop coming over.

~

Mother was alarmed. 'You resigned in such a huff. What will happen now? Whatever savings you had were spent in buying the house and the car.'

'Did I buy these things on a whim? I did not have any other choice.'

'If you don't have a job how will you manage all this?'

'You don't have to worry about that.'

I managed to turn away from Mother's worried face but the concerns had already begun circling me like vultures. No publisher owed me any more money and neither was any royalty due from anyone. Rather, I was the one obligated to finish the writing projects I had committed to and it was going to take me a couple of years to finish all the books and pay off all my debts. Besides, it was not as if I could finish writing whole books in only a couple of days. Neither could I force myself to write unless I knew what I was going to write. My words required time to organize themselves of their own volition. I could never scold them or beat them into forming sentences for me. The fact of the matter was that I was not a writer. Whatever I had written thus far had been possible because there had been no other way to exorcise the feelings churning inside me without giving them an outlet. I would often cry while writing. While writing about a woman's sorrows, I would find myself in tears as I imagined becoming my own creation and feeling the pain she felt. It had happened while writing *Phera* when I had felt I was Kalyani. Sometimes the pain would become so intense that I would stop writing and curl up with my pillow to weep.

While writing *Nimantran* (The Invitation) I was the young girl who had accepted an invitation from her lover only to be deceived and gang raped by him and six of his friends. Crying, choking on my tears, I had described the rape as if I was the one who had been violated; I could swear to have felt real pain. Having finished writing her journey back home after the ordeal, her decision to tell her father the truth about where she had been, that she had gone on an invitation, I had leaned over the page and cried my heart out. While writing Jamuna's story in *Aparpakkha* I could feel Jamuna's presence deep within me. When she had conceived her child and declared to the world that it was her child, not someone else's and definitely not any man's, it had seemed to me as if I was the one who was carrying a child that was only mine, growing inside me nursed with love. While writing *Sodh* (Vengeance) I became Jhumur, and after vengeance had been exacted from her husband Haroon, a smile of satisfaction like the one she must have smiled had hung on the corners of my lips for the longest time. In *Bhramar Koio Giya* (Let the Bee Tell My Tale) I was the girl who had left her impotent scoundrel of a husband's home and ignored all social censure to fight for an independent life on her own.

I was not a writer. I could not time myself into a ten-to-five schedule and write. No orders or requests that I had to sit down to write could ever make me. Of course, I did write many columns without too much effort and did some commissioned writing too, mostly because I needed the money and had no other choice. But there was no life in such writing. Since I was not a writer my sentences were not always correct and neither were my articles devoid of spelling mistakes. Since I was not a writer I could not describe things properly either. I was aware of my limitations though. In the literary world my experience was akin to that of a peasant who has been picked up from a farm in a village and dropped off in a metal processing plant. Despite not having the credentials, being a writer had somehow become a part of my identity; from a minor component of my life it had gradually grown to occupy a place of significance. I was no longer a writer who wrote during leisure, at least not since I had left my job. There was no way any more to rid myself of this identity.

I owned a house and I did not have to pay rent any more, so I had expected that costs would go down. However, my calculations showed that I was spending more than before. The electricity bill, telephone bill, gas bill, the committee maintenance, the driver's salary, in all it added up to quite a bit. Regardless of my wishes my uncertainties settled on me like a cloak. As usual, Mother was trying to save my expenses. There was no need for her to get things from our old house in Mymensingh, thus keeping open the possibility that someone might one day confront me with the lie that I could never have survived without Father's help. I even explained this to her time and again but try as I might it failed to make a difference. She would go to Abakash to plead with Father and get household things for me—in one haul she brought back a portion of rice from the share we received from the farm in Nandail, a bottle of soyabean oil, some onions and garlic, some lentils bundled in a gamchha, two laukis, some parval and four coconuts from our own tree. She would travel by bus with all this baggage, in the forbidding heat, her skin sticky from the sweat and her sari sticking to her. That is how she had been on this particular day and I did not have the heart to confront her and demand to know why she insisted on getting things from Abakash.

Often the smallest things appear bigger than they really are. At the same time, neither could I get rid of my stubborn resolution that I was not going to live off someone's pity. My financial condition was in dire straits and I could sense that very well. I had resigned from the government job but that did not mean I was no longer a doctor. I began approaching private clinics in the city to see if any of them needed a doctor. Almost all of them did and they were ready to take on even the most inexperienced doctors, like the ones fresh out of medical school. With my experience in gynaecology, obstetrics and anaesthesia, and my long work experience in two of Dhaka's most prestigious institutions of medicine, Mitford and Dhaka Medical, I should have been a catch. And in many ways I was. Hearing my credentials the administrators of many private clinics could scarcely hide the excitement in their eyes. The other shoe usually fell with the next question they asked me: my name. As soon as they heard it their faces turned pale and they invariably asked me to leave behind my details, address, experience, etc. on a piece of paper, or a formal letter of application, with a promise that they were going to consult internally and get back to me. Suffice to say no one ever got back. I was rejected as soon as they saw my name even if they were desperately in need of doctors. I was reduced to a forbidden name.

~

Yasmin had been after me for the longest time to get her a job somewhere. She had cried and insisted a number of times even though there was no way in which I could help. A woman with a master's degree in botany, with good marks and honours, had no job prospects in our country! She had applied to the schools and colleges of Dhaka for a post as a teacher of botany, but to no avail. Entry into such places required the blessings of someone in the upper echelons of power; we did not have such acquaintances, nor did we have relatives who were influential. Yasmin's disappointment at her constant setbacks was palpable. Having assumed that I had numerous connections both Yasmin and Milan depended on me to help them get jobs. Milan was no longer happy with the thankless clerical job he was doing at Adamji Jute Mill and wanted me to help him find a better one. And there I was, having given up my own job and completely unsure how much I was going to be able to help them! Since I had no influence I requested some of those who were close to me to see if something could be done.

It was finally the kharaj addict K who brought news of a new job for Yasmin. Quite honestly I had never expected K to come through at such a time—he was usually quick on the promises, but failed to keep them or did not bother nearly 99 per cent of the time. He would promise to drop by one morning and then never turn up, with days passing or sometimes even a week, without so much as a hello; and then ten days later there he would again be at my door in the evening. Consequently, despite his promise that he was going to look for a job for Yasmin, none of us had been entirely confident in his ability. Besides, our experience with Motaleb had also taught us to be wary of any job K might arrange for her. In the bread factory where he had arranged for a job for Motaleb, my cousin had not even lasted seven days. Every night he had witnessed the owner of the factory getting drunk and beating up workers without any reason. Motaleb had packed his bags and bid the job farewell.

Still, despite our misgivings, K told us about the new job. He was not too excited about it, since he was sure we were going to dislike it and reject it immediately. Just as he had suspected, on hearing the offer the first thing I said was, 'Impossible. This job won't do. See if there is any other job, especially one where she can use her botany degree.' I was convinced Yasmin was going to agree with me too. The job entailed being the private secretary to a garments mill owner. She would have to take calls, connect people to her boss and keep the files and papers in order. Had she spent so many years earning her botany degree for such a job? However, to my utter shock and dismay, Yasmin declared, 'Whatever it is, I'll do it.' While all I could do was stare helplessly at my sister, Milan agreed with Yasmin. 'Bubu, let her do it. These days no one gets a job in the field they have studied. People are becoming bank accountants with a degree in chemistry! One of my friends studied physics and did not get a job anywhere. Now he is a teacher in a madrasa. People get MA degrees in Bengali literature and then take up supervisory posts in factories. What can people do, Bubu? There are no jobs. People do whatever they can manage to get their hands on. Let her do it. If she gets a better offer later she can always leave this one.'

I was unemployed. Yasmin lived in my house with her husband and her child. Almost all of Milan's salary was spent on the baby. They had no savings that they could afford to spend on running the house. Such a life was so painful for her that no matter what sort of a job it was, considering how rare it was to get a job, Yasmin did not hesitate to accept the offer. She would leave for her office in the morning and return in the afternoon, for 2000 taka at the end of the month. To her it was a princely sum. Soon I noticed Yasmin had begun to dress up more before going to office. She would wear brightly coloured saris, put lots of kohl in her eyes and paint her lips stark red. Not particularly happy about it I could not help but ask her about it one day. 'Why do you deck up so much?'

'Why? Is there a problem if I do?'

'Is there a problem if you don't?'

'Everyone does it, so I do it too.'

'You never used to deck up like a ghost before. What's gotten into you?'

'Nothing's happened. You don't have to worry about what I am doing.'

She finished and walked out in a huff and I was left behind to sigh and feel lost. I could understand that she was only trying to secure her job with such tactics. The talent that she possessed was not what was required for the job of a private secretary; what it required was beauty and physical appeal. She was only blatantly trying to prove to her employers that she had what it took to be good at her job, so that no one in her office could accuse her of being ugly and unattractive and consider laying her off.

Fatwa

Protests against me were becoming increasingly frequent across the country. Posters had been put up on the boundary wall of Abakash and also on the walls of Arogya Bitan. 'Come together in a movement against a fallen woman, a sexual fiend and sinner, an anti-Islamic atheist like Taslima Nasrin.' As if a game had started with me where anyone could say anything they wished since there was no one to stop them. Besides, it was not as if I was part of a political organization which was going to defend me or crack their heads on my behalf.

I came across a news report that in an open public address in Sylhet, Maulana Habibur Rahman, the chairman of the Sahaba Sainik Parisad, had declared a price of 50,000 taka for my head. Whoever was going to hand over my head to the maulana was going to receive the sum as reward. In Bangladesh, 50,000 taka was not a small amount and I did not pay too much attention to the report initially. Every day there was something or the other against me in the papers so there was no reason to give special credence to a news item in *Banglabazar Patrika*. Besides, Motiur Rahman Chowdhury, the journalist behind the report, had been after me for the longest time and I was convinced the report was something he had fabricated. So I tossed the paper aside and concentrated on what I was doing. However, a little later something forced me to pull the paper towards me and read the report again.

Motiur Rahman Chowdhury was from Sylhet and perhaps knew more about the region than any other journalist in the business. He had published the news of the fatwa in an inset box on the front page of the newspaper. It was not a rumour because it was important enough to have made the front page. In an instant it seemed like ice was spreading through my veins. There was a movement against me, I was being abused in the mosques after the Friday prayers nearly every week, leaflets were being distributed and posters were being put up, unspeakable things were being said about me in public meetings, protest marches, Waz mehfils and other Islamic gatherings where I was being chewed up and spat out with every new vicious accusation. I was unmoved by all this, especially because I was aware that the right to offend was a democratic right too. But how could they declare a price on my head? Who had given them the authority to do such a thing?

Maulana Habibur Rahman had also called for a half-day bandh in Sylhet demanding my hanging. I was confident there was going to be no strike because of a random organization like the Sahaba Sainik Parisad. Unless it was a big political party calling for a general strike such calls were hardly ever successful. So one could imagine my surprise when I found out that the intended strike was a success. Sylhet had been shut down, all the shops were closed and no transport was available either. What was the reason behind the strike? The people of Sylhet wished to see me hanged. Even if the government was not willing to take such a step it did not matter to them. There was already a price on my head, so anyone could take up the offer to chop my head off. I pulled the curtains closed in all the rooms so that no one could shoot me from outside and stayed inside, trembling with bated breath in the darkness. In the end, it was Ahmed Sharif who convinced me that this strategy was not going to work in the long run. He called me and asked, 'What arrangements have you made?'

'Nothing. I'm just sitting at home.'

'How is that helpful?' he admonished. 'Don't you see what is happening! You must immediately make arrangements for police protection.'

'Police protection? How do I do that?'

'Write to the Motijheel police station. Tell them that a price of 50,000 taka has been declared on your head and you require security. I am sending someone over who will take your letter to the police station.'

Ahmed Sharif was a professor in a university, a philosopher and an author, and a staunch critic of religion; the mullahs had once taken to the streets demanding his hanging as well. Sharif was well aware that these mullahs had influence much beyond the mosques. He had once invited me to a weekly discussion session held at his house to discuss possible ways of exposing the despicable schemes of such charlatans. There are some erudite people whose mere acquaintance, even a chance at basking in their reflected glory, is enough to rid one of the most stubborn misconceptions. Sharif was one such person and encouraging words from such a wise man were like blessings to me.

Sharif sent a man named Gaznavi who took my letter to the Motijheel police station. A couple of days passed which eventually extended to a week, but I received no word from the police about security. I was effectively house-bound and stayed frozen in fear nearly the entire time. Everyone at home was told to never open the door to a stranger and the guards downstairs were instructed to always make sure to talk to me via the intercom before letting anyone come up. This was already an existing protocol but I requested them to be extra careful, without going into too many details about why I wanted security to be tightened. One good thing was that I had bought a car immediately after buying the house so I did not have to risk my life by taking rickshaws. Otherwise, on many an occasion, I had faced people shouting and running in pursuit after recognizing me while travelling by rickshaws.

'See, there she goes, Taslima Nasrin!'
'Catch that bitch! Catch that bitch!'
'Get her!'
'Drag her down from the rickshaw! Beat the shit out of her!'
'See, there goes an atheist!'
'The slut!'

I was certain they would not have hesitated to drag me down from the rickshaw and rip me apart if they had managed to catch hold of me. Besides, it was not as if I could go on long drives in my car. I could not go to shops or fairs, nor attend any events, or go to the cinema, the theatre, the park or even a meeting; I could not venture out anywhere! Even before I could understand what was happening my movements had become restricted; I was effectively under house arrest. My poet friends did not invite me anywhere any more. Rather, they attended poetry events and then dropped by to tell me how great they had been. They attended special programmes organized for writers, or rallies held by artists and authors, and narrated to me all they had done there.

Everyone was busy with festivals, seasonal fairs and music programmes. There were week-long cultural programmes but not one person was sad that I could not attend them. It was as if everyone had accepted my absence as a fundamental reality and if I was to ever tell them that I wished to go somewhere they would get startled and say, 'What are you saying! Have you gone mad! Don't go outside. You never know where danger lurks.' So the only alternative was to stay at home like a good girl and let them have all the fun. Everything that was happening was meant for them and not for me. All I needed was security, not fun and festivities.

Was it depressing for me to stay at home? At least I was alive and that was all that was important. Yes, that was important, but I doubt any of them had any idea how it felt to live the way I was living. They did visit me often, though, and I also went to their houses frequently and that was how we managed to meet. Whenever my friends came over they were visibly nervous; most were afraid of the Special Branch people keeping watch over me. Visiting me was akin to getting one's name registered in the government books—they had to leave their names and addresses with the guards downstairs from whom the Special Branch officers received daily updates. Whenever my friends came we usually sat and chatted for hours and ate a lot of food, with the hours stretching from afternoon to evening and often late into the night. But everything happened indoors, not outside. The world outside was out of bounds for me almost entirely.

I received word that the fundamentalists were joining forces. A call for an uprising had gone out from the mosques and madrasas, public meetings were being held and there were rumours that a massive protest rally was in the works. One afternoon I was alone at home with Minu; Yasmin and Milan were away and Mother was at Mymensingh. Suddenly there was a knock on the door. Through the spyhole I saw six men in fez caps standing outside. Unsure of their intentions I asked Minu not to open the door; instead I told her to ask them what they wanted.

'Whom do you want to see?' Minu shouted.

'Open the door.'

'First tell me what you want.'

'Open the door first. You'll see what we want.'

I signalled to Minu to not open the door and tell them no one was home. Minu obeyed my orders but the men refused to go away. Instead they began kicking at the door, while one of them pressed the doorbell. For the next fifteen to twenty minutes the punishing blows on the door and the sound of the bell continued relentlessly. I was sitting inside, sweating profusely. The intercom was not working, the phone lines were dead and we were on the ninth floor so no one would have heard me even if I had shouted. We closed every possible bolt, went into my study and locked ourselves in. The men were trying to break the main door down. After that it was only the door to the study standing between them and me. Then five of them were going to hold me down, allowing the sixth to take out the chopper concealed under his kurta and behead me. I clutched at my throat in fear and my body began to go into shock from the terror. Soon my grip loosened, my hands fell away and my limp body curled up on the floor, with Minu—dark, gaunt, toothy, our maid and my own first cousin—sitting silently near my head. Neither of us could hear the other breathe and I was suddenly very drowsy . . .

I woke up to a house full of people. Yasmin and Milan were back. I learnt from Minu that the men had continued their home invasion long after I had lost consciousness. How long? Nearly half an hour? An hour? I had no desire to know any further. I sent Milan to buy strong locks for the door and questioned the security guards downstairs as to why they had let six bearded men in caps come upstairs to the apartment. The guards informed me that the men had not told them where they were headed. They had said they were visiting someone in Building 2. This meant anyone could claim to want to meet Abdul Zalil or Mannan Tarafdar and come up to my floor instead. The guards were supposed to inform me via the intercom but, like it happened, it often did not work. I told the guards that if strangers wished to see me henceforth and if the intercom was not functional then instead of letting the person come up alone one of the guards had to come up with them. The one who looked like the leader of the guards informed me, 'Madam, we don't have so many extra people with us who can go up every time.'

You still have time. Repent and become a true Mussulman again or convert and become a Hindu once and for all. Unless you choose one there will be consequences. Someone had left the chit in the letterbox. Besides such notes, there were also the anonymous letters full of threats. *If you write even one line against religion any more, from that day your life will become hell.* Harsh unrecognizable voices were making nasty telephone calls threatening to break my head, chop off my limbs, slice open my veins, gang rape me on the open road, decapitate me, so on and so forth. I could sense they were lying in wait somewhere very close by. An endless series of gifts had been bestowed on me and I did not know what to do with the largesse. In despair and in terrible danger, my senses outraged as well as disjointed, there was nothing for me to do but mope.

When K arrived at such a juncture, instead of his face my eyes went straight towards the black bag he always carried under his arm. I took the bag from him and took out the black pistol I knew was in there. The coldness of the metal made a shiver run down my spine even though K never kept the gun loaded. That very instant I knew that I needed to procure a weapon for self-defence. Earlier Annada Shankar Roy had remarked in the papers, 'The sort of danger Taslima is in, she should keep a pistol with her.' When I had read it I had failed to fathom the weight of his words and laughed it off as a bizarre suggestion. This time, I kept K's pistol with me, not because I wanted to kill someone but because I needed something I could use to defend myself. If someone came to attack me and I had the pistol at hand, it might possibly save my life. There were particularly bad days when nothing appeared certain and one had to depend solely on uncertainties and possibilities.

The day I decided to keep K's pistol with me I received a call from a journalist informing me that police officers from the Motijheel police station were on their way to my house to search the place, although he could not tell me why. Mother was petrified. 'What are you going to do? Where will you move this thing now?' She took the pistol out from under the stacks of clothes in the cupboard and began running around looking for a hiding place, tucking it under the mattress one moment and running to the kitchen to hide it among the dishes the next. Exasperated, I spat out, 'Ma, if they search the place, wherever you keep it they will drag it out. There's no point hiding it.' It seemed the police had finally found the excuse they had been looking for all along to come for me.

Around the same time Dr Rashid, out for a stroll on a breezy afternoon, decided to drop by. I told him everything; we had to act fast and remove the pistol before the police got there. His dark face lost the smile that he had entered with, growing even darker and without even pausing to think I put the entire responsibility of getting rid of the pistol on Dr Rashid's shoulders. I had no other choice and he did not hesitate in my time of need either. He paused for a moment to consider where he could hide the pistol—inside his shirt, in his trousers—and how he was going to carry it out of the complex. In the end, having come to the conclusion that hiding it would only draw more attention to it, he decided to simply carry the bag in his hand, like a bag of documents or money. In plain sight no one was going to suspect what he was carrying with him. Taking Milan along, Dr Rashid left at once, telling me not to open the door to the police immediately and to check their identity cards and appropriate search warrants first before letting them in. Walking unhurriedly and carrying on a casual conversation the two hailed a rickshaw—if they had taken my car instead and run into the police on their way out then that would have been the end of the charade.

They had got off the rickshaw at Dhaka Medical only to be met with the sight of a throng of policemen, students and doctors in the crowded courtyard. For a moment they teetered on the edge of going ahead or turning back, before Dr Rashid decisively took the call of going ahead with the plan. They met another doctor on the way who informed them that there had been a fight among students and one student had been shot dead. Terrified, both of them could only croak out barely comprehensible words. With the police standing only a few feet away, the other doctor looked at the bag Rashid was carrying and asked with a wink, 'What's that? A bottle is it!' Forcing a genial 'Don't be silly' smile on his perspiring face Dr Rashid kept walking ahead like doctors usually walked beside their patients, heading straight to the operation theatre and the cupboard at the back. That night the police never turned up at my house. But I learnt a valuable lesson regarding how they could turn up just about any day and there was no way I could risk keeping an unlicensed firearm in the house. Despite all my anxieties and misgivings I returned the troublesome object to its rightful owner with alacrity and managed to breathe a sigh of relief.

Ultimately the police had to provide me with security. The feather-light appeal I had submitted at the Motijheel police station had been tossed aside with the excuse that they required a court order for the same. For that I needed a lawyer to take up my case. There were two big lawyers fighting human rights cases in the country: Dr Kamal Hossain and Amirul Islam. Even though I was not acquainted with Dr Hossain personally I had recently met his daughter Sara Hossain. She had got in touch with me when two human rights advocates from abroad had come to Dhaka and expressed an interest in meeting me; Sara had arranged a meeting between us at Dr Hossain's office in Motijheel.

Sara was a barrister herself. Having earned her law degree from Oxford she was working as an assistant to her famous father. A stunningly beautiful girl, she always wore a white salwar kameez and was fit as a fiddle. She spoke in Bangla, but the way she deliberately used only Bangla words while speaking made it clear that she was more comfortable in English. She used Bangla for such English words for which the Bangla version was not too commonplace: judge, high court, lower court, justice, among others. If one had to translate all legal words into Bangla I was certain most people would not understand a word of what was being said. Many of the words she used struck my ears as distinctively odd. While talking to her it seemed to me I was that rickshaw-puller I had heard of who had told his passenger he did not know where the university was and when the person had directed him to the place he had turned around and said, 'Oh, you wanted to come to the university! You should have just said that!'

Sara was the one who finally registered a case against the fatwa. The court told us that to fight a case against the Sahaba Sainik Parisad I had to go to Sylhet; it could not be done from the courts in Dhaka. Since going to Sylhet was as good as impossible for me and because the court was not keen on doing anything in my absence, I had to

risk an appearance at the lower courts in Dhaka. If the government
had displayed even an iota of morals they would have lodged a case
against the Sahaba Sainik Parisad immediately. But they remained
silent, as if the Parisad had done nothing wrong and I deserved the
fatwa because it was my fault.

There were a crowd of people at the court, their eyes trained on
me, and I could not help but wonder how so many people knew I was
going to be attending. It seemed an invisible hand was at work that
was keeping tabs on all my movements and I could not be sure about
the motives of the many people who were there that day. Obviously
we had to work fast. The magistrate presiding over the case gravely
remarked, 'If you write such things, is it any wonder that they declared
a fatwa!' Despite his obvious reluctance he had to instruct the police
to post security at my place.

We returned from the court and began our wait for the promised
policemen but days passed without any sign of them. I did not know
that the police could flout a direct court order. The security personnel
were finally deployed from Motijheel police station on 14 October.
Whether this was a consequence of the earlier court order or the
harsh letter regarding my security sent to the Bangladesh government
by Amnesty International that had been published in the newspapers
the day before, I could not tell. Not just Amnesty International,
most international human rights organizations had requested the
government to make arrangements for my security, thirty-six writers
and intellectuals of the country had issued a statement against the
fatwa and a furious debate was on in the newspaper columns over the
issue.

Two large policemen were posted at the main gate of my house
where they sat and mostly dozed. Despite their less than active
presence everyone at home finally breathed a sigh of relief. Mother
was especially kind towards the policemen, sending out tea for them
at regular intervals. Two chairs were also placed in the corridor for
them. Pavel Rahman, a portly photographer working for Associated
Press, arrived one day to take photographs of the guarding policemen.
Perhaps it was a lark for him but I failed to see the joke in all this;
instead I could not help but be discomfited by the indolence on
display on the part of the policemen. Our neighbours too had begun

talking about how the police were making them uncomfortable and apprehensive about another imminent attack on the house. Yasmin spoke to one such outraged neighbour and told them they should then be happy that the police were there in case an attack actually did happen. No one really felt safe, though, and as soon as I stepped out of my apartment I could feel numerous eyes on me. If there was security posted at home then there were sleuths posted outside as well. Wherever I went they followed me, recording every single move I made for the government's records.

~

I could sense something bizarre was about to happen in the country, I could almost smell it brewing. Influential fundamentalist leaders were banding together and numerous meetings were being held on streets, highways and bylanes, all of them about one particular issue: Taslima Nasrin. Politicians were calling press conferences and public gatherings were being held all round. All of them wanted harsh punishment for me and they were summoning people from all strata of society to answer their call. War had already been declared against me in the various mosques and hundreds of students from the madrasas were poised to take to the streets with swords and shields. There were posters everywhere—Islam was in danger and the country was going to face devastation unless I was punished at once. Milan often went to the Shantinagar mosque for the Friday prayers and returned with the leaflets being distributed there. Not just in the mosques, such leaflets were being distributed among the people on the roads too. One day Milan handed me a leaflet about a protest rally, a huge demonstration that was in the works.

Naara-e-Takbeer	=	Allahu Akbar
An insult to Islam	=	The Muslim will not tolerate
An insult to the Prophet	=	Shall not be, shall not be
The BPJ's tout	=	Taslima beware
Rushdie's accomplice	=	Taslima beware
Down with Taslima	=	We want justice
Atheist, Murtad, Traitor	=	Beware, beware

We demand that the one who has rained terrible abuses on the
holy Quran, Islam and the Prophet, the one who has hatched a
wicked plot to undermine our continued harmony and freedom,
the notorious *murtad*, traitor to Allah, enemy of the prophets,
an accomplice of the vile Rushdie, a pawn of India's right-wing
communal party BJP, and a shame to all women

MURTAD, SHAMELESS TASLIMA NASRIN

♦Arrest♦Strict Punishment♦Immediate Confiscation of All
Offensive Writings
Public Forum
Location: Baitul Mokarram South Gate
Date: 18 November 1993, Thursday
Time: 2 pm

Let us come together imbued with honest thoughts and love for the
nation, our race and the Prophet in a protest march.

A Supplication by:
On behalf of all ulemas and mashaikhs
(Saidul Hadis Maulana) Azizul Haque
(Maulana Gazi) Ishhaq
Saidul Hadis, Patia Madrasa, Chattagram
(Maulana Mufti) Abdur Rahman
Director General, Islamic Research Centre, Dhaka
(Maulana) Mahiuddin Khan
Editor, *Mashik Medina*, Dhaka
(Maulana Poet) Ruhul Amin Khan
(Maulana) Abdul Gaffar
Mufassir-e Quran, Dhaka
(Maulana Mufti) Wahiduzzaman
Mohaddis, Barkatra Madrasa, Dhaka
(Maulana) Abdul Jabbar
Chief Secretary, Befaqul Madarisil, Bangladesh
(Maulana) Noor Hossain Kasemi
Muhtamim, Baridhara Madrasa, Dhaka

(Maulana Kwari) Obaidullah
Khatib, Chakbazar Shahi Masjid
(Maulana) Muhammad Habibur Rahman
Convener, Bangladesh Chhahaba Sainik Parisad

A handful of scholars mounted a passionate defence of freedom of expression and wrote in support of me. Mustafa Nurul Islam wrote:

> We are living in contentious times, in a weird country, where they have decided that no one is going to be allowed to think freely, or dream. I reserve my rebukes for us, that these sins are being committed with impunity in a country whose legacy is the Liberation War. Taslima Nasrin writes, and she writes about her beliefs and her thoughts—who are these alternate legal authorities who seem to possess the right to issue a fatwa against her demanding her assassination? What is her fault? That she has dared to strike at the dark roots of centuries-old superstitions and spoken out against opportunists. Her only fault is that she writes what she feels and is open about discussing her trusted experiences . . . It is possible that many of us may not agree with her opinions all the time. But it does not imply that we can let a writer's fundamental rights be violated . . . Nazrul was once termed a kaffir and sentenced to death. Abul Hossain and Kazi Abdul Wadud, proponents of the Freedom of Intellect Movement (Buddhir Mukti Andolan), were made to sign an indenture. I fear we are facing a revival of such medieval instances of prejudice. The final truth that must be acknowledged is that the wheel of history can never turn back.

Professor Sirajul Islam Chowdhury observed:

> What is happening around Taslima is no longer a literary issue, it's political. We are no longer discussing literature, we are discussing causes for possible fundamentalist attacks. For the fanatics this is a political issue, they are not interested in books at all. Yet it is these sorts of issues they wait for. Neither are they interested in a logically sound counter-argument. That is exactly what has happened in this case. Whenever these fundamentalist parties get

an opportunity they try to capitalize on such issues. Everyone is entitled to a right to express their opinion. Those who are attacking this freedom are enemies of progress.

Leftist thinker Badruddin Umar did not agree with most of my writings but even he was of the opinion that religious reactionaries were using me as a tool for stoking communal tension. Decisively opposing them, he opined that it was an important duty of every progressive force in the country to resist religious barbarism. K.M. Sobhan wrote:

The freedoms of speech and expression are fundamental rights guaranteed by the Constitution to every citizen. It is the duty of the state to ensure security of its citizens and make sure that every citizen can move about freely without restrictions. The fundamental rights guaranteed to every citizen by the Constitution ascertain that unless there are strong legal grounds no action can be taken that jeopardizes a person's life, freedom, body, reputation and property. The language that the conservatives and fundamentalists have used to attack Taslima Nasrin's private life has undoubtedly caused harm to her reputation. They misrepresent her opinions and one cannot help but ask if they are actually aware of the opinions they so vociferously distort. The people who cannot seem to stand Taslima's talent and her literary acumen are the ones who threaten her and spread rumours about her.

An editorial was published in *Bhorer Kagaj*.

Time progresses, the world progresses, but Bangladeshi society shows no signs of progress. Instead our society is constantly being pulled backwards by communal differences, fundamentalism and our reactionary attitudes. Back in 1971 these fundamentalist forces had dubbed the muktijoddhas as kaffirs. Their latest target is Taslima Nasrin and her writings are what have sparked the ire of these fatwaphilic fanatics. Some sections might deem a book objectionable; it is not a given that everyone will accept all forms of writing. Similarly there is controversy around Taslima's work and there is a multiplicity of strong opinions both for and against them. But the so-called Sahaba Sainik Parisad of Sylhet has shown extreme disregard and contempt for all legal and social tenets of the country by calling for her head in a public gathering, declaring a cash reward of 50,000 taka for anyone willing to accomplish the task. Ultimately they wish to re-establish the Middle Ages in Bangladesh. It is indeed difficult to comprehend how a group of people can declare a reward for someone's murder in a country where there is a legally elected government, a judicial system and the rule of law in place.

Meanwhile, London-based Amnesty International has already expressed their concerns regarding the matter. Taslima Nasrin has sought legal recourse and the court has ordered the police to ensure her security. But those religious traders have not ceased their activities. These elements that are pushing the country towards chaos and anarchy by repeatedly undermining our established laws, how do they manage to carry on with their undertakings in broad daylight with such complete impunity? We believe in the religious freedom of every citizen of this country. We must similarly stand for the freedom of a writer. Our Constitution guarantees us the right to life and the freedom of speech and expression.

'Balance' was the *mot du jour* doing the rounds in the papers, especially the progressive ones. In this editorial as well the conclusion was dedicated to finding a delicate balance.

It is not a sign of good health of a nation when someone instigates others to murder an author. This is against the central tenets of Islam as well. (Was it though, completely against the tenets of Islam?) At the same time, the idea that a writer's freedom to write does not imply a freedom to write whatever they wish to (so I was supposed to write according to whose wishes?) and that a writer automatically develops a sense of responsibility (had I done something irresponsible?) are facts that no true writer (so was I not a true writer?) needs to be reminded of. No sensible writer (I was being insensitive too?) will want their work to be used for unscrupulous political ends (how is a writer supposed to know if their work is going to be used for unscrupulous political ends).

It was a good piece of writing. Especially at a time when there was a crisis of good writing, this was surely one to remember. I call it a crisis because at the time most of the articles being written were in favour of the fatwa. Flashes of fiery dissent from the liberals and rationalists were few and far between. In an article Shamsur Rahman expressed his heartfelt disappointment at the state of affairs.

> It has become difficult to envisage a scenario where I can live in Bangladesh and not be disappointed by it from time to time. The very act of reading the newspaper is a source of disappointment. And why shouldn't it be so? Road accidents, police violence of peaceful picketers, terror activities in educational institutions, interfering in a writer's freedom of expression, a free rein given to fatwa-wielding goons, harassment of women in the villages that often leads to murder, a spike in the rate of robberies and thefts, growing influence of fundamentalists and the dilemma facing freethinking individuals—these are reasons enough to wound, disappoint and outrage any open-minded rationalist. But it is dangerous to express this outrage and anyone who speaks up against such evils risks severe repercussions. When people wear their ignorance like a crown, in a system where prejudices, superstitions and orthodoxy are well established, is it any wonder that rational individuals do not find a space to articulate their thoughts! It is even more disappointing when one sees a freethinking writer becoming a target for reactionaries and fundamentalists and most other writers remaining indifferent to her plight. One cannot expect that everyone will agree all the time with something an aggrieved author has to say. However, despite differences of opinion if the literary community does not write in favour of a fellow writer's freedoms, then who will?

It was not as if the literary community answered Shamsur Rahman's call and applied themselves to write in my favour all at once. Some were of the opinion that I had gone too far with my views on religion and there was no point siding with me. Some said I wrote such things deliberately to instigate the zealots, that I had created the issues that had brought them together. Many believed fundamentalism was on the rise in the country solely because of me, because I had deliberately made myself the centre of controversy. Others opined that I had a tendency to go overboard while talking about women's rights and it was not right for them to comment in my favour. Despite these faultlines some opinions were still emerging; if there were a hundred things written against me, there was usually one in solidarity.

The fundamentalists had banded together and declared jihad, which was an easy thing to do since they had the support of those in power. They were utilizing this support to the hilt and their dailies, weeklies and bimonthlies, despite there being no love lost among them, were constantly writing against me. Most of it was lies, fake stories, dirty and obscene things meant to engender hatred in the mind of the reader and nourish that hatred to such an extent that the reader was forced to admit that my death was necessary for the greater good. Not just readers who already harboured prejudice but the common man too, who would be shocked and aghast at such things and demand my hanging at once.

In comparison, the progressive journals and papers that were usually quite vocal about their opposition of communal and fundamentalist politics were also rather quiet on the matter. The attitude was as if the fundamentalist attack on me was a stray incident and entirely my personal issue in which they could not interfere. Roads were being blocked for public meetings, thousands of people were marching in protest during which traffic came to a standstill and it was being called Taslima Nasrin's personal matter! It made sense in a way. The fanatics were not after them, so the progressive journals and papers did not feel the need to stick up for me. Unfortunately when renowned authors wrote in protest they had no choice but to publish such articles, more because of the author's name than in solidarity with me. Nevertheless, sometimes some voices of conscience cried out from the dark.

Shakina Hossain of *Dainik Sambad*, like the chorus in a tragedy, declared:

> No, this is not Taslima Nasrin's personal matter because throughout the country fundamentalist and communal forces, individuals, groups and media houses have declared jihad. Every progressive writer must rise above petty self-interests and treat this as an assault on their freedoms too. By sticking to their usual stance of non-interference, to save their skins and their votebanks, progressive political forces are turning a blind eye to all that is happening. But

no matter how dumb and blind they pretend to be they will not be able to avoid these flames themselves and that is something they better figure out at the earliest.

According to Shakina such progressive voices had to realize what exactly was at stake before things got very late. Unfortunately none of the political parties showed any interest in understanding this and the issues remained, for the most part, my personal matter. Typically the Awami League would be at the forefront whenever forces of communalism were on the rise but in my case the League too took a vow of silence. Even if they did not wish to speak in support of me, they could still have denounced the fatwa. But since that could not be done without mentioning my name it was not something they wanted to commit to. Atheism was inextricably linked with Taslima Nasrin's name and perhaps the League was afraid that its recently acquired religious façade would slip off if it were to utter my name.

That meant if an atheist had a fatwa hanging over her head, she had to take care of it by herself. The attitude was simple—no matter what the ideology of our founding fathers had been, the progressive leftist intellectuals wished to toe the line of Islam and the Prophet. Thus there was no way I could expect their support. Of the other political parties JASAD must be mentioned. The National Socialist Party had been founded in the 1970s primarily to oppose Sheikh Mujibur Rahman. After Sheikh Mujib's death, even though there had been no reason for the continued survival of such an organization, it had survived. Since mere survival hardly amounted to anything, many of its leaders had joined other parties over time, some even migrating to the Awami League.

During the elections the JASAD and factions like the JSD that had broken away from it were part of the eight-party coalition headed by the Awami League. Of the other remaining parties the biggest was the nationalist party, the BNP, which was no different from any other fundamentalist party. Especially after the 1991 elections, when they came to power thanks to the assistance and largesse of the Jamaat, whatever little difference had been there previously was on the verge of being eradicated. With eighteen seats in Parliament Jamaat wielded considerable influence, bolstered by the more than forty lakh votes they had received.

Ershad was in jail but one could not be sure that he would not have joined the fundamentalists with his supporters had he been free. The Jatiya Party had no character of its own; its politicians who had joined the BNP or the Awami League as soon as Ershad was put in jail had proved this irrevocably. Changing one's party affiliations was like second nature in Bangladesh and it all depended on whether an arrangement was suiting someone or not—a classic side-effect of not having any ethics or ideology. On the other hand the fundamentalists never wavered from their ideology and no one could accuse members of the Jamaat of changing sides. Usually, the Awami League was more than ready to exploit any weakness on the part of the BNP. When the Ekattorer Ghatak Dalal Nirmul Committee was holding mock trials and sentencing Golam Azam, the League had swooped in and joined forces with the committee. But when the government was wilfully ignoring a fatwa issued against a writer by Jamaat-backed fundamentalists, when the BNP had nothing to say against the outpouring of communal tensions across the country, even the League was strangely quiet. The fatwa issue could have been a huge opportunity for them to build an anti-BNP mass movement but even the usually resourceful Awami League did not want to go down that road. And there was only one reason behind that: Taslima Nasrin.

Ulemas across the country were gearing up for a larger movement and were busy mustering forces at the ground level. No ulemas, alams, imams, maulanas, pirs, mashaikhs were sitting idle and a united Muslim front had been established. A protest committee too was established to oppose anti-government and anti-religious activities. All religious organizations, political or not, had come together for the United Front. Despite numerous differences of opinions among them they were all united on this one issue. Despite five to ten thousand people taking out protest marches and the fundamentalists blocking roads and thoroughfares, no political party was ready to take up the initiative of a movement against communalism.

When no political party, no human rights organizations, no writers' groups or women's rights groups appeared willing to do anything, my friends Nahid, Jhunu, Mitun and Neepa formed a group called Taslima Sapakkha Goshthi (Pro-Taslima Front) and took to the streets in a silent protest march from the TSC to the Press Club

with a banner emblazoned with 'Resist Communalism'. The group
also printed and handed out a leaflet appealing to all progressive and
conscientious people who had faith in the ideals of independence and
the Liberation War:

> Let us all rise above our party affiliations and ideologies to stand
> by Taslima Nasrin. Let us unite on her behalf and appeal to the
> government, to ensure the safety of those who have spoken out
> in support of Taslima Nasrin and the larger movement for the
> rights of women and universal human freedom, to restore all of
> Nasrin's rights as a citizen and to take strict punitive action against
> communal forces.

How many people joined the silent march? Hardly a hundred to a
hundred and fifty! Most were girls, and some of the women from the
garments factories joined in too. Jhunu was a gifted public speaker
and her rousing speech in front of the Press Club was enough to draw
a crowd. Jhunu was a brave girl. With her short hair and her penchant
for wearing shirts and pants she was subjected to a lot of comments
on the road regarding her appearance, but she cared two hoots about
such things.

One big attraction of the protest march, from what I heard later,
was the renowned sculptor Shamim Sikdar who chanced upon the
rally at the TSC crossing, joined in and held the banner aloft. There
were few people in Bangladesh gutsier than Shamim Akhtar. A
professor at the Dhaka Art School, a group of her colleagues had once
joined forces and carried on a long campaign demanding her removal
from her post. Sikdar had not broken down in the face of such a
concentrated assault, had not buckled and cried. She had fought and
won and she used to walk past her belligerent colleagues with her
spine stiff with pride.

Like her own unwavering stance her massive sculptures too
dotted the landscape of Dhaka. To Sikdar self-respect was paramount
and she was not willing to compromise on that front under any
circumstances, just like she had not compromised as a child when,
on her way to school on a bicycle, a local boy had snatched away her
stole. Not only had she beaten the boy up, she had also never carried

a stole or worn a salwar kameez again, let alone a sari. She wore pants, shirts and hard shoes, and kept a revolver at hand for emergencies. Since my adolescence I had heard about and idolized Sikdar. At one point I had even aspired to be like her, but that could never be because I was always held back by my shame and fear.

Sikdar, Goon and some of the latter's friends and followers finished the silent march and went to Sakura. They called me from the restaurant and asked me to join them there. I had never had the opportunity to meet Sikdar in person, having only seen her from a distance working with her tools on the giant sculpture 'Shoparjito Shadhinota' (Self-earned Independence) at the TSC. My intense fascination for her drove me to Sakura. On my way out I ran into Chotda and took him along too. The group had occupied a large table at the back of the restaurant. As usual Sikdar was wearing a shirt, pants, a hard leather belt and boots. As soon as she saw me she said, 'We have just come from a rally in solidarity with you. It went well.' What ensued was a long description of the march although I was so overwhelmed by her presence that I had scant interest in any rallies or such. Patting my shoulder Sikdar said, 'Don't be afraid. The mullah bastards will not be able to do anything. It's not that easy! If you become afraid they will try to capitalize on that. Write whatever you wish, we are all here for you. Send me word if there's any problem. I'll see which scoundrel dares to do anything to you! I'll break all their bones.'

Sikdar pushed her cigarette packet towards me. In a society where a woman smoking was an unthinkable act she used to smoke in public all the time, on the road and in restaurants and bars, never bothering about what others were saying about her. I was offered alcohol too, but not being used to it, I had to rush to the washroom to throw up after only a couple of sips. I was careful to hide this from the rest, afraid that Sikdar was going to scoff and say, 'Little girl, you can't even hold down a little alcohol!' She had already said to me, 'I had assumed you are a tough girl! But you are as shy as a housewife! I can't understand why the mullahs are after someone as meek and innocent as you!' She pointed at the sari I was wearing and said, 'Why do you wear the sari? Is it even a dress? Can you fight the cap-wearing goons in a sari? One pull and the entire thing unravels! You have to grow out of it!' Hearing me express my concerns over the protest marches by the mullahs, Sikdar stopped me and remarked, 'You are so scared! You are a scared little girl! When they wanted to demolish Shoparjito Shadhinota I went to TSC alone to guard it. I was ready to face whoever would have come. None of the scoundrels dared to come anywhere near it.' She was looking at me and her eyes were awash with compassion. 'Do you know judo or karate?'

'No.'

'You have learnt nothing in life!'

'What use will it come to? I am not going to go down to the field and fight them!'

'Oh, I understand, you fight with your pen. But they have not just taken up pens, have they? They have taken up much more and they are flexing their muscles. They are showing you how masculine they are. You don't go out in fear. Is that even justifiable? If you can knock out at least two or three of them, if you can tear off their caps and robes and make them run on the road naked, they will never dare utter your name again.'

I was well aware that I could never be as courageous as her. There was only one Shamim Sikdar in Bangladesh and as unique an individual as she was, not everyone could be like her. Fear, shame, slander, there was nothing she cared about and I felt blessed to have been in the company of such a daring and audacious woman.

~

My columns were being published regularly in *Khabarer Kagaj*, *Samikkhan*, *Bhorer Kagaj*, *Ananya* and *Jai Jai Din*. I had been writing non-stop since my resignation. *Jai Jai Din*, edited by Shafeeq Rahman, was the most popular weekly around that time. Rahman had lived in London for years before returning to Bangladesh a few years back and starting the journal. During Ershad's rule he was once stopped from entering the country and sent back from Dhaka airport. After Ershad was overthrown he had come back and settled in rather well. I used to write in *Jai Jai Din* because of his request but I was not very satisfied with it. Rahman would simply expunge any mention of religion from whatever I wrote.

In fact this was a common trend in most papers and journals of the time—it was fine as long as I was writing against communalism but I was not allowed to attack religion. Previously such restrictions had not been there and I could write whatever I wished to and no one edited lines from my articles. But I could sense that my freedom to write my thoughts was gradually being regulated and the editors were removing lines and words at will without seeking my permission, presenting the distorted product to the readers. The serialized essay titled 'The Vedas, the Bible, and Women' I was writing for *Bhorer Kagaj* was abruptly discontinued because of this. They had no problem with anything else I wanted to write as long as it was not about religion. Religion was tearing the country apart but one was not allowed to criticize it.

As it is the only reason there was so much demand for my articles was because my articles increased sales; even though I could not be sure how many of these editors truly believed in what I was writing none of them had the courage to terminate my services and put their circulation at risk. Saju Ahmed, the editor of the magazine *Robbar*, had requested me for an article once, which I had obliged and he had printed with a lot of care. He sent a representative of his with a letter asking me to write for his magazine regularly. Even though I did regularly write for many, I had to turn him down since I had no time to give to another column. Strangely enough, a few weeks later he published a special issue of *Robbar* on me with my photo on the cover and more photos inside. Every single line of every single article of the special issue was replete with nothing but abuse directed at me. I had never known abuse could be so dirty, insults could be so cruel, disrespect could be so terrible and jealousy could be so dangerous.

Ishaq Khan, R's friend, had written an article, not about my writing but about my sexual life—how many men I had slept with, when, where, how, including detailed descriptions of everything. It included accounts of my many lovers in Mymensingh even before I had met R, all of whom I had also slept with according to Khan. He had mentioned the advertisements I had put when the personal advertisement section was first started in *Bichitra* back during my college days, only so he could invent a few obscene sentences that he wanted to pass off as wordings from my advertisement. The readers were obviously not going to go through issues of *Bichitra* from sixteen years ago to verify if I had indeed written such an advertisement.

Looking at his innocent and unassuming appearance most people would not have imagined the sort of malice Ishaq Khan harboured within him. His goal in life had been to become a writer of short stories but he had been unsuccessful thus far. Thanks to the efforts of Saju Ahmed, Ishaq Khan's salacious assassination of my character did exceedingly well with the public and brought him instant fame. The issue had to be published thrice due to public demand. Papers would have sold whether I was being praised or vilified—*Robbar*, which used to sell 2000 copies, sold nearly 20,000—so the gloves came off! The magazine was filled with nothing but denigration and the failed writer tasted success for the first time.

As it was there were too many publications in the country that had popped up like mushrooms—dailies, weeklies, bimonthlies, monthlies, those published every two or three months, and so on. The ones with low circulation began running stories about me to up their sales, with my photographs on the cover and largely imaginary fiction inside. I don't recall speaking to a single journalist but long interviews of mine were published and jokes about the fatwa became routine. Rumours were doing the rounds that Habibur Rahman wished to marry me and I had said yes. While I was being driven out of my mind by a 50,000-taka fatwa swinging over my head, I was made into a laughing stock, a source of entertainment, in the papers.

What Motiur Rahman Chowdhury had wished to do via his report on the fatwa proved once and for all how intensely I was hated in my own country. But when the intelligentsia made statements against the extra-judicial fatwa and numerous people began writing about it both in Bangladesh and abroad, fearing that there was a genuine risk of a cohesive public opinion forming in my favour, the maulana Habibur Rahman began claiming that he had issued no such fatwa; even if he had, he claimed it had been revoked long ago. Obviously, he pretended to not be the sort of person who randomly issued fatwas, even though there had been a successful strike in Sylhet—called by him—in support of the fatwa only a while ago. Attempting to brush the term under the carpet Habibur Rahman launched a new vocal campaign accompanied by incendiary public

addresses. A press conference was organized on 21 October at the
Cicily Restaurant in Dhaka by ulemas and mashaikhs of all levels
demanding the 'immediate confiscation of all works of the notorious
Taslima Nasrin, her arrest, and exemplary punishment'. At the press
conference a statement was made in front of the journalists.

> The name Taslima might mislead one to think of her as a Muslim.
> But in her beliefs, her creed and her mentality she is anything but.
> She has been constantly waging a war against Allah by making
> the most vile observations vis-à-vis the Quran, the Prophet and
> the Islamic sharia . . . Because of her shameless, arrogant and
> objectionable writing obscenity, debauchery and immorality
> have spread like an epidemic both in the state and abroad. This
> is severely detrimental to the image of Islam and the Prophet.
> This woman has referred to specific verses of the Quran—sura
> Al Imran, sura An-Nisa, sura Al-Baqara, sura Al-Hujurat, sura
> Al-Waqi'a, sura Ar-Rahman—and has ridiculed and distorted
> Allah's dictums. Similarly she has mocked the Prophet using the
> most terrible of words and has decried man's faith in religion as
> a falsity. She has gone on to claim that religion turns humanity
> inhuman and insults and denigrates women. She has declared
> that she holds the great Allah and His messengers responsible
> for oppression of women, inequality between the sexes and all
> social troubles. She has heaped scorn upon all believers and has
> claimed that she holds nothing but contempt for women who
> adhere to the Prophet's hadith. Sexual excesses and depravity are
> considered sins in all faiths but Taslima has repeatedly sought
> to encourage society to embrace free sex and dissolution and
> to that end she has written, "I believe a woman can sleep with
> ten men and still remain chaste." It is not difficult to envisage
> how terrible the consequences of such limitless opinions and
> their free proliferation in society can be. It is a truth universally
> acknowledged that if a person is to be found guilty of treason, if
> they are found to be openly engaging in conspiring against the
> state, then their only possible punishment is death. Similarly if
> a person with a Muslim name ridicules Islam, the holy Quran,
> and the great Prophet, if they seek to bring disruption to society

by their misrepresentations, then they will be considered heretics and according to the sharia their only punishment is death.

After the address the Sahaba Sainik Parisad proudly declared that through conferences, a protest rally and a half-day strike, all undertaken in Sylhet, they had presented the government with a set of three demands:

1. Immediate arrest of Taslima Nasrin; 2. Immediate confiscation of all her work; and 3. Exemplary punishment for her. These reflect what is in the hearts of the faithful populace and the government has to accept these demands. The government has already impounded Taslima's *Lajja*, and now it is time to do the same to her other more harmful books and do justice by the Parishad. We are also going to generate a larger popular movement to demand the institution of capital punishment for offences committed against Islam, the holy Quran and the great Prophet.

And it was already happening, I could see that with my own eyes. The movement was not simply growing, it was slowly taking on monstrous proportions.

There was a rally coming down the road. Not a few hundred people, there were a few thousand, marching from the Kankrail crossing to Shantinagar. Sitting at my window I could clearly see the banner they were carrying, 'We demand the noose for Taslima' written across it in bold letters. They were coming down the road shouting 'Naara-e-Takbeer Allahu Akbar'. Mother was reading suras from the Quran. Her muttering froze mid-sura seeing me standing at the window; in a flash I was dragged away to the safety of shadows. Unsure whether suras were going to help she rushed to her prayer mat and bent over in namaz hoping her entreaties would reach Allah's ears and He would save me from public fury in time. The rally stopped at the Shantinagar crossing. A few uniformed policemen had been posted there and they were not letting the rally pass. The roars of 'Naara-e-Takbeer' shook the entire building.

Rallies such as this were a regular fixture from Baitul Mukarram to Shantinagar. Each time, I stayed frozen in fright, my heart about to leap out of my chest. All I could wonder was what would happen if the mob managed to ever find their way to my apartment. The two policemen sitting at the door were hardly going to be able to stop them. With each passing day the rallies were swelling like an angry river.

~

Sheikhul Hadis was a well-known name. He founded a new committee, the Committee for the Prevention of Seditious and Heretical Activities, and muftis and maulanas signed up in hordes. They organized huge protest rallies with gigantic banners, especially after the Jumu'ah prayers on Fridays. They did not stop at protest marches only and presented a deposition to the Speaker of Parliament.

Respected Speaker
Bangladesh Jatiya Sangsad
Sangsad Bhavan
Shere Bangla Nagar
Dhaka

Janaab,
We humbly request:

1. It is common knowledge that the people of Bangladesh are deeply religious and people of all communities in this country have always been aware and vigilant about preserving communal harmony among each other. But a few confused factions have assumed that hurting the religious sentiments of others is a sign of progress and have continued with their devious plan of attacking people's religious principles as well as the unity among the different communities.
2. A notorious writer named Taslima Nasrin has repeatedly hurt the religious sentiments of the people of Bangladesh via her books, novels and columns in various magazines and journals. On the other hand she is also engaged in a well-planned and cunning campaign of propagating hate and strife among communities.

3. By writing *Lajja*, a novel of nefarious intentions full of lies
    and misinformation, Taslima Nasrin has sought to smear the
    history of communal harmony in this country, hurt the image
    of Bangladesh in the international arena, and instigated some
    national and international communal groups to harbour ideas
    of revenge against Muslims. However, the government has
    only banned *Lajja* and not taken any other legal steps, despite
    there being numerous instances where Nasrin has made
    many comments which are contrary to the independence,
    sovereignty and cohesion of Bangladesh, veering dangerously
    close to treason. The patriotic people of Bangladesh are deeply
    outraged and hurt by the government's attitude regarding the
    matter.

4. Even though according to the Constitution and the rule of law,
    hurting a citizen's religious sentiments and causing discord
    between people of different faiths is a punishable offence,
    since there are no specific guidelines regarding a speedy and
    strict system of punishment for actions against the state and
    religion, traitors and heretics are brashly carrying on their
    misdemeanours and instigating social unrest and dissonance.

5. Nearly 90 per cent of the people of Bangladesh are Muslims.
    Through her various books and writings Taslima Nasrin has
    repeatedly shown disrespect towards their holy Quran, the
    hadith of the Prophet and the sharia of Islam. Despite vocal
    protests from religious groups all across the country against
    her sacrilegious activities the government has mysteriously
    continued to toe the line of inaction by taking refuge in weak
    laws. Consequently, most pious Muslims of the country have
    lost their faith in the government and the judiciary.

6. Taslima Nasrin has not only targeted our religion, contrary
    to the value systems prevalent in our society she has stridently
    attempted to upset social stability by encouraging debauchery,
    free sex, premarital and extramarital sexual relationships, and
    with exaggerated stories of patriarchal oppression of women
    in relationships. Her writing is no better than pornography,
    whose only purpose is to drive our youth towards depravity
    and moral decay.

In such a scenario, mindful of the feelings of the patriotic and religious citizens of our nation, we strongly demand: 1) laws that will guarantee the death penalty alongside other stern punishments for all traitors and heretics, 2) immediate arrest and exemplary punishment of Taslima Nasrin, and 3) immediate confiscation of all her objectionable literature.

(Sheikhul Hadis Maulana Azizul Haque)
Convener, Committee for the Prevention of Seditious and
Heretical Activities
Saat Masjid, Muhammadpur, Dhaka

An almost similar letter was sent to the home minister too.

Janaab, we are writing to you outraged and in despair regarding a notorious writer named Taslima Nasrin who has insulted and injured the beliefs and sensibilities of twelve crore patriotic and devout citizens of Bangladesh . . .

~

There was a price on a writer's head in Bangladesh—especially in Europe and America this was huge news. After the fatwa fracas with Salman Rushdie the media abroad was more than eager for such a story. A fatwa had been declared on a writer because of her writings, Muslim fundamentalists were demanding her head, for which protest rallies were being held. People across the world read this news and support began to pour in from many quarters, all in solidarity with a writer's freedom of expression. Human rights activists, women's rights activists and writers held demonstrations in front of the consulate offices of Bangladesh in many places across Europe and America. The prime minister's office too received numerous appeals from various foreign organizations requesting security for me as well as appropriate actions against the radicals.

I received a request to write a co-editorial for the *New York Times*. Writing a few sentences in English was fine, but to write an entire article in a foreign language was an entirely different thing. Neither could I turn it down and say it was not possible for me. As if to make the impossible happen, Farid Hossain, a journalist for Associated Press, came forward. Having been tasked by foreign newspapers to handle news related to me, Farid Hossain had already been to my house quite a few times. A highly educated journalist and an unassuming, warm and courteous man, Hossain did not simply visit me for news, he also stepped up as a friend in need. I wrote the co-editorial in Bengali and Hossain translated it into English. Since getting transferred from Dhaka Medical to Maulavibazar in Sylhet, whenever Dr Rashid visited Dhaka he used to stay at my house. Arrangements would be made for him in my study and he would, much like an older brother, shower me with advice and also reply to all the letters I received from various foreign organizations.

Meredith Tax from PEN, an international association of writers, had been trying to get in touch with me for some time. She had been calling me numerous times a day. The first time I had taken the call, unable to understand a word of what she was saying, I had been forced to hang up. Since then, whenever she called I had made someone tell her I was not at home or was indisposed. I could not begin to imagine how she had managed to get my phone number. Eventually she found out from someone about my lawyer and inundated Dr Kamal Hossain with telephone calls and faxes. Meredith was head of the female writers' branch of PEN; her responsibilities included assisting women writers under persecution across the world. I did not know what help Meredith could be from far away in New York!

I was also certain that the depositions the government had received from various organizations across the globe had all ended up in the trash. Khaleda Zia was impassive to such requests. People were calling from France, Germany, Australia, Norway, Canada, England, India and elsewhere to ask how I was doing, what I was feeling, thinking, and whether I had enough security. Many were not satisfied with a phone call and eventually flew down to Bangladesh to meet me in person. The first world was on a sudden rush to the third. People from television, radio and newspapers were thronging my house all day.

A reporter from the BBC came to take an interview for a documentary that the BBC wanted to produce. A team came from a German television channel; they did not just want an interview, they shot enough material for an entire documentary. Another team from France came to shoot a two-hour documentary too. Shibnarayan Roy was at home that day and when the conversation inevitably turned to comparisons between me and Salman Rushdie he firmly replied, 'There are many differences between Salman Rushdie and Taslima. Rushdie is not fighting for social change, Taslima is.'

The film crew was headed to Sylhet afterwards to interview Habibur Rahman, although they were so cautious about it that they did not breathe a word about it to me. Unfortunately, while heading towards Old Dhaka to interview a Hindu family, they were caught on camera and the photo was published in *Inquilab*. Police detectives had followed them because the government was concerned that foreigners had come to shoot a documentary with dishonest intentions. Answering *Inquilab*'s call, a thorough search was conducted of the entire team and they were forced to leave the country. Thankfully they had already sent a copy of the film to Paris secretly via the French consulate.

After this incident no foreign journalists planning to interview me were allowed to enter the country. The smart ones began using myriad other excuses to get past security. Catherine Bédarida of the French magazine *Le Monde* came to meet me, as did Antoine de Gaudemar of *Libération*. I quite liked Gaudemar. It was not difficult to understand what he was saying; he spoke a halting and broken sort of English. Being a Bengali through and through—forget French, the do-not-know-English-well kind of Bengali—my English was as tattered as his. During his visit we drove to the river Dholeswari one day. Gaudemar was concerned that something might happen if I were to go out, but I was suffocated after being confined to the house for so long and wanted to go out somewhere.

When Jill Saucier from a French photo agency came to take my photographs and requested a visit to Mymensingh I had to agree. Jill wanted to take photographs of the house I had spent my childhood in and the school I had attended. I was thankful for these sudden trips even though we were in a car and there were no impromptu halts on the way at a shop or a marketplace. At least you could see people zipping past the car window! After being confined within the four walls of my house for days on end my room seemed to me like my own mausoleum. I was going to die one day for certain but that did not mean I had to sit in my grave and wait. I would keep repeating to myself Sikdar's counsel. 'Don't be afraid!'

Journalists from *Sunday* and the *Statesman* came to me from India for interviews. There were conferences being held across India in condemnation of the fatwa. Statements were being issued, many sensible writers were writing on my behalf and editorials were being published in the newspapers. A group of authors in Calcutta, led by Annada Shankar Roy, had gone to the Bangladeshi consulate with a deposition only to be rudely turned away. A forum in defence of my right to life and freedom of expression was organized at University of Calcutta by the Bangladesh Bharat Maitri Samiti (Committee for Indo-Bangladesh Unity). Many renowned scholars including Annada Shankar Roy were present there, although there was no one from Bangladesh in attendance. At the forum Roy opined that I was a child of the twenty-first century who had been born in the twentieth by mistake; I should have been born in France or England instead of Bangladesh. He also remarked, 'Taslima is an Angry Young Woman while the mullahs are a group of Angry Old Men. An accord between the two is impossible. Besides, we must admit that we can hardly hope to sway public opinion in Bangladesh from here in West Bengal. That task can only be performed by leading intellectuals over there and all we can do is pledge our support to them.'

Meanwhile, the English translation of *Lajja* was published by Penguin India. Publishers from various countries were calling me and expressing their interest in translating and publishing the book in other foreign languages. Ever since the news of the fatwa had been taken up by Western media people were convinced that since I was a writer I must have written a truly objectionable book for the fundamentalists to be so incensed by me. Since *The Satanic Verses* was responsible for Salman Rushdie's fatwa, there had to be a book in my case too. It had been some time since the government had banned *Lajja*. But a few journalists erroneously cited the book as the primary cause of the fatwa, purely to satisfy the curiosity of their readers. Was *Lajja* truly the main reason behind the ire of the fundamentalists? No, it was not. The fundamentalists had been upset with me for some time; the ban had only managed to add fuel to the fire that had been simmering for a long time. This explained the fatwa. The government's inaction had bolstered their courage and further fanned the flames. This explained the nationwide movement. For me the English translation had made sense. Even though the story was set entirely in Bangladesh, since communal riots were not an uncommon thing in India it was not going to be incomprehensible to the readers there. But what were German and French readers going to glean from the book? A little piqued, I asked one of the publishers one day, 'Do you know what *Lajja* is about?'

'No, I don't, not really.'

'It's entirely about certain regions of Bangladesh. There is a lot of data in it. Your readers won't like to read it. It's not that good as a novel.'

'Don't even worry about that. Just let us publish it.'

'I don't think I have written anything till date that can be translated into a foreign language. I have written about the social problems around me. There is no international flavour to it. Let me write something decent, I will surely let you publish it.'

'Of course we can print whatever you write in the future. But we really want to publish *Lajja* now.'

'Why *Lajja* of all things?'

'Because it was banned by the government of Bangladesh! Isn't the fatwa because of that too?'

'No, the fatwa was not declared because of *Lajja*. The fundamentalists had been grumbling since its publication. The fatwa was declared much after the ban. The book was out in the market for three months here after it was published. No radical ever demanded that *Lajja* be banned.'

'Still, we want to publish it.'

'This book won't do well in your country.'

'We will take care of that. Just give us your permission. We will give you an advance on the royalty.'

'Royalty isn't an issue here. What matters is the reader's interest. Why would your readers be interested in Hindu–Muslim issues in Bangladesh?'

'They are interested. You leave that to us, we will take care of all that.'

They would just not listen. Michèle Idele from the French publishing house Édition des Femmes was calling me three times a day for the same. 'Taslima, you have fought relentlessly for women's rights. Our organization too has been involved in a similar endeavour for many years. We are protesting on your behalf here. Give us permission to publish *Lajja*. We are sending you the contract, please sign it.'

'But *Lajja* is not about women's rights. I have a few books about women; see if you can publish any of those. Although I am not sure if the problems of the women of Bangladesh will resonate with . . .'

'Don't think about that. Of course we want to know about women from other countries. We will print those too. But we will print *Lajja* first.'

'*Lajja* has already been published in English. Read that first and see if it is fit to be translated and published. I am confident you will not want to publish it after reading it.'

'We won't want to publish it! What are you saying? We are desperate to get the book!'

'Why? What is it about the book?'

'You have criticized Islam in it. Which is why the Muslims are angry!'

'That's completely wrong,' I replied bitterly. 'There's no criticism of Islam in *Lajja*.'

'Taslima, we don't believe in religion. For us every religion is the same. Women are oppressed by every religion.'

'That even I believe.'

'Don't think that the only reason we wish to publish the book is because you have been critical of Islam in it. A feminist writer, far away in Bangladesh, has written a book that has been banned by her government and she has been publicly sentenced to death for it. We want to read this book. Our readers want to read this book too.'

'Let me repeat, they don't want to hang me because of *Lajja*, they want to hang me because of my comments on Islam.'

'It's the same thing. They want to hang you because of your writing.'

It was never-ending and the more such requests poured in the more awkward it became for me. Two French publishers, Michèle Idele and Christian Besse, were both adamant about getting my permission to publish *Lajja* in French and a tussle ensued between them regarding it. Both of them sent me the contract form, Michelle offering me 5000 francs as advance and Besse offering me 30,000.

They were calling me from France every day much to my chagrin. *Lajja* had become a source of embarrassment for me. I could not fathom what interest French readers might have regarding what was happening deep in the heart of Bhola or Manikgunje. From time to time Besse would manage to get hold of me on a sudden telephone call. 'Taslima, you are a writer. There are many publishers who publish books that have caused a storm and then conveniently forget about the writer after it. But we respect you as a writer. We publish books by good authors regardless of whether the books sell or not. We don't wish to publish a suddenly famous author simply based on a whim. We have been printing books by renowned authors from across the world in French. The other French publisher you have mentioned publishes feminist literature, but *Lajja* is not a feminist work! They want to publish it simply because so many magazines are writing about your book.'

I had to agree with him on that count. 'How do you know I am a good writer? You haven't read my work. The truth is, I can't really write well. There are numerous authors in this country who are far better writers than I ever will be. I am a doctor, I was never a student of Bengali literature. I haven't yet learnt how to write a proper novel! I have mainly written about social problems I see in my country. And sometimes I write angry pieces about injustice, oppression and discrimination. That's about it!'

In a tone that evoked a heartfelt familiarity Besse disagreed with my assessment. 'Don't pull your own writing down! You say you can't write, if that were true why are so many people angry with you? Surely you have touched a raw nerve. Not everyone is capable of doing something like that. Just like good literature is important, literature that acts as a catalyst to social change is also equally important. Be confident and you will be able to write great books. Even if you don't want to be called a writer, that is who you are and you must continue to write. We the publishers, we don't just want to publish popular and famous authors, we want to inspire writers to write more. That is our job too, we make writers. We try and inspire those who show immense promise. You have a lot of potential, Taslima.'

~

The state religion of Bangladesh was still Islam. Even though passing a fatwa was illegal as per the laws of the country, it was allowed within the tenets of Islam. Islam has certain punishments specified for certain crimes. If someone commits adultery they are to be stoned and if one is accused of something that is not Islamic then they are to be caned a hundred and one times. In my country fundamentalism was on the rise and the winds were blowing in their favour. As usual, women were the first to fall victim to the fatwas issued by fatwaphilic maulanas in villages across the country.

In a village called Hathkachhra in Sylhet, Noorjahan had gotten married for the second time. Maulana Manna declared the marriage against Islamic tenets because she was yet to get a talaq from her first husband. The man in question had left her years back and she had sent the relevant documents for a talaq to his address before her second marriage. Nevertheless, it was decreed that Noorjahan was to be stoned. A huge pit was dug in the courtyard of her house and she was made to stand in it. Then the maulanas stoned her in the name of Allah while the entire village stood around and watched without a word of protest. Bloodied, humiliated, Noorjahan climbed out of the pit, walked to her house and committed suicide by consuming poison.

In Faridpur, another Noorjahan had gone on a trip with her lover despite having a husband. Adultery being a sin in Islam, the maulana declared a fatwa against her and Noorjahan was tied up and burnt alive. In Kalikapur, under the Kaligunje police station of Saatkhira, Khalek Mistry's sixteen-year-old daughter Feroza used to catch tiny shrimps from the river to sell and help her father out. One day she met fisherman Haripada Mandal's son Uday from the adjoining village of Bandakati and the two of them began a relationship. The chairman of the local council tried Feroza because of the grave offence and according to the sharia she was tied to a post and struck with a broom a hundred and one times. After the ordeal Feroza limped home on her sister's shoulder and committed suicide soon after. A punishment was decided for Uday too because he was Hindu.

Not all such incidents of fatwas made it to the papers; it was not easy to find out about all the girls dying because of random fatwas declared on them in one of the 68,000 villages in Bangladesh. If an incident was to cause exceptional outrage only then did it come under the radar of a local journalist. Besides, it also depended on the newspaper the journalist was from. Those belonging to the *Inquilab* faction never printed such news, unwilling to give the public any chance to complain about anything. Rather, if such news got published elsewhere and inspired criticism, they immediately jumped to the defence of the clerics and produced opaque arguments against the women in question to legitimize what had happened. *Inquilab* was the highest selling and most ghoulish newspaper of the country; it had surpassed *Ittefaq* which used to enjoy the most circulation previously.

When the news broke all of a sudden that fundamentalists had incinerated 112 schools for girls constructed by BRAC, an NGO, and also declared a fatwa against girls attending school, *Inquilab* took up the task of defending the perpetrators. They argued that the NGO schools had been trying to convert the girls to Christianity, since BRAC was primarily financed by Christian nations. Even the women of the villages who used to work for the NGO had fatwas slapped on them forbidding them to leave their houses, and if they were to disobey then their husbands were going to be forced to give them talaq.

Not just fatwas, the village arbitration councils too were charting new heights of barbarism. Such councils had been a common feature in villages for centuries. In Badekusha of Sirajgunje, a council led by the imam of the mosque and the village elders ostracized thirty-five women because they had dared to follow family planning procedures. Family planning was against the tenets of Allah, so the axe of religion had fallen on their heads and the thirty-five were consigned to spend the rest of their lives as outcasts. They had to accept the judgement in silence, since religion had been reduced to a personal fiefdom of the maulanas. A long flowing robe, a fez cap, dark lines on the forehead from regularly reading the namaz, chanting the *tasbih* a few times, these had been enough for them to fashion religion into their own property. Using faith as a tool of fear they were controlling the people. No one had ever heard of cases or complaints being lodged against a maulana, an imam or an elder and neither did any of them ever get punished for their crimes.

Jashne Julus processions marking the birth anniversary of Hazrat Muhammad were being organized across the city and trucks full of cap-wearing men could be seen everywhere in Dhaka. The entire city was gearing up for festivities. When the Hindus had taken out a Janmashtami procession they had been attacked by the BNP's stick-wielding goons; members of their Yuva Command had assaulted women, torn off their saris and cracked the skull of the boy who had been put on the float as Krishna. Ultimately the procession had dispersed and the police, standing at a distance as mute spectators, had not raised a finger during the whole episode.

While the fanatics were on a rampage across the country, in an unparalleled show of thoughtlessness the courts declared their leader Golam Azam innocent of all charges, paving the way for his release from prison. The murderer walked out of jail and was publicly greeted with flowers and garlands. The traitor whose citizenship had once been revoked was set to get back his rights as a citizen of Bangladesh again. It seemed to me a strong possibility that soon the government was going to accord Golam Azam and his felon cronies—who had been responsible for the death of millions of Bengalis, who had set fire to millions of homes and raped countless Bengali women—the status of muktijoddhas.

Around the time Golam Azam was released, the people's court of the Ghatak Dalal Nirmul Committee was vandalized, mikes were torn off and the police beat back the crowd with sticks, injuring numerous innocent people. It seemed the country did not belong to us any more—we who were trying to hold on to the ideals represented by Rafiq, Salam, Barkat and Jabbar, the martyrs of the Language Movement in 1952, and the numerous muktijoddhas who had fought for the independence of Bangladesh. The country was gradually becoming Golam Azam's and spinning out of control. The enemies of freedom defaced lines by Rabindranath, Jibanananda Das and Nazrul written on the wall beside the Sahid Minar, darkening the slogan 'Banglar Hindu, Banglar Bouddho, Banglar Krishtan, Banglar Mussalman, Amra Sobai Bangali' (Hindus of Bengal, Buddhists of Bengal, Christians of Bengal, Muslims of Bengal, we are all Bengali). It seemed there was much

more destruction in store for us, and I could not help but wish we
went deaf or blind before anything else happened.

~

To protest the fatwas declared on women in the various villages the
Mahila Parisad took out a protest rally. The women sat down on
the road in front of the Press Club holding placards with slogans of
the Parisad, while their leaders took to the stage and gave powerful
speeches naming all the women on whom random fatwas had been
declared. Not a single person mentioned my name. The Mahila
Sangram Parisad was the biggest women's rights organization in the
country. Even though Sufia Kamal was its titular head it was Maleka
Begum who ran things. Begum was a writer on women's issues, had
written quite a few books on the subject and was a long-time women's
rights activist. She could be described as one among the few feminist
leaders of the country.

    One day she paid me a sudden visit. I was so overwhelmed that
I almost hugged her in joy! Back in the day when I had just begun
writing columns we had run into each other a few times and she
had always encouraged me with 'You are writing so well, keep at
it, keep writing'. Her husband Motiur Rahman had been the editor
of the Communist Party's paper *Ekata* before becoming the editor
of *Bhorer Kagaj*. Both were renowned socialist leaders and I used
to admire them no end but on many occasions some incidents
concerning them had been nothing short of shocking. After winning
the Ananda Puraskar when I had gone to Maleka Begum's house
to share my happiness with her she had acerbically remarked, 'It's
common knowledge how easy awards are to come by when you are
on good terms with Sunil.' She had not been happy with my win,
had been convinced that since I was not fit for such an award on
my own merit Sunil Gangopadhyay must have pulled strings on my
behalf. I had felt terribly alone all of a sudden and walked out of her
house in silence.

    The Ananda Puraskar had been a double-edged sword; it had
cut a swathe through a large chunk of my well-wishers, slashing the
number almost down to zero. On another occasion, seeing her at

a demonstration at the court with her group demanding the death penalty for Khuku, I had been too stunned to fathom what Maleka Begum was after. After the papers had published details of Khuku's 'illicit' relationship with Munir everyone had turned against the woman and demanded her death. Instead of standing by Khuku the representatives of the Mahila Parisad had gone and vocally demanded capital punishment for her. The same Maleka Begum was at my house!

'I've come to see you. How are you?'

I smiled weakly. Surely she could guess how I was.

'I thought I should drop by once. With all that is happening around the country I am so worried about you. The mullahs are going way too far.'

'Yes. Who knows what will happen to this country.'

Suddenly she began to laugh. I was staring at her in astonishment. Composing herself, she said, 'I have been associated with the women's movement for thirty years, and it's you whose name spreads across the world as a feminist activist.'

Embarrassed by my own fame I did not know where to look. As if becoming famous was the worst and most shameful thing I could have done. I would have been happiest had I been able to deny my fame. It was my fault that everyone knew my name.

Maleka Begum was a very intelligent woman, or else how could she have known what was in my heart! 'No, it's not your fault. It's the mullahs who are making you famous.' Laughing again she continued, 'In fact you should thank them.'

Trying to dispel my discomfort I stood up from the chair saying, 'You must have tea. Let me go and ask them to make some.'

After finishing the tea she said, 'Taslima, at such a time we can support you and fight on your behalf, only if you join our organization.'

'Your organization? You want me to join the Parisad?'

'Yes.'

After a moment of strained silence I replied, 'Maleka aapa, are you saying unless I join the Parisad you can't protest the fatwa against me or the movement that the mullahs have begun? You fight for women, I write on behalf of women . . .'

'It's just that you're a little controversial.'

'So what? Don't speak up for me if you don't wish to, but can't you even protest an injustice?'

After some time Maleka Begum excused herself and got up to leave. She had understood that I was not going to join the Mahila Parisad just to get their support. Despite that, on her way out she offered me time to reconsider. I had read many of Maleka Begum's books but not once had it seemed to me that she was someone who could make compromises easily or be starkly irrational under trying circumstances.

~

I received an invitation from Reporters Sans Frontières and Arte TV of France to visit Paris to attend a television special on the freedom of the press. I had only read about Paris and heard about it from others; never had I dreamt that I would one day get an opportunity to go there. I informed the organizers that I would be unable to attend since I did not have a passport. It had been a year and a half since they had taken it away and chances were slim that they were going to give it back to me any time soon. But to my immense surprise my passport was returned to me. After the news of the fatwa spread around the world it was the most surprising thing that happened to me.

Around the time when protests were being held abroad in support of my freedom of expression and my rights as a citizen, an officer from the American consulate named Andrew came to meet me one day. He asked me a bunch of questions regarding how my passport was taken away, when, by whom, and then left just as suddenly as he had arrived. Then on another occasion he visited me again to speak about the passport. Barely two weeks after that Andrew called me and asked me to pick up my passport from the passport office. Never had I seen this sort of magic before and I could not help but wonder how the US consulate had managed to achieve something I had failed at accomplishing in a year and a half! I was ecstatic on getting my passport back, not because I could go abroad but because my rights as a citizen had finally been restored to me.

~

The fatwa was creating a lot of uproar everywhere. Editorials were being written in well-known foreign papers on the issue, writers, journalists and scholars were protesting and members of women's groups, human rights organizations and writers' associations were eager to offer me their help. This fatwa managed to make me a known name the world over, but the other fatwa that no one got to know about was the one declared on Mother from the pir's house.

The place had been Mother's refuge. For years she had gone there to listen to stories of Allah and forget about her own troubles. Ever since Hasina had taken up the reins of the family Mother had effectively been reduced to an extra person in Abakash. After I moved to Shantibag she would visit me to forget her sorrows, not that she managed to find that elusive happiness in my company either. So even from Dhaka she would often go off to the pir's house. After Bhalobasha was born Yasmin had spent a few months in Abakash with her infant daughter and then moved to Dhaka. In order to take care of the child Mother had moved too. However, after settling in, Mother had realized that besides the lack of space for so many people the commotion of a baby in the house was not letting me write or sleep. So she had decided to return to Mymensingh.

Of course, the other reason behind her decision to return was a desire to save my money. Whether it was Yasmin taking care of the expenses or I, certain overheads had to be met and raising a baby was not cheap. After Suhrid was born he had been Mother's responsibility and the same had been the case for Bhalobasha. Mother had assumed that the way Father had helped out with Suhrid—with pure milk and chicken soup for the baby—would also happen with Bhalobasha. She was not completely unnecessary at Abakash despite the reins of the family having passed to someone else, she had a granddaughter to raise and she was still going to be accorded some respect—all these were things she had assumed. But her status as an unimportant and peripheral member of the family had not changed. The way a grandson had been important to Father had not been reflected in his attitude towards Bhalobasha. As for Hasina, effectively the new matriarch of the family, no one was more important to her than her two children—in fact, other children were only an inconvenience.

Her husband's and her daughter-in-law's behaviour used to drive Mother to the pir's fairly often.

After the passing of Pir Besharatullah the mantle had passed to his son Musa. But even Musa could not live to enjoy the life of a pir for long and died of heart disease abruptly, passing the responsibility on to Besharatullah's grandson, Fajli khala's son Mohammad. It was Mohammad who issued a fatwa on Mother that was supported by all the other members of the house. The fatwa: Mother was not allowed to enter the pir's house any more. Her crime? She had given birth to a kaffir named Taslima Nasrin and was yet to cut all familial ties with her. These were her crimes and she was given a choice: cast me aside or cut ties with the pir's house.

Mother took Fajli khala aside and inquired, 'Fajli, how can I cut ties with my own daughter? Is that even possible?'

'You have cut ties with her, borobu! Your daughter is a kaffir. You can't have relations with a kaffir! Then you will be a kaffir too.'

'You are calling me a kaffir?'

'Children are nothing but illusions in this world. In the end you have to return to Allah. For the sake of blood if you accept a kaffir as a daughter then let me tell you Allah won't forgive you. It's in the Quran, if you keep relations with them I will cast you to the fires of *dokhaj*.'

'Nasrin is very kind to people. She is so generous. She writes against offences and injustices committed against women. She helps so many poor girls with money. Will she not get Allah's forgiveness?'

Fajli khala's voice hardened. 'No. There is no forgiveness. She will go to hell. She does not believe in Allah. Borobu, you know very well she has written horrible things about the Quran. She has said the Quran was written by men. That our Prophet was a libertine. That Allah doesn't exist. *Astaghfirullah!*'

'Fajli, your brother doesn't give me any money. He keeps driving me away from Mymensingh time and again. If I don't go to Nasrin where will I go?'

'What do I know of that! The simple thing is, if you want to continue coming to this house then even glancing at a kaffir's face is forbidden. And if you maintain relations with a kaffir then this house is forbidden.'

Unable to bear it any more Mother broke down in tears. She wept and lamented, but none of it made any difference to Fajli khala. She was thrown out of the pir's house and was asked never to go anywhere near it again.

This and That

Mother moved to Dhaka with Bhalobasha. Since Yasmin kept nine-to-five hours, the child was mostly Mother's responsibility. Bhalobasha—Srotosshini Bhalobasha. I had chosen the name although Milan had been none too happy about it at first.

'How is that even a name? I have never heard of a name like Bhalobasha.'

'So what?'

'People will laugh.'

'So what?'

'Once she grows up boys will tease her.'

'So what?'

Milan's mother had chosen Mosammat Afisa Khatun and had Yasmin not changed her mind at the last minute that would have stuck. Almost waging a rebellion in favour of my choice she had managed to get her way in the end. Everyone adoringly called the cherubic girl Bhalobasha. The sight of her tottering about the house on her tiny feet gladdened my heart. She would climb on to my lap, press a key on the computer and erase my writing. But I could feel no anger towards her; for Bhalobasha I only ever felt love.

~

Mother's nomadic life did not quite find the stability she had expected in the Shantinagar apartment. She wanted stability but there was no one to give it to her. At Abakash she had to live by Father's rules and at Shantinagar she had to live by mine. Trapped in the middle she continued to drift like she always had. She did not like Nahid. The foremost reason for that was that Nahid smoked and was getting me

471

to smoke too; on top of that Mother was convinced Nahid was not a trustworthy friend. I usually told her off and asked her to not say such things against Nahid, and Mother would dip out of sight and cry. I had given her instructions that Nahid could come and go as she pleased and that she should never be disrespected. To be fair, no one had ever shown any disrespect to Nahid in my house, but it was Nahid who always looked for opportunities to tell me how none of my family members had shown her any courtesy, how it had taken them a long time to let her in, or how they had not given her anything to eat or shown her disdain in some way.

Usually Mother bore the brunt of my anger after such conversations. However, one day it was Nahid who I got annoyed with. One night Neepa and her mother came by the house to complain about Nahid. After the two of them had met at my house Nahid and Neepa had become friends and Nahid spent the night at Neepa's on occasion. The last time she had stayed over, while sleeping on the same bed at night, Nahid had repeatedly touched Neepa in the dark and had at one point tried to take her clothes off. After hearing about the whole incident Neepa's mother had come to ask me to tell Nahid never to set foot in their house again. This was not reason enough to be suspicious of Nahid or to be angry with her. Nahid was possibly homosexual, something I had been unaware of. Nahid had never told me, she had chosen to conceal it. She had every right to conceal personal information and there was nothing wrong with that.

What sparked my suspicion, though, was an article about my relationship with K that came out in the papers. Such pieces were hardly surprising given how everyone knew about the two of us. But the article described an incident where I had hit K and he had left my house with his shirt torn. Not this exact incident but something quite similar had actually happened and Nahid had been a witness to it. There had been no one else at home at that point of time who could have taken the story to the papers. The moment I read the story I lost all faith in Nahid. She was no longer welcome at home. She tried everything to get in touch with me but failed to change my mind.

It was fine if they were writing about my personal life in the papers. That was a regular thing for them and it barely made any difference to me any more. The yellow press was usually adept at mixing one kernel of truth with several fragments from various lies to concoct salacious stories about my personal life. In the beginning I used to get upset and angry, or at least worried, but eventually I could only spare a passing glance at such stories. I had accepted Nahid as a friend but I did not want her to remain in my life as a spy. She could have written about me herself or spoken to a journalist—I would not have minded the ensuing criticism. But why hide it from me? As soon as I realized that she was saying one set of things to me and a completely contrary set of things to other people, I also realized that no matter what else, she could not be my friend. I did not like people who changed their statements depending on who they were talking to, and neither did I want such people coming to my house.

When I let Gauri Rani Das stay at my house, Mother warned me, 'Letting a perfect stranger live here, is that wise?' I snapped at her and asked her to be quiet. 'You don't have to worry about who I am going to allow in this house. It's my house.' Even to my ears my voice sounded like Father's. Father too used to remind me at least twice a day that Abakash was his house. Gauri Rani Das was a gang rape survivor and I had written a column in the newspaper in her support asking for suitable punishment for the accused. Somehow word about me had reached Gauri Rani and she came to my house for shelter. She had filed a case against the rapists and needed a place to stay in Dhaka and it was impossible for me to turn the helpless woman away. So I asked her to stay and eat at my house for as long as she needed to; if she required financial assistance for the case that too she could ask without hesitation.

Gauri Rani moved into my house and was given a queen's welcome. In a week or two, Mother complained about a smell in the house that refused to lessen no matter what was done. According to her the smell was coming off Gauri Rani and I shouted at her for being mean and narrow-minded and asked her to shut up. Then one day I realized that the smell was indeed coming off Gauri Rani and even after she would take baths the stench remained. I had sensed the smell before too but had never expected that Mother's deduction could be so accurate. Although the stench continued to grow stronger it was impossible for me to ask Gauri to leave. Instead I made arrangements to have her clothes washed, which Minu did with her nose covered. But the smell remained, disappearing only the day Gauri left.

'Organize a huge dinner, my friends are coming over.'

'Cooking's done! But there are seven more people joining us. Seven girls from the garment mills are coming to eat at home.'

'You'll have to leave for a while. Someone is coming from Calcutta and will stay here for five days.'

'We need to get some alcohol. My poet friends want to drink.'

'There will be loud music. Very loud, as loud as my heart desires.'

'Don't make any noise. It disturbs my writing.'

'There's a party going on till two in the night! Who cares! This is my house, this will go on all night if need be.'

'Give the driver some food. Not in the kitchen, make him sit at the dining table.'

Mother had no problems with whatever I wanted. Even when K and I would go inside the bedroom and lock the door in the middle of the day, Mother did not have a problem. From time to time she would leave and go back to Mymensingh. As long as Mother was in the house it felt like home. Everything was usually spic and span; there would be no water on the bathroom floor, no crumpled sheets or dirty clothes. Food would be ready even before someone could ask for it, usually all my favourite dishes. No one had to be told to give me tea at regular intervals in my study and everything in the house would always be effortlessly beautiful. When Mother was at home I could barely sense her presence, but when she was not there I could acutely feel her absence. One day when she was not at home I asked Yasmin about her.

'She was angry so she left.'

'Why was she angry?'

'Apparently you said too much money was being spent on the groceries.'

'Yes, I did. But it was not meant for Ma.'

'She thought it was.'

Mother had no issues with my independence. The only thing that made her cry was when I behaved badly with her and it made her go back to her nomadic life again. She would get upset about my scolding and move back to Abakash. There, Father behaved the same way and she again came back to me. Mother did not have a stable roof over her head, she had no home. What I never noticed was how I could suddenly turn into Father while speaking to her. I had always respected him irrespective of what a cruel man he could be; perhaps even while I was berating his cruelty I had nursed a secret admiration for his authority, a fascination I had failed to recognize then for what it was.

When I finally learnt to stand on my own feet, when life became comfortable, quite unconsciously I became like Father, authoritarian and powerful. Mother's poverty, her wretchedness, her lack of beauty, her inferiority complex, her docile nature, her pain, her foolishness, her religiosity, her superstitions, all these were anathema to me and it ensured the growing distance between us. She tried her best to become a relevant member of my household; I could only think of her as an extra person just like Father did back in Abakash. During Eid I would head over to Abakash laden with gifts for him while completely forgetting her. Then if I had to give her something it would be an old sari from my wardrobe, something I used to wear often but did not fancy any more. Even then Mother would be ecstatic. She would refuse initially. 'You bought it for yourself, you wear it. Whatever I have is enough.'

'No, I don't wear this any more.'

'Still! What if you feel like wearing it? Keep it.'

'No. I don't like this sari any more.'

She would be forced to take it in the end but she would go around showing it to everyone nonetheless. 'Nasrin just gave this to me. She loves this sari. Did not wear it even once!'

~

I never asked Mother to save on household expenses but she did it nonetheless. If we were to buy some chicken for one day she would try and make it last for two. I never compromised with my share so she would give me her portion and eat dal and rice with the maid instead. She was far more concerned about my financial troubles than I. She was also perennially afraid whenever Bhalobasha tried to walk, afraid that the toddler would fall and hurt herself. If I went and stood in the balcony Mother would be terrified that some unknown assailant was watching me from the road or from one of the neighbouring buildings. It was horrible to see Mother so afraid all the time. The police posted at my gate were no longer there; one fine day they had simply not turned up. Only when the protest rallies came anywhere near Shantinagar were police posted on the road in front of my house. I could walk out of the house at odd hours whenever fancy struck me and Mother would always try and stop me. 'Don't go out now. Anything can happen any time, who knows?' Most of the time I would not even turn back and she would go on trying. 'At least take someone with you. Don't go alone.'

Quite honestly, after being afraid for days and months on end it was all becoming too intolerable for me. Even if I could abruptly leave the house it's not as if I could go anywhere. So I usually headed out of the city. Sahabuddin, courteous, reticent and extremely honest, would ask me, 'Aapa, which way should I go?'

'Whichever, wherever you want to go.'

I had nowhere to go so Sahabuddin usually drove south. There was no destination southward; it was simply quieter, far from the noisy city, towards the villages, forests and rivers. I liked the speed, the sense of escape and I adored my hair getting all mussed up by the rushing wind. All I wanted was to walk alone through the forest, perhaps find a tiny earthen hut surrounded by a fence of banana leaves, bathe in a pond or swim in the river, go fishing or play gollachhut with the girls in the village. But I quashed such feelings deep down, acutely aware that with my urban style of draping the sari, my car, my shoe-clad feet and my short hair, I would stick out like a sore thumb there and be ogled at like a circus clown. So I would simply ask him to stop the car at a quiet spot and sit inside.

Occasionally I asked Sahabuddin about his home, his wife, his children and he bashfully and hesitantly answered my questions. When I asked if the salary I paid him was enough he usually said it was. When I asked if there was anything he wanted he usually said there was nothing as such. Other drivers usually got around 1500 to 2000 taka per month but I paid Sahabuddin 2500. It was my choice to pay him that much and not something he had demanded. Besides, he had lunch at my place every day. Even though he had the usual

ten-to-five hours, on most days he had to stay back till eight or nine
and sometimes even as late as two in the night; he never complained.
When I tried giving him money for the extra hours he would shrink
in embarrassment and I had to force him to accept it. Altogether he
earned around 3000 taka per month.

My previous driver had been young and used to drive very fast;
when sent to pick someone up he would usually stop midway and sell
fuel from the car. After replacing the young man with Sahabuddin
I never had to worry about a driver again. He would wash the car
and keep it sparkling clean. The other drivers used to park their cars
in the garage of Eastern Housing to chat and play cards there but I
never saw Sahabuddin with them. He usually sat inside the car and
read booklets on the namaz and such things. Once he informed me
fearfully that some men were coming around to the garage every day
to look for him. He was afraid the strangers were going to try to harm
me and they were looking for him to warn him not to drive my car
any more or perhaps to hide bombs inside. Sahabuddin would not
step out of the car at all and he also informed the guards that he did
not know the men so under no circumstances were they to be allowed
inside the garage. A lanky, clean-shaven, pyjama kurta–clad sixty-
five-year-old man was my protector without my knowledge.

I had never told him what was happening in the country around
me but he knew regardless, although he never let on that he knew.
If he were to notice individuals or a rally advancing towards my car
he automatically sped up without my prompting him to do so and I
did not have to tell him to avoid roads where anti-Taslima rallies or
meetings were being held. On one such occasion I asked him, 'Why
are you taking a detour?'

'There's a rally that way today.'

'What rally?'

Sahabuddin was quiet. He was not aware that I knew what the
demonstration was about.

'Who all are marching?'

'They are not nice people.'

It was the briefest answer he could have given—bad people were
marching that side so I had no reason to go there.

'Do you need to refuel?'

'No.'

The car did not need too much fuel. Given what little use it was put to, not much fuel was consumed.

'Sahabuddin, do you need money?'

'No.'

'You had spoken to me about your son's matric exam. Do let me know if you ever need anything.'

'No, I don't need anything.'

Sahabuddin got awkward whenever it came to money. There were limits to how polite and devoid of greed one could be and Sahabuddin time and again tested such limits. Often it seemed to me he was not a human being at all but an extraterrestrial who had somehow ended up on our dirty planet and I could not help but wonder how different our country would have been if everyone was as honest as him. A handful of rich men had taken enormous loans from banks and were showing no signs of returning the money. They were also friends with those in high places and the government usually forgave their defaulter friends. In fact no matter who was in power this arrangement remained the same and there was no space for honesty in any sphere of life.

Teachers used to be honest but seeds of deceit were growing among them too. They were demanding heavy tuition fees from students and assuring them success in examinations in exchange. Police personnel, engineers, civil servants—everyone was taking bribes. Roads were being constructed one day and showing wear and tear in a matter of weeks. Everything was being adulterated. Greedy doctors were recommending patients to private clinics for operations to perform surgeries that were not required simply for the sake of money. It was the same with ministers and bureaucrats. The ones who already had enough to eat wanted more to consume, the ones who had nothing were going hungry and being forced to watch. If there was even an iota of honesty left it was among the poor. But why were they all silent? Why were they not demanding what was rightfully theirs?

Rickshaw-pullers braved the rain and the sun for the meagre amount of money they made, silently tolerating abuse and even violence from their customers. Along the periphery of five-star hotels and tall apartments of Baridhara there were numerous people living in rundown slums who were not protesting the injustices being meted out to them. Hungry beggars were watching rich men stuffing themselves with food in restaurants and then burping in contentment but despite that they were not ready to snatch food away from them.

Once I had gone to the Kawran market at night when trucks laden with fresh vegetables and greens would be parked there for the workers to unload things. On my way back after buying some vegetables I had chanced upon workers sleeping on the pavements. None of them had homes of their own or even a roof to sleep under, no fans during summer, no nets to ward off mosquitos. After a day of back-breaking work they were happy as long as they got a sliver of place to sleep in at night; they did not know how to protest.

Although my first reaction at such stark differences between the rich and the poor was anger, I had to stop to ask myself what right I had to be angry. To anyone who was homeless and destitute was I not just the same, a rich person with privileges? I had an expensive apartment and a car, so I was rich. I told myself I had done nothing dishonest to earn my wealth—I did not have an illegal business, neither was I a conman nor did I dabble in the black market. However, the self-loathing was not that easy to shake off. Was I supposed to renounce everything and become a pavement dweller, or go and live in a slum? Was I supposed to give away all my wealth, live on one square meal or none at times, like most people did? Would that address the inequalities between the rich and the poor? Perhaps not. Would I be able to address these inequalities through my writing? No, I would not. Corruption had seeped into society's veins. No politician was interested in thinking about changing the living conditions of the poor, let alone doing something about it. Whichever party came to power through the democratic machinery had but one objective: to abuse their power as much as possible to serve their personal gains. Concerns like the good of the country and its citizens or rectifying social inequalities were farthest from their mind.

I had once asked a poor man from the slums adjoining Baridhara how he felt about all these rich people around him and their endless wealth. Why were they willing to accept such inequalities that ensured happiness for the rich and absolutely nothing for them? Why did they not protest against the rich? The man had replied, 'Allah has given them, He hasn't given us. If we suffer in this world Allah will make sure we have everything we want in the hereafter. Thus, one must have integrity. That's what Allah is testing, our integrity, through all this suffering. If we can pass this test Allah will come to our aid.' I was convinced these were not his words. He had parroted what our politicians had taught him.

Our politicians used religion to keep the poor at bay. Otherwise if even 80 per cent of the suffering masses were to take to the streets in protest, the rich would not have been able to go on with their lives of privilege and luxury. Religion was effectively a weapon used by the rich to perpetuate their privileges, just as it was a weapon for politicians to keep the poor quiet and to win elections. Religion could be used to stoke religious sentiments, it could be used to hide the death of thousands of people in the hurricane at Uri Char and make the homeless live under the open sky. Religion could be used to explain to the people who lost their houses and their possessions to the floods every year that Allah was testing their integrity. The question no one had the gumption to ask was why only the poor had to repeatedly prove their honesty. It was the upper and middle classes that reaped the benefits; the middle class harboured aspirations of becoming the upper class and conveniently adopted all the latter's practices. At the same time all movements against social injustices invariably arose from among the educated and conscious middle class, which was why perhaps most such movements failed to solidify into anything larger and significant in the long run.

Despite being socially conscious, despite their keenness to fight for the betterment of society, the middle class was not a victim of this systematic inequality. When victims fought, they fought for their lives. Obviously, movements by victims fighting for justice were disrupted all the time. None of the factories in the country adhered to international labour laws. Workers were made to work well past their hours, they were paid less and not given any of the benefits due to them. Whenever they threatened to organize and fight for their rights their leaders were poached away by the owners and bribed with a lot of money to sabotage the movement. That is how the country was running.

Despite wide-ranging advancements in agricultural technology across the world, in a primarily agrarian country like Bangladesh ploughs were still the main tool for tilling land. Farmers who were producing crops did not get the returns they deserved because middlemen between the farmers and the buyers took away nearly half the profit. Was it not possible to institute a system where this chasm between the rich and the poor could be bridged? Where the rich would not be able to keep on increasing their wealth at the expense of the poor and the latter would not be forced to live under inhuman conditions?

There was hardly anyone in the country who could hope to become rich through honest means anyway. The ones who were very rich had mostly earned their wealth through dishonest means, by swindling other people; most did not pay their taxes either. The honesty and dedication required to work towards true equity between the rich and the poor was not something most people had in them. Even if individuals wished to walk the path of honesty, institutionalized dishonesty on the part of the government made sure no one remained honest for long. If the upper echelons were corrupt was it any wonder that it would trickle down below too?

Ours was a poor country. We did not possess wealth below our earth with which all of us could become rich overnight. The population was expanding at a rapid rate; numerous people were dying every year because of natural disasters; buses, trucks, cars and trains were overturning every other day while ships and boats were getting lost at sea—calamities that were claiming hundreds of lives in a matter of minutes. Despite everything, the population numbers showed no signs of slowing down. Children were dying of malnutrition every other day but even as their mortality rate went up, so did their birth rate. Uncertainties were on the rise and so was the lack of proper education, both contributing to fostering misconceptions, superstitions, poverty and blindness. As anxiety and despair increased, so did the reliance on religion. Even in an urban space like Dhaka there was more than one Islamic gathering organized every day. Religion was a booming industry and the ones investing in it were earning well too. In fact, anyone whose livelihood was all about conning other people was bound to flourish in such a system—the more the number of gullible victims the more their income. There was not a single honest leader in the country for the people to place their trust in and neither were any of the political leaders interested in thinking about the good of the people. Everyone was busy watching over their own stockpiles instead.

Dr Kamal Hossain started his own political party called Gono Forum (People's Forum). Once a trusted aide to Sheikh Mujib, he was the one who had drafted the secular constitution of Bangladesh. Having fallen out with Sheikh Hasina over a difference of opinion he had left the Awami League. The forum did not have too many members and most of the affiliates were highly educated scholars and legal professionals, including a few hardened leftist leaders. If the forum could ever lay claim to power then there was a possibility of real change in the country, but Dr Kamal was yet to find much success in making the forum popular among the people. Neither was it possible, since to be a popular political outfit one had to employ political agents, maintain goons on the roster and be ready to cheat people. All this was hardly possible for someone who wished to be an idealistic politician. In the last election Dr Hossain had lost by a significant margin to Haroon Molla, an uneducated businessman dealing in trucks. A celebrated jurist, an adviser to the United Nations, highly educated, honest, secular, and yet such a candidate had lost to a politically inexperienced man—this could hardly be the sign of a properly functioning democracy. One had to only give false assurances to 80 per cent of the populace as well as give them some money, and it ensured votes no matter what manner of criminal the candidate was. The more the money, the bigger the lies, the more the votes!

Often, while out on one of my long drives I would be so immersed in thought, with my head resting on the window pensively, that I would fail to notice when we reached home. The sound of Sahabuddin's voice would wake me out of my reverie; he would be there holding the car door open for me. Time and again I asked him not to open the door for me but Sahabuddin would only lower his head in response. On my way to my apartment I often wondered if the courtesy I was showing Sahabuddin was for his sake or for mine. Probably it was for myself to make myself feel as if I was generous.

For Sahabuddin, holding the door open was not a chore. He did it to keep me satisfied, so that one day I would not be able to casually tell him that his services were no longer required. Sahabuddin needed the job. He was not stealing fuel from the car or trying to hoodwink me into giving him money because he was an innately honest man who as a child had perhaps been taught aphorisms like 'never do evil', 'never hurt anyone' or 'never be dishonest'. He was old but he was still living his life based on lessons learnt in childhood that most others had forgotten. Even if they remembered they had no interest in adhering to such tired maxims, with the corruption around them not making things any easier.

After one such long drive I returned to my study, switched the fan on and lay back on my chair. A thousand thoughts were still buzzing through my brain like tiny insects. I had so many pieces lying around incomplete, articles I had lost interest in finishing. I could not figure out what would be the point of it all, what would be the point of going on writing. A terrible despair enveloped me. If my writing was not going to succeed in changing anything in society then what was the point of writing any more? Eighty per cent of the people did not know how to read or write. Only the educated got the chance to read what I had to say; besides, I wrote primarily about the problems of the educated middle class, the class I belonged to.

Consequently, neither physically nor mentally, I could never reach the lives of the poor; all I could do was imagine their lives but I could never become one of them. I had written about Noorjahan because I could identify with her pain. But I had not experienced that pain by living her life and there was a world of difference between the two. Was I using Noorjahan only for my own benefit or was I truly moved by her plight? Why had I written about her? How many women like her could read what I wrote and gather strength from my words? Not even one! So was I then writing only for the educated middle class so they would praise me? Or was I truly invested in what I felt and wanted to share that feeling with others so they could awake and arise and try to do something good? I was not sure what exactly the country needed. Was economic change automatically going to lead to social change, where religion was going to lose primacy and all civic amenities including health and education were going to be rapidly developed? Or did the key lie in a stable and healthy political atmosphere? Or did everything have to start with the eradication of religion? Which of these could get rid of systematic inequalities between men and women, the rich and the poor, the majority and the minority? Was one of them going to be enough, given how intricately connected all three were? Or did one have to fight each battle separately but simultaneously? Unable to think any more I cursed and got off the chair. I wanted tea and I called out to Minu. Even Minu could have been working in a garments factory but I was not letting her because that would have hindered my comfortable life. Or was it because I was trying to save her from the uncertainties that came with such a job?

Yes, I definitely needed tea.

While I was sipping tea the five girls arrived. All of them students of Jahangirnagar University, they had come to meet me once before. Simple, sari-clad, pigtailed girls; however, their views were anything but straight and narrow. They had the same thing to say as before—according to them all the things I was trying to achieve by way of women's rights through my writing, none of it amounted to anything in the long run as long as capitalism remained the dominant mode of production. The solution according to them was joining the Communist Party and becoming an active member. If the party came to power, only then could I hope to bring my dreams to fruition, or so they believed. I did not wish to join any political party, though. Why? Because I barely understood politics. The girls did not agree when I told them that. Tea arrived. It was set before them but the five were much more interested in talking than having tea.

Why was I writing about secularism and women's rights separately? Why was I not writing only about communism? With the advent of communism, secularism and women rights were going to be automatic developments. So the problems I was concerned with were superficial ones. I was only writing about certain issues without trying to explore what the core of the problem was. The girls mentioned a host of other social, economic and political problems and claimed that capitalism was at the source of all of it. I coughed and then felt an insane urge to laugh when the five of them asked in unison, 'What happened?' I almost replied, 'It's this capitalist mode of production!' While listening to them I could not help but think how beautiful their sentences were. I also noticed the sentences were not from their hearts, they were emerging from their brains as if they had learnt a host of such beautiful sentences by heart. None of them were disagreeing with each other; when one was speaking the other four were nodding in agreement. All five seemed like simple robots to me.

They gave me tonnes of advice before taking their leave.

I lounged on the sofa for a long time. Yasmin had changed the TV channel to Zee TV, where Hindi songs were playing. I was staring at the screen, my thoughts miles away. Even when Saju, Lovely and Jaheda came and called and asked how I was, my mind was still wandering. The spell broke on hearing the news they had brought: that Jaheda and Saju had lost their jobs. They had been heading a movement against the owner of their garments factory, something they had been working towards for a long time. To that end they had visited the homes of all the workers, explained to them the benefits they were not getting, made them aware of how the owner was cheating them and inspired thousands of workers to take to the streets in protest. The owner had hired goons to attack the rally, beat up the protesters and break their limbs, while the police had stood by and watched.

I already knew about the terrible conditions under which they were forced to work: fifteen hours of work, no holidays, not even weekends off, two toilets for 3000 workers with a rule prohibiting its use more than twice, termination of services in case of pregnancy, salary deduction for absence if any of them got ill, and no extra money for the overtime they were made to do. I had written about their troubles but what good was a column! What they urgently needed was the movement they had tried to begin on their own. Expectedly, the owner was happy having dismissed the leaders and crushed their movement, along with their heads and limbs. The government had taken no steps against such heinous crimes and the courts too had refused to let them file a case.

'At least the factory will be shut,' I said.

Jaheda corrected me. 'The factory will reopen tomorrow, aapa.'

'How can they reopen the factory if workers refuse to work?'

'Most workers will accept the terms set by the owner.'

'Not everyone surely!'

'They have already dismissed the ones who won't. It won't matter to the owner. There are too many poor people in the country and he will get labour easily. Most are ready to work under any conditions.'

I could see the awareness in Jaheda's eyes, her hands clenching into fists and her teeth gnashing in anger. After their secret nightly meetings with the workers Jaheda and her group would come over to my house and I would hurriedly arrange for food for the hungry lot. Over dinner they would describe to me how things were going and how much longer they had to wait. Jaheda and Saju had lost their jobs some time ago. Lovely was still employed but it was not certain how long that was going to last. Despite their experience in working in garment mills, Jaheda and Saju had not gotten a job elsewhere. I heard everything they had to say. At one point I got up, tore out the last remaining leaf from my chequebook, wrote a cheque for the last 4000 taka remaining in my account and handed it to Jaheda.

'What's the money for?'

'Buy a sewing machine. Work from home and try and earn for now.'

I had been to Jaheda's small shanty in the slums of Pallavi. The room had enough space for a bed and a small table. Sitting on that bed I had heard the stories of their fight for survival. Jaheda had moved to the city from the village to earn a living. Having been educated only till class eight there had been nothing else for her to do other than working in a garments factory. Saju used to like studying and had even passed his matriculation exam. But without any money there had been no way for him to go to college and so he too had taken up a job in the factory. As for Lovely, after the death of her parents she had joined the factory in order to support her family. Saju and Jaheda had been living together for the past couple of years and they had a child too. Since both of them spent most of the day outside and there was no one to take care of the baby they had sent the child to be brought up by Jaheda's mother in the village. Saju would proudly declare, 'We live together. Marriage is an unreasonable arrangement!'

'Don't you face trouble living together without marrying?'

'No, living together is not a problem for the rich and the poor. It's only a problem for the middle class,' Saju had told me.

I could not help but agree with him. It was the middle class that had issues with such an arrangement. They were the ones who had the most shame, the most fear and the most superstitions.

Since Saju was interested in studies he would read whichever paper or journal he could get his hands on. That was how he had come across my writing. Reading my columns every week was a must for him and he would make Jaheda and Lovely read them too. Then one day he had brought Jaheda to meet me, who in turn had brought Lovely, and through them other workers of the factory had found their way to my place. Their company gave me courage and I enjoyed spending time with them far more than I did with the girls from Jahangirpur University. Their resilience and daring was what astounded me the most. They would travel from one place to another hanging from the door of the bus, or if they did not have money then they walked mile after mile, uncaring of the scorching noon sun or the uncertainty of the night.

They knew nothing about capitalism or socialism but they were aware of their rights, they knew how to work hard and they were prepared to do everything necessary to earn every last farthing of what they deserved. Their poverty had failed to break them and no conspiracies or attacks were going to succeed in pushing them back. Perhaps there were many things they did not know but they weren't stupid. They had enthusiasm and they could not afford to be afraid or overwhelmed. They could not afford to live by the differences observed in society between the sexes and among various religious affiliations. They did not follow the path travelled by others but chose to fashion their own, and every moment was a new fight for them—a fight for food, clothes or survival. I was infamous for being rebellious but I was acutely aware that even ten Taslimas like me were nothing in comparison to the rebel that Jaheda was, or the sheer courage she displayed. I was not as proud of my own achievements as I was of Jaheda's.

As soon as they left with the cheque a thought struck me—did I just douse the fire burning within them a little with my gesture? Was my money only going to calm them down? Were they not going to talk to any of the workers any more about how the factory owner was exploiting them? Were they no longer going to organize to fight for

workers' rights? Henceforth were they only going to sew clothes in
their new sewing machine and think about how to turn things around
for themselves, just the two of them? Did I just turn Saju and Jaheda
away from a collective struggle for their rights? A chill set in my bones
at the thought.

~

The year was almost over. Things were usually very hectic around
this time and I was either writing tirelessly or proofreading finished
pieces. February was just around the corner. February meant the
book fair and publishers going mad over new books they wished to
release. Kakali Prakashani was about to bring out a compilation of
my columns titled *Chhoto Chhoto Dukkho Kotha* (Slight Stories of
Sorrow). Selim Ahmed of Kakali had kept my request and published
Phyan Dao (Famine!), a collection of old poems about the famine of
1950 that I had compiled from journals and newspapers of the time
and edited. Nikhil Sarkar was the inspiration behind the project. He
had asked three people to work on three books: Bilal Chowdhury was
tasked with compiling short stories about the famine, I was asked to
work on poetry and Sarkar had taken upon himself the responsibility
of compiling a book on images of the famine. To that effect he
gathered paintings on the famine by artists of the time and also wrote
a long essay on the same. The volume was titled *Dai* (Responsibility)
and was published by a small publication house called Punashcha.
Despite being well aware that *Phyan Dao* was not going to sell well
Selim Ahmed had honoured my request and published it, perhaps
out of hope that in the near future his faith was going to be rewarded.
So I had to make sure to give him a new book to publish at the book
fair. Pearl Publications was not as lucky and I could only give them
Lajja Ebong Onyanyo (Lajja and Others), not an original work, but
a collection of what other authors had written about *Lajja*. Minu of
Pearl Publications was justifiably upset.

'Give me something original.'

'Where can I get you something original?'

I had been busy working on *Koraner Naari* and reading the Bible,
the Vedas and the Quran for it. I had not managed to finish the novel

Aamar Meyebela (My Girlhood) that I was writing. Obviously I could not give him something incomplete to publish! In the end I suggested Minu collect four old novellas of mine and publish them together as *Chaar Konya* (Four Women). It managed to mollify him to some extent but he still made sure to remind me that I had not given him a new book to publish. I also gave the responsibility of the books Khoka had published earlier to various other publishers. *Dukkhobati Meye* (The Girl Who Feels the Blues), a book of short stories, went to Maola Brothers who had been after me for the longest time for a book. I did not wish to disappoint anyone, I wanted to publish with everyone who approached me, but that was hardly possible.

The Gyankosh publisher was a very affable man to whom I had given the reprint rights of *Nirbachito Kolam*; despite it being an old work he was elated. With the others I had to make do with promises for the moment. I felt especially bad seeing the pitiful look Mezbauddin Ahmed of Ankur Prakashani gave me. He told me all about how he had paid an advance to MHI nearly five years ago for a novel but MHI was yet to give him anything in return. He used to publish a weekly journal called *Samikkhan* where I was a regular columnist, which is how we had met initially. He had asked me for a book as soon as he had launched his publishing house. In the end I managed to pacify him with a temporary fix—I suggested he collect the debates written for or against me in *Samikkhan* and compile them into a book. When asked whether I had no books at all, I told him I did—*Koraner Naari*. Most publishers recoiled in shock at the very mention of the name and none of them had the courage to take up the challenge.

Faced with publishers clamouring for my work I could not help but be reminded of the old days when there used to be one writer and one publisher working on a book through the various stages of production, a labour of love. I was reminded of the excitement of my initial years with Khoka, which had been far more beautiful than the busy times I was living in. I was frequently reminded of Khoka too, the person who had been my closest confidant during some of my most difficult times. But when better days had finally arrived I had everyone except him in my life. I had never expected that my relationship with Khoka would ever turn sour but it had happened and I must say the fault had been entirely his.

One day he had suddenly grabbed hold of my hand and cried, 'Don't you understand anything? Don't you see how much I love you?' I had been too dumbstruck to respond to something like that. I had experienced many humiliating, insulting and disgusting scenes in life but I had never imagined even in my wildest dreams that I would face something like that with Khoka. Feeling dizzy I had snatched my hand away, moved away from him and asked him to leave. After throwing him out I had wept my heart out, like how people cry, rage and feel empty when their dreams shatter. Khoka had never gotten in touch with me ever again. A few months before this incident when his wife had begun suspecting there was something going on between the two of us he had requested me to go to his house and explain the truth of our relationship to her. To allay her fears I had done that too. Ever since that incident his wife would come over to my place often, with him or on her own, and we spent hours chatting over food. Even the newspapers had gotten the two of us married on numerous occasions and *Banglabazar Patrika* had even insulted Khoka in its pages. No amount of gossip had managed to cause a dent in our relationship. In the end he had done that all by himself.

My old life, one of exhilaration, no longer existed. Samar Majumdar and Dhrubo Esh had done great work with covers back then and I was fortunate to have followed their work closely. I used to visit Samar at his Elephant Road residence to see him at work. Dhrubo Esh used to live in the Art College hostel and he would stay up late into the night making sketches to accompany the poems on every page. With Samar I used to compare our ideas to understand what the final result was going to look like. If it did not make sense we moved to the next and then to another tirelessly. Racing against deadlines, I would go around town trying to locate Dhrubo, to suggest alterations like adding a splash of colour here or something else there. However, I no longer cared who was doing the cover or how it was coming along. The more my world was expanding the more my movements were getting restricted. Even if I wanted to I could no longer hope for the same passion and enthusiasm that had been distinctive of my earlier days.

~

February brought with it the festivities. There were events planned through the month—the book fair, the National Poetry Festival, poetry readings and recitals, music fairs and drama festivals. Writers, artists as well as readers waited the entire year eagerly for this one month. Once I used to wait for February too. But I was sitting at home, not having been invited anywhere since I was not allowed to go anywhere in the first place. No one had called me to their event and I was not welcome even as a member of the general audience. Poets were finishing one event and moving to the next, riding the festive wave from one joy to another, while I was locked away in a dark room. Everyone was out and about, the events scheduled to last from afternoon till midnight. I was well aware that if I were to go to the book fair there would be a crowd of people around me in the blink of an eye, with half wanting to kill me on the spot and the other half wishing to touch my feet. One group would approach me with knives and the other with books for me to sign. Even then I wanted to run to the fair, to join the celebrations outside without letting the fear of death hold me back. If I had to die so be it but I still wanted to go. But there were invisible shackles on my feet and they would not let me.

All my poet friends were busy and none of them had time to see how I was doing or how I was feeling. The National Poetry Festival was under way, so were the book fair and myriad poetry recitals. I asked people about the book fair, only to be met with glowing accounts of how fantastic everything was and lengthy descriptions of events that were happening. Some of the new boys and girls who were reciting my poetry had even made audiobooks of my novels and columns, copies of which they sent to me. My publishers were sending me word on how well my books were doing, with some already on their second or third editions. Sales were so high that many of them were not being able to keep up with the growing demand. They also informed me many visitors were coming to the stalls hoping to meet the author and get her autograph.

'I really want to go,' I eagerly told them.

They immediately stuck out their tongue in disapproval and said, 'Don't even say that out loud. There is danger everywhere. Besides, the organizers of the fair have also declared that they will not allow you inside.'

Early in the morning on 21 February I stood on my balcony to watch scores of boys and girls dressed in white, flowers cupped in their palms and 'Amar bhaier rokte rangano' on their lips, walking towards the Sahid Minar. I used to march to the Sahid Minar every year to offer flowers. Every poet, artist and writer was usually busy on this day, signing autographs, attending events, reciting poetry and chatting with their admirers or friends over tea. They were meeting friends they had not met for a long time; writers' conferences were being held on the Biswa Sahitya Parisad and the Bangla Academy grounds. Only I was alone, kept out of everything and not allowed to partake of the joy. With my head pressed against the grille on the window I could see people walking past, singing—as far as the eye could see there was a sea of them. It was amazing how this particular Falgun day never ceased to be anything short of stunning! The flaming red of the flamboyant tree was smeared across everything, the colour mixing with the strains of the tragic song they were singing. The song made me cry and I lay on my bed as if I had been shot through the heart. A hand touched me lightly just then. Mother said softly, 'I'll go and place a red rose at the Sahid Minar on your behalf today.'

There was nothing wrong with falling in love. On and off I could feel the desire to fall in love taking hold of me; I wished if I could lose myself in its turbulence again! Somewhere deep within me this desire stayed hidden, so well that even I did not realize it existed. At times, alone, when I was overcome with despondency I could feel the yearning within me; I would pick it up and pet it tenderly, wishing to shield its defenceless body from the harshness and cruelty of life.

For a few days the handsome, refined and witty AR had caught my fancy. Having just come out of a broken marriage and with the door to his heart wide open, he had been looking around for a new love and perhaps another shot at marriage. But I liked his company and that was about it. With K too, my relationship was one of simple physical need; I wanted him but I did not need him. As the desire to fall in love again slowly began to hum a new tune in my ear I was suddenly reminded of H from back when I was in college.

He had been madly in love with me and when he had found out that I did not love him back, that I loved R instead, he had not taken it too well. One day he had run into R and attacked him, actually attacked him, and threatened to murder him if R came near my college in the future! H, the one man who had truly loved me! Suddenly, after so many years, all I desired was to recapture that love again. I had no clue as to H's whereabouts. Acting on instinct I began looking for him and finally managed to locate a lead. Dr H, previously a student of Mymensingh Medical, was a doctor in a hospital for the disabled in Dhaka. I called the hospital and managed to get through to him and it did not take me long to be convinced that I had the person I was looking for. Unexpected as it was, I invited him to my house and he came to see me one evening. He looked the same to me; nothing about him seemed to have changed at all. However, something was definitely not the same because try as we might we could not go back to the way we had been with each other. I tried speaking without using a direct pronoun for some time but the entire conversation soon became stilted. Much to my surprise, H told me about his wife and two children. Why was I surprised? Had I expected him to wait for me all these years? As deluded as it might sound, that was exactly what I had hope.

'I told your bhabi that I am going to meet an old college friend . . .'

'My bhabi?' I was astonished. When had he managed to meet Geeta or Hasina?

Smiling shyly, H replied, 'My wife.'

'Oh!' I had a bland smile plastered on my face as he spoke about his job and his new family. Looking around the house, his eyes wide with surprise, he asked, 'Have you bought this place?'

'Yes.'

'Must have cost you a pretty penny. Will I ever be able to afford a house?'

'Why not? Of course you will be able to!'

'No. Whatever I earn is spent on food. I live in my father's house, that's the only saving grace.'

'But what's wrong with that? Is it necessary that you have to have your own house?'

'I'm sure you have a car too.'

'Yes, I do.'

'You have made quite a bit of money.'

'No, nothing much. Besides, does money bring happiness? Isn't happiness the most important thing? They are not mutually inclusive.'

'Your bhabi is a very nice girl. I am very happy with her. So I guess you can say that.'

'Was it a love marriage?'

'No, an arranged one.'

'Is your wife a doctor too?'

'No. She has done her BA.'

'Does she work?'

'No, she's a housewife.' He took out a photo of her and their children from his wallet and showed it to me.

'Your wife is very beautiful!'

Laughing, he replied, 'She was even more beautiful. After having the kids . . .'

H did not look at me with love any more. Neither did he talk about the past. In fact, the more I tried returning to the past the more he stayed firmly rooted in the present, where his wife and two children were. No trace of his old love for me remained and I brushed my yearnings aside silently.

Still smiling shyly, he said, 'If I ask something of you, will you do it for me?'

'What is it?' I was eager to know, certain he was going to tell me that he still felt something for me deep within his heart.

'I know you can do it, if you wish to.' The shy sweet smile was fixed on his lips.

'What is it? I have to hear it first!' My heart was beginning to beat faster. Something stirred in the quietness and a wave passed over the calm waters.

H's smile turned awkward. 'Make some arrangements for me to go to America.'

The wave died and the stillness returned with force. His words had come as a huge surprise and a very bitter one at that.

'Me? Send you to America? How can I do that?' I asked dispassionately.

'You can. You have so many connections abroad. If you want you can do anything. In this country you can't make money even if you are a doctor. If I can go to America my luck will surely change.'

Even though I insisted I held no such power to send him anywhere H would not listen. He was convinced that I was someone immensely influential. Just like before Mother sat him down to a lavish dinner. Even she had once harboured dreams regarding me and him. While eating H casually remarked, 'My wife is a great cook too, khalamma!' She did not seem too happy hearing about the wife either. I had not told a soul about what was in my heart but Mother had somehow peered inside my heart and figured out my secret. On his way out H finally said, 'See if you can do something for this brother of yours.'

My lover had morphed into my brother! Such was fate!

I sat by myself on the dark balcony and stared at the starry sky for a long time. I felt terribly alone. The house was full of people, every one of them my relatives, my kin, and yet it seemed there was no one more alone than I. Twelve years had passed but like a stubborn adolescent girl I had tried to rekindle an old love story. Twelve years was a really long time. My loneliness was whispering to me, 'You are a foolish girl. You have spent your entire youth running after glittery things, things that were not even gold to begin with.'

I wished H all the happiness with his wife and children. It always made me happy whenever married men showed fidelity towards their wives. This was perhaps why my relationship with K often caused me a lot of discomfort. I had even said to him on occasion, 'Don't come to me any more. Live happily with your wife. There's no reason for you to go to another woman.' K came nonetheless, even if only once a week, even if for only an hour. K's wife called me one day. 'How can you keep seeing my husband? Aren't you ashamed? You write about women, don't you! Then how can you destroy another woman's life?' For an instant I was speechless and could find nothing to say to her allegations. Then, my voice dry, I said to her decisively, 'Speak to your husband, sort it out with him. Tell him never to come see me again.'

All my friends and well-wishers were either much older than me or much younger. I had no friends my age. Besides, it was not as if only people from the literary world were my friends. Be it a hardened garment trader like Yahya Khan or a consummate poet like Nirmalendu Goon, I had friends from all walks of life. Yahya Khan at least had some acquaintance with the literary world since he was an amateur poet too. Khusro on the other hand was a businessman through and through and had nothing to do with literature. Neither did Dr Rashid, but I could talk to him for hours about anything under the sun. I was not in touch with any of my friends from school or college.

I had heard from Jhunu khala that my school friend Sara was a Bengali teacher at Bhikharunnesa School. Since then I had been excited at the prospect of reconnecting with her. One day Sara came over to my house; we sat across each other and spoke for a long time but it was a conversation entirely devoid of life. I had so many wonderful memories with Sara from childhood but as we spoke I realized there was nothing left for us to talk about any more. We spoke about our other friends, we spoke about her husband and her children and then realized there was nothing else for us to do but sit awkwardly in silence the rest of the time.

Papri from Vidyamoyee had visited me in Shantibag once and with her too there had been nothing to talk about. Our lives were too different, while I had no husband or children all of them were married. They were working, taking care of the children, leading busy lives and it was no longer possible to keep in touch with an old friend, especially one who was still single. Obviously there was a hint of apprehension there, a suspicion that their friend might get involved with their husbands! Married people preferred to stay in touch with other married people.

I was not aware where all my doctor friends were or what they were doing either. While I was sure many were still in Dhaka I never ran into any of them. Perhaps we would have managed to stay in touch if I had remained a practising doctor in an established hospital. But there was no hospital to go to any more. Sometimes I could not help but wonder who exactly had drifted apart from whom. Had they drifted apart or had I? Or was it that time had simply come between us? That was what life was all about, a constant irrevocable progression towards the new.

Nonetheless, it felt nice to reminisce about the old days and dream about recapturing that time again. Although I never imagined going back to exactly as I was, I wished to go back to the person I had been all those years ago, a younger me from a younger time. Of course, reminiscing about the past and carrying the past along like a

burden were entirely different things. Abakash had been such a dear
place but I no longer spent too much time there. Something always
seemed missing and I would keep wondering what it was. Was it
my childhood that was missing? Or were people different? Perhaps
they had changed just like everything else had. Whatever it was, the
passing of time was an irrefutable truth. Things that were lost were
usually lost forever while we inexorably marched towards our future,
growing up and growing old in the process. Our time was very brief
and the very thought was enough to make me want to scream about
the injustice of it all. But there was no one who I could share my
anxieties with. Life to me represented different things at different
points of time—sometimes beautiful, sometimes ugly, at times
tolerable and mostly not. Most of the time though I was so absorbed
in the bounties life had to offer that all I could do was clutch them
with every ounce of strength I had.

~

I could hear the drums. A procession to mark Poila Boishakh
celebrations was making its way down the road. Boys in dhotis
were beating the drums while girls in traditionally draped saris were
dancing with pitchers tucked at their hips. People were marching
down the road holding aloft giant paper elephants, horses, tigers and
bears, many wearing masks resembling characters from fairy tales.
Under the banyan trees of Ramna Park the performers of Chayanot
had gathered since morning. Music permeated the air; amidst strains
of 'Baandh bhenge dao' (Break these barriers down) sung in chorus
people were bidding farewell to the past year and welcoming the
new. All of Dhaka was at Ramna or its neighbouring areas. People
had spread *nakshi katha* on the grass and were fanning themselves
with palm leaf fans while gorging on munchies, listening to Fakir
Alamgir singing songs of freedom at Suhrawardy Udyan. Earlier
Poila Boishakh eve would pass in long addas while watching the stage
being constructed for Fakir Alamgir. There were only two days in
the entire year that I considered as festivals: Poila Boishakh and 21
February. I had no Eid, Shab-e-Baraat, Shab-e-Qadr, Fateha Doaz
Daham, Fateha Yazdaham, or Milad-un-Nabi. In fact, no sooner

had I developed a sense of reason than I had stopped attending religious events. But unlike others I was no longer allowed to be part of either Poila Boishakh or 21 February, or go for any of the musical programmes.

Sanjida Khatun's Chayanot was performing Rabindrasangeet at Ramna. There were fairs all around—handicrafts, Bengali books, music and dance, and the air was heady with the aroma of revelry. I was all by myself at home, old and redundant and consigned to my loneliness, no longer allowed the right to welcome the new with the others. Misery had me in its thrall.

In the afternoon Mother peeked into my room, pursed her lips and said, 'The Poila Boishakh fairs this year aren't any good.'

'Who told you?'

'Chumki's mother from the other apartment. She'd gone. There were hardly any people.'

Some time later she came back to the room with ginger tea and dry-roasted puffed rice, a smile of contentment playing on her lips.

'Chayanot is performing, did she say anything?' I looked at her eagerly.

Without looking me in the eye Mother responded, 'Who goes to listen to music in this horrid heat? Might as well stay at home and listen to music.' She turned around and left in a hurry, looking distinctly uncomfortable, as if she was hiding something. Was she lying to me to ease my pain of not being able to go to the fair? For a moment I contemplated calling Chumki's mother in the apartment next door and asking her whether the Poila Boishakh fairs were truly no good. Munching on the puffed rice between sips of tea I could hear the song 'Charidike dekho chahi hriday prashari, khudro dukkho shob tuchcho maani' (Look around you with an open heart and cast aside the trivial sorrows) that Mother had put on.

I let it be. The fair probably wasn't any good after all.

Notes

1. Vidyamoyee Government Girls High School is a school for girls in Mymensingh, Bangladesh.
2. Ananda Mohan College is a university college in Mymensingh, Bangladesh. It is one of the old educational institutions in the country.
3. Hussain Muhammad Ershad was a Bangladeshi politician who served as the tenth President of Bangladesh. He seized power as the head of the army during a bloodless coup against President Abdus Sattar on 24 April 1982 by imposing martial law.
4. Ziaur Rahman was a Bangladeshi politician and army general who declared the independence of Bangladesh on behalf of its first interim head of state, Sheikh Mujibur Rahman. He later served as the seventh President of Bangladesh from 21 April 1977 until his assassination on 30 May 1981.
5. Golam (or Ghulam) Azam was a Bangladeshi politician convicted of war crimes. During the Bangladesh Liberation War in 1971, he led the Bangladesh Jamaat-e-Islami, which opposed the independence of Bangladesh, and together with the Pakistani military establishment, perpetrated the 1971 genocide and was instrumental in the killing of Bengali intellectuals. He led the party until the year 2000.
6. The Bangladesh Jamaat-e-Islami, or Jamaat for short, is the largest Islamist political party in Bangladesh. On 1 August 2013 the Bangladesh Supreme Court declared the registration of the Bangladesh Jamaat-e-Islami illegal, ruling the party unfit to contest national elections.
7. 25 March marks the beginning of the Bangladesh Liberation War after the Pakistani military junta based in West Pakistan launched

Operation Searchlight against the people of East Pakistan on the night of 25 March 1971, during which time there was a systematic execution-style purge of nationalist Bengali civilians, students, intelligentsia, religious minorities and armed personnel.

8. 16 December is celebrated as Victory Day in Bangladesh to commemorate the triumph of the Allied Forces over the Pakistani forces in the Bangladesh Liberation War of 1971.

9. 'Amar bhaier rokte rangano ekushe February, ami ki bhulite pari' is a song sung during International Mother Language Day celebrations on 21 February in Bangladesh—it roughly translates as 'How can I forget 21 February, coloured by the blood of my brothers'.

10. Abul Barkat, Rafiq Uddin Ahmed and Abdus Salam were demonstrators who died during the Bengali Language Movement demonstrations in erstwhile East Bengal (now Bangladesh) in 1952. On 21 February 1952, students in Dhaka defied the Section 144 curfew and organized rallies demanding the induction of Bengali as the state language. The processions were joined by other members of the public besides students and the police fired on the gathered crowds, killing a number of protesters and wounding numerous others. They are considered martyrs in the history of modern Bangladesh.

11. Jatin Sarkar is a Bengali intellectual, researcher and biographer of Bangladesh, and a renowned Marxist intellectual who was awarded the prestigious Bangla Academy Award in 2008 for his 'research and essays'.

12. Swadhin Bangla Betar Kendra was the radio broadcasting centre of Bengali nationalist forces during the Bangladesh Liberation War. The station played a vital role in the war, later broadcasting the declaration of independence too. In 1971 radio was the only media reaching the farthest ends of Bangladesh and it ran a propaganda campaign throughout the duration of the war to boost morale.

13. 'Shahid Noor Hossain Day Being Observed, *Prothom Alo*, 10 November 2017, http://en.prothom-alo.com/bangladesh/news/165951/Shaheed-Noor-Hossain-Day-being-observed and 'What Does Democracy Mean to Bangladeshis?', *Daily*

Star, 6 December 2016, http://www.thedailystar.net/op-ed/
what-does-democracy-mean-bangladeshis-1325527.

14. The Urdu word 'dozakh' is translated as hell.

15. The Urdu word 'hawiya' is translated as the deepest pit of hell.

16. 'Shokal' is the Bengali word for morning.

17. Gollachhut is a Bangladeshi variation of tag played between two teams comprising an equal number of players, with the 'king's team' running to cross over to the other side of the playing field, without being tagged by the opponents trying to prevent them.

18. Baticharchari is a quintessential part of everyday Bengali cuisine, made of vegetables, or in some variants even fish and prawns, cooked in a little oil and minimal spices.

19. The Muslim League formed its government in East Bengal immediately after the partition. Problems in East Pakistan for the League began following the adoption of the constitution of Pakistan in 1956. Furthermore, the Bhasa Andolan (Language Movement) proved to be the last straw, causing the Muslim League to lose its mandate. It remained a minor party in East Pakistan but participated with full rigour during the general elections again in 1970.

20. The Razakar was an anti-Bangladesh paramilitary force organized by the Pakistani army in Bangladesh during the Bangladesh Liberation War. Since then it has become a pejorative term (implying traitor) in Bangladesh due to the numerous atrocities committed by the Razakars during the war. The Razakar force was composed of mostly anti-Bangladesh and pro-Pakistan Bengalis and Urdu-speaking migrants who lived in Bangladesh at the time.

21. The Shanti Committee was one of several committees formed in East Pakistan in 1971 by the Pakistani army to aid its efforts in crushing the rebellion for independence. Nurul Amin, as a leader of the Pakistan Democratic Party, led the formation of the Shanti Committee to thwart the Mukti Bahini, the force behind the Liberation War.

22. TSC, or the Teacher–Student Centre, University of Dhaka, was where many historically important political meetings and

discussions were held during the Liberation War. Many academic and social events are still held here.

23. Purabi Basu is a Bangladeshi short story writer, pharmacologist and activist who won the Bangla Academy Literary Award in 2013.

24. Bangabandhu Sheikh Mujib Medical University is essentially an upgrade of the Institute of Postgraduate Medicine and Research (IPGMR), popularly referred to as PG.

25. Hazrat Maulana Hashmatullah Faridpuri, widely known as Atroshi Pir, started his spiritual career at a very early age. Founder of the Naqshbandya-Mujaddidia brotherhood, his hermitage at Atroshi in Faridpur was a large institution attracting numerous followers from all over the country. The growth of the Atroshi Pir's stature is explained lucidly in *Embodying Charisma: Modernity, Locality and the Performance of Emotion in Sufi Cults* by Helene Basu and Pnina Werbner, eds (Kentucky: Routledge, 1998).

26. 'Shahid Noor Hossain Day Being Observed', *Prothom Alo*, 10 November 2017, http://en.prothom-alo.com/bangladesh/news/165951/Shaheed-Noor-Hossain-Day-being-observed and 'Daughter's Fight for a Hero's Due', *Daily Star*, 28 February 2017, http://www.thedailystar.net/frontpage/daughters-fight-heros-due-1368457.

27. President Sheikh Mujibur Rahman of Bangladesh was assassinated at his residence in Dhaka, along with his wife, three of his sons, two daughters-in-law and his brother, and twelve other people during a coup d'état led by Major Syed Faruque Rahman. The original six conspirators, all military officers, had met on 6 August and the decision was made to act before 1 September, when the nation's district governors would be given control over the police and armed forces. Nearly thirty-five years later, on 28 January 2010, five of the coup leaders were hanged after their convictions in 1998, including Syed Faruque, and the man who actually shot President Mujib, Major Bazlul Huda.

28. The Buriganga (old Ganges) is a river that flows past the southwest outskirts of Dhaka.

29. The electoral symbol of the Awami League is a boat.

30. Naznin Tithi, 'Gano Adalot', *Daily Star*, 23 January 2016, http://www.thedailystar.net/in-focus/gano-adalot-205765.
31. Basanta Utsab is the Bengali cognate of Holi.
32. 'Bangal' refers to the people of erstwhile East Bengal, marked by the distinct accent of Dhaka and Barisal, who migrated to West Bengal during the partition. By contrast 'ghoti' was the term used to describe the Bengalis already living in West Bengal during and before that time. Primarily used now as social subgroups, the ghoti–bangal antagonism has been a defining feature of the Bengali socio-cultural milieu in West Bengal post independence.
33. Perhaps the most well-known and oft-sung song of the Basanta Utsab, the Rabindrasangeet is a call to the householders to throw open their gates and come out to play with colours during Holi in Santiniketan.
34. A tax on agricultural land and its produce according to Islamic law that was first levied on non-Muslims by their conquering Muslim rulers.
35. Jatiya Samajtantrik Dal or National Socialist Party, shortened to JSD or JASAD, is a left-wing political party in Bangladesh.
36. 'Malaun', translated as 'accursed' or 'deprived of God's mercy', is an ethnic slur used against the Hindu minority in Bangladesh.